T0134661

The Quest to Cyber Superiority

Nir Kshetri

The Quest to Cyber Superiority

Cybersecurity Regulations, Frameworks, and Strategies of Major Economies

 Springer

Nir Kshetri
University of North Carolina
Greensboro, North Carolina
USA

ISBN 978-3-319-82128-3   ISBN 978-3-319-40554-4   (eBook)
DOI 10.1007/978-3-319-40554-4

Printed on acid-free paper

This Springer imprint is published by Springer Nature
The registered company is Springer International Publishing AG Switzerland

Preface and Acknowledgments

Cybersecurity (CS) currently is in a nascent stage of institutionalization and policy development in most economies. Nonetheless, national governments, supranational institutions, and other actors are engaged in a variety of actions that can potentially have far-reaching social, political, and economic implications. It is this nature of the global CS that makes it a field wide open for research, in which new and interesting questions can be raised and unexpected insights can be uncovered.

One key idea in this book is that the state is the obvious agent with the credibility, legitimacy, and resources to ensure that proper CS measures are in place to protect citizens and organizations from cyber-threats. It thus examines the key drivers and effects of nations' CS regulations, frameworks, standards, and strategies. It provides a detailed analysis and description of formal and informal institutions and key institutional actors involved in the CS debate. It explores how significant variation across countries in CS-related regulations can be attributed to differences in political, cultural, and economic factors. It sheds light on the current cyber-conflicts and intense competition among nations to develop cyber-defense and cyber-offense capabilities in the quest to establish superiority in the cyberspace. The book also examines how CS is affected by the externalities of nations' past and current engagement in internal and external wars and conflicts and compares such externalities for major economies such as China (Mao Zedong's Guerrilla warfare) and the USA (the "war on terror"). It discusses multifaceted and multidimensional aspect of CS and examines military security, political security, economic security, and cultural security on the cyber front. It also compares similarities and differences between CS and conventional security. While the state constitutes the principal focus of the book, it also explores the roles of other key actors in managing cyber-risks.

The book investigates drawbacks and shortcomings of some economies' CS frameworks. Drawing on the experiences of economies such as Japan and the EU, it shows how nations are likely to face a tricky trade-off between using emerging technologies in economically productive ways and ensuring CS. Also analyzed are the impacts on trades, investment, international relations, and diplomacy. A close look is taken on how CS-related concerns have led to protectionism in and diversion of trade and investment and how such measures have affected firms involved in storing, processing, and transmitting data. The book covers CS issues in relation to recent conflicts shaping relationships among major economies and explains how the attempts to secure the cyber domain have been limited by the lack of an international consensus on key issues, questions, and concepts. It suggests some institutions solutions that may ameliorate some of the conflicts.

It emphasizes the need for a multi-prolonged approach that includes international cooperation, government–industry collaboration, measures to address the shortage of CS-related skills, and the creation and development of CS culture and awareness at the organizational, national, and international levels in order to protect vital national and global infrastructures. The analysis is also expected to help separate and sort out the hype from the reality and understand factors relevant to a firm's environment in making CS-related decisions. In this way, firms can make a better focused investment decisions based on the risks faced.

The key ideas, concepts, and theories are explored, illustrated, and contrasted through in-depth case studies of major economies and regions with different institutional frameworks and different levels of development and available resources such as the EU, the USA, China, India, Japan, South Korea, Brazil, and Russia. The case studies provide rich stories and research findings about the key elements of these economies' CS frameworks, driving forces, visions and priorities, and impacts on business and consumers, international relations, and trades and investments.

In light of the above observations, the major goals of this book are to (a) review the theoretical rationales for and factors affecting the institutionalization of CS; (b) provide an authoritative and up-to-date account of the global diffusion pattern of CS; (c) analyze the effects of new technologies such as cloud computing, big data, and analytical tools on issues related to CS; (d) evaluate the effects of CS regulations on international trade and investment politics; (e) show why an economy's global integration is linked to its adoption of CS regulation; (f) document and evaluate the current state of CS regulations in major world economies; (g) investigate the links between formal and informal institutions and CS regulations; (h) provide a framework for explaining how actors in the firm's nonmarket environment may provide a possible mechanism by which a firm may face barriers to trade and investment associated with CS-related issues; (i) develop systematic knowledge about the characteristics of various models of data privacy and security protection; (j) provide some examples of situations in which the private sector and special interest groups can play key roles in shaping CS regulations; (k) discuss implications of the findings of this book for businesses, governments, and consumers; and (l) identify areas of research needed to improve our understanding of the global diffusion of CS.

Given its complex, multifaceted, and multidimensional nature, no single academic discipline is capable of capturing a full understanding of national CS frameworks and strategies. This book thus draws upon theory and research in many interrelated fields including developmental studies, criminology, computer science, economics, law, military studies, security studies, political science, international studies, business, management, organizational theory, and sociology to look at the key issues, dilemmas, and challenges that nations face today on the CS front.

Undergraduate and graduate students and CS researchers from a wide range of disciplines represent the primary audience groups for this book. It is also useful for policy makers and practitioners, who need an informed understanding of the key elements of global CS. However, anyone with a broad interest in world affairs would find the book a useful reading and reference source.

I would like to thank a number of people and organizations for their help and support. This book could not have been written without the generous support of a one-semester research assignment provided by the University of North Carolina-Greensboro (UNCG). I would like to acknowledge Kohler Fund support for this study from the UNCG's International Programs Center and a grant from the Ritsumeikan Asia Pacific University.

Springer's Senior Editor Katharina Wetzel-Vandai has been supportive and encouraging in guiding and managing this book project. I also received help from my talented graduate assistant Minjing Sun at UNCG. Finally, my wife Maya deserves special thanks for her understanding and support.

Greensboro, NC   Nir Kshetri

Contents

About the Author

Nir Kshetri is Professor at Bryan School of Business and Economics, The University of North Carolina-Greensboro and a research fellow at Research Institute for Economics & Business Administration—Kobe University, Japan. He is the author of five books and about 100 journal articles. His 2014 book, *Global Entrepreneurship: Environment and Strategy*, was selected as an Outstanding Academic Title by *Choice* Magazine. Nir participated as lead discussant at the Peer Review meeting of the UNCTAD's *Information Economy Report 2013* and *Information Economy Report 2015*. Nir has taught classes or presented research papers in about fifty countries. He has been interviewed by and/or quoted in over 60 TV channels, magazines, and newspapers.

Abbreviation

ACLU	American Civil Liberties Union
AFBF	American Farm Bureau Federation
AICPA	American Institute of Certified Public Accountants
APEC	Asia-Pacific Economic Cooperation
APT	Advanced Persistent Threat
ASEAN	Association of Southeast Asian Nations
BD	Big Data
BPO	Business Process Outsourcing
BRIC	Brazil, Russia, India, China
BRICS	Brazil, Russia, India, China and South Africa
BSI	Bundesamt für Sicherheit in der Informationstechnik
CCP	Chinese Communist Party
CCYL	China Communist Youth League
CDU	Cyber Defense Unit
CERT	Computer Emergency Response Team
CFTC	Commodity Futures Trading Commission
CISPA	Cyber Intelligence Sharing and Protection Act
CoE	Council of Europe
CoECoC	Council of Europe Convention on Cybercrime
CPO	Corporate Privacy Officer
CS	Cybersecurity
CSA	Cloud Security Alliance
CSP	Cloud Service Provider
CUO	Cloud User Organization
DDoS	Distributed Denial of Service
DFS	Department of Financial Services
DHC	Dubai Healthcare City
DHS	Department of Homeland Security
DIFC	Dubai International Financial Center
DNS	Domain Name System
DoD	Department of Defense

DPA	Data Protection Authority
DPDC	Department of Consumer Protection and Defense
DSCI	Data Security Council of India
EC	European Commission
ENISA	European Network and Information Security Agency
EO	Executive Order
EPIC	Electronic Privacy Information Center
ETNO	European Telecommunications Network Operator's Association
EU	European Union
FBI	Federal Bureau of Investigation
FCC	Federal Communications Commission
FDA	Food and Drug Administration
Febraban	Federação Brasileira de Bancos
FIP	Fair Information Practices
FISMA	Federal Information Security Management Act
FTC	Federal Trade Commission
GCC	Gulf Cooperation Council
HIPAA	Health Insurance Portability and Accountability Act
IBSA	India, Brazil, South Africa
ICANN	Internet Corporation for Assigned Names and Numbers
ICT	Information and communications technology
IFA	International Franchise Association
IGF	Internet Governance Forum
IP	Intellectual Property
IPR	Intellectual Property Rights
IRGC	Iranian Revolutionary Guard Corp
ISC	Internet Society of China
IT&BPM	IT and Business Process Management
ITU	International Telecommunication Union
JSDF	Japan Self-Defense Forces
KISA	Korea Internet and Security Agency
KPA	Korean People's Army
MCTI	Ministry of Science Technology and Innovation
METI	Ministry of Economy, Trade and Industry
MIAC	Ministry of Internal Affairs and Communications
MoD	Ministry of Defense
NASSCOM	National Association of Software and Services Companies
NATO	North Atlantic Treaty Organization
NCSA	National Cyber Security Alliance
NCSP	National Cyber Security Policy
NIC	National Informatics Centre
NIS	National Intelligence Service
NIST	National Institute of Standards and Technology
NPA	National Police Agency

NSA	National Security Agency
OECD	Organisation for Economic Co-operation and Development
OSS	Open-Source Software
PBOC	People's Bank of China
PFI	Personal Financial Information
PII	Personally Identifiable Information
PLA	People's Liberation Army
PPP	Public–Private Partnership
PwC	PricewaterhouseCoopers
QFC	Qatar Financial Centre
RBI	Reserve Bank of India
SBU	Sluzhba Bespeky Ukrayiny
SCO	Shanghai Cooperation Organization
SEC	Securities and Exchange Commission
SERPRO	Serviço Federal de Processamento de Dados
SOCA	Serious Organized Crime Agency
SOX	Sarbanes-Oxley Act
SSN	Social Security Number
SKDM	South Korean Defense Ministry
TCO	Total Cost of Ownership
UN	United Nations
VC	Venture Capital

List of Figures

List of Tables

Chapter 1
Global Cybersecurity: Key Issues and Concepts

1.1 Introduction

Cyber-attacks are touted as a critical national security threat and among the greatest risks nations face today. Due to the rapid growth in number and sophistication of cyber-attacks, security of the cyberspace is accentuating rather than improving. A 2009 *Science* article noted: "[c]yberspace is less secure than it was 40 years ago" (Wulf and Jones 2009).

Proponents have put forward some compelling arguments for government interventions to deal with cyber-threats. The lack of effective CS practices among businesses and consumers and the failure of the private sector to secure itself increase the importance of government intervention. Several theoretical points are held up to explain the failure of the market. First, the fact that infrastructure providers are not held legally accountable and liable for CS failures, they lack incentives to invest in CS security measures. Second, it is difficult to judge the relative responsibility of any individual party in case of a CS breach due to the interdependence among various subsystems, components and equipment. Finally, due primarily to the newness, the CS industry and market lack practical signals to measure CS quality. These factors make it difficult to assess the effectiveness of investments in CS infrastructure (Friedman 2013).

Unsurprisingly most governments are reorganizing, retooling and rebuilding security institutions to grapple with the new challenges of the Internet era and are taking major steps to strengthen CS. For instance, the French government announced plans to spend 1 billion euros from 2015 to 2019 on CS-related issues (Fouquet and Mawad 2014).

One the cyber front, nations' development of cyber-warfare capabilities has been a notable trend. An *Economist* article asserted: "After land, sea, air and space, warfare has entered the fifth domain: cyberspace" (economist.com 2010). As of 2013, 20 nations were reported to have military units dedicated to cyberwar (Nye 2013). In September 2014, Israel established a National Authority for Cyber-

© Springer International Publishing Switzerland 2016

N. Kshetri, *The Quest to Cyber Superiority*, DOI 10.1007/978-3-319-40554-4_1

Defense to strengthen cyber protection for institutes, defense agencies and citizens. The new authority is described as an 'Air Force' against new cyber-threats (Dvorin 2014). CS strategy has been a key component of the national security frameworks of most major nations. According to the NATO's Cooperative Cyber-Defense Center of Excellence, as of 2012, more than 50 countries had published a CS strategy (Klimberg 2012).

1.2   Gulf Between Hype and Reality

It is important to point out that the gulf between hype and reality makes it difficult for many stakeholders to assess the extent for various cyber-risks. Potential reasons for this gap between hype and reality are many, and predominant among them is security and consulting companies' tendency to exaggerate cyber-risks. It is also possible that, as is the case of most underground economies, law enforcement agencies may be tempted to use "purported evidence" of rapid cybercrime growth "to justify larger budgets and more arbitrary powers" (Naylor 2005).

Some categories of cyber-threats are associated with a higher degree of bias. For instance, most cyber-attack-related intelligence on North Korea largely comes from the U.S. and South Korea, both of which have a clear political bias against the North (theguardian.com 2014). Overall, the perception of cyber-risks among some politicians is far greater than it actually might be. Martin Libicki observes: "These days, most of Washington seems to believe that a major cyber-attack on U.S. critical infrastructure is inevitable" (Libicki 2013).

The hype of cyber-risks has also led to an exponential growth in investments in CS-related entrepreneurial activities. Two partners at the CS Venture Capital (VC) firm, YL Ventures, with experience in the U.S. and the Israeli markets, noted that while the CS threats are "real and escalating for many corporations", the fears might have been" overplayed". They went on to say that "[f]or the past two years, consumer curiosity and fear, often unjustified, has fueled mainstream media coverage of CS breaches causing more fear and more coverage, resulting in hype". They argue most investors lack experience in CS and have viewed the CS as the next big thing, which has led to a massive over-investment in the CS industry without paying much attention to sound financial metrics such as the total potential market, growth rate, and possible market share. They reported dramatic increase during 2012–2014 in the number of new CS companies looking for funding, the size of early-stage funding rounds and pre-money valuations (Leitersdorf 2014). Such overinvestment would normally be expected to result in a desperate marketing strategy by CS firms.

1.3 Definitions of Major Terms

Before proceeding, we offer some clarifying definitions of important terms used in the book.

1.3.1 Cybersecurity

CS involves technologies, concepts, policies, processes and practices used to protect assets (e.g., computers, infrastructure, applications, services, telecommunications systems, and information) and the cyber environment from attack, damage and unauthorized access (ITU 2008). From a nation's perspective, put simply, CS is the "ability to protect itself and its institutions against cyber-threats" (Choucri 2012).

1.3.2 Cybersecurity Strategy

CS strategy involves plans and actions taken in order to facilitate the achievement of national competitive advantage on the CS front and superior CS performance. Implementation of a CS strategy involves the development of technology and training CS workforce to work within the defined CS strategy.

1.3.3 Cybercrime

We define a cybercrime as a criminal activity in which computers or computer networks are the principal means of committing an offense (Kshetri 2009). Examples include cyber-theft, cyber-trespass, cyber-obscenity, critical infrastructure attacks and cyber-extortions.

1.3.4 Cyber Power

We use Daniel T. Kuehl's definition of cyber power as "the ability to use cyber-space to create advantages and influence events in other operational environments and across the instruments of power" (Kuehl 2009). The idea here is that a nation's cyber power can enable it to produce preferred outcomes in the cyberspace or in other domains (Nye 2011).

1.3.5 Institutionalization

Institutionalization is defined as the process by which a practice (e.g., CS) acquires legitimacy and achieves a taken for-granted status.

1.3.6 Cloud Computing

Cloud computing (hereinafter: cloud) involves hosting IT applications on servers and delivering software and services via the Internet. In the cloud model, companies access computing power and resources on the "cloud" and pay for services based on the usage. Cloud service providers (CSPs), which are suppliers of cloud services, deliver value to users through various offerings such as software as a service (SaaS), platform as a service (PaaS) and infrastructure as a service (IaaS). SaaS is a software distribution model, in which applications are hosted by a vendor and made available to customers over a network. It is considered to be the most mature type of cloud computing. In PaaS, applications are developed and executed through platforms provided by CSPs. This model allows a quick and cost-effective development and deployment of applications. Some well-known PaaS vendors include Google (Google App Engine), Salesforce.com (Force.com), and Microsoft (Windows Azure platform). Some facilities provided under PaaS model include database management, security, workflow management, and application serving. In IaaS, compute power and storage space are offered on demand. IaaS can provide server, operating system, disk storage and database, among other things. Amazon.com is the biggest IaaS provider. Its Elastic Computer Cloud (EC2) allows subscribers to run cloud application programs. IBM, Vmware and HP also offer IaaS.

1.3.7 Strategic Asymmetry

Strategic asymmetry involves employing "some sort of differences to gain an advantage over an adversary" (Metz 2001). It could be real as well as perceived. Positive asymmetry involves capitalizing on differences with an adversary to gain an advantage. Positive asymmetry, on the other hand, is a difference an adversary is likely to use to exploit a weakness or vulnerability.

1.3.8 Trade and Investment Barriers

A CS-related barrier to international trade and investment is defined as any issue related to real and perceived security risks in the cyber environment that either directly or indirectly hinders the growth of international trade and investment.

1.3.9 Big Data

Following the research company Gartner, big data (BD) is defined as "high-volume, high-velocity and high-variety information assets that demand cost-effective, innovative forms of information processing for enhanced insight and decision making" (gartner.com 2013). In Gartner's three Vs—volume, velocity and variety—the software company, SAS, has suggested two additional BD dimensions: variability and complexity (sas.com 2013). Recent research has indicated that the various characteristics or dimensions of BD identified by Gartner and SAS are tightly linked to privacy and security issues.

1.3.10 Opportunistic and Targeted Cyber-Attacks

There are two basic types of cyber-threats. In opportunistic attacks, the cybercriminals care less about who they attack. More secure networks are less likely to be attacked. In targeted attacks such as advanced persistent threat (APT), the perpetrators are interested in attacking a particular network. The idea here is that it is "almost impossible to secure a network against a sufficiently skilled and tenacious adversary" (Schneier 2012).

1.4 The Nature of Cyber-Threats and Some Key Challenges

1.4.1 Difficulty of Dominance in the Cyberspace

Now let us make some observations from the perspective of the world's big industrialized democracies that are especially interesting, significant and relevant to the context of this book. A close look at some nations' relative cyber capabilities and their alleged engagement in cyber-attacks and cyber-warfare reveals patterns and trends that are rather counter-intuitive and contradictory to the assumptions of many analysts. Before proceeding further, an observation is worth making. As F. Kramer points out, in contrast to sea, air and space, cyber-warfare is more similar to land warfare in terms of "the number of players, ease of entry, and opportunity for concealment" (Kramer 2009). He concluded that "[o]n land, dominance is not a readily achievable criterion". Unlike in sea warfare and air warfare, dominance thus is not an achievable goal in cyberspace.

Some analysts predicted that technologically backward states may face greater challenges and difficulties to fight a cyber-war (Gartzke 2013). Yet contrary to these stereotypes, so called "rogue" and economically backward regimes have not been passive observers of cyber-attacks and cyber-warfare. Indeed, quite the opposite, some such nations have advanced cyber-warfare capabilities and potential to inflict harm and damage to their adversaries.

From the Western perspective, cyber capabilities of Iran and North Korea are especially interesting and relevant. Also what may concern the West as well as North Korea's Asian adversaries is that in 2012, these two countries signed an agreement to cooperate on scientific and IT security issues (Perlroth 2014a). The Iranian Revolutionary Guard Corp (IRGC) proposed the development of Cyber Army in 2005, mainly to tackle internal threats. Iran is believed to have the world's one of the most powerful cyber armies (strategicstudiesinstitute.army.mil 2014). The country made a big push to strengthen its cyber capabilities in 2010, when the Stuxnet worm damaged some of its uranium processing capacity. In 2012, Iran's Supreme Leader Ayatollah Ali Khameni announced the creation of a Supreme Council of Cyberspace, which is charged "to oversee the defense of the Islamic Republic's computer networks and develop new ways of infiltrating or attacking the computer networks of its enemies" (Harris 2014). Iran has demonstrated the capability of launching sophisticated cyber-attacks. A National Post article, citing iSight, reported that a 3 year campaign of an Iranian hacking network used social networks to develop friendships with U.S. lawmakers, defense contractors and a general in an attempt to extract data from them. The espionage group allegedly created a fake news organization with fabricated journalist and attempted to interact with some 2000 military, government and diplomatic officials over Facebook and other social media sites (Riley 2014). The hackers used the 14 personas to make connections, six of which appeared to work for a fake news site, *NewsOnAir.org*. Eight personas purportedly worked for defense contractors and other organizations (Afternoon Voice (India) 2014).

Cyber-attacks from North Korea are considered among the most significant threats to South Korea as well as some Western economies. South Korean security officials believe that, in addition to the huge cyber-warfare force, North Korea has about 12,000 highly skilled civilian hackers (chosun.com 2013). According to the South Korea's National Intelligence Service (NIS), North Korea has developed cyber-attack capability to take over South Korea's power supply systems. Referring to the cyber arms race between the two Koreas, a *Huffington Post* article noted that "by some counts the North [Korea] is winning" and the attacks from the North highlighted a "shocking weakness" in the South's defensive capabilities (Rundle 2013).

Likewise, CS experts and the U.S. government linked the hacking group, "Guardians of Peace" or GOP which launched cyber-attacks on Sony Pictures

Entertainment in November 2014 to the North Korean government (Gale 2014). The malware reportedly contained Korean language code (Strohm 2014). Analysts believed that the attacks could have been in response to Sony's movie "The Interview", in which the storyline involves a plot to assassinate North Korea's leader Kim Jong-Un. Symantec's analysis indicated that that techniques and component names in the code used in cyber-attacks against Sony had similarities with those used in 2013 attacks on South Korean banks and media companies, which were attributed to DarkSeoul, a hacking group with alleged links to North Korea (Robertson et al. 2014). Another similarity in the two attacks was the deployment of a command and control server in Bolivia.

The above features of the recent competition in the cyberspace indicate that a nation's technologically advancement may not necessarily lead to cyber superiority. One view is that big industrialized democracies are on the losing end of cyberwar. For instance, speaking at a Bloomberg Government cybersecurity conference in October 2013, Mike McConnell, a former National Security Agency (NSA) director and vice chairman of Booz Allen Hamilton asserted that the U.S. is fighting and losing a "cyberwar" (Salant and Holmes 2013).

In order to better understand the above observations, it is important to take a closer look at nations' engagement in a cyber-attacks and the development of cyber-warfare capabilities. Table 1.1 compares some indicators related to cyber-warfare capabilities of the U.S. and two of its key allies with those of its major adversaries.

It is important to consider the significance of Table 1.1 in the context of symmetric and asymmetric threats, which would help us further understand the real and perceived risks associated with cyber-warfare. For this, the above facts need to be considered in relation to conventional threats posed to the West by economies such as Iran and North Korea. Experts say that only "desperate" adversary depends entirely on asymmetric methods. That is, integrated approaches that appropriately combine symmetric and asymmetric methods are essential in defeating an adversary (Metz 2001). In particular, given the limitations of information and communications technologies (ICTs), approaches that combine non-ICT and ICT tools are more effective. Large and powerful nations such as China and Russia and those with nuclear capabilities such as Iran and North Korea may thus pose the most severe threats to the West because of their cyber-warfare powers as well as capabilities to combine ICTs with non-ICT resources. Note that both Iran and North Korea are believed to be pursuing clandestine nuclear activities.

1.4.2 Difficulty of Attribution

In a cyber-attack, attribution can be defined as "determining the identity or location of an attacker or an attacker's intermediary" (David 2003). The fact that the Internet was designed for ease of use without considering security puts the offense at an obviously advantageous position over the defense. Due to the attacker's anonymity

Table 1.1 Cyber-warfare forces: A comparison of U.S. and its allies versus adversaries

Country	Cyber-warfare forces	Country	Cyber-warfare forces
The U.S.	The Defense Department's Cyber Command had about 900 personnel in 2013 (Nakashima 2013). The Command's plan is to recruit 6000 cyber-personnel by 2016. As of October 2014, it had hired about 2000 personnel (blogs.wsj.com 2014).	China	Quoting a Taiwanese information security official, Japan's *Mainichi Daily* noted that, in 2011, China had about 900,000 hackers with "close ties to the …government or military". Of these, about 70,000–80,000 were from the PLA or law enforcement agencies and 500,000–600,000 were civilians organized like military units and are rewarded for carrying out cyber-attacks (Mainichi Japan 2011). Other estimates suggested that there were over 60,000 cyberwar fighters in the PLA in 2009 (Bronk 2009).
Japan	In March 2014, the Ministry of Defense (MoD) set up a Cyber-Defense Unit (CDU) with 90 Japan Self-Defense Forces (JSDF) personnel. CDU is responsible for collecting information about malware and viruses and identifying ways to respond to cyber-threats.	Iran	According to the Defense Tech institute, Iran had cyber force size of 2400 and reserves and militia of 1200 hackers in 2008. The IRGC cyber-warfare budget was estimated at US$76 million in 2008 (Carroll 2008). It spent U$1 billion in 2011 to develop cyber-attack capabilities (Clayton 2014).
South Korea	The Cyber Command force consisted of around 400 personnel in 2013 (globalpost.com 2013), which increased to 600 by the end of 2014. In July 2013, South Korea announced that it would double the CS budget and spend US$8.8 billion by 2017. It also plans to train 5000 CS experts by that time.	North Korea	The Korean People's Army (KPA) is reported to have a cyber-warfare unit in the Reconnaissance General Bureau known as "Unit 121". According to an ex-chief of South Korea's NIS, in 2010, there were 1000 professional hackers in the Unit. In 2009, then-leader Kim Jong Il ordered an expansion. In 2013 the Unit was estimated to have 3000–4000 personnel engaged in cyber-warfare (Bechtol 2013). Another estimate put the number at 5900 in July 2014 (english.yonhapnews.co.kr 2014).

and problems associated with attribution, it is extremely difficult to use punishment as a threat to deter a potential offender from attacking (Lindsay 2013). Whereas retaliation requires knowing the attackers with full certainty, equivalents of DNA sample, fingerprint, and other offender information to identify a cyber-perpetrator do not exist (Summers 2014; Clark and Landau 2011). In most case, traces lead only to botnets, which consist of businesses' and consumers' computers worldwide. Most cyber-offenders thus believe, and often rightly, that they cannot be traced and can cause a widespread destruction without prompting a response from the victim (Sanger and Perlroth 2014).

In order to illustrate the near impossibility of detecting cyber-attack sources, consider the 2014 high profile hacks on JPMorgan Chase, Bank of America and Citibank. Trend Micro's chief CS officer and others believed the attacks were linked to U.S. sanctions on Russia (Dave 2014). A *New York Times* article asserted that the hackers allegedly operated from Russia and had "at least loose connections with officials of the Russian government" (Goldstein et al. 2014). Investigations of U.S. law enforcement officials, however, ruled out the possibility that the Russian government sponsored the attacks (reuters.com 2014).

1.4.3 Vulnerability of Critical and Sensitive Sectors

We can also observe intersectoral and inter-industry heterogeneity in the cyber-threats faced and CS measures taken. Government, energy and banking industries often face high profile cyber-attacks compared to other sectors. Especially cyber-attacks on the energy sector entail major risks, which may stop the flow of natural gas through pipelines, or cause a petrochemical facility's explosion and oil spill (Pwc 2014).

In 2013, researchers at several U.S. CS companies discovered cyberespionage campaign, which targeted Western oil and gas companies and energy investment firms. According to the CS company, CrowdStrike more than 1000 organizations from over 84 countries were victimized by the hacking group. The group's modus operandi was described as a "watering hole attack", which involved infecting the websites the targets often visit. Workers and investors unknowingly downloaded the malware, when they visited the infected websites, which allowed the hackers to penetrate the victims' computers. According to a report released by Symantec, the had "the Stuxnet-like remote control capability" (Perlroth 2014b).

In 2013, researchers at several U.S. CS companies discovered a cyberespionage campaign in which hackers allegedly from Russia attacked the networks of over 1000 companies. Experts believed that industrial espionage was a key motive given Russia's dependence on oil and gas industry. By looking at the manner in which the targets had been chosen, analysts believed that hackers also wanted to remotely control the industrial control systems (Sanger and Perlroth 2014).

Banks represent a highly attractive target since they have highly sensitive information about customers such as social security numbers (SSN) and detailed records of past spending. Cyber-attacks facing banks include disruption of websites, payment card fraud, and infiltration of their networks to steal money.

Likewise, healthcare companies store financial, medical and other types of personal information. Especially medical information is highly attractive for cybercriminals since the information can be used in a variety of ways and it takes victims longer to realize that their information has been stolen. Cybercriminals can also use medical information to impersonate patients with specific diseases and obtain prescriptions for substances that are controlled by regulators such as the Food and Drug Administration (FDA) (Finkle 2014).

1.5 Elements of National CS Strategies

In order to examine national CS strategies, this book draws from the rich literature on strategy, mainly so called the "design school", which was developed in the 1960s, primarily in the corporate setting. Nonetheless, it is recognized that the basic concepts and frameworks of the design school can be extended to other settings such as government agencies, universities, and non-profit organizations. A simple paraphrasing may be required to do so such as changing the terminology to "corporate strategy" for government agencies, "organizational strategy" or "agency strategy" (Behn 1980).

This school has proposed a general framework that provides a basis for the study of strategy formulation and implementation (Mintzberg 1990). Strategy involves determining the long-run objectives, purposes or goals and the adoption of policies, courses of actions and the allocation of the resources necessary for achieving the goals (Andrews 1967; Chandler 1962).

The model proposed by this school views the process of strategy formulation as a design to achieve a fit between external environment and internal competence (Mintzberg 1990). Other relevant factors that influence the evaluation and choice of a strategy are organizational values (internal) and social responsibilities (external). The proposed model of national CS strategy based on these elements is presented in Fig. 1.1.

1.5.1 Strengths

Some nations have developed key strengths in a number of CS areas. One country cashing in on the trend of rapidly rising cybercrime is Israel, which has spawned numerous globally competitive CS firms. Israel is making attempts to build an image of the country as the center of global CS excellence. The CEO of CyberArk put the issue this way: "Everybody understands that you buy Swiss watches from Switzerland and information security from Israel" (Leichman 2013). Israel-based firms have achieved the depth needed in cyber protection expertise. Some high-profile CS firms from the country include the financial data security firm Trusteer (acquired by IBM in 2013), CyberArk (specialized in securing and managing privileged passwords and identities), NativeFlow (specialized to manage the Bring Your Own Device (BYOD) problem), Check Point Software Technologies Ltd, Actimize (which provides solutions to global financial institutions to detect fraud, prevent money laundering, and manage risk) and Aorato (which learns and graphs people's network behavior and identifies suspicious activity) (Miller 2014).

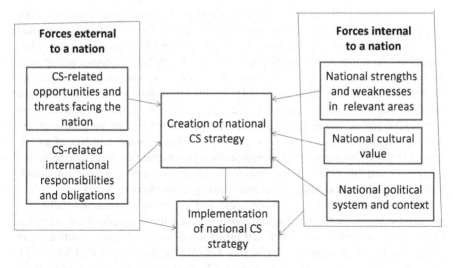

Fig. 1.1 A design model for a national CS strategy

1.5.2 Weaknesses

Most organizations and nations suffer from a low level of CS preparedness. In a Ponemon Institute's survey of about 4900 IT security practitioners in 15 countries, which was released in April 2014, 57 % of the respondents did not think that their organizations were protected from advanced cyber-attacks. 48 % said that their board-level executives had a "sub-par" understanding of CS issues (Ponemon Institute 2014). A shortage of CS specialists is a common weakness facing most economies. According to Cisco's *2014 Annual Security Report*, there was a shortage of over 1 million security professionals across the globe. The report noted that most organizations lack people or systems needed for CS (cisco.com 2014). According to the European Commission (EC), the U.K. will need 750,000 more CS specialists by 2017 (Warrell 2014). Developing economies have an even more acute shortage of such specialists. In 2014, Thailand (population: 67 million) was estimated to have 200–300 CS specialists compared to 1500 in Singapore (population: 5.3 million) (Leesa-nguansuk 2014).

This shortage can be attributed to the nascent stage of the field. CS-related educational, training and certification processes are highly decentralized and are taking place in non-standard ways, without using a formal basis and a clear model (Vijayan 2014). CS is only just being recognized as a profession and the "routes" to jobs are less well-understood than the potential threats (Warrell 2014).

A high dependence on digital technologies can be considered as a weakness for industrialized economies. These economies' proficiency in collecting, processing, analyzing and disseminating information to facilitate rapid and effective decision making and the achievement of information superiority have made them attractive cyber-attack targets. A big concern is also a general lack of CS orientation among individuals, businesses, and government agencies. In many cases employees are easily manipulated by cybercriminals due to factors such as their desire and pressure to be helpful, high turnover rates, low pay and the lack of training. Most employees do not want to run the potential risk of making a customer unhappy or angry. For instance, a CS expert reportedly called a big investment-management firm to test the latter's CS readiness. He told the customer service representative that he was going through a divorce and asked if his wife had opened an account with a false name. The representative readily provided him with account numbers and other details. In another case, the expert pretended to be an employee of a well-known IT company gathering information for a government contract and called the company's satellite office. In less than half an hour, an employee gave him details about the company's operating and anti-virus systems (Kapner 2011).

Likewise, in South Korea, businesses' and government agencies' failure to adequately invest in CS has been a concern, given the widespread use of ICTs. For instance, according to the National Information Society Agency, South Korean government's CS budget for 2013 was US$214 million (beSUCCESS 2013). According to Panda Labs' *Annual report 2012*, South Korea had the world's second highest percentage of computers infected with malware (54.2 %) only behind China (54.9 %). A simulated cyber-attack carried out by the Korea Advanced Institute of Science and Technology (KAIST) in an agreement with a Korean bank indicated that its security mechanisms could be broken in a few weeks (beSUCCESS 2013). Observers have also noted that the South Korean military is unprepared to deal with cyber-threats (Hickey 2012).

1.5.3 Opportunities

Political elites of some nations have framed the use of cyber-attack as an opportunity that could help establish their relative superiority vis-à-vis other nations. For instance, two senior colonels of the Chinese military Qiao Liang and Wang Xiangsui, in their 1999 book, Unrestricted Warfare, have argued that since China's People's Liberation Army (PLA) lacks resources to compete with the U.S. in conventional weapons it should focus on the development of new information and cyberwar technologies and viruses to neutralize or erode an enemy's political, economic and military information and command and control infrastructures. The authors have forcefully made a case for developing a means of challenging through asymmetry rather than matching the U.S. in terms of all types of resources (Waller 2000).

Likewise, North Korean rulers view that the development of cyber-capabilities can overcome the adverse effects of economic sanctions facing the country. According to a South Korean official, North Korean leader Kim Jong-un in February 2013 said: "If we have strong information technology and brave warriors like the Reconnaissance General Bureau, we will be able to break any sanctions and have no problem building a strong and prosperous country" (chosun.com 2013).

Table 1.2 Actions of state and non-state actors that have the potential to affect national security

	State actors	Non-state actors
Military/ Political	Cyber-attack initiated by state actors (e.g., Stuxnet, cyber-attacks on Estonia in 2007 and Georgia in 2008).	Non-state actors weakening tyrannical governments (Anonymous attacks on North Korea's intranet).
Economic	Economic espionage involving state actors: An ex-head of the U.S. NSA argued that IP thefts of U.S. organizations have resulted in the "greatest transfer of wealth in history". He estimated the cost of IP theft to the U.S. companies at US$250 billion annually (Joye 2013). State actors have been blamed for a large proportion of this alleged theft.	Cybercrime gangs involved in financially motivated crimes (e.g., The creators of Zeus Trojan horse compromised banking information and stole US$70 million by September 2010 in the U.S., over US$9 million in 3 months in the U.K.) (Ducklin 2011).

1.5.4 Cyber-Threats: Sources, Nature and Characteristics

Some U.S. observers have long believed that China, Iran, Russia, and North Korea have developed cyber-attack capabilities, trained hackers in cyber-warfare, and have been systematically probing the U.S. computer networks in order to exploit the weaknesses (Lenzner and Vardi 2004).

Rival states are not the only threats nations face. Table 1.2 presents a sample of CS-related actions of state and non-state actors that have the potential to affect national security. Individuals and non-state actors are using cyberspace to further their interests through malicious actions and behaviors (Reveron 2012). In June 2013, the collective hacker group, Anonymous, claimed that it hacked into North Korea's intranet and downloaded secret military documents. While some analysts (Fisher 2013) have disputed this claim and pointed out physical separation of North Korea's intranet from the rest of the Internet makes the validity of this claim extremely doubtful, there was some visible impact. According to U.S. officials, for instance, domestic North Korean sites were taken down following Anonymous's announcement of the hacking attacks (Keck 2013) .

There are various security concerns. Prior researchers have proposed five key security issues: political, economic, military, societal/socio-cultural and environmental (Albert and Buzan 2011). Since environmental security is of little relevance in the context of CS, we mainly focus on the first four threats.

1.5.4.1 Military Security Threats

The military security of states depends on their ability to protect from forceful coercion, and fight wars. A powerful example is the Stuxnet worm, which appeared in the second half of 2010. It was programmed to damage Iran's centrifuges at the Natanz nuclear site. While the nature of the cyberspace makes it impossible to trace the actual origin of the software, Israel and the U.S. have been blamed as creators of the Stuxnet (Choucri and Goldsmith 2012). As a further example, speaking at a military conference in August 2012, a former ground commander in Afghanistan acknowledged that he used cyber-attacks against an adversary in 2010: "I was able to use my cyber operations against my adversary with great impact. I was able to get inside his nets, infect his command-and-control, and in fact defend myself against his almost constant incursions to get inside my wire, to affect my operations" (Gjelten 2013). Another example could be the 2007 cyber-attacks on Estonia's Internet infrastructure. CS specialists believed that pro-Putin Russian hackers and political activists of the so called Nashi variety teamed up with the Kremlin to launch the attacks (Glenny and Kavanagh 2012).

1.5.4.2   Political Security Threats

The political security concerns with a government's political authority, governing capacity, and the capability of being recognized. From the standpoint of political security, cyber-attacks that are launched to express political or social protest, known as hacktivism deserve mention. These types of attacks have become a major headache for the governments of a number of countries (e.g., Brazil, North Korea, Russia, the U.S.) and companies. According to Amnesty International, in countries such as Bahrain, Azerbaijan and Egypt, Internet users are persecuted for the Internet's political use (Boiten 2014). North Korea has closed down access to Twitter and Facebook (Boiten 2014).

1.5.4.3   Economic Security Threats

The economic security deals trade, production and finance (Albert and Buzan 2011). Developed and developing countries have different viewpoints regarding the economic security threats associated with CS. For instance, the U.S. is concerned about IP theft and other problems associated with economic espionage (Table 1.2). BRICS states (Brazil, Russia, India, China and South Africa), on the other hand, have argued that developing countries' dependence on Western technologies as a threat to economic security.

1.5.4.4   Societal, Socio-Cultural or Cultural Security Threats

The societal, socio-cultural or cultural security involves the sustainability of collective identities and value. For instance, China's stated goal of creating a healthy cyberspace, which is defined as "porn-free" and "crime-free", reflects an emphasis on cultural security.

It is reasonable to suggest that not all of these concerns are equally relevant, important and applicable to the context of the cyberspace. Concerns regarding cyber-attacks' impacts on military, political and economic securities have been increasingly found at the center of international debates. Therefore, in Table 1.2, we focus on some examples of activities in the cyberspace carried out by state and non-state actors to illustrate how cyber-attacks could affect nations' military/political and economic securities. As Table 1.2 makes it clear, the actions of state and non-state actors have the potential to affect the global security as well as international relations positively as well as negatively.

1.5.5 National Cultural Value

Just like organizational values, which involve the beliefs, preferences and expectations of those leading the organization or the top management team (Mintzberg 1990) , affect corporate strategy, national cultural values are likely to be reflected in a national CS strategy. A country's CS strategy may not necessarily represent the value system of most citizens, which is especially the case in the CS of authoritarian regimes. For instance, the Chinese value system and norms are reflected in the Chinese government's emphasis on healthy and harmonious Internet environment. A healthy cyberspace is "porn-free" and "crime-free" and "harmonious" means that it does not threaten to destabilize the state's social and political order. However, any cyber activity that challenges the CCP's right to rule may be considered as a non-harmonious behavior.

1.5.6 National Political System and Context

The nature of a nation's CS strategy and its implementation can be linked to the national political system and context. For instance, the U.S. lacks a comprehensive CS legislation, which in large part, is a product of a substantial Democrat-Republican divide. While most Republicans emphasize national security and information-sharing, they are against imposing regulations that may increase costs to private firms and require them to follow government-set security standards. Democrats, on the other hand, like to limit the state's power to access citizens' data held by Internet firms but are worried relatively less about regulatory burden on the private sector (The Economist 2013).

A comparison of Brazil and China may offer important insight regarding the influence of national political system and context on CS strategy. A computer crime bill was pending in the Brazilian Congress since 2005 for over 7 years, which became unpopular with lawmakers due to a concern that it may facilitate government spying on citizens. China is less likely to face such constraints due to its authoritarian political structure.

1.5.7   International Responsibilities and Obligations

International responsibilities and obligations can be considered as the equivalent of social responsibilities in the formulation of corporate strategies. Most nations consider a moral responsibility and obligation to cooperate with other nations and contribute to global CS. International CS-related cooperation is increasingly embraced in numerous international discourses involving CS. In a letter to the editor of the *Financial Times*, Dai Qingli, Spokesperson, Chinese Embassy in the U.K., when responding to the complaint that China did not cooperate with other countries in CS-related matters, noted that Chinese police helped 41 countries investigate 721 cases related to cybercrimes between 2004 and 2010. She also said that China had inter-police co-operation with more than 30 countries (Qingli 2011).

1.5.8   Implementation of Strategy

While a well-formulated strategy is an important prerequisite to a successful implementation, there are a number of factors that drive the success of the implementation process. Prior research in the corporate setting has suggested that it is essential to communicate effectively with and increase the commitment and involvement of employees (Alexander 1985). The implementation of a national CS strategy should focus on broader stakeholders. The process of strategy implementation can be facilitated by proactively engaging and communicating with key stakeholders regarding the CS strategy and explaining what it is all about and the rationales behind it. Finally, it is important to think about what the critical resources and how sufficient resources can be made available in order to implement the strategy (Smircich and Stubbart 1985). Prior research has identified at least four different kinds of resources: money, manpower, technical expertise (in-house expertise or hiring new employees with required skills in order to implement CS) and time (adequate time and attention to the CS efforts) (Alexander 1985).

1.6   The Roles of the Private Sector

In a strategy, commitment of resources is the key to achieving the goals and objectives (Husted and Allen 2000). The private sector's CS spending and CS-related entrepreneurial activities deserve mention for two reasons. First, the government's role has decreased significantly in CS compared to the traditional security (Cavelty 2008). Second, in many cases, commercial interests and national interests are tightly linked and the boundary between national security and commercial security is blurred. Analysts have noted that techniques once found in state-sponsored cyber-warfare are being deployed against corporate targets. Likewise, increasingly evolving nature of industrial espionage is being expanded to control physical assets via hacking, which used to be deployed only to capture commercial secrets and intellectual property (IP) in the past (Binham 2013).

Many organizations are devoting substantial resources and efforts to strengthen CS due to increased perception of cyber-threats. For instance, in a survey conducted by ESG research among organizations with more than 1000 employees, 57 % of security professionals believed that the CS threat landscape was "significantly worse" or "somewhat worse" than in 2012 (Oltsik 2014). According to Gartner, organizations worldwide spent US$67 billion on CS in 2013 (economist.com 2014). Likewise, a study of the research company Markets and Market indicated that the global CS will reach US$120.1 billion in 2017 (saudigazette.com.sa 2014). The Asia-Pacific CS market is expected to reach US$26 billion by 2017 (Loh 2014). Federal agencies and contractors annually spend US$10 billion to protect sensitive government data from cyber-attacks (foxnews.com 2014).

Especially a number of large firms in sensitive and critical sectors have substantially increased CS spending. The Brazilian oil giant Petrobras is an illuminating example of a firm with strong CS measures, which in 2013, announced a CS investment of US$1.8 billion. Likewise, JPMorgan's CS spending was estimated at US$250 million in 2014. In the same vain, while global CS budgets fell by 4 % in 2014, CS spending in the healthcare sector increased by two-thirds that year due primarily to the threat of cybercriminals targeting patient data (Kuchler 2014a).

The surge in entrepreneurial activities and investments in CS have improved the flow of critical resources in CS. According to the financial data provider PrivCo, VC firms are expected to invest US$788 million into early stage CS startups in 2014 compared to US$452 million in 2013 (Oltsik 2014). According to PrivCo, in the first 8 months of 2014, investment in CS start-ups exceeded the total of 2013, which was US$1.1 billion (Kuchler 2014b). Major banks are also investing in CS start-ups. For instance, Citibank's VC arm has taken stakes in vArmour, Pindrop security, and Click Security. Likewise, Wells Fargo-backed Norwest Venture Partners has invested in Shape Security and FireEye (Kuchler 2014c).

Another indirect indicator of the private sector's emphasis on CS concerns lobbying activities on this issue. According to a review by Capitol Metrics, a lobbying analytics firm, during 2008–14, the number of companies, associations and other groups lobbying on data and CS issues nearly tripled. The number of lobby firms advocating on behalf of clients on data and CS issues also tripled during the period. Between 2008 and 2012, the number of companies, trade associations and other groups lobbying on data or CS matters climbed steadily from 108 to 321, and dipped slightly in 2013 to 314. Those figures reflect lobbying activity by companies' in-house lobbyists who listed "data security," "cybersecurity" or "cyber security" on lobbying disclosure forms. Between 2008 and 2012, the number of lobby firms that advocated on behalf of clients on data and CS issues ballooned from 74 to 220, and dropped off slightly in 2013 to 216. The rise in lobbying activity appears partly tied to corporations responding to high-profile data breaches.

Target, Michaels Stores and Neiman Marcus, hired outside lobbyists immediately after disclosing the cyber-attacks they faced (Ho 2014).

At the same time, market forces are evolving that may enhance firms' CS performances. For instance, the cyber liability insurance (data breach insurance) industry and market are currently in the infant stage, but are growing fast. A company is required to strengthen CS in order to buy coverage at a lower rate. A system that requires CS insurance thus raises CS standards. That is, such insurance could help companies improve their CS systems and put efforts to help secure policies (businessinsurance.com 2014). Cyber liability insurance provides coverage for the theft or loss of first-party and third-party data. For the loss or theft of first-party data, an insurer may cover expenses related to notifying clients regarding the data breach, purchasing credit monitoring services for affected customers and launching a public relations campaign to restore the company's reputation. Third-party coverage includes claims related to unlawful disclosure of a third-party's information and infringement of intellectual property rights (IPR) (natlawreview.com 2014).

Many companies have relied on private sector threat intelligence services. These services rely on technologies that do not necessarily communicate with other companies which have not bought the same technology. In order to address this challenge, the financial services industry in the U.S. is leading an effort to encourage banks and companies in critical infrastructure sectors to improve information sharing. The Financial Services Information Sharing and Analysis Center (FS-ISAC) would facilitate sharing information about cyber-attacks (Kuchler 2014d). This measure is expected to prevent hackers from using the same malware against several companies over time.

1.7   Discussion and Concluding Remarks

It can be argued that, to some extent, the current fear and heightened concerns about cyber-attacks and cyber-warfare may have been driven by an exaggerated assessment of the threats by the media, government officials and CS companies. In some ways, they may have even presented misleading accounts of such threats. Nonetheless cyber-threat is undoubtedly a serious and growing problem.

Real and perceived threats of cyber-attacks have slowed down the capture of value from modern ICTs such as cloud computing, big data, mobile technologies, and health-care technologies. According to McKinsey Global Institute's (MGI) cyber risk-maturity survey, about 70 % of the respondents reported that CS concerns had delayed the adoption of public cloud computing by at least a year. The same survey found that for 40 % of the respondents CS concerns delayed enterprise-mobility capabilities by at least a year. MGI analysis of data on the technologies that will be critically linked to business strategy during the coming decade indicated that robustness of the CS environment will determine US$9–21 trillion of economic-value creation worldwide over the next 5–7 years (Bailey et al. 2014).

An appropriate national CS strategy is likely to address some of the concerns and accelerate the diffusion of these ICTs.

Nations must be prepared to deal with unexpected problems that may arise in the implementation of a CS strategy. To illustrate this argument, we can consider Israel's CS strategy. In an effort to foster cooperation and coordination in CS-related issues among the private sector, academia, CS experts and government agencies and to promote long-term research and analysis of cyber-threats, in 2011, Israel created the National Cyber Bureau (NCB). While it was a welcome addition for the Israeli CS landscape, the NCB's creation produced internal conflicts and turf wars with the intelligence agency Shabak (also known as ShinBet). The creation of the National Authority for Cyber-Defense, a new cyber-defense authority created in September 2014 to protect civilian networks is expected to resolve the conflict. The new agency reports to the head of the NCB. It is also likely to decrease the influence of Israel's intelligence community in civilian cyber-defense issues (Sugarman 2014). This provides an important lesson for policy makers in other countries to adequately prepare for dealing with unexpected problems.

There has been a lack of comprehensive, integrated and holistic efforts to fight cyber-attacks. The German company Siemens and the Swiss company ABB, which dominate the global market for power grid and industrial equipment, are taking measures to make their designs secure. But infrastructure companies have been slow to upgrade their equipment. While a security breach could have catastrophic consequences, they tend to view the upgrades as "sunk cost" and their willingness to pay the price to improve security is often low. Put differently, these companies are not incentivized to achieve the highest CS levels (Vinton 2014). The executive director of a Brazilian company, which specializes in securing industrial control systems, put the issue this way: "The [power] industry has 20-year-old devices—we have to think of other kinds of tools" (Simonite 2013). More emphasis thus needs to be placed on strengthening CS measures of the entire value chain of critical infrastructures.

A nation's CS strategy has important international spillover effects. That is, in today's dynamic, interconnected, and interdependent global society, cyber-attacks, cyber-frauds and CS trends in a given country are of interest to other countries. Hackers and cybercriminals are highly motivated and skilled, who are constantly morphing, reconfiguring and developing their crafts. In the words of Brian Finch, they "act like water" and "follow the path of least resistance" (Finch 2014). This means that if a country's private sector, government agencies and other actors strengthen their CS measures, more vulnerable targets in other countries become more attractive from the cyber-offender's risk-return perspective. A related point is that nations' CS strategies, as well as insecure systems, also have serious international spillover effects. For instance, the Stuxnet worm damaged a number of unintended targets.

The risks associated with cyber-warfare are similar to and different from those of conventional military warfare. A key difference is that unlike nuclear weapons, cyberwar is less likely to pose the "existential threat to humanity" (Nye 2013).

However, a strong similarity is that conventional military attacks and cyber-attacks may employ different means to achieve the same or similar end.

References

Afternoon Voice (India). (2014). *Iranian hackers used fake Facebook accounts to Spy on US. Others: iSight.*

Albert, M., & Buzan, B. (2011). Securitization, sectors and functional differentiation. *Security Dialogue, 42*(4–5), 413–425.

Alexander, L. D. (1985). Successfully implementing strategic decisions. *Long Range Planning, 37* (3), 201–218.

Andrews, K. R. (1967). *The concept of corporate strategy.* Homewood, IL: Dow Jones-Irwin.

Bailey, T., Miglio, A. D., & Richter, W. (2014). The rising strategic risks of cyberattacks. *McKinsey Quarterly, 2,* 17–22.

Bechtol, B. E. (2013). *South Korea: Responding to the North Korean threat.* American Enterprise Institute.   http://www.aei.org/outlook/foreign-and-defense-policy/defense/south-korea-responding-to-the-north-korean-threat/

Behn, R. D. (1980). Leadership for cut-back management: The use of corporate strategy. *Public Administration Review, 40*(6), 613–620.

beSUCCESS. (2013). *South Korea cyber security concerns go far beyond financial industry.* http:// e27.co/south-korea-cyber-security-concerns-go-far-beyond-financial-industry/

Binham, C. (2013). *The hacker hunters.* http://www.ft.com/intl/cms/s/2/bccc8f3c-523c-11e3-8c42-00144feabdc0.html#axzz37vVS6Nvw

blogs.wsj.com. (2014). *Army bolsters cybersecurity force amid shifts in threats, technology.* http:// blogs.wsj.com/washwire/2014/10/14/army-bolsters-cybersecurity-force-amid-shifts-in-threats-technology/

Boiten, E. (2014). *Nations want to be the ruler of the internet – at least within their own borders.* http://phys.org/news/2014-11-nations-ruler-internet-borders.html

Bronk, C. (2009). *Time to move toward a more secure cyberspace.* http://www.worldpoliticsreview.com/article.aspx?id=4194

businessinsurance.com. (2014). *N.Y. state financial regulator will focus on cyber security.* http:// www.businessinsurance.com/article/20140923/NEWS07/140929962?tags=l338l299l69l80l83l 302l303

Carroll, W. (2008). *Iranian cyber warfare threat assessment.* http://defensetech.org/2008/09/23/ iranian-cyber-warfare-threat-assessment/

Cavelty, M. D. (2008). *Cyber-security and threat politics.* London, New York: Routledge.

Chandler, A. D., Jr. (1962). *Strategy and structure: Chapters in the history of the American industrial enterprise.* Cambridge, MA: MIT Press.

chosun.com. (2013). *N. Korea 'confident' in cyber warfare capabilities.* http://english.chosun. com/site/data/html_dir/2013/04/08/2013040801313.html

Choucri, N. (2012). *Cyberpolitics in international relations: Context, connectivity, and content* (p. 39). Cambridge, MA: MIT Press.

Choucri, N., & Goldsmith, D. (2012). Lost in cyberspace, Harnessing the internet, international relations, and global security. *The Atomic Scientists, 68*(2), 70–77.

cisco.com. (2014). *South African businesses face unprecedented levels of cyber attacks,* March 20. http://www.cisco.com/web/ZA/press/2014/032014.html

Clark, D. D., & Landau, S. (2011). Untangling attribution. *Harvard National Security Journal, 2* (2), 25–40.

Clayton, M. (2014). *Cyber-war: In deed and desire, Iran emerging as a major power*. http://www. csmonitor.com/World/Security-Watch/Cyber-Conflict-Monitor/2014/0316/Cyber-war-In-deed-and-desire-Iran-emerging-as-a-major-power

Dave, P. (2014). No fraud in bank cyberattacks; But experts urge financial institutions to spend more on defense systems. *Los Angeles Times* Part B, 2.

David, A. (2003). *Wheeler and Gregory N. Larsen, techniques for cyber attack attribution*. Institute for Defense Analysis, IDA Paper P-3792, 1.

Ducklin, P. (2011). *Busted! Ukrainian cybercrime duo who ripped off $4.5 million sent to prison in UK*, November 2. http://nakedsecurity.sophos.com/2011/11/02/busted-ukrainian-cybercrime-duo-who-ripped-off-4-5-million-sent-to-prison-in-uk/

Dvorin, T. (2014). *Israel launches national Cyber-Defense authority*. http://www. israelnationalnews.com/News/News.aspx/185349#.VCm0pVfNJmc

economist.com. (2010). *War in the fifth domain: Are the mouse and keyboard the new weapons of conflict?* http://www.economist.com/node/16478792

economist.com. (2014). *Defending the digital frontier*. http://www.economist.com/news/special-report/21606416-companies-markets-and-countries-are-increasingly-under-attack-cyber-criminals

english.yonhapnews.co.kr. (2014). *N. Korea attempts to hack into S. Koreans' smartphones*: NIS. http://english.yonhapnews.co.kr/northkorea/2014/10/29/29/0401000000AEN20141029003300315F.html

Finch, B. (2014). *Why cybersecurity must be defined by process, not tech*, December 11. http://blogs.wsj.com/cio/2014/12/11/why-cybersecurity-must-be-defined-by-process-not-tech/

Finkle, J. (2014). *Exclusive: FBI warns healthcare sector vulnerable to cyber attacks*. http://www. reuters.com/article/2014/04/23/us-cybersecurity-healthcare-fbi-exclusiv-idUSBREA3M1Q920140423

Fisher, M. (2013). *Hacker group Anonymous is no match for North Korea*. http://www. washingtonpost.com/blogs/worldviews/wp/2013/06/27/hacker-group-anonymous-is-no-match-for-north-korea/

Fouquet, H., & Mawad, M. (2014). *France demonstrates security savoir faire as it enforces new cyber-security law*. http://www.chicagotribune.com/sns-wp-blm-news-bc-france-cyber06-20141006-story.html#page=1

foxnews.com. (2014). *Federal workers, contractors reportedly behind many cyber breaches – often by accident*. http://www.foxnews.com/politics/2014/11/10/federal-firewall-reportedly-struggles-against-increasing-number-cyberattacks/

Friedman, A. A. (2013). *Cybersecurity and trade: National policies, global and local consequences*. Center for Technology and Innovation at Brookings.

Gale, A. (2014). *North Korea denies direct role in hacking sony pictures*. http://www.wsj.com/articles/north-korea-denies-role-in-hacking-sony-pictures-1417931200

gartner.com. 2013. *Big data*. http://www.gartner.com/it-glossary/big-data/

Gartzke, E. (2013). The myth of cyberwar: Bringing war in cyberspace back down to earth. *International Security, 38*(2), 41–73. doi:10.1162/ISEC_a_00136.

Gjelten, T. (2013). *First strike: US cyber warriors seize the offensive*, January/February. http://www.worldaffairsjournal.org/article/first-strike-us-cyber-warriors-seize-offensive

Glenny, M., & Kavanagh, C. (2012). 800 titles but no policy—thoughts on cyber warfare. *American Foreign Policy Interests, 34*(6), 287–294.

globalpost.com. (2013). *Damage from N.K. cyber attacks estimated at 860 bln won: lawmaker*. http://www.globalpost.com/dispatch/news/yonhap-news-agency/131015/damage-nk-cyber-attacks-estimated-at-860-bln-won-lawmaker

Goldstein, M., Perlroth, N., & Sanger, D. E. (2014). *Hackers' attach cracked 10 financial firms in major assault*. http://dealbook.nytimes.com/2014/10/03/hackers-attack-cracked-10-banks-in-major-assault/?_php=true&_type=blogs&_php=true&_type=blogs&_r=1&#

Harris, S. (2014). Forget China: Iran's hackers are America's newest cyber threat. *Foreign Policy*.

Hickey, W. (2012). *Cyber war: North Korea is getting dangerously good at knocking out networks.* http://www.businessinsider.com/cyber-war-north-korea-is-getting-dangerously-good-at-knocking-out-networks-2012-6

Ho, C. (2014). Lobbying on data, cybersecurity has tripled. *The Washington Post*, P. A13.

Husted, B. W., & Allen, D. B. (2000). Is it ethical to use ethics as strategy? *Journal of Business Ethics, 27*(1), 21–31.

ITU. (2008). *Overview of cybersecurity, Recommendation ITU–T X.1205* (http://tinyurl.com/boys7dj). The ITU Plenipotentiary Conference 2010 held in Guadalajara, Mexico, approved the definition of cybersecurity.

Joye, C. (2013). *It's global cyber war out there*, January 1. http://afr.com/f/free/national/it_global_cyber_war_out_there_94da3CY7Avufi9jp5d0JTI

Kapner, S. (2011). *Hackers press the 'schmooze' button*, October 31. http://online.wsj.com/article/SB10001424052970203911804576653393584528906.html?mod=WSJ_article_onespot

Keck, Z. (2013). *Anonymous: We have Stolen North Korean military documents.* http://thediplomat.com/2013/06/anonymous-we-have-stolen-north-korean-military-documents/

Klimberg, A. (2012). *National cyber security framework manual.* http://www.ccdcoe.org/publications/books/NationalCyberSecurityFrameworkManual.Pdf

Kramer, F. (2009). Cyberpower and national security. In F. D. Kramer, S. Starr, & L. K. Wentz (Eds.), *Cyberpower and national security* (p. 12). Washington, DC: National Defense UP.

Kshetri, N. (2009). Positive externality, increasing returns and the rise in cybercrimes. *Communications of the ACM, 52*(12), 141–144.

Kuchler, H. (2014a). *Businesses spend less on cyber security despite rise in attacks.* http://www.ft.com/intl/cms/s/0/1f8d1436-45c9-11e4-ab10-00144feabdc0.html#axzz3EtjFVeJE

Kuchler, H. (2014b). *Cyber security group vArmour raises $35m.* http://www.ft.com/intl/cms/s/0/f9c0c6dc-27ee-11e4-b7a9-00144feabdc0.html#axzz3B2mHAZPk

Kuchler, H. (2014c). *Banks join wave of investors in cyber security start-ups.* http://www.ft.com/cms/s/0/63d7798e-5b03-11e4-b449-00144feab7de.html#axzz3HIndeXlL

Kuchler, H. (2014d). *US financial industry launches platform to thwart cyber attacks.* http://www.ft.com/intl/cms/s/0/080092b2-437a-11e4-8a43-00144feabdc0.html#axzz3GYSHXxLM

Kuehl, D. T. (2009). From cyberspace to cyberpower: Defining the problem. In F. D. Kramer, S. Starr, & L. K. Wentz (Eds.), *Cyberpower and national security* (p. 38). Washington, DC: Center for Technology and National Security, National Defense University.

Leesa-nguansuk, S. (2014). Thai cybersecurity slammed. *The Bangkok Post*, August 2.

Leichman, A. K. (2013). *Israel is the go-to address for cyber-security.* http://www.israel21c.org/technology/israel-is-the-go-to-address-for-cyber-security/

Leitersdorf, Y. (2014). *Ofer Schreiber. Is a cybersecurity bubble brewing?* http://fortune.com/2014/06/17/is-a-cybersecurity-bubble-brewing/

Lenzner, R., & Vardi, N. (2004). The next threat. *Forbes*, 70.

Libicki, M. C. (2013). *Don't buy the Cyberhype: How to prevent Cyberwars from becoming real ones.* http://www.foreignaffairs.com/articles/139819/martin-c-libicki/dont-buy-the-cyberhype

Lindsay, J. R. (2013). Stuxnet and the limits of cyber warfare. *Security Studies, 22*(3), 365–404.

Loh, D. (2014). *Cyber security industry has potential to grow further: Analysts.* http://www.channelnewsasia.com/news/business/singapore/cyber-security-industry/1390432.html

Mainichi Japan. (2011). *Japan not alone as victim of Chinese cyber attacks.* http://mdn.mainichi.jp/features/archive/news/2011/10/20111031p2g00m0fe042000c.html

Metz, S. (2001). Strategic asymmetry. *Military Review*, 23–31 (July–August).

Miller, Z. (2014). *7 Israeli security companies who could help Putin protect the Sochi Olympics.* http://www.forbes.com/sites/zackmiller/2014/01/29/7-israeli-security-companies-who-could-help-putin-protect-the-sochi-olympics/

Mintzberg, H. (1990). The design school: Reconsidering the basic premises of strategic management. *Strategic Management Journal, 11*, 171–195.

Nakashima, E. (2013). *Pentagon to boost cybersecurity force.* http://www.washingtonpost.com/world/national-security/pentagon-to-boost-cybersecurity-force/2013/01/19/d87d9dc2-5fec-11e2-b05a-605528f6b712_story.html?hpid=z4

natlawreview.com. (2014). *What is cyber liability insurance?* http://www.natlawreview.com/article/what-cyber-liability-insurance

Naylor, R. T. (2005). The rise and fall of the underground economy. *BJWA, 11,* 131–143. http://www.mdpi.com/2078-2489/4/1/117/htm#sthash.dm28Mr92.dpuf

Nye, J. S., Jr. (2011). *The future of power.* New York: Public Affairs Press.

Nye, J. S. (2013). From bombs to bytes: Can our nuclear history inform our cyber future? *Bulletin of the Atomic Scientists, 69*(5), 8–14.

Oltsik, J. (2014). *Cybersecurity startup gold rush for venture capitalists.* http://www.networkworld.com/article/2459150/cisco-subnet/cybersecurity-startup-gold-rush-for-venture-capitalists.html

Perlroth, N. (2014a). *Cybersecurity breaches raise questions,* December 3, http://www.nytimes.com/times-insider/2014/12/03/cybersecurity-breaches-raise-questions/

Perlroth, N. (2014b). Energy sector faces attacks from hackers in Russia. *The New York Times,* July 1, B1, B7.

Ponemon Institute. (2014). *Exposing the cybersecurity cracks: A global perspective: Part I: Deficient, disconnected & in the dark,* Sponsored by Websense, Inc.

Pwc. (2014). *How oil & gas is affected by Mega trends.* The Norwegian Oil and Gas Association.

Qingli, D. (2011). *China itself is facing growing cybercrime and attacks.* http://www.ft.com/intl/cms/s/0/2a134f8c-f5be-11e0-bcc2-00144feab49a.html#axzz1dOy0Cfug

reuters.com. (2014). *Russia ruled out as culprit in Chase cyber security breach, U.S. officials say.* http://www.reuters.com/article/2014/10/21/cybersecurity-jpmorgan-idUSL2N0SF30M20141021

Reveron, D. S. (Ed.). (2012). *Cyberspace and national security threats, opportunities, and power in a virtual world.* Washington, DC: Georgetown University Press.

Riley, M. (2014). Iranian hacking network used fake news group to spy on U.S. officials; Facebook Links National Post (f/k/a The Financial Post) (Canada), A10.

Robertson, J., Lawrence, D., & Strohm, C. (2014). *Sony's breach stretched from Thai hotel to Hollywood.* http://www.bloomberg.com/news/2014-12-07/sony-s-darkseoul-breach-stretched-from-thai-hotel-to-hollywood.html

Rundle, M. (2013). *Cyber war threatens real-world conflict In Korean Peninsula – And The North might be winning.* http://www.huffingtonpost.co.uk/2013/04/10/north-korea-cyber-war-threatens-real-war_n_3052026.html

Salant, J. D., & Holmes, A. (2013). *Pearl harbor looms for vulnerable networks, McConnell says.* http://www.businessweek.com/news/2013-10-30/pearl-harbor-looms-for-vulnerable-networks-mcconnell-says-3

Sanger, D. E., & Perlroth, N. (2014). *New Russian boldness revives a cold war tradition: Testing the other side.* http://www.nytimes.com/2014/10/31/world/europe/new-russian-boldness-revives-a-cold-war-tradition-testing-the-other-side-.html?_r=0

sas.com. (2013). *Big Data: What it is and why it matters.* https://www.sas.com/en_us/insights/big-data/what-is-big-data.html

saudigazette.com.sa. (2014). *Cyber security solutions demand on the rise in M.* http://www.saudigazette.com.sa/index.cfm?method=home.regcon&contentid=20141001219958

Schneier, B. (2012). Securing medical research: A cybersecurity point of view. *Science, 336* (6088), 1527–1529. doi:10.1126/science.1224321.

Simonite, T. (2013). *Protecting power grids from hackers is a huge challenge.* http://www.technologyreview.com/news/511851/protecting-power-grids-from-hackers-is-a-huge-challenge/

Smircich, L., & Stubbart, C. (1985). Strategic management in an enacted world. *Academy of Management Review, 10*(4), 724–736.

strategicstudiesinstitute.army.mil. (2014). *Iran's emergence as a cyber power.* http://www.strategicstudiesinstitute.army.mil/index.cfm/articles/Irans-emergence-as-cyber-power/2014/08/20

Strohm, C. (2014). *Hack that crippled Sony Pictures' computers highlights growing threat of malware as cyber weapons.* http://business.financialpost.com/2014/12/04/hack-that-crippled-sony-pictures-computers-highlights-growing-threat-of-malware-as-cyber-weapons/?__lsa=8c2b-c5b1

Sugarman, E. (2014). *What the United States can learn from Israel about Cybersecurity.* http://www.forbes.com/sites/elisugarman/2014/10/07/what-the-united-states-can-learn-from-israel-about-cybersecurity/

Summers, D. J. (2014). *Fighting in the cyber trenches.* http://fortune.com/2014/10/13/cold-war-on-business-cyber-warfare/

The Economist. (2013). To the barricades: How America and Europe are trying to bolster their cyber-defences. http://tinyurl.com/cnflnbz

theguardian.com. (2014). *Sony Pictures hack: how much damage can North Korea's cyber army do?* http://www.theguardian.com/technology/2014/dec/05/sony-pictures-hack-north-korea-cyber-army

Vijayan, A. (2014). *Cybersecurity should be professionalized.* http://www.computerworld.com/s/article/9250174/Cybersecurity_should_be_professionalized

Vinton, K. (2014). *Hacking gets physical: Utilities at risk for Cyber attacks.* http://www.forbes.com/sites/katevinton/2014/07/10/hacking-gets-physical-utilities-at-risk-for-cyber-attacks/

Waller, J. M. (2000). PLA revises the art of war. *Insight on the News,* 21–23 (February 28).

Warrell, H. (2014). *Cyber security industry sends recruiting officers into schools.* http://www.ft.com/intl/cms/s/0/ae43a730-5a00-11e4-8771-00144feab7de.html#axzz3GzOK0fXN

Wulf, W. A., & Jones, A. K. (2009). Reflections on cybersecurity. *Science, New Series, 326*(5955), 943–944.

Chapter 2
The Evolution of Rules and Institutions in Cybersecurity: Cloud Computing and Big Data

2.1 Introduction

The cloud and big data (BD) are described in the popular press as the Next Big Things and major technology disruptions (Weber 2011; Bunge 2014). They are likened and equated to the Industrial Revolution in terms of implications for technological innovations and economic growth (Price 2011). Their transformational nature is, however, associated with significant CS risks.

Regulators are taking a closer look at cloud and BD security. It was reported that due to concerns related to cloud security, as of August 2014, over a dozen countries, including Germany, Brazil, and India had already introduced or were actively discussing data localization laws (Strauss 2014). It is important to note that this requirement goes against the efficiency and innovative capacity of BD and the cloud. For instance, according to the National Institute of Standards and Technology (NIST), "there is a sense of location independence in that the customer generally has no control or knowledge over the exact location of the provided resources but may be able to specify location at a higher level of abstraction (e.g., country, state, or datacenter)" (Mell and Grance 2011). This means that regulations that require locating facilities in a given jurisdiction may force CSPs to select a sub-optimal location or avoid a market (Berry and Reisman 2012). Especially the EU has proposed strict regulations aimed at strengthening cloud security. According to the cloud security company, Skyhigh Networks analysis of more than 7000 CSPs in the European market, only 1 % would meet regulations currently being proposed (Brown 2014).

Organizations also worry about hidden costs associated with security breaches or lawsuits tied to data breach. Failure to take sufficient CS measures, for instance, can lead to a number of problems such as financial loss, regulatory noncompliance, brand and reputation damage, the loss of competitive advantage. Businesses and consumers are cautious in using it to store high-value or sensitive data and information (Goodburn and Hill 2011).

© Springer International Publishing Switzerland 2016
N. Kshetri, *The Quest to Cyber Superiority*, DOI 10.1007/978-3-319-40554-4_2

The importance of this issue is being recognized even in least developed countries. To take an example, consider the use of cloud and BD by emergency workers in the coordination and allocation of medical resources in West African countries that were hard hit by Ebola in 2014. In order to provide actionable insights to government agencies to help contain the disease, IBM developed the cloud and analytics platform for this purpose and teamed up with local Telecom firms such as Orange and Airtel, Sierra Leone's Open Government Initiative and Kenya's Echo Mobile. In order to protect privacy and security of consumer information, Echo Mobile anonymizes the SMS data (businesscloudnews.com 2014).

The idea in this chapter is that security and privacy issues in the BD and cloud, which are real as well as perceived phenomena, can be better understood by examining the evolutions of rules as well as formal and informal institutions. That is, a clearer understanding of various institutional actors, their actions and how they are shifting would help organizations navigate the complex, turbulent and rapidly evolving technological landscape.

2.2   CS Issues in Cloud Computing, and Big Data

2.2.1   The Cloud

A significant gap remains between vendors' claims and users' views of the cloud's security, privacy and transparency. The cloud industry's response has been: "Clouds are more secure than whatever you're using now" (Talbot 2010). But many users do not agree. Issues such as security, privacy and availability are among the topmost concerns in organizations' cloud adoption decisions rather than efficiency and the total cost of ownership (TCO) (Brodkin 2010; McCreary 2008). Due primarily to concerns related to security, privacy and confidentiality critics have argued that the cloud's perceived costs may outweigh the benefits.

Most CSPs are bigger than their clients and deal with higher data volumes. Information stored in the cloud is a potential gold mine for cybercriminals. Storing data in the cloud does not remove organizations' responsibility for protecting both from regulatory and reputational perspectives. In general it is often cloud user organizations' (CUOs) responsibility to make sure that personal data are protected and are only used according to legal provisions. This is further illustrated in Chap. 6 with a comparison of the responsibilities of CUOs and CSPs in the EU's five biggest economies

If an organization dealing with customer data stores them in the cloud provided by a vendor, it is likely that, the organization rather than the vendor is likely to be legally responsible if customer data are compromised. In February 2014, in such a case, the New York Supreme Court ruled in favor of Sony Corp. of America's insurers- Zurich American and Mitsui Sumitomo. In 2011, hackers had attacked Sony's PlayStation Network and extracted Personally Identifiable Information (PII) of more than 77 million people. The hacker had used Amazon's EC2 to attack Sony's system. The court ruled that the insurers are not required to defend Sony against such attacks (Katz 2014).

Sony faced eight class-action lawsuits. Sony's case indicates that a vendor may not be legally responsible under the existing institutional arrangements even if organizations using technologies and services provided by the vendor experience CS breaches. Some commentators have argued that there has been arguably a "disturbing lack of respect for essential privacy" among CSPs (Larkin 2010). For instance, in a complaint filed with the Federal Trade Commission (FTC), the Electronic Privacy Information Center (EPIC) argued that Google misrepresented privacy and security of its users' data stored in Google clouds (Wittow and Buller 2010). CSPs have also been criticized on the ground that they do not conduct adequate background checks of their employees (Wilshusen 2012).

2.2.2   Big Data

BD's characteristics are tightly linked to privacy and security. For instance, a huge amount of data means that security breaches and privacy violations often lead to more severe consequences and losses via reputational damage, legal liability, ethical harms and other issues, which is also referred as an amplified technical impact (ISACA 2014). Second, a large proportion of BD entails high-velocity data such as those related to click-stream and GPS data from mobile devices, which can be used to make a short-term prediction with high level of accuracies (Taylor et al. 2014) . Businesses' initiatives to collect such data have met stiff resistance from consumers. Consumers have expressed growing concern over organizations' data collection methods, especially the use of tracking technologies, such as cookies and GPS trackers (Table 2.1). Yet a number of companies are engaged in questionable data collection and sharing practices. In 2012, a security blogger revealed that Nissan, without warning the owners, reported location, speed and direction of its Leaf brand cars to websites that other users could access through a built-in RSS reader. Likewise, there are reports that iPhones and Android phones have been secretly sending information about users' locations to Apple and Google (Cohen 2013).

Third, data comes in multiple formats such as structured and unstructured. Of special concern is much of the unstructured data such as Word and Excel documents, emails, instant messages, road traffic information and Binary Large Objects (BLOBs) (e.g., multimedia objects such as images, audio and video), which is sensitive in nature and may contain PII and IP (Truxillo 2013). To take an example, in 2010, an Italian court found three YouTube executives guilty of violating a child's privacy. The child had autism and was shown being bullied in a YouTube video (Hooper 2010).

In addition to privacy and security risks of high volume of data from multiple sources, there are also complex data sharing and accessibility issues. The existing

Table 2.1 BD characteristics in relation to security and privacy

Characteristic	Explanation	Security and privacy concerns
Volume	Huge amount of data is created from a wide range of sources such as transactions, unstructured streaming from text, images, audio, voice, VoIP, video, TV and other media, sensor and machine-to data.	• High data volume would likely attract a great deal of attention from cybercriminals. • Amplified technical impact • Violation of transparency principle of FIPs. • Firms may need to outsource to CSPs which may give rise to privacy and security *issues*.
Velocity	Some data is time-sensitive for which speed is more important than volume. Data needs to be stored, processed and analyzed quickly.	• Increasing consumer concerns over privacy in the context of behavioral advertising based on real-time profiling and tracking technologies such as cookies. • Violation of the individual participation principle of FIPs. • Increase in the supply and demand of location-based real time personal information, which has negative spillover effects (e.g., stalking people in real time). • Physical security risks.
Variety	Data comes in multiple formats such as structured, numeric data in traditional database and unstructured text documents, email, video, audio, financial transactions.	• Unstructured data is more likely to conceal PII. • A large variety of information would make it more difficult to detect security breaches, react appropriately and respond to attacks (freepatentsonline.com 2003). • Most organizations lack mechanisms to ensure that employees and third-parties have appropriate access to unstructured data and they are in compliance with data protection regulations (Varonis Systems 2008).
Variability	Data flows can vary greatly with periodic peaks and troughs. These are related to social media trends, daily, seasonal and event-triggered peak data loads and other factors.	• Organizations may lack capabilities to securely store huge amounts of data and manage the collected data during peak data traffic. • Attractiveness as a crime target increases during peak data traffic. • Peak data traffic may cause higher needs to outsource to CSPs which give rise to important privacy and security issues.
Complexity	Data comes from multiple sources which require linking, matching, cleansing and transforming across systems.	• Resulting data is often more personal than the set of data the person would consent to give. • A party with whom de-identified

(continued)

Table 2.1 (continued)

Characteristic	Explanation	Security and privacy concerns
		personal data is shared may combine data from other sources to re-identify. • Violation of the security provision of FIPs.

non-BD security solutions are not designed to handle the scale, speed, variety and complexity of BD. Most organizations lack systematic approaches for ensuring appropriate data access mechanisms. The time-variant nature of data flow means that some of these issues are of more significance during the peak data traffic. For instance, organizations may lack capabilities to securely store huge amounts of data and manage the collected data during peak data traffic. A peak data flow may also increase the need for outsourcing to cloud service CSPs. Commenting on these complex challenges, the Commissioner of the U.S. FTC put the issue this way: "The potential benefits of Big Data are many, consumer understanding is lacking, and the potential risks are considerable" (Brill 2013).

As presented in Table 2.1, the various characteristics of BD are tightly linked to CS (Kshetri 2014).

2.2.2.1   Volume

An organization is often required to store all data in one location in order to facilitate analysis. High volume and concentration of data attract hackers. Moreover, a high data volume increases the probability that the data files and documents may contain inherently valuable and sensitive information. Information stored for the purpose of BD analytics is thus a potential goldmine for cybercriminals. A huge amount of data also means that security breaches and privacy violations lead to more severe consequences and losses via reputational damage, legal liability, ethical harms and other issues. This phenomenon is also referred as an amplified technical impact (ISACA 2014).

If inappropriately used, information contained in huge data volume may lead to psychological, emotional, economic, or social harm to consumers. For instance, BD predictive analysis may improve the accuracy of predictions of a customer's purchasing requirements or preferences. Highly customized offerings based on predicted preference and requirement data may, however, lead to unpleasant, creepy and frightening experiences for consumers. This phenomenon is also referred as predictive privacy harm (Crawford and Schultz 2013). The example most often cited is that of a man's high school aged daughter tracked by the U.S. retailer, Target. The company's pregnancy prediction score indicated that she was pregnant before her father knew and sent promotional mails for products that pregnant women need (Duhigg 2012).

The availability of a huge amount of data also increases the possibility that personal data can be put to new uses to create value. The U.S. FTC Commissioner pointed out the possibility that firms, "without our knowledge or consent, can amass large amounts of private information about people to use for purposes we don't expect or understand" (Brill 2013). Such uses often violate the transparency principle of Fair Information Practices (FIP) (Teufel 2008).

A huge data volume is also related to the demand or even the necessity of outsourcing. An issue of more pressing concern is determining relevance within large data volumes and how to use analytics to create value from relevant data. Firms may thus rely on CSPs for analytic solutions.

2.2.2.2   Velocity

The quickly degrading quality of real-time data is noteworthy . In particular, clickstream data, which constitute the route chosen by visitors when they click/ navigate through a site, is typically collected by online advertisers, retailers, and ISPs. The fact that such data can be collected, stored, and reused indefinitely poses significant privacy risks (Skok 2000). Some tracking tools can manipulate clickstreams to build a detailed database of personal profiles in order to target Internet advertising (CDT 2000).

An important use of BD is real-time consumer profile-driven campaigns such as serving customized ads. For instance, location tracking technologies allow marketers to serve SMS and other forms of ads based on real-time location. This process often involves passive data collection without any overt consumer interaction. The lack of individual consent for the collection, use, and dissemination of such information means that such a practice violates the individual participation principle of FIPs (Teufel 2008).

Recent studies show that there is an increasing consumer concern over privacy in the context of real time behavioral advertising and tracking technologies such as cookies (King and Jessen 2010). In the U.S., consumer complaints related to unauthorized consumer profiles creation increased by 193 % from 2007 to 2008 (Gomez et al. 2009). The Internet advertising firms DoubleClick and Avenue A, the software firm, Intuit and the web-tracking firm Pharmatrak have faced lawsuits for using cookies to target advertising.

BD initiatives have led to an increase in both the supply and demand of location-based real time personal information. Data created and made available for use in the implementation of BD initiatives also have negative spillover effects. Particularly, the availability of location information to third parties may have some dangerous aspects. One example is the use of location data for stalking people in real time. For instance, the iOS app Girls Around Me, which was developed by the Russian company I-Free, leveraged data from Foursquare to scan and detect women checking into a user's neighborhood. The user could identify a woman he liked to talk, connect with her through Facebook, see her full name, profile photos and also send her a message. The woman being tracked however would have no idea that someone was "snooping" on her (Bilton 2012). As of march 2012, the app was downloaded over 70,000 times (Austin and Dowell 2012).

There is also a physical risk of (near) real time data. In China, for instance, illegal companies buy databases from malicious actors and provide services to their clients, which include private investigation, illegal debt collection, asset investigation, and even kidnapping (Yan 2012).

2.2.2.3   Variety

By combining structured and unstructured data from multiple sources, firms can uncover hidden connections between seemingly unrelated pieces of data. In addition to the amount, a high variety of information in BD makes it more difficult to detect security breaches, react appropriately and respond to attacks (freepatentsonline.com 2003).

One estimate suggested that only about 10 % of available data is in a structured form (e.g., transactional data on customers, time-series data from statistical agencies on various macroeconomic and financial indicators) which can be presented in rows and columns (Gens 2011). Especially because of the relative newness, most organizations lack capability to manage unstructured data, which arguably contains more sensitive information. Processes and technology solutions for securing unstructured data are still in nascent phase and governance issues are not addressed.

For instance, organizations often lack mechanisms to ensure that permanent and temporary employees and third-parties have appropriate access to unstructured data and they are in compliance with data protection regulations (Varonis Systems 2008). In a survey conducted by Ponemon among IT professionals, only 23 % of the respondents believed that unstructured data in their companies was properly secured and protected (Fonseca 2008). Another study of DiscoverOrg indicated that over 50 % of organizations were not focused on managing unstructured data and only 20 % had unstructured data governance processes and procedures (Rosenbush 2014).

2.2.2.4   Variability

The variability characteristic is related to the time-variant nature of security and privacy risks. The volume of data collected and stored, which need protection, will grow during the peak data collection and flow periods. It is during such periods that organizations may lack internal capacity and tools to manage and protect information. A related point is that the attractiveness as a crime target is high during such periods. In December 2013, Target announced that its high-profile security breach, which compromised 40 million credit and debit-card accounts and 70 million people's personal data, occurred during the peak holiday shopping season from November 27 to December 15. The virus tried to steal card data during peak customer visit times (10 AM–5 PM local times) of target stores (Yadron 2014a).

The variability characteristic of BD may also necessitate the outsourcing of hardware, software and business-critical applications to CSPs. Applications such as ERP and accounting systems are required to be configured for peak loads during daily and seasonal business periods or when quarterly and annual financial statements are prepared.

2.2.2.5   Complexity

BD often constitutes aggregated data from various sources that are not necessarily identifiable. There is thus no process to request the consent of a person for the resulting data, which is often more personal than the set of data the person would consent to give (Pirlot 2014). A related privacy risk involves re-identification. It is possible to use a data aggregation process to convert semi-anonymous or certain personally non-identifiable information into non-anonymous or PII (ISACA 2014). Health-related data is of special concern. Based on a consumer's search terms for disease symptoms, online purchases of medical supplies, and RFID tagging of drug packages can provide marketers with information about the consumer's health (Talbot 2013). Access to such information would enable an insurance underwriter to predict certain disease and disorder probabilities, which would not be possible using information voluntarily disclosed by consumers.

Many of the innovations involving BD use multiple data sources and involve transferring data to third parties. Many organizations believe that making data anonymous before sharing with third parties would make it impossible to identify. This is often a convenient but possibly false assumption. Researchers have presented a variety of methods and techniques that can be used to de-identify personal data and reassociate with specific consumers (Brill 2013). BD processes can generate predictive models that have a high probability of revealing PII (Crawford and Schultz 2013) and thus make anonymization impossible. Failure to protect PII and unintended or inappropriate disclosure violate the security provision of FIPs (Teufel 2008). In some cases, the identified person may suffer physical, psychological, or economic harm. For instance, in 2011, customers of the U.S. drugstore Walgreens filed a lawsuit accusing the drugstore of illegally selling medical information from patient prescriptions. Walgreen allegedly sold the prescription information to data mining companies, which de-identified the data and then sold to pharmaceutical companies. The plaintiffs argued that Walgreens unfairly benefitted from the commercial value of their prescription information (Manos 2011).

2.3   The Theoretical Framework: Rules and Institutions

In this section we start by reviewing definitions of rules and institutions and discussing their relevance in the context of BD and cloud industry and market. One of the earliest scholars to write about rules was Max Black (Black 1962). In his philosophical treatment of this concept, he identified four different ways "rules" is used in everyday conversations: regulations, instructions, precepts, and principles. In order to better understand how institutions are related to rules, we consider Nobel Laureate Douglas North's definition of institutions. He defined institutions as the "macro-level rules of the game" (North 1990) which include "formal constraints (rules, laws, constitutions), informal constraints (norms of behavior, conventions, and self-imposed codes of conduct), and their enforcement characteristics" (North 1996).

Among the four uses of rules, instructions (strategies for solving a problem) and principles (physical laws or behavioral models) are not related to the ways institutionalists approach the term, rules. As an example of a use of the rules as instructions, the Brazilian oil giant, Petrobras makes some uses of private clouds but not public clouds due to CS concerns. Petrobras also prefers to deploy proprietary systems and software developed in Brazil. Likewise, as an example of principle in the context of CS could be Finch's law, which is proposed by Brian Finch, co-leader of the law firm Pillsbury Winthrop Shaw Pittman's Global Security practice, "Cyber defense cannot keep pace with the increasing sophistication or creativity of cyber-attacks" (blogs.wsj.com 2014b).

The macro-level rules proposed by Douglas North can be considered as consisting of regulations and precepts. Institutions thus can be considered as a conceptual subset of the rules as defined by Max Black. According to this view, this section builds on the definition of institutions and .comprehensive taxonomy of rules provided and laid out by Elinor Ostrom, who was awarded the Nobel Prize in Economic Sciences in 2009 (Ostrom 2005). Black's regulations and precepts have guided Ostrom in her formulation of the definition of institutions, which she defines as "the rules, norms, and strategies used by humans in repetitive situations" (Ostrom 2005). When used as regulation, rules are something that are "laid down by an authority (a legislature, judge, magistrate, board of directors, university president, and parent) as required of certain persons (or, alternatively, forbidden or permitted)" (Black 1962). An example is: CSPs must keep sensitive data belonging to a U.S. federal agency within the country [the Federal Information Security Management Act (FISMA)]. When used in a regulation-sense, one can refer to activities such as the rule "being announced, put into effect, enforced (energetically, strictly, laxly, invariably, occasionally), disobeyed, broken, rescinded, changed, revoked, reinstated" (Black 1962). Whereas CS regulations are reasonably strictly enforced in the U.S., the existing legislation aimed at curbing cybercrimes is laxly enforced in countries that lack resources. A Saudi official noted that while cybercrime laws in Saudi Arabia offers basic legal measures, they lack details of technical and procedural measures required to prosecute cybercriminals (Pinaroc 2009).

Ostrom describes rules as used in the (moral) precept sense as "generally accepted moral fabric of a community" and "cultural prescriptions" and refers them as norms (Ostrom 2005). Norms are "shared prescriptions known and accepted by most of the participants themselves involving intrinsic costs and benefits rather than material sanctions or inducements" (Ostrom 2005). In order to better understand moral precepts related to cybercrimes and CS, consider the following example, Following the Israel Defense Forces' (IDF) interception of a flotilla carrying humanitarian aid to Gaza in May 2010, tens of thousands of email addresses, passwords and personal details of Israelis were allegedly stolen by Turkish hackers. It was reported that there was dispute amongst the Turkish hackers in the online forum about the appropriateness of using the information for financial gain. Some hackers felt that using the information to steal money would undermine their political agenda. There was also a discussion of what the Koran says is permissible to do with the money of "infidels" (haaretz.com 2010).

Norms encompass a wide range of meanings and operate at various levels of the social system. For instance, social norms govern or reflect people's expectations of behavior in the entire society (Williamson 1993). Differentiating from use of rules in the regulation sense, Ostrom (p. 831) notes that "one would not speak of enforcing, rescinding, or reinstating a rule in the precept sense" (Ostrom 2005). A precept can also be understood as a "maxim for prudential or moral behavior" (Ostrom 2005). An example is: A good rule is not to store data in clouds provided by CSPs from country X.

Norms are related to informal institutions and are "rules-in-use" rather than "rules-in-form". It is important to note that rules-in-use are the "do's and don'ts" that may not exist in any written document and sometimes may actually be contrary to the "do's and don'ts" written in formal documents (Ostrom 2005). Industrial norms and individual transaction norms are also examples of institutionalized norms. Industrial norms govern the functioning of an industry. Individual transaction norms, on the other hand, are developed between individual firms.

We use W.R. Scott's (2001) institutional framework for analyzing the evolution of institutions around BD and cloud security. Scott has conceptualized institutions as composed of three pillars: regulatory, normative and cultural-cognitive, which relate to "legally sanctioned," "morally governed," and "recognizable, taken-for-granted" behaviors, respectively (Scott et al. 2000).

2.3.1   Regulative Institutions

Regulative institutions are related to regulatory bodies and the existing laws and rules related to BD and the cloud. Adhering to these institutions, individuals and organizations would not suffer the penalty for noncompliance (Hoffman 1999).

2.3.1.1   Laws Governing BD and the Cloud

The importance of regulative institutions such as laws, contracts and courts in the BD and the cloud environment should be obvious if these technologies are viewed against the backdrop of the current state of security standards. In the absence of radical improvements in security, such institutions become even more important because cloud users can rely on these institutions in case a cloud provider's failure to deliver a given level of security.

Especially sensitive data have caught the attention of regulators. For instance, localization requirements are most often associated with sensitive sectors such as finance, healthcare and government (e.g., contactors, manufacturers, and federal agencies providing products or services to government organizations, military branches or departments). For instance, according to the SMA, CSPs are required to keep sensitive data belonging to a federal agency within the country. Google Apps used by government agencies are FISMA certified (Brodkin 2010).

Overall, the BD- and cloud-related legal system and enforcement mechanisms are evolving more slowly compared to the technological development. Compliance frameworks such as the Sarbanes-Oxley Act of 2002 (SOX) and the Health Insurance Portability and Accountability Act (HIPAA) were developed for the non-cloud environment and thus do not clearly define the guidelines and requirements for data in the cloud (Bradley 2010). BD and the cloud thus pose various challenges for companies that have responsibilities to meet stringent compliance related to these frameworks such as IT disaster recovery and data security.

2.3.1.2   International Harmonization of Regulative Institutions

National governments are facing international pressures to harmonize and align legal systems and enforcement mechanisms. They are also increasingly turning to supra-national institutions to resolve transnational problems (Smith and Wiest 2005).

BD and the cloud linked in an important way to national competitiveness and security. Governments are thus enacting new laws and revising existing regulations to enhance their firms' international competitiveness (Table 2.2). In many cases, these actions have been in response to interest group pressures. For instance, industry associations such as the European Telecommunications Network Operator's Association (ETNO) (Chap. 6) as well as organizations such as Oracle, Cisco Systems, SAP, Apple, Google and Microsoft have been engaged in organized lobbying efforts to influence BD- and cloud- related policies of the EU and its members. In response to these and other pressures, the EU and its members have shown willingness to enact cloud friendly laws, revise existing laws and collaborate with other institutional actors. The EC Vice-President responsible for the Digital Agenda, Neelie Kroes, for instance, emphasized the critical role the cloud can play

Table 2.2 A sample of actions and responses of various actors in shaping BD- and cloud- related institutions

Actor	Nature and sources of powers	A sample of actions
Consumers	Relative power vis-a-vis the vendors has increased with an intense competition. Consumers have expressed growing concern over organizations' data collection methods, such as the use of tracking technologies (e.g., cookies and GPS trackers).	• After users' complaints about data security and ownership issues, Dropbox updated its user terms/conditions.
Organizations dealing with consumer data	Facing pressures from consumers to re-evaluate privacy and security implications of their offerings and take corrective actions.	• Foursquare revoked API access to the iOS app Girls Around Me, which forced the developers to pull the product from Apple's iTunes Store.
BD and cloud vendors	Decreasing relative power but attempting to increase "potential power" by offering users with new, innovative and potentially attractive value propositions.	• To win federal-government deals, AWS and Google undertook efforts to improve security to achieve certification for FISMA. • U.S.-based food and agricultural companies such as Monsanto, DuPont and other corporations claim that they do not use data for purposes other than providing services requested by farmers, keep the data secure and do not sold (foxnews.com 2014a).
Associations and interest groups representing users	Norms, informal rules, ethical codes and expert power	• AICPA's official endorsements to Paychex, Intacct and Copanion. • CSA: as an independent voice promotes the use of best practices for providing security assurance and provides education for users. • The AFBF has put together a "privacy expectation guide" to educate its members. In addition, it has drafted a policy which has emphasized that data should remain the farmer's property (foxnews.com 2014a).
Inter-organizational bodies representing BD and cloud vendors	The power of collective actions	• **ETNO: lobbied for** an international privacy standard, simplification of rules governing data transfers, and others-- expected to enable European companies to compete with those in the U.S. (Ingthorsson 2011).
National governments	Coercive power over citizens and businesses	• FISMA in the U.S.: CSPs are required to keep sensitive data

(continued)

Table 2.2 (continued)

Actor	Nature and sources of powers	A sample of actions
		belonging to a federal agency within the country. • Germany, Brazil, India and other countries have introduced or are actively discussing data localization laws. • China, South Korea, the U.S. and the U.K.: Legislations governing the location of storage for personal, financial and medical data.
Supra-national institutions	Nations mostly observe principles of international law and obligations: can resolve transnational problems	• EU planning to make mandatory to notify customers of data breaches. • European Parliament's Civil Liberties Committee: recommended making easier for users to access, amend and delete data and appointing dedicated data protection officers in companies (Worth 2011). • EC: emphasizing the importance of easing users to change cloud provider by developing de facto standard for moving data among different clouds. • EU members working to align privacy laws and close jurisdictional gaps (European Commission 2010).

in the economic growth of the member countries and emphasized the need to develop appropriate regulative framework (Thiel and Valpuesta 2011).

2.3.2 Normative Institutions

Normative components deal with "a prescriptive, evaluative, and obligatory dimension" (Scott 1995). Elements of normative institutions also include trade/professional associations (e.g., the American Institute of Certified Public Accountants (AICPA), and the ETNO), industry groups or non-profit organizations (e.g., the EPIC) that can use social/professional obligation requirements (e.g., ethical codes of conduct) to induce certain behaviors in the cloud industry and market.

A lesson from other economic sectors is that professional and trade associations are likely to emerge to play unique roles in shaping the industry in the absence of well-developed regulative institutions (Greenwood and Hinings 1996). There have been some successful attempts at the association and inter-organizational levels to challenge the appropriateness of the current institutional arrangement. In the future even higher, broader and more significant institutional changes can be anticipated if only for the fact that the cloud has brought transformational shifts.

2.3.2.1   Trade Associations and Other Interest Groups Representing, and Advocating for, Users

Trade associations and other interest groups representing, and advocating for, users are constantly emerging and influencing security and privacy issues in BD and the cloud in new ways as a result of their expertise and interests in this issue. An example is the Cloud Security Alliance (CSA) (www.cloudsecurityalliance.org), a vendor-neutral group of information security professionals. The CSA is working on a set of best practices as well as information security standards and vendor risk management processes for providers (Crosman 2009) . The CSA has prepared a list of over 200 questions that cover key issues such as data integrity, security architecture, audits, legal/regulatory compliance, governance, and physical security.

Some Europe-based rights groups such as the UK's NGO Privacy International have expressed concerns related to risk of loss of data sovereignty and argued that the U.S. has been a potential threat to data privacy. For instance, the Foreign Intelligence and Surveillance Amendments Act (FISAA) requires U.S. companies to hand over of EU citizens' data stored on their clouds regardless of EU data protection laws (Nielsen 2013).

Some established trade and professional associations have a vested interest in security and privacy issues in the cloud. The AICPA is making efforts to accelerate cloud adoption among its over 400,000 members. The AICPA's resources, expertise and experience would make it easier for it to assess and monitor the performance of CSPs. Paychex, a payroll-solutions provider, was the first CSP to win the AICPA's official endorsement. The AICPA also endorsed bill.com for invoice management and payment in 2008. The AICPA's endorsements are based on an extensive due diligence on CSPs' CS practices. Another example is the American Farm Bureau Federation (AFBF), which has put together a "privacy expectation guide" to educate its members. In addition, it has drafted a policy which has emphasized that data should remain the farmer's property (foxnews.com 2014b).

2.3.2.2   Inter-organizational Bodies Representing Technology Vendors

An inter-organizational system gives the vendors the power of collective action and cooperative endeavor to pursue shared goals which may not be possible if each vendor acts in isolation. Prior research in economics indicates that political processes tend to have built-in biases that often favor organized groups compared to those that are unorganized (Mitra 1999). To take an example, consider Brazil's proposed regulation to force foreign companies to hold data in data centers in Brazil. It faced strong resistance and criticism from foreign companies. In October 2013, 47 organizations representing diverse industries worldwide sent a letter to selected Brazilian Congress members, which pointed out several unintended consequences of the proposed data center localization plan. Their criticism focused on four main points: decreased security (data security depends on how data is protected and a focus on physical location may distract from the reality), higher costs (not being able to enjoy economies of scale, which would increase costs for end users), decreased competitiveness (isolation from the world's innovative and efficient cloud services and strong computing power around the world) and harm to consumers (denial of cloud services available around the world). This protest played a key role in the Brazilian government's withdrawal of the provision in the final version of the bill (Ribeiro 2014).

A related point is that in industries such as cloud computing, which is likely to benefit from compatibility, the choice of industry standards is often the result of complex negotiation among industry participants (Farrell 1987). A goal of such negotiation would be to strengthen security and privacy issues and enhance the trustworthiness of this industry.

The BD and cloud industries have learned from some of the high-profile security breaches of vendors. Industry best practices are continuously developing. Some examples include the Data Centre Tier certifications by Uptime Institute and the ISO27001 standard for security management (The Business Times Singapore 2013).

2.3.3   Cultural-Cognitive Institutions

Cognitive institutions can be considered as culturally ethical precepts. They are built on the mental maps of individuals. An organization's cloud and BD adoption decisions may also depend on its perception of the providers' ability to protect data from a third party, make them available when needed and a trust that the provider would not engage in opportunistic behavior.

2.3.3.1   Perception of Vendor's Integrity and Capability

BD and the cloud raise issues related to privacy, security and confidentiality if only for the fact that the users may think that service provider may deliberately or accidentally disclose the data or use for malicious purposes. Of particular concern is thus the users' perception of the dependability of cloud vendors' security assurances and practices. As noted earlier, issues such as confidentiality, integrity, and availability of data related to ineffective or noncompliant controls of service providers, data backup and third-party backup locations are of concerns to users (Table 2.3). Organizations are also concerned that CSPs may use insecure ways

Table 2.3 Principal findings of surveys conducted with businesses regarding their perceptions of and responses to BD and cloud computing

Survey conducted by	Conducted/Released in	Major findings
IDC	October 2008	• Security concern was the most serious barrier to cloud adoption for organizations.
InformationWeek	2009 and 2010	• 31 % of companies in 2010 viewed SaaS Apps as less secure than the internal systems compared to 35 % in 2009 (Ely 2011).
IDC (conducted in Asia Pacific)	April 2010	• Less than 10 % of respondents were confident about cloud security measures
Harris Interactive survey for Novell	October 2010	• 90 % were concerned about cloud security. • 50 viewed security concerns as the primary barrier to cloud adoption. • 76 % thought private data more secure when stored on the premises. • 81 % were worried about regulatory compliance.
InformationWeek Analytics SaaS Survey	2011	• <A third of IT executives feel the benefits of cloud exceed risks. • About a quarter did not fully understand the regulatory and compliance issues in cloud computing. • 47 % concerned about a security threat (Ricadela 2011).
Cisco's CloudWatch 2011 report for the U. K.	September 2011	• 76 % cited security and privacy a top barrier to cloud adoption. • 64 % concerned about location of data (Nguyen 2011).
Dell	Released in November 2014	• Security is a barrier for 52 % for cloud adoption and 35 % to leverage BD (Chanthadavong 2014).
, Informatica	2012	• Data security and privacy raised concerns for 38 % (Hernandez 2012).
BARC Institute	Second half of 2012 (Germany, Austria, Switzerland, France, the U.K.)	• 25 % of the respondents expected to encounter data privacy issues (BARC Institute 2013).
Information Systems Audit and Control Association (ISACA)	2013 IT Risk/Reward Barometer among IT professionals from Australia and New Zealand (BD)	• 5 % were "very prepared" to ensure effective governance and privacy, 45 % reported "adequately prepared" and 25 % "not

(continued)

Table 2.3 (continued)

Survey conducted by	Conducted/Released in	Major findings
		prepared at all" (CSO Online 2013).
Voltage Security	April 2013	• 76 % concerned about inability to secure BD. • 56 % could not start or finish cloud/BD projects due to security concerns (darkreading.com 2013).
SAP	2014 (at GSMA Mobile World Congress in Barcelona, Spain)	• 38 % said that security and privacy prevented their organizations from fully unlocking BD's potential (SAP 2014).
Ovum	Early 2014 (the U.K., France, Germany)	• 53 % were concerned about the security issues in the BD environment (Savvas 2014).

to delete data once services have been provided (e.g., disposing hard disks without deleting data).

Malicious insider risks are also among the most important risks that organizations face. According to a report released by the Federal Bureau of Investigation (FBI) in 2006, over 40 % of attacks originated inside an organization (Regan 2006) . One fear has been that IP and other sensitive information stored in the cloud could be stolen. Worse still, CSPs may not notify their clients about security breaches. Evidence indicates that many businesses tend to underreport cybercrimes due to embarrassment, concerns related to credibility and reputation damages and fears of stock price drops. An organization's data in the cloud may be stolen but it may not ever be aware that such incidents had happened.

A final point concerns attitude and perception of the country of origin of cloud vendors. Since the 2013 revelations of U.S. spying, German politicians have viewed Google and other U.S. cloud vendors as threats to Germans' personal freedom. One official reportedly said that from viewpoint of the Germans' personal freedom, Google was more dangerous than the U.S. NSA (Jervell and Gummer 2014).

2.3.3.2 Users' and Technology Providers' Inertia Effects

Organizational inertia may affect the lens through which users view security and privacy issues in the BD and the cloud environments. For instance, an inertia effect may adversely influence organizations' assessment of the cloud from the security and privacy standpoints because they may not be comfortable about losing some of the features of the non-cloud environment such as control on data.

Reduction in control due to the shared and dynamic resources in the cloud environment is a concern. Cloud users have no access to and physical control over the hardware and other resources that store and process their data and information. Just as important is the need for change in preference for localness. From the standpoint of security, most users tend to prefer computing functions locally on site (Brynjolfsson et al. 2010).

2.4 Forces and Nature of Institutional Changes

2.4.1 *Institutional Field Around BD and the Cloud*

CS issues are shaped by expectations, values, positions, power, influence, resources, roles, concerns, orientation and interests of various institutional actors that have different levels of understanding and are affected differentially by these issues. In this regard, we introduce the concept of institutional field, which can be helpful in understanding institutions and institutional changes associated with BD and the cloud.

An institutional field is "formed around the issues that become important to the interests and objectives of specific collectives of organizations" (Hoffman 1999) . For BD and the cloud industries, this institutional field includes national governments, supra-national organizations, industry bodies, trade and professional associations as well as cloud vendors, cloud clients and the organizations of these clients (Table 2.2).

Institutional theorists view a field as a dynamic system characterized by the entry and exit of various players and constituencies that have competing interests (Barnett and Carroll 1993). The last column of Table 2.2 provides a sample of actions. Purdy and Gray have noted that fields evolve through three stages: innovation, mobilization and structuration (Purdy and Gray 2009). In the innovation stage, new logics related to security and privacy concerns in BD and the cloud are introduced and are drawn into debate. It can be argued that the CS issues in BD and the cloud are in the mobilization stage, in which field development is characterized by a complex power dynamics. For instance, CSPs are attempting to exercise their power based on expertise, experience and knowledge and are engaged in technology push without sufficiently addressing the CS concerns. Many users, on the other hand, are exercising their bargaining power and voicing frustration with vendors' failures to address these issues. Some governments, on the other hand, are using the coercive power of the state to use BD and the cloud in spying on citizens. Institutional actors such as technology vendors, organizations using BD and the cloud and regulators in this mobilization stage compete to validate and implement their logics. For instance, cloud vendors are relying on the economic logic of the cloud's low TCO to persuade users. Some users' logics are based on the idea that the cloud's costs are likely to outweigh the benefits in the absence of strong security measures. The final stage is the structuration stage, in which logics are translated into practices (Reay et al. 2006). In this stage, norms and structures are standardized and institutions deepen their taken-for-grantedness. It is clear that institutional fields around security in BD and the cloud have not yet reached the structuration stage.

Drawing from the scholarship in institutional theory, we outline three broad, inter-related, and non-exhaustive mechanisms of institutional change and field formation in the context of CS: "jolts" or exogenous shocks (Meyer 1982), changes in organizational logics (Friedland and Alford 1991), and gradual change in field structure (Clemens and Cook 1999).

In many cases institutional changes are associated with and facilitated by initiating events or triggers also known as disruptive events. Such events are also referred to as shocks, jolts, or discontinuities, which can overcome the effects of institutional inertia (Meyer 1982) . Measures taken by U.S. regulators following high profile cyber-attacks on JPMorgan Chase in multiple stages between June and August of 2014, which affected 76 million households and 7 million small businesses, provide a good example to illustrate our point. Following the attacks, state and federal regulators such as the Commodity Futures Trading Commission (CFTC) and New York's Department of Financial Services (DFS) have raised the urgency and importance of strengthening CS measures.

CS issues have forced organizations to change their organizational logics. Examples of such logics include those connected to organizational identity (e.g., what the organization is and what it stands for). Organizations may require to change the components of organizational identity such as organizational objectives, values and practices. For instance, in order to strengthen their CS practices, Indian firms engaged in outsourcing have taken measures to prevent insider cyber-attacks go against the values and norms of Indian culture. For instance, call center employees have to undergo security checks which are considered as "undignified" (The Economist 2005). Likewise, due to a growing CS concern, organizations may change business logic related to risk management. In addition to cyber risk, there are other categories of business risks that need to be considered in an organization. It is thus important to frame them up together and convey how CS risk stands vis a vis the other risks (e.g., the risk of making employees and customers dissatisfied and disappointed) (Yadron 2014b).

Structure of an institutional field may change over time due to gradual changes in practices, beliefs, habits and policies related to CS. For instance, consumers may experience CS-related situations that may lead them to question their beliefs about CS. For instance, a large proportion of Internet users are questioning the honesty of Internet companies in the handling of their personal data (e.g., see Table 2.4). The importance of this issue is underscored by the strikingly high proportion of consumers that consider privacy of their personal data as a top issue and prefer not to be monitored.

Table 2.4 Principal findings of surveys assessing consumers' perceptions of and responses to BD

Cable Forum (cableforum.co.uk)	2008	Forum visitors	95 % of the respondents said that they would opt out of monitoring (even anonymous) of online activities by a third party (Arthur 2008).
Pew Internet & American Life Project.	2012 (March 15– April 3).	National survey among 2254 U.S. adults	30 % of smartphone owners said that they turned off location tracking features due to concerns that others would access this information (USA Today 2012).
BCG	2013 Global Consumer Sentiment Survey.	10,000 consumers in 12 countries	Privacy of personal data was a "top issue" for 75 %. Only 7 % were willing to allow their information to be used for purposes other than it was originally collected (Rose et al. 2013).
Ovum	2013	11,000 people across 11 countries	68 % would use a do-not-track feature if it was easily available on a search engine. Only 14 % believed Internet companies were honest about the use of personal data (Coyne 2013).

2.4.2 The Driving Forces and Mechanisms of Institutional Changes

We focus on three inter-related issues associated with BD and the cloud: dense networks of actors created by these technologies' transformative nature, power dynamics, and contradictions that have emerged with the diffusion of these technologies.

2.4.3 Development of Dense Networks and Relationships

BD and the cloud are drawing diverse actors, and a trend towards collaboration, coordination and communication is emerging. BD and the cloud have generated new interactions among private sector agents. Powerful vendors are also encouraging public-private interactions, leading the coordination efforts and influencing national and international policy-making processes. For instance, in 2011, Microsoft general counsel spoke to the French National Assembly to emphasize the importance of lowering the barriers to cloud diffusion (O'brien 2012).

The above activities are indicative of the formation of a dense network of relationships among various actors in the institutional field formed around BD and cloud security, which is likely to reduce incentives for opportunism (Axelrod and Cohen 2001). Dense relationships and interactions are also likely to generate a lot of "gossips", which would help enhance trust. For instance, if formal mechanisms are created to provide trust on the cloud, vendors and users do not have to depend on personal or organizational characteristics or past exchange history. This phenomenon is also referred as the production of institutionally based trust (Zucker 1986).

2.4.4   The Power Dynamics

In social science, the concept of "A's power over B" is used to describe the "policy possibilities open to A" (Harsanyi 1971). That is, an actor with more power is more likely to get compliance from other actors. A powerful actor can also deprive another actor of options, change the relative costs of actions and change the probability that an action will result in a given outcome (Dowding 1996) . The sources and nature of powers of various key actors are presented in Table 2.2.

It is first important to recognize the concerns and dissatisfaction that BD and cloud users have. Consumers are concerned about potential abuses and misuses of personal data. Especially businesses' initiatives to collect high-velocity data (e.g., click-stream, GPS data from mobile devices, social media usage, etc.) have met resistance from consumers. A 2013 national survey conducted in the U.S. by the Pew Internet & American Life Project found that a large proportion of respondents have taken actions such as turning off location tracking features. Likewise, in a survey conducted by the non-profit Cable Forum 95 % of the respondents said they would opt out of even anonymous monitoring of their online activities by a third party. Consumers are also concerned about the secondary uses of personal data. A key idea is that businesses store huge volume of personal data so that potential innovative uses can be discovered in the future. That is, when the data is first collected organizations may not be aware of the most innovative secondary uses. As Table 2.4 shows, most consumers are against the secondary uses of their personal data.

Consumers have shown a marked tendency towards exercising their power. Dropbox's updates in its terms and conditions in response to user pressures (Table 2.2) and other similar examples indicate that users' relative power vis-a-vis providers has increased with intense competition. Consumers are leveraging this increased power to force BD and cloud vendors and organizations using their data to take measures to enhance privacy and security. As an example, in 2011, customers of the U.S. drugstore Walgreens filed a lawsuit accusing the drugstore of illegally selling medical information from patient prescriptions. Walgreen allegedly sold the prescription information to data mining companies, which de-identified the data and sold to pharmaceutical companies. The plaintiffs argued that Walgreens unfairly benefitted from the commercial value of their information (Manos 2011) . We can say that consumer have employed "power tactics" in an attempt to strengthen their power vis-a-vis the providers (Kim et al. 2005).

Technology vendors, on the other hand, are increasing their capacity to negotiate with and influence the users by offering them new, innovative and potentially attractive value propositions. Put differently, they are attempting to increase their "potential power" (Kim et al. 2005). Cloud and BD vendors are thus reacting to a perceived decline in power by engaging in proactive behaviors to develop more secure products.

2.4.5   Contradictions Associated with BD and the Cloud

A simple approach to understand institutional changes associated with BD and the cloud would be to look at the various contradictions and dilemmas these technologies cloud produce with the existing institutional arrangements. If we look from this viewpoint, institutional changes can be seen as an outcome of the dynamic interactions of contradictions and "praxis" (Seo and Creed 2002) .

First, conformance to the existing institutions may lower technical and functional efficiency, which is likely to lead to ab institutional changes. For instance, economies such as Japan and the EU are working to develop appropriate regulative framework due to the critical role of BD and the cloud in the economic growth. This type of contradiction is referred as "legitimacy that undermines functional inefficiency" Seo and Creed 2002).

Service providers respond to the rapidly changing IT environment by making adaptations that help them to maintain competitive advantage in the new technological landscape. The continuous adaptation has resulted in a competency trap whereby IT service providers attempt to pursue cost management programs such as minimizing the TCO. Many services providers have shown an inability to adapt to the environment of the cloud, which poses unique security problems. This phenomenon is also known as "adaptation that undermines adaptability" in which "adaptive moves make adopters less able to adapt over the long run" (Seo and Creed 2002). As security and privacy issues are becoming more important, BD and cloud users are demanding an explicit guarantee of data security and liability clauses in contracts with their vendors. Users' pressures to Dropbox to update its terms and conditions regarding data security and ownership can serve as an example to illustrate this point (Table 2.2).

Third, the legitimacy seeking process may require appeasing multiple institutions that are conflicting and inconsistent. This type of contradiction is referred as "isomorphism that conflicts with divergent interests" which may act as a trigger for institutional change (Seo and Creed 2002).

Finally, businesses, industry bodies and government organizations in some countries have achieved some progress towards developing institutions that are more or less compatible with other prevailing institutions in their countries. These intra-national measures are in conflict with the frameworks adopted by other countries. Such inconsistencies are described as "intra-institutional conformity that creates inter-institutional incompatibilities", which are likely to bring about pressures for changes (Seo and Creed 2002). To take an example, the EU is working to align privacy laws among the member states and close the existing jurisdictional gaps across them.

2.5 Discussion and Concluding Remarks

A number of existing key institutional structures are inadequate and obsolete to deal with the security and privacy problems facing BD and the cloud. While technological development to address the security concerns is critical, institutional measures such as clearer regulatory frameworks and other trust producing initiatives are no less important. Due to the transformative and far-reaching impacts and significance of BD and the cloud, they have drawn diverse actors and participants with different perspectives that have broad social and economic demands and interests. These participants vary widely in resources, expertise, experience and power and their actions are aimed at accomplishing multiple political, social and economic goals, which are far from congruent.

The vast storage and analytical capabilities and availability of an array of contents and applications of BD and the cloud also pose monumental risks related to privacy and security. This issue is extremely important in that organizations are increasingly using BD and the cloud to perform strategic and mission critical functions. BD and cloud providers are facing pressures and challenges to protect information assets of their customers and other sensitive data. A related point is that there is currently a big gap between what vendors claim and what the existing and potential adopters think about the security of these technologies. On the plus side, industry players are realizing a need to develop standards to provide the guidance necessary for security and privacy. BD and cloud users are becoming educated and are bringing more holistic perspectives to incorporate all the relevant issues that are important to them such as cost saving, productivity gain, security and privacy issues and, voice and control over data. By engaging in actions such as lawsuits, filing of complaints with regulatory bodies and applying formal pressures on businesses to use BD and the cloud responsibly and ethically, consumers are helping develop favorable formal and informal institutions around these technologies. As a result of various organized efforts, positive changes in institutional arrangements can be anticipated.

Despite some discussions concerning privacy and security issues in BD and the cloud environments in the context of developing economies, most of the current discussion on this subject has been focused on industrialized countries. One commentator noted that about 90 % of the discussion at the 2013 Internet Governance Forum (IGF) held in Bali, Indonesia referred to BD as a surveillance tool. On the other hand, the debate focusing on developing countries treated BD as a means to observe people to fight poverty. The argument provided by IGF participants was that data can help provide access to clean drinking water, healthcare and other necessities. Some have challenged this view and noted that poor people have no less reason than rich people to be worried about surveillance (linnettaylor 2013).

In fast developing technologies such as BD and the cloud, the institutional change patterns may not reflect the linearity observed in mature industries. National governments' and supra-national agencies' roles in the development of institutions related to these technologies have been mostly passive and reactive rather than active and self-initiated. Since some non-profit organizations and industry bodies as well as various associations representing vendors and users have been relatively active and some of them are also engaged in organized lobbying efforts to influence national/international policy making, it is reasonable to expect that the development of normative institutions is likely to be followed by the development of regulative institutions. As is the case of the Internet Domain Name System (DNS), the development of regulative institutions in BD and the cloud industries are likely to be an ex post facto legitimation of a the codification of industry norms. It is anticipated that the salience of an institutional component may also vary over time. For instance, barriers associated with newness and inertia effects are likely to decline over time. On the other hand, as the penetration level, width and depth of BD and the cloud increase, they may be more attractive cybercrime targets which would mean that the importance of security would further increase.

Nation states and international actors are also facing unprecedented demands, challenges and pressures to introduce new regulations, change the existing regulations and in some cases, close loopholes in the regulations. They hope that these measures would help enhance national security as well as security and privacy of user data, increase national competitiveness in technology and facilitate cloud adoption by consumers and organizations.

References

Arthur, C. (2008). *Phorm fires privacy row for ISPs.* http://www.theguardian.com/technology/2008/mar/06/internet.privacy

Austin, S., & Dowell, A. (2012). *Girls around me' developer defends app after foursquare dismissal.* http://blogs.wsj.com/digits/2012/03/31/girls-around-me-developer-defends-app-after-foursquare-dismissal/

Axelrod, R., & Cohen, M. D. (2001). *Harnessing complexity: Organizational implications of a scientific frontier.* New York: Basic Books.

BARC Institute. (2013). *Big data survey Europe, usage, technology and budgets in European best-practice companies,* Wuerzburg, Germany.

Barnett, W. P., & Carroll, G. R. (1993). How institutional constraints affected the organization of early US telephonies. *Journal of Law, Economics and Organization, 9,* 98–126.

Berry, R., & Reisman, M. (2012). Policy challenges of cross-border cloud computing. *Journal of International Commerce and Economics, 4*(2), 1–38.

Bilton, N. (2012). *Girls around me: An app takes creepy to a new level.* http://bits.blogs.nytimes.com/2012/03/30/girls-around-me-ios-app-takes-creepy-to-a-new-level/

Black, M. (1962). *Models and metaphors.* Ithaca, NY: Cornell University Press.

blogs.wsj.com. (2014b). *Steps directors and CIOs can take to minimize Cyberattack losses.* http://blogs.wsj.com/cio/2014/10/06/steps-directors-and-cios-can-take-to-minimize-cyberattack-losses/

Bradley, T. (2010). Build your own private azure cloud with new Microsoft appliance. *PC World.* http://www.pcworld.com/businesscenter/article/200988/build_your_own_private_azure_clouc_with_new_microsoft_appliance.html?tk=hp_blg

Brill, J. (2013). Demanding transparency from data brokers. *Washington Post Opinions.* http://www.washingtonpost.com/opinions/demanding-transparency-from-data-brokers/2013/08/15/00609680-0382-11e3-9259-e2aafe5a5f84_story.html

Brodkin, J. (2010). 5 problems with SaaS security. *Network World, 27*(18), 1–27.

Brown, M. (2014). *Europe's new data laws will affect MSPs.* http://mspmentor.net/infocenter-cloud-based-file-sharing/082514/europe-s-new-data-laws-will-affect-msps; http://www.zdnet.com/europes-new-data-laws-just-how-many-cloud-vendors-would-comply-7000032499/

Brynjolfsson, E., Hofmann, P., & Jordan, J. (2010). Cloud computing and electricity: Beyond the utility model. *Communications of the ACM, 53*(5), 32–34.

Bunge, J. (2014). Big data comes to the farm, sowing mistrust; seed makers barrel into technology business. *Wall Street Journal (Online)* 26 February.

businesscloudnews.com. (2014). *Mobile, cloud, big data platform helping to contain Ebola outbreak.* http://www.businesscloudnews.com/2014/10/27/mobile-cloud-big-data-platform-helping-to-contain-ebola-outbreak/

CDT. (2000). *CDT's guide to online privacy.* Center for Democracy & Technology. http://www.cdt.org/privacy/guide/start.

Chanthadavong, A. (2014). *Security holds technology adoption back: Dell.* http://www.zdnet.com/security-holds-technology-adoption-back-dell-7000035430/

Clemens, E., & Cook, J. (1999). Politics and institutionalism: Explaining durability and change. *Annual Review of Sociology, 25*, 441–466.

Cohen, A. (2013). *Will 'stalking apps' be stopped?* http://ideas.time.com/2013/02/04/will-stalking-apps-be-stopped/

Coyne, T. (2013). *Avoiding the big data crisis: Managing disclosure.* http://in2.holmesreport.com/2013/09/avoiding-the-big-data-crisis-managing-disclosure/

Crawford, K., & Schultz, J. M. (2013). *Big data and due process: toward a framework to redress predictive privacy harms.* New York University Public Law and Legal Theory Working Papers, 429, http://lsr.nellco.org/nyu_plltwp/429/

Crosman, P. (2009). Securing the clouds. *Wall Street & Technology*, December, 23.

CSO Online. (2013). *Big data policies lacking in Australian and New Zealand organisations: Survey.* http://www.cso.com.au/article/532590/big_data_policies_lacking_australian_new_zealand_organisations_survey/

darkreading.com. (2013). *Over half of big data & cloud projects stall because of security concerns.* http://www.darkreading.com/management/over-half-of-big-data-cloud-projects-st/240155524

Dowding, K. (1996). *Power.* Minneapolis, MN: University of Minnesota Press.

Duhigg, C. (2012). How companies learn your secrets. *New York Times.* http://www.nytimes.com/2012/02/19/magazine/shopping-habits.html?_r=1&pagewanted=all

Ely, A. (2011). 5 Steps to secure SaaS. *Information Week*, p. 17. http://www.informationweek.com/news/security/management/showArticle.jhtml?articleID=229300176

European Commission. (2010). *The future of cloud computing – Opportunities for European cloud computing beyond.* http://ec.europa.eu/information_society/newsroom/cf/itemdetail.cfm?item_id=6993

Farrell, J. (1987). Cheap talk, coordination, and entry. *The RAND Journal of Economics, 18*(1), 34–39.

Fonseca, B. (2008). *Unstructured data at risk in most firms, survey finds, Computerworld.* http://www.computerworld.com/article/2534496/data-center/unstructured-data-at-risk-in-most-firms--survey-finds.html

foxnews.com. (2014a). *Federal workers, contractors reportedly behind many cyber breaches -- often by accident.* http://www.foxnews.com/politics/2014/11/10/federal-firewall-reportedly-struggles-against-increasing-number-cyberattacks/

foxnews.com. (2014b). *American farmers confront big data revolution.* http://www.foxnews.com/us/2014/03/29/american-farmers-confront-big-data-revolution/

freepatentsonline.com. (2003). *Secure auditing of information systems.* United States Patent Application 20030220940. http://www.freepatentsonline.com/y2003/0220940.html

Friedland, R., & Alford, R. R. (1991). Bringing society back in: Symbols, practices, and institutional contradictions. In W. W. Powell & P. J. DiMaggio (Eds.), *The new institutionalism in organizational analysis* (pp. 232–263). Chicago: University of Chicago Press.

Gens, F. (2011). IDC predictions 2012: Competing for 2020. *IDC Analyze the Future.* http://cdn.idc.com/research/Predictions12/Main/downloads/IDCTOP10Predictions2012.p

Gomez, J., Pinnick, T., & Soltani, A. (2009). Know privacy report, U.C. Berkeley School of Information, 5. http://knowprivacy.org/report/KnowPrivacy_Final_Report.pdf.

Goodburn, M. A., & Hill, S. (2011). The cloud transforms business. *Financial Executive, 26*(10), 34–39.

Greenwood, R., & Hinings, C. R. (1996). Understanding radical organizational change: Bringing together the old and the new institutionalism. *Academy of Management Review, 21,* 1022–1054.

haaretz.com. (2010). *Turkish hackers steal personal details of tens of thousands of Israelis.* http://www.haaretz.com/news/diplomacy-defense/turkish-hackers-steal-personal-details-of-tens-of-thousands-of-israelis-1.302494

Harsanyi, J. (1971). *The dimension and measurement of social power,* reprinted in K. W. Rothschild, *Power in economics.* Harmondsworth: Penguin Books, p. 80.

Hernandez, P. (2012). *Survey: 70 percent of organizations have big plans for big data.* http://www.enterpriseappstoday.com/data-management/survey-70-percent-enterprises-big-plans-for-big-data.html

Hoffman, A. J. (1999). Institutional evolution and change: Environmentalism and the US chemical industry. *Academy of Management Journal, 42*(4), 351–371.

Hooper, J. (2010). *Google executives convicted in Italy over abuse video, The Guardian.* http://www.theguardian.com/technology/2010/feb/24/google-video-italy-privacy-convictions

Ingthorsson, O. (2011). *Regulations a barrier to cloud growth in Europe.* http://www.datacenterknowledge.com/archives/2011/08/29/enhancing-cloud-development-in-europe/

ISACA. (2014). *Generating value from big data analytics, White Paper.* http://www.isaca.org/Knowledge-Center/Research/ResearchDeliverables/Pages/Generating-Value-From-Big-Data-Analytics.aspx

Jervell, E. E., & Gummer, C. (2014). *U.S. web firms' expansion leaves Germans conflicted.* http://online.wsj.com/articles/amazon-to-launch-web-hosting-in-germany-1414075728

Katz, D. M. (2014). *The cyber liability shell game.* http://ww2.cfo.com/risk-management/2014/09/cyber-liability-shell-game/

Kim, P. H., Pinkley, R. L., & Fragale, A. R. (2005). Power dynamics in negotiation. *Academy of Management Review, 30*(4), 799–822.

King, N. J., & Jessen, P. W. (2010). Profiling the mobile customer – privacy concerns when behavioural advertisers target mobile phones – part i. *Computer Law and Security Review, 26*(6), 595–612.

Kshetri, N. (2014). Big data's impact on privacy, security and consumer welfare. *Telecommunications Policy, 38,* 1134–1145.

Larkin, E. (2010). Will cloud computing kill privacy? *PC World, 28*(3), 44.

linnettaylor. (2013). *Surveil the rich, observe the poor: Big data at the Internet Governance Forum 2013.* http://linnettaylor.wordpress.com/2013/10/25/surveil-the-rich-observe-the-poor-big-data-at-the-internet-governance-forum-2013/

Manos, D. (2011). *Patients sue Walgreens for making money on their data, healthcareitnews.com.* http://www.healthcareitnews.com/news/patients-sue-walgreens-making-money-their-data

McCreary, L. (2008). What was privacy? *Harvard Business Review, 86*(10), 123–131.

Mell, P., & Grance, T. (2011). *The NIST definition of cloud computing: Recommendations of the national institute of standards and technology.* Special Publication, 800–145.

Meyer, A. (1982). Adapting to environmental jolts. *Administrative Science Quarterly, 27,* 515–537.

Mitra, D. (1999). Endogenous lobby formation and endogenous protection: A long-run model of trade policy determination. *American Economic Review, 89*(5), 1116–1134.

Nguyen, A. (2011). *Only seven percent of UK it services in the cloud, says survey, Computerworld.* http://www.itworld.com/cloud-computing/200657/only-seven-percent-uk-it-services-cloud-says-survey

Nielsen, N. (2013). *US cloud snoops pose questions for EU cybercrime body.* http://euobserver.com/justice/118677

North, D. C. (1990). *Institutions, institutional change and economic performance.* Cambridge, MA: Cambridge University Press.

North, D. C. (1996). Epilogue: Economic performance through time. In L. J. Alston, T. Eggertsson, & D. C. North (Eds.), *Empirical studies in institutional change* (pp. 342–355). Cambridge, MA: Cambridge University Press.

O'brien, K. J. (2012). *Dismayed at Google's Privacy Policy, European Group Is Weighing Censure.* http://tinyurl.com/bgxwt8b

Ostrom, E. (2005). Doing institutional analysis: Digging deeper than markets and hierarchies. In C. Ménard & M. M. Shirley (Eds.), *Handbook of new institutional economics* (pp. 819–848). Dordrecht, The Netherlands: Springer.

Pinaroc, J. D. (2009). *Saudi faces tough time with cybercrimes, ZDNet Asia.* http://www.zdnetasia.com/news/security/0,39044215,62058637,00.htm

Pirlot, A. (2014). *Big data: A tool for development or threat to privacy?* https://www.privacyinternational.org/blog/big-data-a-tool-for-development-or-threat-to-privacy

Price, M. (2011). Pinning down the cloud. *The Wall Street Journal, R3.*

Purdy, J. M., & Gray, B. (2009). Conflicting logics, mechanisms of diffusion, and multilevel dynamics in emerging institutional fields. *Academy of Management Journal, 52*(2), 355–380.

Reay, R., Golden-Biddle, K., & GermAnn, K. (2006). Legitimizing a new role: Small wins and microprocesses of change. *Academy of Management Journal, 49,* 977–998.

Regan, K. (2006). FBI: Cybercrime causes financial pain for many businesses, *technewsworld.* http://www.technewsworld.com/story/48417.html

Ribeiro, J. (2014). *Brazil to drop requirement that Internet firms store data locally.* http://www.networkworld.com/article/2175352/data-center/brazil-to-drop-requirement-that-internet-firms-store-data-locally.html

Ricadela, A. (2011). *Cloud security is looking overcast.* http://www.businessweek.com/magazine/cloud-security-is-looking-overcast-09012011.html

Rose, J., Barton, C., Souza, R., & Platt, J. (2013). *The trust advantage: How to win with big data,* November. Boston: Consulting Group (BCG).

Rosenbush, S. (2014). *Few businesses are focused on unstructured data.* http://blogs.wsj.com/cio/2014/04/02/few-businesses-are-focused-on-unstructured-data/

SAP. (2014). *SAP survey reveals big data-driven customer insight and real-time offers to open new revenue opportunities for operators.* http://www.news-sap.com/sap-survey-reveals-big-data-driven-customer-insight-and-real-time-offers-to-open-new-revenue-opportunities-for-operators/

Savvas, A. (2014). *Cloud, big data raises spectre of insider data theft: Ovum.* http://www.computerworld.in/news/cloud,-big-data-raises-spectre-of-insider-data-theft%3A-ovum

Scott, W. R. (1995). *Institutions and organizations.* Thousand Oaks, CA: Sage.

Scott, W. R. (2001). *Institutions and organizations* (2nd ed.). Thousand Oaks, CA: Sage.

Scott, W. R., Ruef, M., Mendel, P. J., & Caronna, C. A. (2000). *Institutional change and healthcare organizations: From professional dominance to managed care.* Chicago, IL: University of Chicago Press.

Seo, M. G., & Creed, W. E. D. (2002). Institutional contradictions, praxis, and institutional change: A dialectical perspective. *Academy of Management Review, 27*(2), 222–47.

Skok, G. (2000). Establishing a legitimate expectation of privacy in clickstream data. *Michigan Telecommunications & Technology Law Review*. http://cyber.law.harvard.edu/privacy/PrivacyInClickstream%28Skok%29.htm

Smith, J., & Wiest, D. (2005). The uneven geography of global civil society: National and global influences on transnational association. *Social Forces, 84*(2), 621–651.

Strauss, M. (2014). *The U.S. economy is a casualty of NSA surveillance programs*. http://io9.com/the-u-s-economy-is-a-casualty-of-nsa-surveillance-prog-1612667629

Talbot, D. (2010). Security in the ether. *Technology Review, 113*(1), 36–42.

Talbot, D. (2013). *Data discrimination means the poor may experience a different Internet*. http://www.technologyreview.com/news/520131/data-discrimination-means-the-poor-may-experience-a-different-internet/

Taylor, L., Meyer, E. T., & Schroeder, R. (2014). Bigger and better, or more of the same? Emerging practices and perspectives on big data analysis in economics. *Big Data and Society*, 1, http://bds.sagepub.com/content/1/2/2053951714536877

Teufel, H. II. (2008). *Privacy policy guidance memorandum, Memorandum Number*. The Privacy Office U.S. Department of Homeland Security.

The Business Times Singapore. (2013). No need for cloud data to be equally secure.

The Economist. (2005). Business: Busy signals; Indian call centres. 376(8443), 66.

Thiel, S., & Valpuesta, R. (2011). *U.K. Trails U.S. in public cloud adoption, Sales force CEO Says*. http://www.sfgate.com/cgi-bin/article.cgi?f=/g/a/2011/09/13/bloomberg1376-LRILRH0YHQ0X01-3L8HOVDU01DK87C6RGOVTSL63E.DTL

Truxillo, C. (2013). *Five myths about unstructured data and five good reasons you should be analyzing it*. http://blogs.sas.com/content/sastraining/2013/07/08/five-myths-about-unstructured-data-and-five-good-reasons-you-should-be-analyzing-it/

USA Today. (2012). Survey: Cellphone users concerned about privacy in apps. http://usatoday30.usatoday.com/tech/products/story/2012-09-05/mobile-app-privacy/57599260/1

Varonis Systems. (2008). *Ponemon study – Survey on the governance of unstructured data*. http://www.varonis.com/metadata/ponemon-study/

Weber, T. (2011). *Cloud computing: How to get your business ready*. http://www.bbc.co.uk/news/business-12779201

Williamson, O. E. (1993). Calculativeness, trust and economic organization, in the Mechanisms of Governance. *Journal of Law and Economics, 36*(1), 453–486.

Wilshusen, G. C. (2012). Cyber threats facilitate ability to commit economic espionage. *GAO Reports Proceeding*. June 28, 1–16, 20.

Wittow, M. H., & Buller, D. J. (2010). Cloud computing: Emerging legal issues for access to data, anywhere, anytime. *Journal of Internet Law, 14*(1), 1–10.

Worth, D. (2011). *European Parliament calls for stronger data protection rules*. http://www.v3.co.uk/v3-uk/news/2079420/european-parliament-calls-stonger-protection-rules

Yadron, D. (2014a). *Target hackers wrote partly in Russian, displayed high skill, report finds*. http://online.wsj.com/news/articles/SB10001424052702304419104579324902602426862

Yadron, D. (2014b). *Miscommunication as a Cybersecurity threat*. http://online.wsj.com/articles/miscommunication-as-a-cybersecurity-threat-1413751067

Yan, Z. (2012). *Personal data crimes set to be defined*. www.chinadaily.com.cn/china/2012-07/04/content_15546503.htm

Zucker, L. (1986). Production of trust: Institutional sources of economic structure 1840–1920. *Research in Organizational Behaviour, 8*, 3–11.

Chapter 3
Cybersecurity in National Security and International Relations

3.1 Introduction

In the post-cold-war security environment, cyber-threats have been a critical policy and defense issue (Eriksson and Giacomello 2006). Some argue that cyber-conflicts are the most serious security threats facing nations since the development of nuclear weapons in the 1940s (Cobb 1999). In recent years, CS has become a far more prominent and explicit element in national security and international relations. Cyber-attacks, cybercrimes and cyber-warfare have generated much debate and a number of international institutional frameworks and initiatives have evolved to address these threats.

Stressing the seriousness of cybercrime and appreciating the importance of appropriate legislative measures and international cooperation, the member states of the Council of Europe (CoE) and other non-member states recognized the importance of a formal multilateral institutional framework on this issue. Consequently, the CoE Convention on Cybercrime (CoECoC) was signed in Budapest in 2001, which entered into force in 2004. As of December 2014, the Convention had been signed by 53 states. In addition, international and regional organizations and other relevant bodies and fora such as the UN, the IGF, which is a UN-mandated global multi-stakeholder policy forum, the International Telecommunication Union (ITU), which is a UN specialized agency dealing with ICT issues, the Internet Corporation for Assigned Names and Numbers (ICANN), regional development and security organizations such as the Shanghai Cooperation Organization (SCO), and the Association of Southeast Asian Nations (ASEAN) have introduced a number of initiatives and measures that are directed towards reducing cyber-threats.

While these attempts are highly encouraging, CS-related international legal regimes, institutional frameworks and instruments are in a nascent phase of development. CS has become one of the most prominent international relations challenges facing nations. CS experts such as F-Secure's Chief Research Officer, Mikko

© Springer International Publishing Switzerland 2016   53
N. Kshetri, *The Quest to Cyber Superiority*, DOI 10.1007/978-3-319-40554-4_3

Hypponen and Stonesoft's director of CS, Jarno Limnéll argue that a number of nations are currently engaged in the cyberwar arms race.

Nations are competing against one another and groups in different nations are forming alliances in developing cyber-defense and cyber-offense capabilities in their quest to establish superiority in the cyberspace. A close observation of nations' relative cyber-warfare capabilities reveals patterns and trends that are rather counter-intuitive and contradictory to our assumptions. For instance, some analysts have predicted that technologically backward states may face greater challenges and difficulties to fight a war in the cyberspace (Gartzke 2013). Yet, as discussed in Chap. 1, contrary to these stereotypes, so called rogue and economically backward regimes have not been passive observers of cyber-attacks and cyber-warfare. This feature of the recent competition in the cyberspace seems to indicate that a nation's technological advancement may not necessarily lead to superiority in cyber-warfare.

The cyberspace dynamics is undergoing a major upheaval due to global forces of competition, cooperation, and pressures. Such changes often create confusion and uncertainty and produce an environment that lacks norms, templates, and models about appropriate strategies and structures (Newman 2000). In such situations, the institutional context may not provide organizing templates for institutional actors.

This chapter examines the effectiveness of the current international legal regimes and institutional frameworks in dealing with various sources of cyber-threats facing nations. It also suggests some measures that can be undertaken to overcome some of the deficiencies of the current international institutions frameworks related to CS.

3.2 Cyber-Warfare Concerns

It is important to make clear at the outset that cyberwar lacks a definition that is generally agreed on, although it has promoted interest for many years. Analysts differ as to whether the current stage of cyber-conflict can be considered as a cyberwar. Thomas Rid maintained that "cyberwar has never happened in the past, it is not occurring in the present, and it is highly unlikely that it will disturb the future" and argued that cyber-attacks "diminish rather than accentuate political violence (Rid 2013a). He also believed that cyber-attacks are more likely to bring world peace rather than warfare (Rid 2013b). Others such as Mike McConnell, a former NSA director and vice chairman of Booz Allen Hamilton think that industrialized nations such as the U.S. have been fighting a cyberwar (Salant and Holmes 2013). Likewise, according to a survey of the Pew Research Center released in October 2014, about two-third of respondents expected a "major" cyber-attack in the world by 2025, which is likely to lead to significant loss of life or property losses of tens of billions of dollars (Rainie et al. 2014). The survey was conducted with over 1600 technology experts.

Cyber-warfare experts, however, debate over whether these qualify as cyber-warfare. According to the strictest definition, a cyber-attack is considered as a cyberwar only if it causes "widespread harm, rather than mere inconvenience" (The Economist 2008). Some analysts use potential human casualty as an indicator to measure the cyber-attack-related risks faced by nations. For instance, denying the seriousness of cyber-attacks, M.C. Libicki notes: "No person has ever died from a cyberattack" (Libicki 2013). Viewing from this perspective, even the 2008 cyber-attacks against Georgia may not qualify as cyberwar, since unlike the military operations, cyber-attacks did not cause a physical harm.

Some observers, on the other hand, argue that a cyber-attack qualifies as a "cyberwar" if it is combined with conventional military operations. According to this view, the attacks on Georgia would qualify as cyber-warfare but those on Estonia would not (The Economist 2008). Others argue that the effects of the 2007 cyber-attacks in Estonia "were potentially just as disastrous as a conventional attack on this country" (Shackelford 2009).

Now let us define cyber-warfare for the purpose of this book. Analyzing many documents related to war ultimatum and motivations of war such as those of the World War I-era (e.g., statements of British Foreign Minister Edward Grey and German Chancellor Theobald von Bethmann-Hollweg) and the legendary Mongolian warrior and conqueror, Genghis Khan, J. Hirshleifer (Hirshleifer 1998) concluded that wars were fought for material ends as well as for intangible goals such as honor, dominance, reputation and prestige. Based on this, cyber-warfare can be defined as actions in the cyberspace carried out or initiated by a state actor against another state or a non-state entity (an adversary) for economic gains or with an intention to cause material losses or to destruct the glory, honor, prestige and reputation of the adversary. Following Hirshleifer's definition of war, a number of cyber-attacks that are widely believed to be carried out or initiated by nation states qualify as cyber-warfare. Some of them include the 2007 cyber-attacks against Estonia, the 2008 cyber-attacks against Georgia, the Stuxnet worm which was designed to destroy Iran's nuclear enrichment facilities in 2010, the 2012 cyber-attacks against Saudi national oil company Aramco and the 2014 hack on Sony Pictures. The Shamoon malware, for instance, destroyed information on 30,000 computers (material losses of the adversary). Likewise, the cyber-attacks on Sony Pictures were carried out with an intention to embarrass and financially damage the company. The attacks brought Sony Pictures to its knees by harming the company's honor and reputation in addition to the significant financial costs it caused. It was described as the "most embarrassing and all-encompassing hack of internal corporate data ever made public" (buzzfeed.com 2014). The hackers allegedly download 100 TB of data including unreleased films and TV scripts and leaked more than 47,000 SSNs, details on salary negotiations, and other sensitive information.

3.3   International Legal Regimes and Institutional Frameworks Related to CS

The CoECoC is the only multilateral treaty focusing purely on cybercrimes. As of December 2014, 44 countries had signed as well as ratified the Convention in accordance with their national constitutional or legal requirements, making it enforceable. Nine additional countries had signed the CoECoC but had not ratified. Some argue that a key problem of the CoECoC is that it has adopted vague definitions of cybercrime and related concepts that are subject to different interpretations by different states. Many nations that have ratified the CoECoC have done so under a number of reservations. For instance, the U.S. ratified the CoECoC under "more than a half dozen" reservations (Goldsmith 2011). All these have reduced the scope of cybercrimes covered by the Treaty and led to obligations that are less demanding and lack uniformity across countries. A National Research Council study concluded: "[A] signatory nation may decline to cooperate with its obligations under the convention on fairly broad grounds, and the convention lacks an enforcement mechanism to assure that signatories will indeed cooperate in accordance with their obligations" (Owens et al. 2009).

Nations have also relied on the global intergovernmental organizations such as the UN to address cybercrime related issues. For instance, in the first meeting of the Intergovernmental Group of Experts of the UN Crime Prevention and Criminal Justice Program held in January 2011, the Chinese delegation, citing statistics of the China Ministry of Public Security, complained that the country was suffering from foreign-originated cyber-attacks. The delegation noted that in 2010, servers of over 90 % of network sites that were used to commit cyber-frauds such as phishing, pornography and Internet gambling against Chinese targets were located outside China. The delegation also stated that over 70 % of botnet control sites were in foreign countries (Pi 2011).

Formal standards-setting international institutions such as the ITU have also become a venue where these issues are being discussed and debated. For instance, while governments of the U.S. and the EU economies have argued that the ICANN should continue to be the central organization, governments of some of the major economies such as China, Brazil, South Africa, India and several Middle Eastern economies such as Iran and Saudi Arabia want to move the internet management system under the ITU. The economies in the latter group also want to define Internet governance more broadly to include issues such as spam and illegal content as opposed to the ICANN's narrow technical mandate, management of the DNS. Since the ICANN is a U.S.-based organization, many governments do not like the fact that ICANN's central role in governance would put the U.S. in a position of power to regulate and oversee the Internet. These governments think that the U.S. may have exploited its advantage to create Internet malware such as Flame and Stuxnet, which attacked sovereign nations. In the World Conference on International Telecommunications (WCIT-12) was convened by the ITU in December 2012 to amend the International Telecommunication Regulations (ITRs) treaty, which was adopted in 1988. Of the 144 countries with the voting rights at the WCIT-12, 89 countries signed the revised ITRs, which included many countries in Africa and the Middle East, Brazil, Mexico, Argentina, China, Indonesia, Iran, and Russia. Fifty-five countries including Australia, India, EU members, Canada, Japan, and the U.S. did not sign the treaty (ITU 2012). The U.S. considered the ITU and the ITRs as inappropriate international institutions for dealing with CS issues (Kramer 2012).

New regional multilateral exclusive groupings established for politico-security arrangements such as the SCO have also dealt with CS. The SCO economies' approach to CS differs in several important and fundamental ways from the CoECoC signatory countries. The two groups differ in the definition and assessment of the scope of the problem. One such difference is that SCO economies consider it important to focus on the broader problem of information security rather than the narrower CS. In 2008, the SCO Agreement in the field of International Information Security emphasized on and expressed concerns about the "digital gap" between the West and the East. These economies have been particularly concerned about the West's' monopolization in ICT products such as software and hardware and less developed countries' dependence on the West.

Finally, military, political and economic organizations such as the North Atlantic Treaty Organization (NATO), the EU, the Organization for Economic Co-operation and Development (OECD), the ASEAN and Asia Pacific Economic Cooperation (APEC) have also addressed CS issues. For instance, in an attempt to enhance the NATO's cyber defense capability, the NATO Cooperative Cyber Defense Centre of Excellence (NATO CCD COE) was established in 2008. As of April 2014, sponsoring Nations of the NATO CCD COE included Estonia, Latvia, Lithuania, Germany, Hungary, Italy, Poland, Slovakia, Spain, the Netherlands and the U.S. (CCDCOE 2014).

The U.S. and EU countries have also established deep and strong collaborations and partnerships. For instance, the Italy-based European Electronic Crimes Task Force, which has dedicated personnel from the countries involved to investigate and prosecute cybercrimes, provides a forum for law enforcement agencies, the private sector, and academia from the U.S. and EU nations. In the same vein, a virtual forum for ASEAN CS is being formed to develop a common framework to coordinate exchange of information, establishment of standards and cooperation among enforcement agencies.

3.4 Critical Issues and Current Sources of Disagreement Among Nations

There has been a relatively low level of acceptance of the CoECoC. For instance, none of the BRIC states (Brazil, Russia, India and China) is currently a signatory to the CoECoC. Its failure to attract the support of a large number of countries can be attributed to the general Western focus. Many countries have objected to a number of clauses of the Treaty including definitions of cybercrimes, criminalization of IPR violations, mechanisms that involve intrusion of national sovereignty (Goldsmith 2011). Russia's SCO National Coordinator, Ambassador Barsky described the Convention as less than satisfactory (Kizekova 2012).

International cybercrimes in general have alarmingly low prosecution and conviction rates. Some countries that have signed the CoECoC have often not been able to control cyber-attacks originated from them. For instance, while Ukraine has ratified the CoECoC, according to the country's Interior Ministry, 400 people were arrested for Internet and banking fraud charges during 2002–2011 but only eight were convicted (Onyshkiv and Bondarev 2012).

A state victimized by cyber-attacks is likely to encounter several problems in applying formal and informal sanctions. As discussed in Chap. 1, one problem centers around the technical difficulty in attributing the sources of cyber-attacks. For instance, there have been talks in Washington about fines and trade penalties against a country guilty of cyber-attacks (FoxNews.com 2013). The near impossibility of identifying the actual source means that economic and trade sanctions as an instrument of diplomacy in response to cyber-attacks would generally be a bad idea. This means that it is impossible to regulate cyber-weapons in the same manner as nuclear, chemical and biological weapons are controlled and regulated. In this section, we outline key unaddressed issues.

3.4.1   Outdated Legislative Framework and the Lack of Law Enforcement System Capacity

The literatures on the white-collar crime could be particularly helpful for understanding the low levels of cybercrime-related arrests and conviction in countries such as Ukraine, which are signatories to the CoECoC. The system capacity argument maintains that the legal response to a suspected crime is a function of organizational resources and caseload pressures (Pontell et al. 1994). Resource limitations are of particular concern for white-collar crimes due to their complexity, which require substantial amounts of investigative and prosecutorial efforts (Tillman et al. 1996). The limited capacity of criminal justice agencies due to the complexity and hidden nature of white-collar crime and the system overload caused by such crimes reduces state capacity to respond to such crimes (Benson et al. 1990). These constraints also occur in cybercrimes.

A related explanation focusing on an organizational advantage a white-collar crime points out that, offenders that are in "organizationally shielded" positions receive more lenient treatment. An analysis of securities fraud in Canada indicated that employers were less likely to be prosecuted under criminal statutes than were offenders in lower-class positions (Hagan and Parker 1985). The authors concluded that organizational structure of corporations embedded class advantage in such a way that employers were often shielded from prosecution. On account of this remark we can draw a parallel between domestic white collar crimes and international cybercrimes. While the organized crime groups which include "underworld" criminals as well as "overworld" figures from the former Communist Party are in "organizationally shielded" positions as proposed by organizational advantage argument, most international cybercriminals can "jurisdictionally shield" themselves just by operating from economies that lack law enforcement system capacity. Moreover, the primary reason they are not prosecuted may not be because of the difficulty in obtaining direct evidence against them as argued by the system capacity approach. This is in a large part due to outdated regulative institutions and the unwillingness of law enforcement agencies to pursue cyber-fraud cases as the criminals mainly victimize foreigners. In Ukraine's case, for instance, despite international cooperation, crime fighting efforts are hindered by underdeveloped and outdated institutional framework. For instance, while the Security Service of Ukraine (Sluzhba Bespeky Ukrayiny, or SBU) cooperated with the West in 2010 and arrested five alleged kingpins of a criminal group, which stole US$70 million from U.S. bank accounts, they were freed immediately without a court trial. It is also argued that foreigners also account for international cybercrimes originated from Ukraine (Kshetri 2013). Corruption has arguably enabled and generally encouraged them to obtain the right to reside and operate criminal activities in the country.

3.4.2   Concerns Regarding the Fairness of the Procedures and Outcomes of Formal Frameworks

The problem of system capacity is equally applicable to other developing economies that are not signatories to the CoECoC. An additional issue that is important to address in regard to many developing economies relates to their readiness and willingness to join the CoECoC. Some countries are concerned with issues of equity, voice, and just representation and have questioned the fairness of the procedures and outcomes of international regimes. In the first UN forum on Internet governance, countries such as Iran and South Africa complained that they had not been given an opportunity to adequately express their views (Hadoulis 2006). In the India Knowledge Summit in October 2013, the then communications minister Kapil Sibal indicated India would not sign the CoECoC. India and other developing countries have accused that developed countries drafted it without consulting them (Singh 2013).

3.4.3 Disagreement Regarding the Nature and Dimensions of Cyber-Threats

Especially the West's relationship with some major world power such as China and Russia are confronted by issues that are more complex than discussed earlier. In order to understand the disagreements and conflicts, it is important to understand multidimensionality and multiple forms of security risks. The importance placed on a given dimension of security varies across time, space, issue area and according to specific political, geographic and cultural conditions.

Some argue that it is insufficient simply to consider political and military issues as the only dimensions of national security. For instance, developing economies have long emphasized the importance of economic threats in addition to military threats (Ball 1988). In the domain of physical security, secure system of food, health, money and trade are viewed as the essential prerequisite to national security (Thomas 1987). Threats to value and identity are also important source of insecurity (Azar and Moon Chung-in 1998).

It is also important to distinguish between internal security and external security. Most countries tend to view their main security threats as either internal or external. In some states, internal security is the principal and central problem. The task of maintaining peace within the territory or border is a key challenge in such states. One example is Fiji, where the source of primary threat to the nation's stability is internal.

The states have faced a unique governance challenge associated with the Internet. They are finding that the degree of trumping power over internal illicit actors is declining and power over their citizens has reduced due to broader and more diverse flows of information. Some regimes have come under cyber-attacks from their own citizens. For instance, in July 2014, in order to protest about corruption, activists hacked the Twitter accounts of the Kenyan defense forces and its spokesman (bbc. com 2014). Hacking groups such as Anonymous have attacked government websites of a number of countries such as Brazil, Colombia, Ecuador and Venezuela.

When internal security poses a bigger threat, the defense against external attacks is likely to be a less important security goal. In such situation, the government is likely to focus its CS efforts to deal with internal threats. Internal conflicts arise because social and economic and political systems work in the national elites' advantage and they engage in exploitation of the majority of the people in the country (Tickner 1994). Internal security is often desirable for the ruling elites to remain in power, which does not necessarily involve making all citizens equally secure and safe (Ball 1988).

Some governments are leveraging their cyber power to suppress domestic political dissents. To take an example, it was reported that the Government of Burma, used its cyber-warfare department within the police force to track its online critics and send virus-attached e-mails to exiled activists. As another example, according to the Electronic Frontier Foundation, the Vietnam government recruits local hackers in order to spy on journalists, dissidents, and activists (Rayman 2014). Likewise, according to the 2012 annual report of Reporters Without Borders, Iran ranked "the number one enemy of the Internet" due to its strict measures to restrict Internet access, filter contents, and imprison bloggers. On these measures, the country was ahead of countries such as Saudi Arabia, Bahrain, Syria, China, and Belarus.

In some other states, internal security threats are almost non-existent whereas external threats are relatively more prominent. One such example is Japan, which has an orderly a prosperous society with homogeneous population characterized by a high-trust culture. India is another example of a country where external security threats are viewed as more serious, despite significant internal threats associated with poverty, government corruption and illiteracy. Regional security concerns those associated with Pakistan's nuclear weapons, China are viewed as more dangerous than internal threats (Apcss 2001). South Korea is another example in which the threats are primarily external, mainly associated with North Korea.

CS issues need to be understood in light of the above considerations. First, it is important to look at key dimensions of CS such as military, espionage, and cybercrime. The emphasis of the U.S. has been mainly on controlling cybercrimes. Richard Clarke, the former U.S. National Coordinator for Security, Infrastructure Protection, and Counter-terrorism and Robert K. Knake have argued for a treaty that would ban cyber-attacks on civilian targets but not on military targets (Clarke and Knate 2010). According to them, such a treaty would protect the private networks but would allow the lead the U.S. has in cyber-warfare against military targets. Clarke and Knake's proposal does not intend to ban cyber-espionage activities with non-economic motives. The rationale for this approach is that the U.S. relies heavily on electronic spying, and verification of and attribution for espionage are too difficult.

The U.S. has repeatedly emphasized its interest in institutions that set the rules for controlling and punishing cyber-attacks that involve economic espionage. The U.S. believes that non-economic cyber-espionage activities and military attacks are difficult to distinguish and one can be confused with the other. The U.S. opposes international legal regulation on this area because "an arms control agreement limiting cyber espionage is not clearly in [the United States'] interest, might be violated regularly by other nations, and would pose significant compliance-enforcement problems" (Clarke and Knate 2010). Russia, on the other hand, has placed a heavy emphasis on the military dimension. It was reported that Russia and the U.S. had planned a dialogue which would include discussions about how each side's military views the Internet and an effort to establish a hot line that could be used during CS crises (Segal 2012).

It is interesting and relevant to consider China's position on CS. An article published in *China Economic Times* on June 12, 2000 discussed three mechanisms that Xu Guanhua, then Chinese vice minister of Science and Technology, thought high technology would affect national security—military security, economic security and cultural security. There is thus a clear emphasis on the multi-dimensional aspects of CS. Regarding military security, Guanhua forcefully argued that developed countries have put many hi-tech arms into actual battles and discussed the likelihood of ICT-exporting countries installing software for "coercing, attacking or sabotage". Regarding the economic security, a commentary published in the *People's Liberation Army Daily* on February 8, 2000, without directly referring to a specific country, noted that "some countries" with highly developed ICT industries are "taking advantage of their monopolistic position" to "control information technologies, infiltrate information resources" and dump ICT products in underdeveloped countries. According to the article, the goal of these nations is "to attain political, economic and military objectives". The article further noted that through the export of ICT products, the "information powers" dominate information in underdeveloped nations and thereby threaten their economic security.

The issues of value and identity have also been identified as a source of insecurity (Azar and Moon Chung-in 1998). An article in China's People's Liberation Army Daily warned that the "information colonialism" is a real threat to national security, which "will be a major cause of future wars". Due primarily to this concern, the Chinese government, has been building systems based on open-source software (OSS).

The views and positions of China and Russia are reflected in the approach of the SCO, which comprises China, Russia, Kazakhstan, Kyrgyzstan, Tajikistan and Uzbekistan as members. The 2008 SCO Agreement in the field of International Information Security expressed concerns about the "digital gap" between the West and the East. The SCO economies are interested in controlling information that is likely to provoke what they call the three "evils" (terrorism, extremism, separatism). They consider it important to prevent other nations from using their technologies to disrupt economic, social and political stability and national security. Western countries, on the other hand, maintain that too much government regulations and control may harm cyberspace security and emphasize the importance of the private sector in the formulation of international norms (Kizekova 2012). In this way, the SCO economies' approach is characterized by a relatively high emphasis on internal security compared to external security. A clear difference in priority was evident in the meeting between Chinese president Xi Jinping and U.S. president Barack Obama at the APEC Summit held in Beijing in November 2014. For instance, Xi "reaffirmed [China's] firm opposition to terrorism of all forms" including cyber terrorism. Obama, on the other hand, "stressed the importance of protecting IP as well as trade secrets, especially against cyber-threats" (Bennett 2014).

3.4.4 Isolation from Most of the Economies of the World

First, it is important to note that, despite their capabilities, countries such as Russia and China have little incentives to launch cyber-attacks against the West that may cause widespread economic harm. For instance, if Russia and China launch cyber-attacks against the West, due to these economies' global integration, the aftershocks from such attack-led economic disaster in the West are also likely to harm them (Brenner 2013). This is not the case, however, with countries such as North Korea.

Some regimes' political and economic isolation from most of the world economies is clearly the dominant challenge facing the West to integrate them into formal institutional frameworks. Some examples include Iran and North Korea, which present challenges that are unique and different from those associated with China and Russia. For instance, the U.S. and other Western countries have a clearer understanding of the points of view of China and Russia despite occasional tensions and conflicts. China and Russia also maintain diplomatic and economic ties with most countries. The general lack of such understanding and the lack of diplomatic and economic ties with regard to North Korea have increased the complexity (Corbin 2013). Due to the regime's unpredictability and desperation to survive, North Korea arguably poses high threats to its adversaries (Gross 2013). Moreover, unlike China's PLA, which regularly publishes academic journals and policy documents, North Korea's KPA does not publish any documents. Assessing the KPA's advancement in cyber-weapons has thus been an extremely difficult exercise (Waterman 2012).

With the decline of violent geopolitical conflicts, traditional issues such as nuclear war are losing salience and the focus and organizing principle in international relations have been on nontraditional security issues (Collins 2003; Wenping 2007). As noted earlier, the asymmetric nature of cyber-attacks means that entities with limited financial and technical resources or militarily weaker actors can compromise high-value targets (Masters 2011).

This means that so called, "rogue" and economically destitute countries such as North Korea have a higher propensity to engage in cyber-attacks. For instance, North Korea may launch cyber-attacks and avoid sanctions and retaliatory attacks. In this way, the development of cyber-warfare capability would give countries such as North Korea the ability to harm adversaries without potential negative consequences (McGee 2011).

3.5 A Framework for Nations' Strategic Policy Choices for Cyber-Conflicts Associated with Various Sources

The international institutional framework for CS is structurally imperfect and deficient. Based on the above discussion, the relationships among countries from the perspective of CS-related relationships can be divided into four groups that pose different dominant challenges when viewed from a Western country's perspective (Table 3.1). We propose a segmentation approach that groups countries according to the quality and nature of relationship, both in the physical and the cyber domains, and aligning strategic policy development and implementation at the group level.

As noted above nations hold diverse interests, viewpoints and perspectives on CS. While various institutional actors take actions to change institutions, their

Table 3.1 Strategic responses to cybercrimes, cyber-attacks and cyber-warfare involving economies with different categories of relationships

Nature of relationship	Some examples	Strategic responses
A. Membership in formal multilateral frameworks related to CS (e.g., CoECoC)	Signatories of CoECoC	• Local capacity building and institutional development
Lack of membership in formal multilateral frameworks related to CS		
B. Cooperative, strong, close, favorable and stable diplomatic and economic ties	Relationships of most CoECoC signatories with India and Indonesia	• Local capacity building and institutional development • Harnessing the power of successful regional organizations that are internally cohesive and have security as a key focus • Providing opportunities for developing economies' voice and participation.
C. Formal diplomatic and economic ties characterized by periodic tension and distrust	China-U.S. Russia-U.S.	• Working on areas of common interests • Help and encouragement to integrate with the West • Establishment of a high level working group made up of policy makers • A 'bricolage' approach to CS
D. No formal diplomatic and economic ties	U.S.-North Korea U.S.-Iran Japan- North Korea	• Development of offensive and defensive capabilities tailored to specific threats.

"actions, intentions, and rationality are conditioned" by the existing institutions (Holm 1995). That is new institutions are built upon older institutions. Nations also have varied levels of resources and capabilities available for developing CS-related capabilities. These differences make it necessary to develop strategic responses to possible cyber-threats associated with a nation based on its individual characteristics as well as the nature of relationship with others (Table 3.1).

3.5.1 Local Capacity Building in Law Enforcement and Institutional Development

Some emerging economies' law enforcement system capacity to deal with cybercrime has become the dominant challenge that limits their ability to fight cybercrimes. EBay's Albena Spasova, who worked in promoting law reforms in Moldova and Bulgaria noted: "Even in 2001, I was meeting judges who thought cyber-crime was someone stealing a computer" (Wylie 2007). Local capacity building and institutional development can produce effective results in strengthening global CS. As an example, consider Romania. In response to the rise of

Romania-originated cybercrimes, the CoE selected the capital city Bucharest for its latest cybercrime program office. As of 2013, the U.S. FBI trained about 600 Romanian investigators in fighting cybercrime (Odobescu 2014).

Some affected private sector players have also contributed to promote institutional and law enforcement capacity development. To take an example, eBay has been educating Romanian prosecutors about cybercrimes including explaining to a judge using layman's language (Wylie 2007).

Western measures to strengthen local capacity and institutions in the country have paid off. Romania's Directorate for Investigating Organized Crime and Terrorism (DIICOT) reported that it exchanged information with law enforcement agencies from more than 50 countries including the U.K.'s Serious Organized Crime Agency (SOCA) and the U.S. FBI (Constantin 2011). There has been a close collaboration between the Romanian police and the FBI agents since the early 2000s. (news24.com2011. December 19) (worked)AAAAs of 2008, Romania's national police and the FBI arrested 90 Romanians engaged in cybercrimes.

3.5.2 Creation of Informal Networks and Agreements

Informal networks and agreements among states and transnational actors are becoming an important feature of the world politics (Lipson 1991). Transgovernmental networks consisting of domestic regulators and public officials—as a form of informal institution—are becoming an increasingly common feature of global governance (Bach and Newman 2010). Such networks are found in a number of areas such as financial markets, aviation, antitrust, data privacy, pharmaceuticals, and the environment (Bach and Newman 2010). State and sub-state officials from a number of countries work together to share information with each other, develop harmonized guidelines and best practices, and reduce friction associated with globalization (Bach and Newman 2010). These networks are arguably "the optimal form of organization for the Information Age" (Slaughter 2004). Despite criticisms by some doubters such as voluntary rather than compulsory participation in such networks, considerable variation of engagement across nations, and the lack formal enforcement powers and mission-critical services to compliance bodies that coordinate such networks (Downs et al. 1996) , informal networks have become increasingly common mechanism for solving trans-border cybercrimes.

As an example, the U.S. FBI announced in 2009 that it would permanently base a cybercrime expert in Estonia to help fight international cybercrimes (Associated Press Worldstream 2009). The FBI worked closely with the Estonian Police and Border Guard, the Dutch National Police and other relevant agencies, which led to the arrest of six Estonians, who allegedly used DNS Changer malware to hijack more than 4 million computers in over 100 countries, which generated at least US $14 million in profits (Kshetri 2013).

Since 2009, the FBI has stationed a special agent at the U.S. Embassy in Kiev for assisting cybercrime investigation (Kirk 2012). The Ukrainian law enforcement agencies have also cooperated with the West. In 2010, the SBU arrested five alleged kingpins of a criminal group, which stole US$70 million from U.S. bank accounts (Onyshkiv and Bondarev 2012).

On the contrary, the system and approach being used by China and the U.S. to fight cybercrime are outdated and inefficient. For instance, if one country needs the help of the other in investigating a cybercrime, a request for assistance takes place through an exchange of letters. It was reported that in 2010, the FBI office in Beijing forwarded 10 letters through the Ministry of Foreign Affairs and received responses to two. This is in sharp contrast to the deeper and stronger collaborations and partnerships between the U.S. and EU countries (e.g., the European Electronic Crimes Task Force).

3.5.3 Providing Opportunities for Developing Economies' Voice and Participation

Treaties involving alliances and broad policy guidelines are sustained only by perceptions of mutual advantage (Baxter 1980). Making efforts to understand developing economies' problems from their point of view and providing opportunities for their voice and participation would help explore mutual advantage and encourage their participation in formal international frameworks. Attempting to achieve too much too rapidly is often counterproductive. One way to gain their cooperation would be exclude issues from formal treaties that are objected by developing countries and are only tangentially related to cybercrime such as software piracy.

3.5.4 Establishment of a High Level Working Group Made Up of Policy Makers

External pressures can do little to force nations to change their cyberspace behaviors since outsiders lack broad legitimacy. In order to find a solution that satisfies both parties, it is important to engage policy makers and national elites with strong commitment to a soft approach to and interested in developing a better relationship with adversaries. We illustrate this with the following observation involving China-U.S. relationships in cyberspace.

At a hearing of the U.S. House Foreign Affairs subcommittee on Asia, James Andrew Lewis, Director and Senior Fellow, Technology and Public Policy Program and director of the technology program at the Center for Strategic and International Studies noted: "We need to persuade the Chinese to change their behavior; we can't coerce them, they're too big. There are factions within China that want to work with us. We need to encourage them" (Freedberg 2013). One way is to use a soft approach with China. It was reported that the Subcommittee chairman, Steve Chabot was willing to adopt a soft strategy. Likewise, while the Chinese leftist leaders and some government officials associate China's global integration with significant socioeconomic costs, there are factions within the Chinese Communist Party (CCP) that consider integration with the world desirable and important. Like-minded policy makers from both countries who prefer "soft" approach and seek to ameliorate the root causes of cybercrime, cyber-attacks and cyber-warfare through negotiation, conciliation and compromise can help incrementally develop formal and informal relationships related to CS.

3.5.5 A 'Bricolage' Approach to CS

The different approaches to protect against cybercrimes discussed earlier do not directly deal with the fundamental sources of the problem. For instance, for most former Soviet Union economies, the basic source of the problem can be traced to the fact that most of them are too small to absorb the existing computer talent (Serio and Gorkin 2003). A large number of cyber-attacks originate from these economies because students there are good at mathematics, physics, and computer and have difficulties finding jobs. A self-described hacker from Moscow noted: "Hacking is one of the few good jobs left here" (Walker 2004).

Combining components from the existing institutional environment and reorganizing them strategically—also known as bricolage—can be an important way to enhance cooperation and generate positive outcomes (Campbell 2004). For instance, working closely with governments to develop the ICT industry would help address the concerns regarding the West's monopolization in ICT products and less developed countries' dependence on the West.

3.5.6 Identifying and Achieving Cooperation on Common Areas of Interest

Identifying and achieving cooperation on common areas of interest may help secure a "foot-in-the-door" for a subsequent more significant collaboration. To take an example, in 2011, Chinese authorities and the U.S. FBI conducted joint operations to dismantle and shut down an illegal website dealing with child pornography (Lan 2011). This can considered as China's gesture to collaborate with the U.S. and at least symbolic actions to collaborate with the U.S. Theorists argue that a symbolic action can lead to more substantive actions subsequently (Forbes and Jermier 2001).

3.5.7   Helping, Encouraging and Providing Incentives to Integrate with the West

As noted earlier, cybercriminals can take advantage of jurisdictional arbitrage by operating from economies with outdated legislative framework and the lack of law enforcement system capacity. Cybercriminals can more effectively shield themselves jurisdictionally by operating from economies with a low degree of cooperation and integration with the West. Extending theories in white-collar crimes, in the context of international cybercrimes, it can be argued that emerging economies' international cooperation and integration would help them modernize CS-related legislative frameworks and enhance system capacity and law enforcement performance (Kshetri 2013). Cyber-offenders are less likely to be jurisdictionally shielded in such economies.

As an alternative way to link integration with the West and reduction in cybercrimes, it can be argued that the existence of reputation mechanisms and multiplex relationships, which involve relationships based on more than one set of roles make sanctions easier to apply (Bardhan 1993). For instance, Russia is making some progress to become a member of the Organization for Economic Cooperation and Development (OECD). If Russia gains an OECD membership, it is likely to experience additional pressures associated with the membership and its engagement in CS-related international cooperation can be expected to improve.

3.5.8   Harnessing the Power of Successful Regional Organizations that Are Internally Cohesive and Have Security as a Key Focus

Given the lack of membership of most developing economies in the CoECoC, one way to compensate some of the deficiencies of the existing CS-related international institutions is to harness the power of regional organizations, especially consisting of developing nations that are not signatories to the CoECoC. Successful regional organizations that are internally cohesive and have security as a key focus are logical candidates for developing meaningful CS relationships. The ASEAN is one example that fits these criteria and has been effective in managing its internal security relations (Narine 1998). Some major economies' engagement with the ASEAN has focused on deepening CS relationship. For instance, since 2009, the ASEAN and Japan have been working to promote CS-related cooperation and collaboration. Relevant ministries and agencies such as Computer Security Incident Response Teams (CSIRTs) of ASEAN Member States and Japan are working towards addressing common concerns through initiatives such as Internet Traffic Monitoring Data Sharing Project (TSUBAME Project) (asean.org 2013). Likewise, in July 2013, a U.S. delegation participated at the 20th Meeting of the ASEAN Regional Forum (ARF) held in Brunei Darussalam. Cyber security is one of the four core areas addressed by the ARF within its work on counterterrorism and transnational crime (state.gov 2013).

3.5.9 Offensive and Defensive Capabilities Tailored to Specific Threats

The responses discussed thus far are appropriate only if the sources of the cyberattacks have formal diplomatic and economic ties. In the absence of such ties, CS may require an appropriate balance of offensive and defensive capabilities. It is argued that many countries including the U.S. have a strong offensive capability but they are weak in defensive power. Some analysts have called for more proactive defense involving the design and implementation of secure software rather than the current focus on reactive defense (McGraw 2012). In order to better clarify and illustrate this point we offer two examples involving economies that are not signatories to CoECoC. In response to North Korea-originated GPS attacks against its commercial flights and maritime navigational units in 2012 and 2013, South Korea is making efforts to enhance its GPS system capability and is working to develop more advanced GPS technology. For instance, the Ministry of Science and Future Planning announced plans to develop systems that can locate the "attack point and impact of jamming attempts" (Lee 2013).

The development of the offensive and defensive capabilities may sometimes require changes in national regulatory frameworks. For instance, the Japanese government is making an attempt to change the interpretation of the war-renouncing Article 9 of the constitution to lift self-imposed ban on exercising the right of collective self-defense. The exercise of "collective self-defense" would include sanctioning counterattacks by Japanese forces against attackers of allied forces. Note that Japan's current constitution prohibits such measures. In October 2013, Japan and the U.S. agreed to revise defense cooperation guidelines by the end of 2014. Cybercrime (along with China's growing military capability and North Korea's nuclear/missile development) was identified as a trigger that prompted its intention to revise the guidelines.

3.6 Discussion and Concluding Remarks

Based on the definition given above, it can be argued that cyberwar is not an occurrence in the distant future, but a phenomenon that is taking place now. Or at least some nations have accused their adversaries of engaging in the act of cyberwarfare.

This chapter outlined a number of sources, challenges, and potential responses related to international cyber-conflicts and disagreements in issues involving such conflicts. While some governments may be willing to fight international cybercrimes originated from their countries (e.g., CoECoC signatories such as Ukraine), they have faced institutional and law enforcement constraints. Cybercriminals find it attractive to operate from economies with a lack of law enforcement system capacity and/or low degree of integration with the West.

While the West faces significant jurisdictional challenges in investigating and prosecuting international cybercriminals, such challenges are more pronounced in dealing with economies with low degrees of modernization of institutional frameworks and/or low degree of cooperation and integration with the West. For instance, in Estonia and Romania, which are among the countries most integrated with the West, cybercriminals are jurisdictionally less shielded compared to those in Russia.

There are some challenges and drawbacks associated with formal international CS treaties. For instance, there is the lack of acceptance of the CoECoC, the only multilateral treaty on CS, among a large number of developing countries. Likewise, a number of reservations have been made regarding the CoECoC by some countries that ratified. There are also low levels of arrest and subsequent conviction of cybercriminals in some economies (e.g., Ukraine) that have ratified the CoECoC. These facts point to insufficiency and deficiency of the existing international legal regimes and institutional frameworks in responding to cyber-threats. The CoECoC is widely viewed as unsuccessful (Goldsmith 2011). Informal networks can be used as an effective alternative to formal treaties. The existence and depth of informal networks may also provide an explanation behind the markedly different levels of success of the U.S. in fighting cybercrimes originated from EU economies and those from China or Russia.

For the above discussion it is clear that one size fits all does not work in international CS. From the perspective of advanced industrial democracies that are signatories to the CoECoC, depending on the categories of the sources and nature of the cyber-threats, this chapter outlined several possible actions. They may vary from contributing to local capacity building and institutional development, creation of informal networks and agreements, providing opportunities for developing economies' voice and participation, harnessing the power of regional organizations, identifying and achieving cooperation on common areas of interest, helping develop the ICT industry, which can absorb qualified workers, encouraging integration with the West, establishment of a high level working group made up of like-minded policy makers and developing offensive and defensive capabilities tailored to specific threats associated with a specific source.

In light of the lack of law enforcement capacity, especially in many developing countries, the complementary roles of informal networks and formal system need to be stressed. For instance, while some of the signatories of the CoECoC have demonstrated willingness and responsibility to cooperate with other members in fighting cybercrimes, they lack resources to do so. Western countries need to provide cyber-security related resources, training and expertise to enhance the system capacity of these countries. Western multinationals also have the potential to contribute to such initiatives. Regarding informal networks, it is also worth noting that the focus of some countries is shifting away from formal multilateral processes towards informal mechanisms. Especially, the Obama administration's approach to international cooperation has been through ad hoc or informal mechanisms that have bypassed and ignored formal institutions and treaties. For instance, through June 2010, the Obama administration had submitted only six treaties to the Senate, only one of which was multilateral in scope. Moreover, except for the bilateral New START Treaty, which seeks to reduce U.S. American and Russian nuclear arsenals, the treaties were minor (Skidmore 2012). Instead of formal treaties, the U.S. is interested in promoting more intimate cooperation among international law-enforcement officials. Informal institutions and networks may hold special promise from the perspective of the U.S. and other countries.

The existing international legal regimes and institutional frameworks are highly insufficient, obsolete, and incapable of preventing cyber-attacks and there remains a lack of consensus on how best to deal with the ongoing and potential conflicts facing nations in the cyber domain. In light of the deficiencies of the international institutional framework, the challenges of cyber-attacks need to be dealt with at the various levels and demand multi-pronged approaches, which may include both improving formal and informal international institutions to promote the global CS and developing defensive and offensive capabilities. Especially industrialized countries need to make deliberate efforts to win cooperation and commitment of developing countries.

References

Apcss. (2001). *Report from the conference on: Domestic determinants of security: Security institutions and policy-making processes in the Asia-pacific region*, January 10–11, Honolulu, Hawaii. http://www.apcss.org/Publications/Report_DomesticDeterminantsOfSecurity.html

asean.org. (2013). Joint Ministerial Statement of the ASEAN-Japan Ministerial Policy Meeting on Cybersecurity Cooperation, September 13. http://www.asean.org/news/asean-statement-communiques/item/joint-ministerial-statement-of-the-asean-japan-ministerial-policy-meeting-on-cybersecurity-cooperation

Associated Press Worldstream. (2009). *FBI to station cybercrime expert in Estonia*. http://www.msnbc.msn.com/id/30683801/ns/technology_and_science-security/t/fbi-station-cybercrime-expert-estonia/#.T3dS7tnLuZQ

Azar, E. E., & Moon Chung-in. (1998). *Legitimacy, integration and policy capacity: The "software" side of third world national security*. National Security in the Third World: The Management of Internal and External Threats, Upleadon: Edward Elgar Publishing.

Bach, D., & Newman, A. L. (2010). Transgovernmental networks and domestic policy convergence: Evidence from insider trading regulation. *International Organization, Summer, 64*(3), 505–528.

Ball, N. (1988). *Security and economy in the third world*. London: Adamantine Press Limited.

Bardhan, P. (1993). Analytics of the institutions of informal cooperation in rural development. *World Development, 21*(4), 633–639.

Baxter, R. R. (1980). International law in "Her Infinite Variety". *International and Comparative Law Quarterly, 29*, 549–566.

bbc.com. (2014). *Kenya defence Twitter account hacked*. http://www.bbc.com/news/world-africa-28398976

Bennett, C. (2014). *US, China see little progress on cybersecurity*. http://thehill.com/policy/cybersecurity/223865-us-china-see-little-progress-on-cybersecurity

Benson, M., Cullen, F., & Maakestad, W. (1990). Local prosecutors and corporate crime. *Crime and Delinquency, 36*, 356–372.

Brenner, J. F. (2013). Eyes wide shut: The growing threat of cyber attacks on industrial control systems. *Bulletin of the Atomic Scientists, 69*(5), 15–20.

buzzfeed.com. (2014). *It gets worse: The newest sony data breach exposes thousands of passwords, December 4*, http://www.buzzfeed.com/charliewarzel/it-gets-worse-the-newest-sony-data-breach-exposes-thousands

Campbell, J. L. (2004). *Institutional change and globalization*. Princeton, NJ: Princeton University Press.

CCDCOE. (2014). *Cyber defence*. https://www.ccdcoe.org/

Clarke, R. A., & Knate, K. R. (2010). *Cyber war: The next threat to national security and what to do about it* (p. 236). New York: Ecco.

Cobb, A. (1999). Electronic Gallipoli? *Australian Journal of International Affairs, 53*(2), 133–149.

Collins, A. (2003). *Security and Southeast Asia: Domestic, regional, and global issues*. Boulder, CO: Lynne Rienner Publishers.

Constantin, L. (2011). *Romania's anti-cybercrime efforts lack a social component*. http://www.csoonline.com/article/690521/romania-s-anti-cybercrime-efforts-lack-a-socialcomponent

Corbin, K. (2013). *Iran is a more volatile cyber threat to U.S. than China or Russia CIO*.

Downs, G. W., Rocke, D. M., & Barsoom, P. N. (1996). Is the good news about compliance good news about cooperation? *International Organization, 50*(3), 379–406.

Eriksson, J., & Giacomello, G. (2006). The information revolution, security, and international relations: (IR) Relevant theory? *International Political Science Review/Revue internationale de science politique, 27*(3), 221–244.

Forbes, L. C., & Jermier, J. M. (2001). The institutionalization of voluntary organizational greening and the ideals of environmentalism: Lessons about official culture from symbolic organization theory. In A. J. Hoffman & M. J. Ventresca (Eds.), *Organizations, policy, and the natural environment: Institutional and strategic perspectives*. Redwood City, CA: Stanford University Press.

FoxNews.com. (2013). *Obama administration reportedly considering fines, trade penalties for cybertheft*. http://www.foxnews.com/politics/2013/02/20/obama-administration-developing-penalties-for-cybertheft/

Freedberg, S. J. (2013). *Back off: How to curb Chinese cyber-theft*. http://breakingdefense.com/2013/07/24/theyre-already-afraid-us-can-scare-china-gently-into-stopping-cyber-theft/

Gartzke, E. (2013). The myth of cyberwar: Bringing war in cyberspace back down to earth. *International Security, 38*(2), 41–73.

Goldsmith, J. (2011). *Cybersecurity treaties: A skeptical view in future challenges in national security and law*. http://www.futurechallengesessays.com

Gross, G. (2013). *Experts: Iran and North Korea are looming cyber-threats to U.S. CIO*, 10.

Hadoulis, J. (2006). *Global Internet forum closes with call vs. online repression*. Agence France-Presse/INQUIRER.net.

Hagan, J., & Parker, P. (1985). White-collar crime and punishment: Class structure and legal sanctioning of securities violations. *American Sociological Review, 50*, 302–316.

Hirshleifer, J. (1998). The bioeconomic causes of war. *Managerial and Decision Economics, 19*(7/8), 457–466.

Holm, P. (1995). The dynamics of institutionalization: Transformation processes in Norwegian fisheries. *Administrative Science Quarterly, 40*(3), 398–422.

ITU. (2012). *WCIT. Signatories of the final acts*. http://www.itu.int/osg/wcit-12/highlights/signatories.html

Kirk, J. (2012). *Ukraine shuts down forum for malware writers*. http://www.computerworld.com/s/article/9225693/Ukraine_shuts_down_forum_for_malware_writers

Kizekova, A. (2012). *The shanghai cooperation organization: Challenges in cyberspace—analysis.* http://www.eurasiareview.com/27022012-the-shanghai-cooperation-organisation-challenges-in-cyberspace-analysis/

Kramer, T. (2012). *World conference on international telecommunications, remarks.* http://www.state.gov/e/eb/rls/rm/2012/202040.htm

Kshetri, N. (2013). Cybercrimes in the former soviet union and central and eastern Europe: Current status and key drivers. *Crime Law and Social Change, 60*(1), 39–65.

Lan, T. (2011). Real rules for virtual space. *Beijing Review, 54*(47), 12–13.

Lee, M. J. (2013). *S. Korea to set up GPS jamming surveillance system.* www.globalpost.com/dispatch/news/asianet/130410/s-korea-set-gps-jamming-surveillance-system

Libicki, M. C. (2013). *Don't buy the Cyberhype: How to prevent Cyberwars from becoming real ones* http://www.foreignaffairs.com/articles/139819/martin-c-libicki/dont-buy-the-cyberhype

Lipson, C. (1991). Why are some international agreements informal? *International Organization, 45*(4), 495–538.

Masters, J. (2011). *Confronting the cyber threat, in Council on foreign relations.* http://www.cfr.org/technology-and-foreign-policy/confronting-cyber-threat/p15577

McGee, J. (2011). *The difficulties of assessing north Korea's cyber strategy.* https://csis.org/blog/difficulties-assessing-north-koreas-cyber-strategy

McGraw, G. (2012). *Proactive defense prudent alternative to cyberwarfare.* http://searchsecurity.techtarget.com/news/2240169976/Gary-McGraw-Proactive-defense-prudent-alternative-to-cyberwarfare

Narine, S. (1998). ASEAN and the management of regional security. *Pacific Affairs, 71*(2), 195–214.

Newman, K. L. (2000). Organizational transformation during institutional upheaval. *The Academy of Management Review, 25*(3), 602–619.

Odobescu, V. (2014). *U.S. data thefts turn spotlight on Romania.* http://www.usatoday.com/story/news/world/2014/01/13/credit-card-hacking-romania/4456491/

Onyshkiv, Y., & Bondarev, A. (2012). *Ukraine thrives as cybercrime haven.* http://www.kyivpost.com/news/nation/detail/123965/

Owens, W. A., Dam, K. W., & Lin, H. S. (Eds.). (2009). *Technology, policy, law, and ethics regarding U.S. acquisition and use of cyberattack capabilities* (pp. 7–24). Washington, DC: National Academies Press.

Pi, Y. I. (2011). *New china criminal legislations in the progress of harmonization of criminal legislation against cybercrime.* http://www.coe.int/t/dghl/cooperation/economiccrime/cybercrime/documents/countryprofiles/Cyber_cp_china_Pi_Yong_Dec11.pdf

Pontell, H., Calavita, K., & Tillman, R. (1994). Corporate crime and criminal justice system capacity: Government response to financial institution fraud. *Justice Quarterly, 11*, 385–410.

Rainie, L., Anderson, J., & Connolly, J. (2014). *Cyber attacks likely to increase.* http://www.pewinternet.org/2014/10/29/cyber-attacks-likely-to-increase/

Rayman, N. (2014). *The world's top 5 Cybercrime hotspots.* http://time.com/3087768/the-worlds-5-cybercrime-hotspots/

Rid, T. (2013a). Cyberwar and peace: Hacking can reduce real-world violence. *Foreign Affairs,* 77–87.

Rid, T. (2013b). *Cyberwar will not take place.* London: Hurst and Co.

Salant, J. D., & Holmes, A. (2013). *Pearl Harbor looms for vulnerable networks, McConnell says.* http://www.businessweek.com/news/2013-10-30/pearl-harbor-looms-for-vulnerable-networks-mcconnell-says-3

Segal, A. (2012). Chinese computer games. *Foreign Affairs, 91*(2), 14–20.

Serio, J. D., & Gorkin, A. (2003). Changing lenses: Striving for sharper focus on the nature of the 'Russian Mafia' and its impact on the computer realm. *International Review of Law, Computers and Technology, 17*(2), 191–202.

Shackelford, S. J. (2009). From nuclear war to net war: Analogizing cyber attacks in international law. *Berkeley Journal of International Law, 27*(1), 192–251.

Singh, P. V. (2013). *India won't sign Budapest pact on cyber security*. http://www.governancenow.com/news/regular-story/india-wont-sign-budapest-pact-cyber-security

Skidmore, D. (2012). The Obama presidency and US Foreign policy: Where's the multilateralism? *International Studies Perspectives, 13*(1), 43–64.

Slaughter, A. M. (2004). *A new world order* (p. 204). Princeton, NJ: Princeton University Press.

state.gov. (2013). *U.S. Engagement in the 2013 ASEAN Regional Forum*, July 2. http://www.state.gov/r/pa/prs/ps/2013/07/211467.htm

The Economist. (2008). Marching off to cyberwar. 389(8609), 20, December 8. http://www.economist.com/node/12673385

Thomas, C. (1987). *In search of security: The third world in international relations*. Boulder, CO: Lynne Reinner.

Tickner, J. A. (1994). *"Re-visioning security," International relations theory today*. University Park, PA: Pennsylvania State University.

Tillman, R., Calavita, K., & Pontell, H. (1996). Criminalizing white-collar misconduct: Determinants of prosecution in savings and loan fraud cases. *Crime, Law and Social Change, 26*(1), 53–76.

Walker, C. (2004). *Russian Mafia extorts gambling websites*. http://www.americanmafia.com/cgi/clickcount.pl?url=www.americanmafia.com/Feature_Articles_270.html

Waterman, S. (2012). North Korean jamming of GPS shows system's weakness. *Washington Times*. www.washingtontimes.com/news/2012/aug/23/north-korean-jamming-gps-shows-systems-weakness

Wenping, H. (2007). The balancing act of China's Africa policy. *China Security, 3*(3), 32–40.

Wylie, I. (2007). Internet; Romania home base for EBay scammers; The auction website has dispatched its own cyber-sleuth to help police crack fraud rings. *Los Angeles Times*, C.1.

Chapter 4
Cybersecurity's Effects on International Trade and Investment

4.1 Introduction

Incorporation of national security issues into the design of trade and investment policy is certainly not a new phenomenon. Studies conducted as early as the 1950s suggested an important role of national security in trade and investment policy debates (Thorp 1960). However, this issue has acquired new prominence and urgency, especially for the contemporary global powers, due to the close links of modern ICTs such as cloud computing and BD to national security concerns.

Most industrialized and many developing economies have laws and regulations in place that restrict foreign direct investment (FDI) based on national security-related concerns (Hemphill 2010). Turning now to the specific context of this chapter, ICTs are becoming more relevant in the national security equation with governments', individuals' and organizations' rapid adoption of such technologies. CS-related allegations have led to various barriers to international trade and investment.

Unsurprisingly CS-related concerns have led to various barriers to international trade and investment in a broad range of countries. For instance, Australian, Indian, and the U.S. governments have accused the Chinese company, Huawei Technologies of cyber-espionage, which hindered the company's internationalization. Likewise, in 2003, Microsoft needed to share its Windows source codes with the governments of 59 countries including those of China, Russian, and the UK in order to address security concerns. Similarly, Vietnam's proposed 2013 law on cryptographic technology requires licenses and certifications to use civil cryptographic products (Article 32). The government will also control the levels of encryption (Article 31). The Semiconductor Industry Association raised concerns related the difficulties in obtaining the licenses and meeting license requirements, and administrative burden, lack of predictability of procedures and certification costs. Moreover, only domestic companies can apply for certification or meet the

© Springer International Publishing Switzerland 2016
N. Kshetri, *The Quest to Cyber Superiority*, DOI 10.1007/978-3-319-40554-4_4

requirements and the possibility that encryption standards may develop into technology mandates (Semiconductor Industry Association).

In addition to these host country initiated barriers, companies also face such barriers in home countries. For instance, the EU countries' strong data privacy laws prevent the movement of identifiable individuals' data to jurisdictions that do not provide the same levels of protection. These laws have prevented EU companies to outsource their business functions to developing countries such as India. Moreover, they have also increased the costs of doing business in EU economies for companies from non-EU countries with less strict data regulations.

Rules and regulations associated with the home and host country governments are not the only-and for some companies, not the biggest-barriers to trade and investments associated with CS. A firm's CS-related behaviors may trigger reactions from actors in the firm's nonmarket environment such as interest groups, the intelligentsia, and public opinion, which may provide a possible mechanism by which a firm may face barriers to trade and investment. For instance, Yahoo and Google faced criticism in the U.S. for helping the Chinese government to pursue its CS goals. Yahoo and its Chinese subsidiary also faced lawsuits in the U.S. for their CS-related actions in China (Nystedt 2008). Likewise, Amnesty International accused U.S.-based Internet companies such as Google, Microsoft and Yahoo of violating the Universal Declaration of Human Rights in their agreement with Chinese government to censor internet use in China (Fed News Service, Including US State News 2005).

While non-government actors are generally less powerful than the governments, they have the ability to influence policies. For instance, public opinion affects political behavior (Boddewyn and Brewer 1994). In the U.S., the enactment of the Global Online Freedom Act 2006 can be considered as a political response to public opinion. The act has increased the U.S. government's power over technology companies.

In the above example, Yahoo faced indirect barriers in its home country. Such indirect barriers related to information availability, differential standards, investor protection, and political risks are associated with the host country (Nishiotis 2006). For instance, Google pulled out of China after it discovered attacks seeking e-mails from human rights activists and the company's source code (Singel 2010).

Countries' responses to cyber-threats have a potential to shape the direction for commercial relations in the global marketplace (Schweizer 1996). In this chapter, we seek to understand governments' motivations associated with CS-related barriers to international trade and investment established against foreign firms and the types of companies are most likely to be affected by such barriers. It also analyzes how the home country and the host country relations may affect the degree of CS-related barriers to international trade and investment faced by a firm.

4.2   CS-Related Barriers to Trade and Investments: Historical Perspectives, Contemporary Developments and Fundamental Concepts

4.2.1   CS-Related Concerns: Some Examples, Observations and Policy Responses

Cyber-espionage related threats, which are real as well as perceived, are becoming pervasive in recent years. Among many sources of cyber-threats include business competitors and foreign nations engaged in espionage and information warfare (Wilshusen 2012). The motives include monetary gain or political/military advantage, among others.

There are many instances and examples of foreign firms' alleged involvement in espionage activities. An obvious example of a firm facing international investment barriers due to CS-related concern would be Huawei. The U.S. and other countries have expressed suspicion regarding Huawei's close ties with the CCP or the military. When Huawei, in a partnership with Bain Capital, proposed to buy 3Com for US$2.2 billion in 2008, the US Committee on Foreign Investment (CFIUS) raised security concerns and put the deal on hold (Gross 2008). Opposing the deal, a House Representative argued that Huawei's stake in 3Com would "gravely compromise" U.S. national security. The three companies were forced to withdraw their joint filing with the CFIUS.

Likewise, in 2012, due to security concerns, Huawei was not allowed to bid for the US$38 billion Australian National Broadband Network. Huawei wanted to secure a US$1.05 billion contract in the project, but was blocked by the Australian attorney general based on advice from the Australian Security Intelligence Organization (Yueyang 2012).

According to the U.S. House Intelligence Committee report released in October 2012, which was based on a 1 year investigation, Huawei and ZTE allegedly pose a threat to U.S. national security. The conclusion was based on concerns over cyber-attacks that were traced to China. The report recommended that U.S. government computer systems should not use equipment manufactured by the two companies. Furthermore, it asked the Committee on Foreign Investments to block acquisitions, takeovers, and mergers that involve the two companies. In addition, Canada, India, and even the U.K. were reported to be investigating the two firms' links to the Chinese government (Muncaster 2013).

In the mid-1990s, the FBI's analysis of 173 nations indicated that 57 were allegedly covertly trying to obtain advanced technologies from the U.S. corporations and 100 countries spent some public funds to acquire them (Schweizer 1996). U.S. intelligence officials have been concerned about foreign governments' growing involvement in unauthorized acquisition of U.S. proprietary or other information (Wilshusen 2012). Some analysts liken the acts of collecting proprietary information and sharing it with domestic producers to economic espionage and argue that such acts can be viewed "at best a subsidy to well-connected domestic companies, at worst theft on a par with piracy" (Schweizer 1996).

Governments across the world are gearing up to respond to the increasing threats of CS. In 1996 the U.S. Congress passed the Economic Espionage Act (EEA): "The impetus for the EEA was the end of the Cold War. Suddenly, the U.S. found that the greatest threat to its well-being had changed from military opposition to economic competition. Considering itself to be a world leader in industrial innovation, the U.S. decided to ensure homegrown secrets of its native corporations would not be made available through theft and espionage to foreign competitors" (Grosso 2000). Likewise, the EU member nations outsourcing to countries that are not certified as data secure are required to follow stringent contractual obligations.

4.3 A Typology of Barriers to Trade and Investment Associated with CS

A trade barrier is defined as any restriction imposed on the free flow of trade and investment. Barriers to trade and investment can be direct as well as indirect and can be attributed to the home country or the host country. Direct barriers to trade and investment are legal inflow and outflow restrictions of goods, services and capital. Indirect investment barriers, on the other hand, include factors such as the availability of information, differential accounting standards, concern related to investor protection, liquidity risk, macroeconomic instability, and political risk (Nishiotis 2006). In this section, we first develop a 2×2 typology of CS-related barriers to trade and investment (Table 4.1).

As noted earlier, the EU's strong data privacy laws prevent date movement by EU-based firms to many non-EU economies such as India, which is a direct barrier imposed by the home country. Some examples of such barriers are presented in Cell II.

Critics have been concerned about some Western companies' compliance with cyber-control measures in authoritarian regimes, which have led to indirect barrier to trade and investment in the home country (Cell III). For instance, Yahoo and its Chinese subsidiary faced at least two major lawsuits by Chinese dissidents, who claimed that the company helped Chinese authorities by handing over e-mails and other information, which led to a prison sentence of a plaintiff. In the first lawsuit, Yahoo settled with the plaintiffs out of the court in November 2007. A second group filed a different lawsuit in the U.S. under the Alien Tort Claims Act of 1789 and additional U.S. and international laws. The use of the act in democracy and human rights related cases is arguably new in U.S. courts (Nystedt 2008). Commenting on backlash faced by Yahoo, due to its Chinese subsidiary's censorship in China and the act of providing user information to the Chinese government officials, J. Nolan

Table 4.1 Some examples of direct and indirect barriers related to CS in the home country and the host country

	Home country	Host country
Direct barrier	*[Cell I]* • The EU Data Protection Directive: illegal to transfer EU citizens' personal data to jurisdictions outside the EU that do not provide an "adequate level of protection". The EC has recognized nine economies—Andorra, Argentina, Canada, the Faeroe Islands, Guernsey, Isle of Man, Israel, Jersey, Switzerland, and Uruguay—that meet the standards set by the Directive. • FISMA: CSPs are required to keep sensitive data belonging to a federal agency in the U.S.	*[Cell II]* • Concerns raised by China, Russia and the U.K. regarding security risks in Microsoft products • Trade and investment barriers faced by Lenovo in the U.S. and by Huawei in India, the U.S., Australia. • U.S. businesses are required to implement new data privacy practices due to EU restrictions. • The EU's investigation indicated that Google operated in Europe without meeting privacy standards. In 2012, EU regulators demanded Google to revise online privacy policy. They indicated the possibility that Google's compliance with national privacy laws may be tested in Ireland, Belgium and Finland where its data centers are located (O'brien 2012).
Indirect barrier	*[Cell III]* • Lawsuits faced by Yahoo in the U.S. • Amnesty International's accusation that Google, Microsoft and Yahoo violated the Universal Declaration of Human Rights by agreeing with Chinese government to censor the Internet.	*[Cell IV]* • Google's withdrawal from China due to risks related to IPR protection and user information. • January 2013: Gus Hosein, head of U.K.-based NGO Privacy International, declared that U.S. surveillance and spying agencies' possible access to EU citizens' data stored in US companies' clouds is "an irreversible loss of data sovereignty."

commented that "... the court of public opinion is less concerned with the artificial legal distinction between.. parent companies and ... subsidiaries" (Nolan 2009).

Google's withdrawal from China can be explained as the result of an indirect barrier associated with CS in the host country (Cell IV). In 2008, Google's CEO said that his company would work with Chinese universities, starting with Tsinghua University, on cloud-related academic programs. The country's unfavorable environment from the CS standpoint, however, led to Google's withdrawal from China. In a 2009 report, Google noted that it had discovered an attack on its infrastructures that originated in China (Information Warfare Monitor/Shadowserver Foundation 2010). The company further noted that the attack was part of a larger operation that infiltrated the infrastructures of at least 20 other large companies.

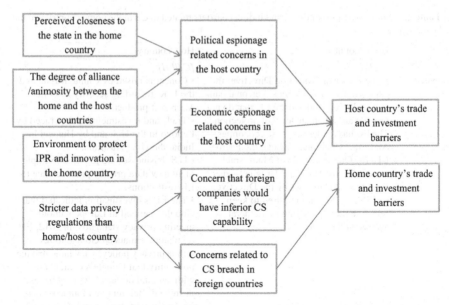

Fig. 4.1 Causes and mechanisms associated with CS-related barriers in trade and investments

4.4   Causes, Mechanisms and Consequences Associated with CS-Related Barriers to Trade and Investments

We focus on the direct trade and investment barriers related to CS in this section. The framework developed in here explains how the characteristics of and relationship between the home and the host countries under consideration and the focal firm's perceived relationship with the home country government give rise to various CS-related concerns, which lead to trade and investment barriers in the home country and the host country. In Fig. 4.1 we depict this framework graphically. As discussed above and presented in the boxes at the right side of Fig. 4.1, trade and investment barriers are imposed by the home as well as the host countries.

Broadly speaking, as the three boxes in the middle show, CS-related barriers to trade and investment encompass at least three categories of concerns: political espionage, economic espionage, privacy and security of citizens' information. Regarding the concerns about political espionage, according to a 2007 report of the U.S. FBI, 108 countries had developed offensive cyber-warfare capabilities. Likewise, with the decline of military confrontation, increasing salience of economic competition in recent years in global affairs, spying for high-tech secrets with commercial applications has grown (Schweizer 1996). Finally, countries across the world are concerned about protecting their citizens' information privacy, which lead to various barriers related to trade and investment.

The rest of this section is devoted to the characteristics of and relationship between the home and the host countries and the focal firm's perceived relationship with the home country government (left boxes).

4.4.1 Perceived Closeness to the State in the Home Country

Nations want to minimize the possible risk of foreign companies spying for their home country government. A picture that emerges when looking into the arguments associated with CS-related trade and investment barrier is that a firm's perceived closeness to the state in its home country is positively associated with the barrier it is likely to face. For instance, due to U.S. lawmakers' concern regarding Huawei's "deep ties" with the Chinese military, its proposal to buy 3Com was given "elevated attention" and put through a 45-day investigation, beyond the standard 30-day review conducted by CFIUS (Karnitschnig et al. 2008). A concern for foreign governments was that its overseas offices spy for China (The Economist 2005). One of the founders of Huawei, Ren Zhengfei, was a PLA officer. According to Rand Corporation, the PLA is a customer of Huawei, a "political patron" as well as a "research and development partner" (Cha 2008). Bain and Huawei were willing to sell the 3Com unit that handled the government security contracts, but that was not enough to assuage the committee's concerns (Karnitschnig et al. 2008).

Similarly, Lenovo's connection to the Chinese government was one of the biggest roadblocks faced in its acquisition of IBM's PC division. Although Lenovo moved its headquarters from Beijing to New York, some U.S. lawmakers argued that the deal could lead to a transfer of IBM's advanced technology and other corporate assets to the Chinese government (Kessler 2006). The issue surfaced again in 2006, when critics challenged Lenovo's sale of 16,000 desktop computers to the U.S. State Department. Politicians and some commentators drew attention to the potential national security implications of placing Chinese computers into government offices. They argued that the company's connections to the Chinese government could pose a security risk (McCarthy 2006).

4.4.2 The Degree of Alliance/Animosity Between the Home and the Host Countries

Nations differ in their CS goals and orientation, which has led the formation of a number of alliances. Most well-known CS-related barriers are established to control trade and investment of firms from countries that belong to a different alliance. This aspect is evident from the barriers faced by Chinese firms in Australia, India and the U.S. and Microsoft in China and Russia. A high degree of animosity between China and the U.S. has led to trade and investment barriers to firms from each country to the other.

Following the World War II, the U.S. approach to national security involved the concept of "collective security" which resulted in a number of defense-related treaties and an engagement in cooperation with other countries to develop military plans and capabilities (Thorp 1960). This approach is still being actively pursued by the U.S. as well as by other countries but the focus has been increasingly on the development of CS-related capabilities.

National security interests influence commercial ties and that alliances promote trade (Gowa 1994). In particular, countries' military alliances are positively related to trade relations (Gowa 1994). This is especially true for countries which belong to the same alliance in a bipolar system with two roughly equal actors or coalitions of actors that divide the world economies into two poles such as during the Cold War. In a system with two major opposing alliance groups, countries that are allies tend to trade more freely among themselves. Trade-related behaviors are driven by possible security externalities which provide fundamental motivation for helping their allies and punishing their enemies (Milner 1999). It is clear that countries such as China, Russia and the U.S. are concerned about externalities of CS on trades and investments in high technology.

CS has been among the major issues in the formation and structure of international alliances. For instance, as discussed in Chap. 3, as of December 2014, the CoECoC had been signed by 53 states. Likewise, the SCO has taken significant steps toward CS cooperation. New and emerging alliances related to CS are likely to shape the development of international political and economic institutions.

The Chinese government suspects that it is under cyber-attack from the U.S. There has been a deep-rooted perception among Chinese policy makers that Microsoft and the U.S. government spy on Chinese computer users through secret "back doors" in Microsoft products. Computer hardware and software imported from the U.S. and its allies are subject to detailed inspection. Chinese technicians take control of such goods and either resist or closely monitor if Western experts install them (Adams 2001). Chinese cryptographers reportedly found an "NSA Key" in Microsoft products, which was interpreted as the National Security Agency. The key allegedly provided the U.S. government back-door access to Microsoft Windows 95, 98, N-T4, and 2000. Although Microsoft denied the allegation and even issued a patch to fix the problem, the Chinese government has not been convinced.

4.4.3   Environment to Protect IPR and Innovation in the Home Country

Economic security associated with high technology is being recognized as a substantial source of national security. A chief CS concern for some Western countries relates to economic espionage. For instance, some U.S. law makers have indicated interest in expanding the definition of 'national security' to include 'economic security' in the evaluation of FDI, which includes cross-border mergers and acquisitions (M&As) (Evenett 2006). The issue of national economic security traditionally encompassed and involved factors such as FDI/equity ownership within specific national industry sectors due to concerns related to infant industries or strategic sectors (Hemphill 2010).

CS is linked to national economic security in new ways and in new contexts. As early as the mid-1990s, it was reported that a large number of nations were involved in actively gathering intelligence on specific industries and companies. They then allegedly shared such information with domestic producers, which would help enhance their companies' competitive advantage (Schweizer 1996).

For instance, some Western analysts argue that the fact that there is the lack of IPR protection and a business environment to support innovations in China makes it attractive for firms in the country to acquire technologies by economic espionage (Kshetri 2013). In 2012 alone, over 100 individuals or corporate defendants were charged by the U.S. Justice Department for stealing trade secrets and dual-use technology for the Chinese government or Chinese entities (Rauhala 2013).

U.S. intelligence officials and CS specialists have argued that China-originated cyber-attacks such as IP and trade secret thefts would have long-term rather than immediate short-term effects with substantial economic damage. Kevin Mandia, CEO of the CS firm, Mandiant has put it strongly and bluntly: "My biggest fear is that in 10 years China will be making everything we [the U.S.] were making—for half the price—because they've stolen all our innovations" (Easton 2012). As noted in Chap. 1, in July 2012, the then head of the NSA and the Pentagon's Cyber Command argued that IP thefts of U.S. organizations have resulted in the "greatest transfer of wealth in history".

4.4.4   Difference in the Strictness of Data Privacy Regulations in the Home and the Host Countries

Countries vary in terms of the strictness of data privacy laws. The U.S., for instance, has stricter privacy laws than some economies in Eastern Europe and Latin America (Kshetri 2007). The EU, on the other hand, is considered to have stricter privacy laws than the U.S. Whereas the U.S. has a more relaxed approach to privacy and in an attempt to encourage marketing innovations, prefers to rely on voluntary self-regulation, the EU tends to enforce privacy rights through legislation (The Economist 1999) (Chap. 6).

A higher degree of strictness of data privacy regulations in the host country than in the home country may act as a barrier to trade and investment. As an example the EU's strong data privacy laws prevent the movement of PII to jurisdictions that do not provide the same levels of protection. Because of these regulations, less data based information is allowed into the hands of companies located outside the EU.

The German Chancellor Merkel expressed a serious concern about the operations of businesses from countries with low levels of data protection (e.g., the U.S.) in nations with more rigorous standards and safeguards (EU economies) (bbc.com 2014). This has put U.S.-based firms at a disadvantage. U.S. vendors' responses to these efforts have sometimes only reaffirmed Europeans' apprehensions. For example, during the Office365 launch in 2011, Microsoft U.K.'s managing director reportedly admitted that the corporation's UK subsidiary was subject to the Patriot Act (Lakatos 2012). Such comments undercut faith in U.S. CSPs. In 2011, for example, the U.K.'s BAE Systems opted not to use Office365 due to concerns about the Patriot Act (Saran 2011).

The situation has further worsened in the post-Snowden era. Some firms are employing their European location as a competitive differentiator vis-à-vis U.S. based firms. The Norwegian company Runbox markets as an alternative to U.S. services such as Gmail. Its selling proposition is that it does not comply with foreign court orders. The company reported a 34 % annual increase in customers after the revelation of the PRISM surveillance (Miller 2014). The U.S. web-hosting company, Servint was reported to lose more than half of its foreign clients following the Snowden revelation (Kim 2014).

India is among the countries that the EU does not consider as data secure. As noted above, under EU laws, the member nations outsourcing to countries that are not certified as data secure are required to follow stringent contractual obligations. Such requirements lead to increased costs. EU-based companies thus hesitate in doing business with countries such as India that have not achieved data secure status. In April 2012, India demanded that the EU designate India as a data secure country and lift the restrictions imposed on the flow of high-end outsourcing businesses to the country. The fact that India has not achieved the status of a data secure country prevents flow of sensitive data, such as patient information for telemedicine, to India. The issue was also raised in the bilateral free trade agreement being negotiated between the two economies. Most of the business process outsourcing (BPO) activities flowing to India from the EU economies consists of low value-added work. Only a small amount of high value added work such as clinical research, engineering design and IPR is outsourced to India. On the other hand, a higher proportion of work outsourced from the U.S. to India is higher-end activities such clinical trials, legal documents and drug discovery, and credit and equity analytics (Sen and Harsimran 2012). This can be attributed to a lower India-U.S. difference compared to the India-EU difference in the strictness of data privacy regulations.

For some firms, stricter data protection laws in the host country than in the home country have been a concern. The EU countries' strong data privacy laws, for instance, have acted as barriers to non-EU firms that want to do business in the EU countries. For instance, U.S. businesses are forced to implement new data privacy practices due to the EU restrictions (Shaffer 2000).

4.5 Discussion and Concluding Remarks

From a firm's perspective, the home country-host country dynamics that determine barriers to international trade and investment are somewhat different in CS-related concerns. The above discussion suggest that differences between the home country and the host country in terms of the economic development level and international political alliances are linked to CS-related barriers to trade and investment. Factors such as geographic distance and cultural differences between the home country and the host country are irrelevant in CS-related barriers.

Home country government support is becoming increasingly important to minimize the impacts associated with CS-related barriers faced by its firms in foreign countries. For instance, in order to overcome EU data transfer restriction and avoid a trade conflict with the EU economies, U.S. regulators have promoted enhanced data privacy self-regulation for U.S. businesses (Shaffer 2000).

Some firms have framed foreign firms' CS-related concerns in terms of cultural differences. For instance, a concern regarding Huawei is the fact that although the firm has claimed to be a 100 % employee-owned private company, it has not revealed information about its shareholders. This is thus being framed as a political issue in the U.S. Chinese companies, however, argue that ownership and other issues are culture specific. In an interview after the U.S. House committee hearing in October 2012, Zhu Jinyun, ZTE's senior vice-president told reporters that it was difficult for him to explain the relationship between the government, the Communist Party and enterprises in China (Tan and Chen 2012).

Prior research indicates that some barriers to investment are asymmetric in nature. For instance, in Errunza and Losq's two-country model of "partial" segmentation country 1's investors are allowed to invest in country 2's securities, but country 2's investors are prohibited from investing in the securities country 1 (Errunza and Losq 1985). There are symmetric as well as asymmetric natures of CS-related barriers to trade and investment. For instance, while political espionage related concerns are symmetric, economic espionage related concerns tend to be less asymmetric and more likely to be raised by governments in industrialized countries to firms from developing countries. Likewise, concerns related to consumer data protection in economies with stricter privacy regulations may lead to asymmetric barriers.

Prior research indicates that threats to resources motivate organizations to conduct broader searches for alternatives that may exist beyond the bounds of social acceptability. They may thus undervalue the risks associated with departing from established ways of doing things and with challenging the legitimacy of established ways, and, as a result, attempt to create the framework for new legitimate forms through non-isomorphic change (George et al. 2006). For instance, the responses of Yahoo, Google and AltaVista are not socially acceptable in their home country. These organizations are likely to lose access to resources if they adhere to current practices.

References

Adams, J. (2001). Virtual defense. *Foreign Affairs* May/June, 98–112.

bbc.com. (2014). *Data protection: Angela Merkel proposes Europe network.* http://www.bbc.com/news/world-europe-26210053

Boddewyn, J. J., & Brewer, T. L. (1994). International-business political behavior: New theoretical directions. *Academy of Management Review, 19*(10), 119–143.

Cha, A. E. (2008). Telecom firm in China sets sights on U.S. Market; Ownership, tactics raise security issues. *The Washington Post,* A.1.

Easton, N. (2012). Fortune's guide to the future. *Fortune, 165*(1), 44.

Errunza, V., & Losq, E. (1985). International asset pricing under mild segmentation: Theory and test. *Journal of Finance, 40,* 105–124.

Evenett, S. J. (2006). Trouble in paradise: Will technocrats review global mergers forever? *CESinfo Forum, Special Issue: Mergers and Acquisitions, 1,* 27–33.

US Fed News Service, Including US State News. (2005). *Cracking down on cybercrime.* Washington, DC.

George, E., Chattopadhyay, P., Sitkin, S. B., & Barden, J. (2006). Cognitive underpinnings of institutional persistence and change: A framing perspective. *Academy of Management Review, 31*(2), 347–385.

Gowa, J. (1994). *Allies, adversaries, and international trade.* Princeton, NJ: Princeton University Press.

Gross, G. (2008). Bain/Huawei's bid to buy 3Com is scuttled by security issues. *Network World, 25*(8), 30.

Grosso, A. (2000). The economic espionage act: Touring the minefields. *Communications of the ACM, 43*(8), 15–18.

Hemphill, T. A. (2010). The 'new protectionism': Industrial policy barriers to cross-border mergers and acquisitions. *Competition and Change, 14*(2), 124–148.

Information Warfare Monitor/Shadowserver Foundation. (2010). Shadows in the Cloud: Investigating Cyber Espionage 2.0, Joint Report: Information Warfare Monitor Shadowserver Foundation, JR03-2010, April 6. www.utoronto.ca/mcis/pdfshadows-in-the-cloud-web.pdf

Karnitschnig, M., Hitt, G., & White, B. (2008). Harsh climate in Washington ices 3Com deal; Hope for buyout revival led by Foreign capital dims amid China jitters. *Wall Street Journal,* February 21: C.1.

Kessler, M. (2006). Lenovo to offer first branded PCs out of China. *USA Today,* February 23: 1B.

Kim, E. (2014). *New report shows Edward Snowden's revelations are seriously damaging US tech firms.* http://www.businessinsider.com/edward-snowden-us-tech-firms-2014-7

Kshetri, N. (2007). Institutional factors affecting offshore business process and information technology outsourcing. *Journal of International Management, 13*(1), 38–56.

Kshetri, N. (2013). *Cybercrime and cybersecurity in the global south.* Houndmills, Basingstoke: Palgrave Macmillan.

Lakatos, A. (2012). *The USA patriot act and the privacy of data stored in the cloud.* http://tinyurl.com/b2bqh53

McCarthy, S. (2006). Lenovo seeks to wean itself from IBM. *The Globe and Mail* (Canada), October 9: B4.

Miller, C. C. (2014). *Revelations of N.S.A Spying cost U.S. Tech companies.* http://www.nytimes.com/2014/03/22/business/fallout-from-snowden-hurting-bottom-line-of-tech-companies.html?_r=0

Milner, H. V. (1999). The political economy of international trade. *Annual Review of Political Science, 2*(91), 114.

Muncaster, P. (2013). *China's computing giants eye overseas growth in 2013.* http://www.technologyreview.com/news/509426/chinas-computing-giants-eye-overseas-growth-in-2013/

Nishiotis, G. P. (2006). Further evidence on closed-end country fund prices and international capital flows. *The Journal of Business, 79*(4), 1727–1754.

Nolan, J. (2009). The China dilemma: Internet censorship and corporate responsibility. Asian Journal of Comparative Law 4(1), UNSW Law Research Paper No. 2008-57.

Nystedt, D. (2008). *Yahoo sued again by Chinese dissidents.* http://abcnews.go.com/Technology/PCWorld/story?id=4364982#.ULfOz2d5iik

O'brien, K. J. (2012). *Dismayed at Google's privacy policy, european group is weighing censure.* http://tinyurl.com/bgxwt8b

Rauhala, E. (2013). Huawei: The Chinese company that scares Washington. http://world.time.com/2013/04/04/huawei-the-chinese-company-that-scares-washington/

Saran, C. (2011). BAE systems: Office365 doesn't fly. *ComputerWeekly.* http://tinyurl.com/bbhjl2a

Schweizer, P. (1996). The growth of economic espionage. *Foreign Affairs, 75*(1), 9–14.

Semiconductor Industry Association. Comments submitted RE: Draft 2.22 law on information security, Issued by National Assembly, Socialist Republic of Vietnam, Filed online via http://mic.gov.vn

Sen, A., & Harsimran, J. (2012). *India seeks 'Data Secure Nation' status, more Hi-end business from European Union.* http://articles.economictimes.indiatimes.com/2012-04-16/news/31349813_1_data-security-council-data-protection-laws-standard-contractual-clauses

Shaffer, G. C. (2000). Globalization and social protection: The impact of EU and international rules in the ratcheting up of US data privacy standards. *Yale Journal of International Law, 25*, 1–88.

Singel, R. (2010). *Google fights China; Will Yahoo and Microsoft Follow?* http://www.wired.com/business/2010/01/yahoo-microsoft-china/

Tan, Y. Z., & Chen, L. M. (2012). *Telecom giants hit back at allegations.* http://usa.chinadaily.com.cn/china/2012-10/09/content_15802157.htm

The Economist. (1999). Crime without punishment: Special article. *Russian Organized Crime, 352* (134), 17–19.

The Economist. (2005). China's champions: The struggle of the champions: China wants to build world-class companies. Can it succeed? http://www.economist.com/node/3535818

Thorp, W. L. (1960). Trade barriers and national security. *American Economic Review, 50*(2), 433–442.

Wilshusen, G. C. (2012). Cyber threats facilitate ability to commit economic espionage. *GAO Reports Proceeding.* June 28, 1–16, 20.

Yueyang, M. L. (2012). *Australia bars Huawei from broadband project.* http://www.nytimes.com/2012/03/27/technology/australia-bars-huawei-from-broadband-project.html?_r=0

Chapter 5
Cybersecurity in the U.S.

5.1 Introduction

Being the world's one of the most digitized countries, the U.S. faces diverse cyber-threats. President Barack Obama described CS as one of the most serious economic and national security challenges the U.S. faces (whitehouse.gov). In the early 2000s, cybercrime and cyber-terrorism were the No. 3 priority for the U.S. behind counterterrorism and counterintelligence. In 2013, the U.S. director of national intelligence declared that cyber-threats were the greatest danger facing the nation. General Martin E. Dempsey, chairman of the U.S. Joint Chiefs of Staff, declared that cyber-attacks had "escalated from an issue of moderate concern to one of the most serious threats to national security" (Nye 2013). A January 2013 report of the Pentagon's Defense Science Board noted that "[t]he cyber-threat is serious, with potential consequences similar in some ways to the nuclear threat of the Cold War" (p. 31) and "[c]yber risk can be managed through the combination of deterrence (up to a nuclear response in the most extreme case) and improved cyber defense" (p. 32) (Department of Defense 2013).

Despite a real and deepening CS crisis facing the country, the U.S. response to this issue has been what *a Washington Post* article described as "alarmingly and inexplicably passive" (washingtonpost.com). While the U.S. government has introduced a number of policy measures in an attempt to strengthen national CS (Table 5.1), the country lacks a clear, effective and comprehensive CS legislation. Lawmakers at the Congress debated a comprehensive CS legislation but failed to reach an agreement. A key challenge has been in balancing competing values and priorities. As discussed in Chap. 1, CS regulation in the U.S. faces a substantial Democrat-Republican divide. Nonetheless, a growing number of lawmakers are pressuring regulators to strengthen CS and taking other measures.

Let us look at some of the comprehensive CS acts which were discussed at the Congress. The Cyber Security Act of 2012 had provisions to ask companies to comply with basic security regulations, but was not passed by the Senate.

© Springer International Publishing Switzerland 2016   89
N. Kshetri, *The Quest to Cyber Superiority*, DOI 10.1007/978-3-319-40554-4_5

Table 5.1 Key events and milestones in the U.S. response to CS

Time	Key document	Explanation
2003	National Strategy for Securing Cyberspace (NSSC) was issued.	It was the Bush administration's first systematic attempt to the CS problems. It emphasized the importance of coordinated national effort to cyber-threats. Its two key components included: (1) the deterrence logic (cyber-threats is similar to nuclear threats in the sense that the cost–benefit logic of mutually assured destruction is applicable); (2) bottom-up policy processes (cooperation with state and local governments and the private sector to develop CS policy) (Harknett and Stever 2011).
2006	National Infrastructure Protection Plan (NIPP) was released (updated in 2009).	The focus was on infrastructure instead of CS. It identified 17 infrastructure sectors (e.g., agriculture, water, energy) and argued that CS was a "dimension" of each sector, rather than an identifiable sector (Department of Homeland Security 2009).
2008	Comprehensive National Cybersecurity Initiative (CNCI) was released.	It recognized the importance of federal government's leadership role in the development of CS technologies and their introduction to the state and local levels as well as in the private sector. It viewed the federal information network as a single entity. It also promoted CS education and emphasized the promotion of federal CS standards throughout the privately owned infrastructure sectors (Harknett and Stever 2011).
March 2009	The Obama administration released Cyberspace Policy Review: Assuring a Trusted and Resilient Information and Communications Infrastructure.	A review team had assessed U.S. policies and structures for CS. It signaled a new top-down orientation compared to the bottom-up approach of the Bush era (Harknett and Stever 2011).
2009	The Pentagon established the U.S. Cyber Command.	The goal is to strengthen cyber-warfare and cyber defense capabilities (blogs.wsj.com 2014).
February 2013	President Barack Obama issued an EO, "Improving Critical Infrastructure Cybersecurity".	The EO was aimed at increasing CS for critical infrastructure vital to the economy, security and daily life such as financial, transportation and communication systems and power plants.

Republican members expressed concerns that enforcement of the act would be too expensive and require too much government oversight (newyorker.com 2013). The Cyber Intelligence Sharing and Protection Act (CISPA) was passed in the House of Representatives in April 2012 but was not passed by the U.S. Senate. Interest groups such as advocates of Internet privacy and civil liberties argued that the CISPA contained too few limits on the government's monitoring of a private individual's information.

In response to the rapidly raising cyber-threats and the lack of a comprehensive legislation, in 2013, President Barack Obama issued an executive order (EO), "Improving Critical Infrastructure Cybersecurity" to respond to the rapidly growing cyber-threats facing the economy. Some federal government agencies are focusing on key CS issues in a proactive manner, in an attempt to institutionalize CS. For instance, by 2015, the Office of Personnel Management, which manages the civil service of the federal government, plans to have every federal government position labeled with a descriptive code detailing the CS functions required for the job (Boyd 2014). Likewise, the CFTC, which is an independent U.S. regulatory agency established to regulate commodity markets, is requiring futures exchanges, swap execution facilities, clearinghouses and other entities under its purview to use risk analysis to identify and minimize sources of cyber risks (forbes.com 2014).

5.2 Cyber-Threats Facing the U.S.

According to PricewaterhouseCoopers' (PwC) 2014 U.S. State of Cybercrime Survey, due to high profile data breaches at companies such as Home depot, Target and JPMorgan, data and information of about half of U.S. adults have been stolen. Computer networks of safety-critical systems such as nuclear reactors have also faced cyber-attacks. The computers of the Nuclear Regulatory Commission (NRC), which oversees the U.S. nuclear power industry, were successfully attacked by foreign hackers twice during 2010–2013. In one of the attacks, phishing emails were sent to about 215 NRC employees, which asked them to verify their user accounts by clicking on a link (Sternstein 2014a).

Many surveys and studies correlate rising cyber-attacks with organizations' and Internet users' low level of CS awareness and orientation. For instance, employees of more than a dozen federal agencies and contractors such as the Department of Defense (DoD), the Department of Education and the National Weather Service are responsible for over half of the federal cyber-incidents during 2010–2014. They reportedly clicked links in phishing emails, opened malware-infected websites and were duped into sharing information (foxnews.com 2014). This example is illustrative of a widespread problem not only in federal agencies but in all types of organizations.

More broadly, according to PwC, less than half of U.S. companies had taken enough precautions to protect consumer data. Only 38 % had prioritized CS investments based on business risks they were facing, and only 31 % had a CS strategy for the mobile sector. Likewise, 54 % of the businesses did not provide CS training to employees (Risen 2014a). A survey conducted by CSO of over 500 private and public sector executives and security experts in the U.S. led to similar findings. Most organizations lacked a strategic approach to CS and had failed to adequately assess and understand supply chain risks. Most organizations were also found to have inadequate mobile device security. The report emphasized the importance of collaboration to share experience and knowledge of threats, strategic spending, especially on CS training for employees (Barker 2014).

Especially Small and medium-sized enterprises (SMEs) tend to have weaker CS mechanisms and thus are likely to be low hanging fruits from cybercriminals' standpoint. According to a survey conducted by PwC, among corporate directors in companies with less than US$1 billion in annual revenue, only 9 % of had discussions regarding CS guidance (Bennett 2014).

5.2.1   Critical Sectors and Important Industries as Attractive Targets

President Obama in his 2013 State of the Union Address noted: "America must also face the rapidly growing threat from cyber-attacks" and "our enemies are also seeking the ability to sabotage our power grid, our financial institutions, and our air traffic control systems" (The White House, Office of the Press Secretary 2013). Let us look at cyber-threats facing some of critical sectors and major industries.

5.2.1.1   Power and Utility

In November 2014, in his testimony before a Congressional panel, the head of the NSA and U.S. Cyber Command said that China and "one or two" other countries possess the ability to launch a cyber-attack that can take the entire U.S. power grid and other critical infrastructure down (Smith 2014). Similarly according to the consulting, construction and engineering firm Black & Veatch's report "2014 Strategic Directions: U.S. Electric Industry", CS ranked the fourth-highest concern for electric utilities (behind reliability, environmental regulation and economic regulation). Note too that CS was ranked sixth in 2013. Black & Veatch's survey indicated that only 32 % of electric utilities had integrated CS systems with the "proper segmentation, monitoring and redundancies", which is needed for dealing with cyber-threat protection. 48 % of the respondents said that they did not have such systems (usnews.com 2014).

Most of the gas and electric utilities rely on Windows XP operating systems at workstations, which are vulnerable and that the electrical grid at large stands susceptible to cyber-attack from abroad and organized criminal networks.

Military leaders have been especially concerned about cyber-attacks on the power grid. They are using scenario planning in order to better understand the risks of cyber-attacks. For instance, in one scenario they considered, in a confrontation over the issue of Taiwan, China tries to cut off the electricity supply o the Fort Bragg military base in North Carolina, which leads to the grounding of the U.S. airborne forces (Mitchell 2014).

5.2.1.2 Financial Sector

Cyber-treats facing the financial sector are an issue of critical importance. In his annual letters to shareholder in April 2014, JPMorgan CEO described hackers' efforts to attack the bank's computers were becoming "more frequent, sophisticated and dangerous". In a "worst case" scenario, in which cyber-attacks lead to a deletion of records, a drain of the account balances and freeze of networks, will produce shocks that will have a severe impact on the economy, which will be on the scale of the attacks of September 11, 2001 (gabonembassyusa.com 2014).

In October 2014, JPMorgan Chase revealed that a cyber-attack which occurred in multiple stages between June and August of that year affected the accounts of 76 million households and 7 million small businesses (Kirk 2014). The hackers accessed over 90 JPMorgan Chase servers for about 2 months before they were detected. They obtained the highest level of administrative privileges to use the system.

Despite the severe threats, firms in the banking and financial industry have failed to increase the defense orientation A 2014 report by the DFS for the state of New York on CS in the banking sector found that most institutions surveyed had experienced cyber-attacks during the past three years. A problem is that many banks' networks run on old systems. Due to the growth in the number of merger and acquisition activities in this sector, banks need to integrate different systems, which pose a huge challenge from a CS standpoint. In addition to cybercriminals targeting consumers' information, banks also face actors with a motivation to disrupt financial industries or engage in economic espionage (Peterson 2014a).

5.2.1.3 Healthcare

The US$3 trillion U.S. healthcare industry has been a lucrative cybercrime target. A study of Ponemon Institute indicated that, the proportion of healthcare organizations reporting cyber-attacks increased from 20 % in 2009 to 40 % in 2013. According to Dell SecureWorks, cybercriminals can get as much as US$20 by selling stolen health insurance credentials in underground markets, compared to US $1–2 for U.S. credit card numbers (Finkle 2014).

In December 2013, cybercriminals accessed a server of Bryan, Texas-based St. Joseph Health System, which contained personal information of 400,000 current and former patients including SSNs, dates of birth, addresses and other medical information (Lee 2014). In August 2014, Franklin, Tennessee-based, Community Health Systems (CHS) said that hackers stole names, addresses, birth dates, telephone numbers and SSNs of 4.5 million patients. In a filing with the U.S. Securities and Exchange Commission (SEC), CHS noted that it experienced APT-type attacks, possibly attributable to China-based hackers, which occurred in April and June of that year (Fields 2014). *Becker's Hospital Review* in July 2013 listed CHS as the second largest for–profit hospital system in the U.S.

Cyber-threats facing healthcare organizations are new, unique, complex and changing rapidly. Some key gaps in the healthcare sector include access to cyber-related intelligence specific to this sector to help in assessing and prioritizing threats and risks. Due primarily to the newness, there is also a lack of education and experience required in consuming and responding to such information (Plus Media Solutions 2014).

Experts say that healthcare providers and hospitals have weak cyber-defense mechanisms. Some U.S. hospitals were reported to use Windows systems over 10 years old without a security patch (Humer and Finkle 2014). In a private notice distributed to healthcare providers in April 2014, the FBI noted: "The healthcare industry is not as resilient to cyber intrusions compared to the financial and retail sectors, therefore the possibility of increased cyber intrusions is likely" (Finkle 2014).

CS in this industry is of special interest for the simple fact that cyber-attacks may pose serious threats to human lives. In a 2011 conference, a CS researcher demonstrated that he could hack his own insulin pump using its serial number. The idea was to prove that sufficient insulin could be delivered to cause death (Kaul 2014). Likewise, a hospital's CS weakness may lead to the theft of sensitive information such as SSN and financial data.

Hackers' alleged penetration into the supply chain of the healthcare industry also remains a significant public health concern. For instance, medical device makers are also attractive targets due to their high-value IP. In 2013, cybercriminals reportedly hacked the computer networks of top U.S.-based medical device makers including Medtronic (the world's largest medical device maker), Boston Scientific and St. Jude Medical. It was suspected that the attacks might have lasted several months (Lee 2014).

5.3   Policy Frameworks and Strategy

Unlike in the EU, the U.S. lacks a comprehensive data security law or a CS legislation. Nonetheless, CS concerns have elicited extensive regulatory responses in recent years. Federal regulatory agencies such as the FTC, the Federal Deposit Insurance Corporation (FDIC), the FDA, the Department of Justice (DOJ) and the SEC, and state agencies such as New York's DFS are weighing in on the CS debate (natlawreview.com 2014).

Compared to the EU, the U.S. provides more autonomy to businesses regarding the way they disclose and store personal information. The U.S. government does relatively little to restrict companies from tracking people and selling information to third-parties. U.S. companies also have more autonomy to decide how much information they want to reveal about their data practices (darkreading.com 2014).

Organizations' data privacy and security framework are subject to a number of federal laws and regulations enacted to protect the privacy, security and confidentiality of specific categories of data and information. A further observation is that there is a substantial heterogeneity in the implementation and interpretation of CS across the U.S. states. It is reported that there are about 47 different state laws in the U.S. regarding how people should be notified in case of data breach involving personal information (King 2013).

The FTC is the key federal agency to regulate how consumers' personal information is handled under Section 5 of the FTC Act. The Act gives it authority to investigate "unfair and deceptive acts and practices in or affecting commerce" (Woods). Other important laws include the HIPAA to protects sensitive health information, the SOX to protect shareholders and the public from accounting errors and frauds in enterprises and to improve the accuracy of corporate disclosures, the Gramm-Leach-Bliley (GLB) Act to regulate financial information, the Fair Credit Reporting Act (FCRA) and the Fair and Accurate Credit Transactions Act (FACTA) to cover information used in credit, insurance and employment decisions and the Children's Online Privacy Protection Act (COPPA) to regulate personal information obtained online from children under the age of 13 (Martinez 2014). For instance, the HIPAA requires healthcare providers to have measures in place to protect patient data privacy, integrity, and availability. Those not complying with the HIPAA standards might face up to US$1.5 million in fines and 10 years in prison. Likewise, to comply with the SOX Act, public companies are required to have IT controls designed to ensure that data is accurate and protected from unauthorized changes.

5.3.1 The CS EO

The NIST, which is an agency of the U.S. Department of Commerce, and the Pentagon are among the key agencies to implement the strategy. The role of the NIST is to develop a "Cybersecurity framework," which involves finalizing voluntary standards and procedures to help companies address CS risks. Likewise, the Pentagon was asked to come up with a recommendation whether CS standards should be considered in contracting decisions.

In order to help organizations manage CS risks, the EO called for a voluntary risk-based CS Framework, comprising of a set of industry standards and best practices. In February 2014, the NIST released the resulting Framework, which was created through collaboration between government agencies and the private sector. The Framework considers CS risks as part of organizations' risk management processes. A goal of the Framework is to help organizations address and manage CS risks in a cost-effective way, taking the business needs into account and without placing additional regulatory burdens. The Framework has three parts: (a) the Framework Core is a set of "cybersecurity activities, outcomes, and informative references", which are common across all critical infrastructure sectors; (b) the Framework Profile will help an organization align CS activities with business requirements, risk tolerances, and resources; and (c) the Framework Implementation Tiers provide a mechanism for organizations to view and understand the characteristics of their approach to managing CS risk (NIST 2014).

5.3.2   Priority in Enforcement

Federal and state regulatory agencies have also intensified enforcement activities in CS-related matters. In October 2014, two telecommunications companies—YourTel America and TerraCom—were fined a record US$10 million by the Federal Communications Commission (FCC). The two companies' neglect in CS allegedly led to as many as 300,000 customers at a risk of identity theft. The two companies accessed sensitive information such as SSNs, addresses, names and driver's license information of their customers and failed to encrypt the data in order to secure. The fine is the FCC's first data security case and its largest privacy violation action (Risen 2014b). In the state of California, banks, companies and large organizations are required to inform the state attorney general's office and consumers about data breach "without unreasonable delay". In 2014, the Kaiser Foundation Health Plan faced a lawsuit from the attorney general of California. The foundation allegedly took over a year to disclose to some employees that their personal data may have been compromised (Goldstein et al. 2014).

5.3.3   CS Regulations to Address Threats Facing Critical Sectors and Important Industries

5.3.3.1   Power and Electricity

In spring 2014, U.S. federal regulators adopted new CS standards for the electric industry. The Department of Energy released guidance to help the industry develop risk management plans shaped by the NIST's framework of CS standards. The *Electricity Subsector Cybersecurity Capability Maturity Model* provides guidance for utility companies to assess CS. The model was developed in consultation with the White House, the Departments of Energy, the Department of Homeland Security (DHS) and power companies (Sternstein 2014b). Likewise, the Senate version of the 2015 National Defense Authorization Act requires the Pentagon to assess the cyber-attack-related vulnerability and risks of the grid (Mitchell 2014).

5.3.3.2   Healthcare

Some regulatory agencies and public gatekeepers are using their regulatory powers to ensure that CS becomes a priority instead of an afterthought. For instance, in October 2014, the FDA which oversees and regulates drug companies directly through its powers to control or approve products' market release, published recommendations for protecting medical devices from cyber-attackers. The guidance suggests medical device makers to take CS risks into account early in the design and development process. They are required to show documentation to the FDA about the risks identified and the steps taken to protect them from such risks. In addition, the FDA asks device manufacturers to submit plans to provide appropriate patches and updates to operating systems and software for newly emerging risks (Miliard 2014). The FDA has also collaborated with the DHS to create public awareness of CS of medical devices (Peterson 2014b).

5.3.3.3   Banks and Financial Institutions

Especially banks and financial institutions are facing unprecedented regulatory pressures to enhance CS measures. Raising concerns about high-profile cyber-attacks facing the U.S. financial system, Senate Banking Committee leaders are pressing financial regulators and the Treasury Department to take regulative measures to strengthen CS (Finkle and Johnson 2014). Senate Banking Committee leaders asked concerned regulators regarding the details of gathering cyber-attack-related information, coordination of efforts across agencies and involvement of the Financial Stability Oversight Council in monitoring risks. As noted above, SMEs often tend to be on the weak end of the CS strength spectrum. The Senate Banking Committee leaders asked about the details of the Federal Financial Institutions Examination Council's plan to help SMEs address CS gaps (Finkle and Johnson 2014).

The SEC, which was established to protect investors as one of its missions, is another federal agency active in the CS arena. While the SEC lacked any binding CS-related rules as of October 2014, it has been sending strong and clear signals regarding the expectation of firms to put in place CS policies and procedures (financial-planning.com). In 2011, the SEC issued guidance which recommended that companies should inform investors of "material" cyber-risks and attacks.

Regulatory measures are also being introduced to strengthen the CS of financial intermediaries and market participants such as brokerage firms. The Financial Industry Regulatory Authority (FINRA), which is a watchdog agency funded by the industry, announced plans to publish examination priorities in January 2015 in an attempt to intensify its scrutiny of CS practices of brokerage firms. The FINRA is expected to hire examiners with technology expertise to examine measures of firms to secure clients' data and test the integrity of firms' technology (Barlyn 2014).

State-level regulatory and administrative agencies are also becoming active. A notable example is New York's Department of Financial Services (DFS), which regulates banks and insurance companies. It was also announced that CS would be a top priority for the DFS in 2015 (Scannell 2014). A new guidance issued by the DFS in December 2014 specifies stricter rules in corporate governance, login security, management of third-party vendors, CS insurance and others (Chon 2014). Before issuing this guidance the DFS was involved in a number of regulatory processes associated with CS. In October 2014, DFS Superintendent talked with industry lawyers and chief executives of financial institutions about cyber-risks. He noted that the agency was considering new regulations which require banks chartered in the state to appoint chief information security officers. The DFS asked financial sector firms to explain the processes and mechanisms used to track potential vulnerabilities at their third-party vendors and suggested them to develop more CS expertise on their boards (Kopan 2014). The DFS head also urged financial companies to invest in cyber-insurance. The idea is that just like the fire insurance has played roles in improving building codes, cyber-insurances can help strengthen cyber-defense (Scannell 2014). In addition, banks may be required to submit quarterly tests of vulnerabilities of their systems (Cumming and Hochstein 2014).

5.4   Initiatives of the Private Sector and Special Interest Groups

About 85 % of the critical infrastructure in the U.S. is owned by the private sector on which the government has a limited authority. Private sector players are thus in a position to take actions and initiatives that are likely to shape the CS ecosystem. Some actors are taking steps to oppose legislation that they view as harmful to the private sector. For instance, the U.S. Chamber of Commerce is taking measures to prevent the SEC from forcing publicly traded firms to share more cyber-attack-related information. Some executives are concerned that disclosing cyber-attacks can make their companies a target for hackers, and expose them to lawsuits and thus could harm corporate profits (Ackerman). While some of these concerns have some basis, they are likely to make companies and the nation less secure in the long run. For instance, firms' failure to disclose CS breaches on the ground that such disclosure would expose them to lawsuits is likely to hinder the efforts of law enforcement agencies and other companies to fight similar attacks in the future.

U.S. technology companies have strongly protested against the NSA surveillance. In July 2014, a coalition of 30 companies and privacy groups wrote a letter to the president asking him to "speak out against" the Cybersecurity Information Sharing Act (CISA) of 2014. The bill was passed by the Senate Intelligence Committee on July 8, 2014. According to the letter the bill would encourage companies to share cyber-threat information with each other and with the federal government, but it fails to provide "a comprehensive solution" to cyber-threats. A concern among civil liberties advocates is that the bill would empower the NSA. In a letter to President Obama, Cisco Systems CEO John Chambers asked to curb NSA's spying activities arguing that the company suffered serious business losses globally by the revelations of the PRISM program (Bent 2014). Other IT firms such as Yahoo, Facebook, Google, Microsoft, and Twitter also called for reforms in the surveillance policies (Clayton 2014).

In order to reduce the financial losses associated with data breaches, U.S. companies are investing in cyber-insurance, which covers the costs associated with notifying customers, negative publicity and extortion. While the U.S. cyber-insurance market is more advanced than the rest of the world, there is still the lack of data on the odds of companies being victimized, which makes it difficult to estimate the costs of cyber-attacks. It is also difficult for companies to measure the nature and extent of cyber-related exposure and to make a decision as to what, and how much, cover to purchase (Gray 2014).

One estimate suggested that in the early 2014 one in four (Gray 2014) to one in three (Fernandes 2014). U.S. companies had insurance to protect against data breach losses. According to Marsh & McLennan, the U.S. cyber-insurance market was US$1 billion in 2013, which could reach US$2 billion in 2014 (Jones 2014). Other estimates suggest that CS insurers will write over US$2.5 billion worth of premiums in 2014 (Gray 2014). It is also worth noting that cyber-insurance is only a small proportion of the total U.S. insurance premiums, which amounted US$1.1 trillion in 2013 (cfo.com 2014). Nonetheless, the U.S. cyber-insurance is much bigger than the European cyber-insurance market, which was estimated to be less than US$150 million in 2014 (Jones 2014).

There have also been initiatives to increase collaboration with the government to fight cyber-threats. In July 2014, the financial industry group, the Securities Industry and Financial Markets Association (Sifm) called for a cyberwar council to fight cyber-attacks. A stated goal of the council was to ward off terrorist attacks that could potentially lead to a financial panic. They proposed that bank executives and representatives from government agencies including the Treasury Department, the NSA and the DHS would be members of the council (Dougherty 2014).

There have also been attempts to foster inter-industry collaboration and networks and knowledge-sharing. For instance, two industry groups—National Cyber Security Alliance (NCSA) and the International Franchise Association (IFA)—have teamed up to help franchise businesses strengthen CS. The NCSA is backed by companies such as Facebook, Google and Microsoft, as well as the DHS. The IFA represents franchisors such as 1-800-Flowers, 7-Eleven, Dairy Queen, Jiffy Lube, Papa John's and KFC (Bennett 2014). In addition, some industries are collaborating with consumers to fight cyber-threats. The banking industry is taking measures to educate consumers about CS and identity theft (wmur.com 2014).

5.5 Impacts on Businesses and Consumers

First, let us analyze the impact of the CS EO on businesses and consumers. The ACLU showed concerns that the CISPA would allow companies to hand over sensitive information to government agencies such as the NSA and the DoD without making a reasonable effort to protect privacy. According to the American Civil Liberties Union (ACLU), the EO would perform better in protecting privacy and security interests of consumers compared to the CISPA. A Legislative Council of the ACLU noted that the EO involves "a privacy-neutral way to distribute critical cyber information" and does not "negatively impact civil liberties". The EO offers less protection to businesses than would be available under the CISPA, which would have legally protected businesses from prosecution if they share information about the online activities of their customers or employees with intelligence agencies. On the plus side, however, information about cyber-threats that businesses receive from government intelligence is likely to support efforts to strengthen CS.

It is important to look at the short-term versus long-term effects of the regulations on firms' CS practices and performances. In light of the findings of recent surveys which indicate companies' failure to spend sufficient resources and efforts to protect their networks, the regulations may force companies to increase spending on CS. For instance, according to a Bloomberg Government study, in order to prevent 95 % of potential cyber-attacks, 172 organizations in critical sectors need to spend US$46.6 billion, which is 774 % higher than their current level of spending (bloombergview.com 2013). In the absence of regulatory requirements and standards, there is no incentive to spend on CS.

The EO is likely to have a heterogeneous impact on the sectoral CS performances. It, for instance, excludes commercial IT products and consumer IT services from critical infrastructures and thus they are less likely to be affected. Hence, for firms in sectors such as media, legal, engineering, consulting, and manufacturing, which are outside of critical infrastructure, the EO does little to enhance CS. In the long run, the EO is likely to place these companies at a disadvantage as they will have to manage CS in their own way. For instance, while personnel in critical infrastructure sectors may be encouraged to get security clearances, those in non-critical-infrastructures may not be in a position to take advantage of such an opportunity (ft.com 2013).

CS specialists think that some examples of standards envisioned by the EO include ensuring up-to-date antivirus programs, knowing all the points where a company's networks are connected to the Internet and limiting individuals and devices that have access to the company networks. In this way, the proposed standards would force companies to take measures to be more secure. Moreover, some argue that, as an increasing number of companies participate in the standards, meeting or exceeding the standards may translate into lower premiums charged by insurance companies (Gorman 2013). Moreover, in case of security breach, companies complying with voluntary standards are likely to have some liability protection (bloombergview.com 2013).

Since not all companies are likely to participate in the voluntary standards and procedures, differences among companies participating versus those not participating can be observed in terms of the CS-related pressures they face, as well as the opportunities they receive for participating. In this way, possible inter-sectoral heterogeneity in CS performances may arise due to the voluntary standards and procedures, which are a key component of the EO's Cybersecurity Framework.

IT companies and some lawmakers have asserted that the balance in the U.S. CS landscape is heavily tilted towards national security and the U.S. government has failed to give enough consideration to economic impacts of its CS measures. In a remark prepared for a Senate Finance Committee event, Senator Ron Wyden noted: "... even today, almost no one in Washington is talking about how overly broad surveillance is hurting the U.S. economy" (washington.cbslocal.com 2014). Some argue that a main drawback is an outdated bureaucratic structure that "empowers military and intelligence agencies over civilian ones". A national security attorney noted that "mistrust of purely military or intelligence agency leadership on CS creates significant challenges for information sharing about threats" (Sugarman 2014).

The U.S. approach to CS has had greater and more dramatic impacts on U.S. technology firms doing businesses in foreign countries. The U.S. Patriot Act has been a concern. There is a deep- rooted perception among some EU-based consumers and activists that U.S. providers are required to disclose cloud data to the government without the owner's consent. Ironically, the truth or falsity of such claims is less relevant than the fear itself, which can be damaging to U.S. CSPs' reputation. While U.S. officials and vendors have emphasized that such concerns are exaggerated and overstated, convincing foreign customers and activists, especially EU-based, that the Patriot Act does not present a risk factor has been a challenge for U.S. CSPs (Rauf 2011).

Some EU vendors have utilized the fear to their advantage, emphasizing that they provide "a safe haven from the reaches of the Patriot Act" (Lakatos 2012). Others have used the EU's strict regulations as a selling proposition. For example, the German CSP, HiDrive, which provides online data storage, emphasizes that its data are hosted in Germany and its services confirm to German laws, which are among the world's strictest (Cooter 2011).

The general atmosphere of distrust further deteriorated following the revelation of PRISM. Some estimates suggest that Snowden effect will slow the growth of the U.S. IT industry by as much as 4 % (Kim 2014). For instance, countries such as Russia, India, Brazil and Germany have argued for data localization and some have already enacted such legislation. Such practices would require ICT companies to store data in the country from which it was collected. For instance, data for a Google user in India, for instance, may be required to remain in that country. There has been an increased interest and discussion regarding the creation of a Europe-only electronic network (also known as a 'Schengen cloud') and also the creation of national-only electronic networks. U.S. officials criticized the plans on the ground that it "could potentially lead to effective exclusion or discrimination against foreign service suppliers that are directly offering network services or dependent on them" (USTR 2014). In general, U.S. companies have argued that storing data internationally would increase company costs for new servers and cut demand for U.S. workers (fortune.com 2014a). Citing *Defense News*, a *Christian Science Monitor* article noted that the United Arab Emirates may cancel the purchase of two spy satellites worth US$926 million from France unless two U.S.-made components are removed from them. It was alleged that the two U.S.-made components contained secret "backdoors" that, if exploited, would provide unauthorized access to sensitive data sent to the UAE's ground station (Clayton 2014).

5.6 Discussion and Concluding Remarks

Recent high profile cyber-attacks have acted as key triggers for strengthening CS measures.

Compared to the EU (Chap. 6), the U.S. CS strategy is driven by somewhat different visions and priorities. Whereas the EU CS strategy relies on a principle-based framework that provides a model for good practice, the U.S. CS strategy places an emphasis on combating CS threats. The U.S. is regulated on an industry specific basis and penalties for violation are less punitive (Brandon 2014).

There is a lack of information sharing among various players in the CS ecosystem which has led to the lack of opportunities to learn about cyber-threats. The U.S. lacks a national, mandatory database of malware "signatures". The availability of such database would allow organizations to set up firewalls against them. For instance, the knowledge about JPMorgan Chase breach would help other banks to look for the signatures of the same type of breach (Bruinius 2014).

U.S. CS strategy is highly inward-oriented, and exhibits a low degree of outward orientation. The U.S.-China Business Council, which represents about 230 U.S. companies with operations in China such as Boeing, Caterpillar, Citigroup and JP Morgan Chase, have asked the U.S. and Chinese governments to work together to address the growing problem of cyber-attacks (Palmer 2013). The absence of international cooperation has also insulated some countries and made them as safe havens for criminals.

As is the case of the rest of the world, the shortage of skilled CS professional is among the most significant barriers in the implementation of CS strategy. Likewise, according to the NIST, more than 700,000 new CS professionals will be needed in the U.S. by 2015 (Coleman 2011). There were more than 30,000 open CS positions to be filled in the federal agencies (fortune.com 2014b).

Businesses in the U.S. differ in terms of the CS-related regulations they face. Businesses that do not belong to critical infrastructures are likely to benefit by implementing the standards suggested by the framework even if they are not required by the regulations to do so. By doing so, they might be able to shield themselves against cyber-attacks and be rewarded with lower insurance premiums.

In general, due to the infant's regulatory system, it is in the interest of businesses to do more to protect their digital assets than required by the law. Finally, consumers can also benefit by the adoption of some elements of the standards such as the deployment of up-to-date antivirus programs and firewalls.

References

Ackerman, A. *UN. U.S. chamber warns Cyberattack disclosures could hurt corporate profits.* http://online.wsj.com/articles/u-s-chamber-warns-cyberattack-disclosures-could-hurt-corporate-profits-1414609209

Barker, I. (2014). *How US organizations are losing the cyber war.* http://betanews.com/2014/10/07/how-us-organizations-are-losing-the-cyber-war/

Barlyn, S. (2014). *Wall Street watchdog to bolster reviews of brokerage cyber security.* http://www.reuters.com/article/2014/10/29/us-finra-cybersecurity-examinations-idUSKBN0II2DA20141029

Bennett, C. (2014). *Cybersecurity help coming for franchises.* http://thehill.com/policy/technology/221649-cybersecurity-help-coming-for-franchise-owners

Bent, K. (2014). *Chambers: We're making it tougher for feds to tamper with Cisco gear.* http://www.crn.com/news/networking/300073635/chambers-were-making-it-tougher-for-feds-to-tamper-with-cisco-gear.htm

blogs.wsj.com. (2014). *Army bolsters cybersecurity force amid shifts in threats, technology.* http://blogs.wsj.com/washwire/2014/10/14/army-bolsters-cybersecurity-force-amid-shifts-in-threats-technology/

bloombergview.com. (2013). *Obama's Sensible Steps on Cybersecurity.* http://tinyurl.com/d46amme

Boyd, A. (2014). *Cybersecurity codes being added to all federal job descriptions.* http://www.federaltimes.com/article/20141107/FEDIT03/311070012/Cybersecurity-codes-being-added-all-federal-job-descriptions

Brandon, J. (2014). *Cloud, IoT, big data require international charter on data privacy, experts claim.* http://www.businesscloudnews.com/2014/09/25/cloud-iot-big-data-require-international-charter-on-data-privacy-experts-claim/

Bruinius, H. (2014). *Cybersecurity mystery at JPMorgan Chase: What were hackers after?* http://www.csmonitor.com/World/Security-Watch/Cyber-Conflict-Monitor/2014/1003/Cybersecurity-mystery-at-JPMorgan-Chase-What-were-hackers-after-video

cfo.com. (2014). *Cyber security spending up, but many uninsured.* http://ww2.cfo.com/applications/2014/11/cyber-security-spending-many-uninsured/

Chon, G. (2014). *NY bank regulator steps up online security demands.* http://www.ft.com/intl/cms/s/0/fe9e020e-7fc9-11e4-acf3-00144feabdc0.html#axzz3LUYJrD7d

Clayton, M. (2014). Five overlooked costs of the NSA surveillance flap. *Christian Science Monitor*, January 12. http://www.csmonitor.com/World/Security-Watch/2014/0112/Five-overlooked-costs-of-the-NSA-surveillance-flap

Coleman, K. (2011). *Government preps next generation of cybersecurity employees.* http://tinyurl.com/c6chf72

Cooter, M. (2011). *Strato launches competitor to Dropbox – with added privacy.* http://www.cloudpro.co.uk/iaas/cloud-storage/1641/strato-launches-competitor-dropbox-added-privacy

Cumming, C., & Hochstein, M. (2014). *N.Y.'s Lawsky considering strict cybersecurity regime for banks.* http://www.americanbanker.com/issues/179_201/nys-lawsky-considering-strict-cybersecurity-regime-for-banks-1070577-1.html darkreading.com. (2014). *Privacy, security & the geography of data protection.* http://www. darkreading.com/cloud/privacy-security-and-the-geography-of-data-protection-/a/d-id/1315480?_ mc=RSS_DR_EDT

Department of Defense. (2013). The Defense Science Board (DSB) Task force report: Resilient military systems and the advanced cyber threat, Department Of Defense.

Department of Homeland Security. (2009). *National infrastructure protection plan: Partnering to enhance protection and resiliency 2009.* https://www.dhs.gov/publication/nipp-2009-partneringenhance-protection-resiliency

Dougherty, C. (2014). *Banks dreading computer hacks call for cyber war council.* http://www. bloomberg.com/news/2014-07-08/banks-dreading-computer-hacks-call-for-cyber-war-council. html

Fernandes, D. (2014). *More firms buying insurance for data breaches.* http://www.bostonglobe. com/business/2014/02/17/more-companies-buying-insurance-against-hackers-and-privacy-breaches/9qYrvlhskcoPEs5b4ch3PP/story.html

Fields, J. (2014). *Cyber security: 5 steps to defend your business.* http://www.tennessean.com/ story/money/2014/09/18/cyber-security-steps-defend-business/15853617/

financial-planning.com. SEC examiners zeroing in on cybersecurity. http://www.financial-plan ning.com/30-days-30-ways/sec-examiners-zeroing-in-on-advisors-cybersecurity-2690777-1. html

Finkle, J. (2014). *Exclusive: FBI warns healthcare sector vulnerable to cyber attacks.* http://www.reuters.com/article/2014/04/23/us-cybersecurity-healthcare-fbi-exclusiv-id USBREA3M1Q920140423

Finkle, V., & Johnson, C. (2014). *Ask regulators for details on cybersecurity measures.* American Banker 179(203).

forbes.com. (2014). *Financial markets need stronger security against cyber attacks – CFTC's Massad.* http://www.forbes.com/sites/kitconews/2014/11/05/financial-markets-need-stronger-security-against-cyber-attacks-cftcs-massad/

fortune.com. (2014a). *Google's Eric Schmidt on NSA spying: 'We're going to break the Internet.'* http://fortune.com/2014/10/08/eric-schmidt-on-nsa-spying/

fortune.com. (2014b). *For Uncle Sam, trouble raising a cyber army.* http://fortune.com/2014/10/ 03/government-cyber-security-shortage/

foxnews.com. (2014). *Federal workers, contractors reportedly behind many cyber breaches – often by accident.* http://www.foxnews.com/politics/2014/11/10/federal-firewall-reportedly-struggles-against-increasing-number-cyberattacks/

ft.com. (2013). *US Cyber Security executive order falls short for the private sector.* http://tinyurl. com/aqu8cmf

gabonembassyusa.com. (2014). *Cyber attacks on banks color terrorism insurance renewal dis pute.* http://www.gabonembassyusa.com/cyber-attacks-on-banks-color-terrorism-insurance-renewal-dispute/

Goldstein, M., Perlroth, N., & Sanger, D. E. (2014). *Hackers attach cracked 10 financial firms in major assault.* http://dealbook.nytimes.com/2014/10/03/hackers-attack-cracked-10-banks-in-major-assault/?_php=true&_type=blogs&_php=true&_type=blogs&_r=1&#

Gorman, S. (2013). *Obama presses cybersecurity effort.* http://tinyurl.com/d45fh98

Gray, A. (2014) *US homeland security chief offers cyber attack insurance.* http://www.ft.com/intl/ cms/s/0/9785647a-4b2d-11e4-8a0e-00144feab7de.html#axzz3FPsY9xJ8

Harknett, R. J., & Stever, J. A. (2011). The new policy world of cybersecurity. *Public Adminis-tration Review, 71*(3), 455–460.

Humer, C., & Finkle, J. (2014). *Your medical record is worth more to hackers than your credit card.* http://www.chicagotribune.com/lifestyles/health/sns-rt-us-cybersecurity-hospitals-20140924-story.html

Jones, S. (2014). *Lloyd's CEO sees cyber insurance to surge after attacks.* http://www.bloomberg. com/news/2014-10-08/lloyd-s-ceo-sees-cyber-insurance-to-surge-after-attacks.html

Kaul, G. (2014). *Medical devices' cybersecurity risks get FDA's attention*. http://www.sfgate.com/health/article/Medical-devices-cybersecurity-risks-get-5867684.php

Kim, E. (2014). New report shows Edward Snowden's revelations are seriously damaging US tech firms. http://www.businessinsider.com/edward-snowden-us-tech-firms-2014-7

King, R. (2013). *New EU cyber security directive to impact U.S. companies*. http://tinyurl.com/cjujzgl

Kirk, J. (2014). *JPMorgan Chase says breach affected 83M customers*. http://www.computerworld.com/article/2691246/jpmorgan-chase-says-breach-affected-83m-customers.html

Kopan, T. (2014). *N.Y. financial chief eyes cybersecurity – Scoop: Rockefeller wants answers from Whisper – Energy sector a cautionary tale on cyber regulation*. http://www.politico.com/morningcybersecurity/1014/morningcybersecurity15793.html

Lakatos, A. (2012). *The USA patriot act and the privacy of data stored in the cloud*. http://tinyurl.com/b2bqh53

Lee, T. (2014). *Hackers break into networks of 3 big medical device makers*. http://www.sfgate.com/news/article/Hackers-break-into-networks-of-3-big-medical-5217780.php

Martinez, R. (2014). *Reasonable doubt: Data privacy, cybersecurity, and the FTC*. http://www.jdsupra.com/legalnews/reasonable-doubt-data-privacy-cybersec-06717/

Miliard, M. (2014). *FDA offers final guidance for medical device cybersecurity*. http://www.govhealthit.com/news/fda-offers-final-guidance-medical-device-cybersecurity

Mitchell, C. (2014). *Cyberwar: Not if. Not when. Now*. http://washingtonexaminer.com/cyberwar-not-if.-not-when.-now./article/2553470

natlawreview.com. (2014). *Cybersecurity: 10 million more reasons to pay attention*. http://www.natlawreview.com/article/cybersecurity-10-million-more-reasons-to-pay-attention

newyorker.com. (2013). *Network insecurity*. http://www.newyorker.com/magazine/2013/05/20/network-insecurity

NIST. (2014). Framework for improving critical infrastructure cybersecurity, Version 1.0 National Institute of Standards and Technology February 12.

Nye, J. S. (2013). From bombs to bytes: Can our nuclear history inform our cyber future? *Bulletin of the Atomic Scientists, 69*(5), 8–14.

Palmer, D. (2013). Trade group wants U.S.-China action on cyber security threats. *Chicago Tribune*. http://tinyurl.com/c7godjg

Peterson, A. (2014a). *JPMorgan Breach Rattles Wall Street*, October 4. http://www.vnews.com/news/business/13816127-95/jpmorgan-breachrattles-wall-street

Peterson, A. (2014b). *The FDA wants to talk about medical device cybersecurity*. http://www.washingtonpost.com/blogs/the-switch/wp/2014/09/23/the-fda-wants-to-talk-about-medical-device-cybersecurity/

Plus Media Solutions. (2014). US official news, healthcare industry still lacking in cyber threat preparedness, while cyber attacks targeted at industry increase.

Rauf, D. S. (2011). *Patriot act clouds picture for tech*. http://tinyurl.com/dy4lhcc

Risen, T. (2014a). *Companies unprepared as hacking increases*. http://www.usnews.com/news/articles/2014/05/28/companies-unprepared-as-hacking-increases

Risen, T. (2014b). *FCC adds cybersecurity to its oversight*. http://www.usnews.com/news/articles/2014/10/24/fcc-adds-cybersecurity-to-its-oversight

Scannell, K. (2014). *NY bank regulator targets cyber threat*. http://www.ft.com/intl/cms/s/0/5a981338-4cdf-11e4-a0d7-00144feab7de.html#axzz3FPsY9xJ8

Smith, A. (2014). *China could shut down U.S. power grid with cyber attack, says NSA Chief*. http://www.newsweek.com/china-could-shut-down-us-power-grid-cyber-attack-says-nsa-chief-286119

Sternstein, A. (2014a). *Exclusive: Nuke regulator hacked by suspected foreign powers*. http://www.nextgov.com/cybersecurity/2014/08/exclusive-nuke-regulator-hacked-suspected-foreign-powers/91643/?oref=ng-relatedstories

Sternstein, A. (2014b). *WH Official: Cyber coverage will be a basic insurance policy by 2020.* http://www.nextgov.com/cybersecurity/2014/09/wh-official-cyber-coverage-will-be-basic-insurance-policy-2020/93503/

Sugarman, E. (2014). *What the United States can learn from Israel about Cybersecurity.* http://www.forbes.com/sites/elisugarman/2014/10/07/what-the-united-states-can-learn-from-israel-about-cybersecurity/

The White House, Office of the Press Secretary. (2013). *President Barack Obama's State of the Union Address.* http://www.whitehouse.gov/the-press-office/2013/02/12/president-barack-obamas-state-union-address

usnews.com. (2014). *Cybersecurity among top energy industry concerns.* http://www.usnews.com/news/articles/2014/08/12/cybersecurity-among-top-energy-industry-concerns

USTR. (2014). 2014 National trade estimate report on foreign trade barriers, United States trade representative, March 31.

washington.cbslocal.com. (2014). *Dem Senator: NSA tech spying hurting US Economy.* http://washington.cbslocal.com/2014/10/08/dem-senator-nsa-tech-spying-hurting-us-economy/

washingtonpost.com UN. *America should not shrug at its cyber vulnerability.* http://www.washingtonpost.com/opinions/home-depots-breach-should-spur-us-to-fight-cyberattacks-vigilantly/2014/09/19/01dc9942-4025-11e4-b03f-de718edeb92f_story.html

whitehouse.gov UD. *Five things to know: The administration's priorities on cybersecurity.* http://tinyurl.com/yexjyz8

wmur.com. (2014). *Local banks promote cyber security.* http://www.wmur.com/news/local-banks-promote-cyber-security/28957370

Woods, J. *Federal trade commission's privacy and data security enforcement under Section 5.* http://www.americanbar.org/groups/young_lawyers/publications/the_101_201_practice_series/federal_trade_commissions_privacy.html

Chapter 6
Cybersecurity in European Union Economies

6.1 Introduction

As is the case of most industrialized countries, cyber-attacks have been growing rapidly in EU economies. The U.K.'s 2010 National Security Strategy rated cyber-attacks as a "Tier 1" threat and one of the four highest-priority risks facing the U.K. 90 % of German companies reported that they experienced cyber-attacks during the first 10 months of 2014 (dw.de 2014).

An underlying problem is that EU-based firms suffer from a low level of CS preparedness and defense mechanisms. A survey of office workers in the U.K., France and Germany revealed that 77 % of the respondent lacked confidence that their organizations complied with current data protection laws. About half of the respondents said that their organizations lacked a data protection policy, or had not told their employees about such policy (computerweekly.com 2014).

One of the most relevant aspects of the EU's CS strategy concerns the 1995 Data Protection Directive, which has been the major legislative instrument for handling consumer data in its members. A key strength of the EU approach is its reliance on a principle-based framework that provides a model for good practice. A further benefit concerns the Directive's technology-neutral principle. The Directive provided flexibility for EU members to vary the requirements to suit their local circumstances. The Directive has also helped increase public awareness of data protection.

Since the Directive was passed, there have been dramatic changes in the ways personal data are accessed, stored, processed, transmitted, shared and used. The evolution of cloud computing and BD is perhaps among the most influential forces to reshape and modify EU CS regulations.

In addition, critics have raised several concerns with the EU approach of data privacy regulations. A major weakness is an unclear link between the concept of personal data and real risks to privacy. Germany's Federal Office for Information Security [Bundesamt für Sicherheit in der Informationstechnik (BSI)], for instance,

© Springer International Publishing Switzerland 2016   107
N. Kshetri, *The Quest to Cyber Superiority*, DOI 10.1007/978-3-319-40554-4_6

has emphasized that since data, applications, systems and cloud services may differ, one-size-fits-all approach might not be appropriate (bsi.bund.de 2011). A second criticism of the EU approach of data privacy regulations is that it lacks consistent and effective measures to provide data processing transparency through information and notification. Another underlying problem concerned the existing inconsistency in interpretation and enforcement of data privacy laws among member countries and Data Protection Authorities' (DPAs) inconsistent roles in accountability and enforcement. A further criticism concerns overly simplistic and static approach to define entities involved in processing and managing data. The outmoded rules and cumbersome procedures have hindered data transfer to other countries for storage and processing. These and other weaknesses pose practical implementation problems (Robinson et al. 2009).

Thus while many privacy advocates consider the EU's data privacy standards defensible and preferable, critics have been concerned that these standards fail to take into account the context of a changing technological landscape. In response to the demands of various interest groups and as its own priority, the EC, which represents the interests of the EU as a whole, has recognized the inappropriateness of the existing framework and announced its new cloud strategy.

After three postponements, the European Parliament's Committee for Civil Liberties, Justice and Home Affairs (LIBE) in October 2013 approved a comprehensive reform of the 1995 Directive, which was proposed by the EC in January 2012 (europa.eu 2013a). The General Data Protection Regulation is expected to replace the 1995 Directive. The 28 EU member states will have 18 months to incorporate the amendments into their national legislation. The new regulations are expected to be enforced starting 2016 or 2017. Until then the 1995 data protection directive will be major legislative instrument for handling consumer data on the cloud. The already strong EU data protection rules, which apply across all economic sectors, and privacy rights are firmly established, are getting stronger. The fines for noncompliance will be up to 100 million euros under the new regulations (Brown 2014).

6.2   EU CS Strategy

In February 2013 the EC released its CS strategy document: "An Open, Safe and Secure Cyberspace" (European Commission 2013c)—and its proposed directive on network and information security (NIS) (European Commission 2013a) represents the EU's comprehensive vision on how best to prevent and respond to cyber disruptions and attacks. The European Network and Information Security Agency (ENISA), which is a center of network and information security expertise for the EU, is the key agency to implement the strategy. Its roles include: (a) assisting the Member States in developing cyber resilience capabilities; (b) examining the feasibility of Computer Security Incident Response Team(s) for Industrial Control

Systems (ICS-CSIRTs); and (c) supporting in carrying Cyber incident exercises to test preparedness and ability to cope with cyber-disruptions.

Table 6.1 compares the EU and U.S. CS strategies. In the EU economies, individuals' privacy and freedom of expression have almost the same level of protection. The Article 8 of the European Convention on Human Rights states the EU's fundamental principle of privacy: "everyone has the right to respect for his private and family life, his home and his correspondence". Especially due to decades of state surveillance by the Nazis and the East German communists,

Table 6.1 A comparison of the EU and U.S. CS strategies

	EU CS strategy	U.S. CS EO
Strategy document	• EC's Cyber Security Strategy and a proposed directive on network and information security (European Commission 2013d).	• An EO signed by the U.S. President (whitehouse.gov 2013).
Key agencies to implement the strategy and their roles	• The ENISA	• The NIST • Pentagon
Constraints that underlie the strategy and next steps	• The Member States have to write the directive into their national legislation. Further changes to the text are likely.	• An EO is on weak legal footing. It cannot compel firms to comply—only legislation can do that.
Vision and priorities	• Achieving cyber resilience • Reducing cybercrime • Developing cyber defense policy and capabilities related to the Common Security and Defense Policy (CSDP) • Developing industrial and technological resources for cyber-security, • Establishing a coherent international cyberspace policy for the EU • Promoting core EU values (europa.eu 2013b).	• Combat cyber-attacks and cyber-espionage on government agencies and critical sectors such as banking, power and transportation industries and U.S. companies.
Key concerns	• Appropriateness of pan-European rules (same rules in all countries) • Compliance costs in member states: concerns of the private sector's confidentiality, extra costs and possible damage to reputation. • Obligation of the Member States to report cyber-attacks are "vague" and do little to protect EU citizens' data stored outside the EU (euractiv.com 2013). • Misdirection of funds away from the police into intelligence agencies (Vaas 2013).	• A process of compiling voluntary standards may turn into mandatory regulations (de facto requirements). • Too much focus on information sharing but little to address the problems related to insecure system. • For firms in sectors outside of critical infrastructure the EO does little to enhance CS.

Germans are more anxious and fearful about the misuse of personal information. A researcher at Deutsche Digital Institut described this as "a deep collective experience" rather than "paranoia" (Jervell and Gummer 2014). A main difference is that the EU has set a baseline common level of privacy in order to protect privacy rights of its citizens irrespective of the data location. The U.S., on the other hand, follows a self-regulatory approach and has sector-specific regulations for sensitive data.

Due partly to the above-mentioned problem of businesses' CS underpreparedness, the EU economies have realized a need for basic competencies in cyber-disaster preparedness and response. The ENISA organized Europe's largest and most complex CS exercise—Cyber Europe 2014. A part of the exercise was that over 200 organizations from 25 EU member states faced virtual cyber-attack on October 30, 2014. The targets of the virtual attacks included security agencies, ministries, telecoms and energy companies, financial institutions and Internet service providers. All EU members except for Belgium, Lithuania and Malta tested their procedures and capabilities against real large-scale CS scenarios. The ENISA announced a plan to carry out over 2000 separate cyber-incidents, which included denial of service (DoS) attacks to online services, and attacks on critical infrastructures (euractiv.com 2014).

Some EU member states have expressed concerns about the compliance costs associated with the EU CS strategy. Especially newer EU members, due to the lack of national administrative, economic and technical capacity, are likely to face higher burdens to comply with the EU regulations. For instance, in an October 2012 questionnaire addressed to the national parliaments of the EU, Romania's Committee for Information Technologies and Communications expressed concerns about financial burdens on private data controllers. The committee also argued that some of the proposed obligations need to be analyzed further to look for the possibility of reducing additional burdens (Parliament of Romania 2012) .

The Directive is also intended to ensure uniform data protection standards across the EU members. Note that, as revealed in a 2003 Gallup survey of European companies collecting personal data, substantial heterogeneity in implementation and interpretation by EU members is prevalent. For example, maximum penalties for the misuse of personal information currently are 600,000 € in Spain, 150,000 € for a first offense plus 5 years in prison in France, and 250,000 € in Germany (Dowling 2009). The EU is introducing stronger CS regulation, and stricter enforcement mechanisms. The proposed fines in the revised EU data protection legislation, which is expected to be ratified by the end of 2015, will be up to 5 % of global turnover a company, or 100 million euros (computerweekly.com 2014).

Individual EU economies have also released national CS strategy documents. France's new CS law will require over 200 entities in critical sector power grid, telecommunications and retail to boost CS using domestic technology. French businesses are also suggested to focus on domestically manufactured certified products. According to new French rules, businesses may face fines of up to 750,000 € if they fail government security audits (Fouquet and Mawad 2014).

6.2.1   The EU Cloud Strategy

The EU considers the cloud computing as a key enabler of national and regional competitiveness. The cloud's evolution is arguably among the most influential forces to reshape and modify EU data regulations. According to an EU press release, the implementation of all the key elements in the new cloud strategy would create 2.5 million jobs and lead to a net annual gain of 160 billion euros to EU GDP by 2020 (European Parliamentary Research Service 2014).

Critics and skeptics argue that the regulatory compliance requirements have imposed inefficiencies and acted as a barrier to incentive for the development the cloud industry. They also note that market fragmentation and the lack of scale economies make unattractive to develop innovative solutions. These concerns are reflected in a slow growth of the EU's cloud industry. According to Gartner, during 2012–2016, North America, led by the U.S., is expected to account for 58 % of public cloud spending of US$779 billion, compared to Western Europe's 22 %.

Europe also has far fewer established cloud providers. While U.S.-based providers need to customize applications to meet EU requirements, they are often in better positions even after considering adaptation costs due to their experiences in the home country.

To address the Directive's various shortcomings, the EC has developed a new cloud strategy (ec.europa.eu 2013) that focuses on key issues such as regulatory framework, standards and certification and model contract terms. The purported fundamental purposes behind the reform included strengthening citizens' online privacy rights and providing a much needed boost to the EU digital economy.

The EC has viewed that its proposed actions outlined in its cloud strategy would address cloud users' risk perceptions. The initiatives and efforts in standardization and certification would make easier to signal and verify compliance.

The EC has addressed cyber security challenges in its Strategy for Cyber Security released recently and will support the development of security standards and assist with EU-wide voluntary certification schemes in the area of cloud computing, while taking in due account the need to ensure data protection (European Commission 2013a). In addition, the possible increase in compliant cloud services due to the new regulation will raise competition and might push the cost of cloud services down for the users in EU.

At the event, Fuelling the European Economy, hosted by Microsoft in Brussels, Neelie Kroes gave a Keynote speech and emphasized that the Commission's proposal would improve privacy and allow for the development and deployment of cloud services (Ashford 2012). Kroes also urged CSPs and users to participate in talks about security and technical/commercial standardization (Thiel and Valpuesta 2011). At the 2012 World Economic Forum in Davos, Switzerland, the EU announced the European Cloud Partnership, which focuses on the public sector's role. The idea in the Partnership is to help make the cloud more appropriate for the public sector and increase the public sector's involvement in the cloud. In a blog, Kroes noted that CSPs, industry bodies and associations such as SAP, Digital

Europe, EuroCloud, OpenForum Europe, TechAmerica Europe, and Google reacted positively to the Partnership (Kroes 2012). This is a sign of an increasing level of public–private interaction. In addition, pressures and ideas generated by various stakeholders are shaping the formulation and implementation of the EU's cloud policy (Table 6.2).

The strategy focuses on three key areas: (a) European Cloud Partnership, which brings together public authorities and industry bodies to develop a common regulatory framework; (b) Cloud Computing Standards and Certification, the main component of which is to introduce pan-European certification schemes; and (c) Model Contract Terms for Cloud Computing, which address issues such as data preservation after the contract is terminated, disclosure and integrity, ownership, location, transfer and inter-provider portability of data and subcontracting in the cloud.

The strategy also to allows DPAs in the Member States to approve Binding Corporate Rules as well as industry codes of conduct that are specifically tailored to the cloud. Further, in light of the concerns related to EU citizens' data handling in non-EU economies, the Commission has emphasized the importance of collaboration and coordination with India, the U.S. and other countries in issues related to law enforcement agencies' access to data and development of appropriate cyber security framework. Finally, the Commission seeks to leverage the expertise and resources of EU's advisory bodies (e.g., the ENISA is expected to facilitate the voluntary certification schemes in the cloud).

It is important to look at the ways national DPAs interpret and understand cloud security because these interpretations and understandings are likely to shape future responses and regulatory developments. While "one continent, one law" is an ultimate goal of the reform (European Commission 2013b), substantial intra-EU differences exist in the implementation and enforcement of privacy laws, which may not disappear in the near future. This is illustrated in Table 6.3 with a comparison of the responsibilities of CUOs and CSPs in the EU's five biggest economies.

No clear regulatory framework for CSPs' roles, responsibilities and functions exists as yet within the EU. In general it is CUOs' responsibility to make sure that personal data are protected and only used according to legal provisions. From Table 6.3, it is explicitly or implicitly clear that it is the CUO's responsibility to take active steps to identify potential risks and preventive measures. The Italian DPA is especially clear on this point and has emphasized that a CUO's employers are viewed as data controllers and hence will be liable for any wrongdoing that may occur due to the CSP's fault (Sforza 2012). Most CUOs, however, are not necessarily aware of this fact. For instance, the U.K.'s ICO is concerned that many businesses fail to realize that they are legally responsible if customer data are compromised, even after passing them to cloud providers (ico.org.uk 2012). CSPs' increased focus on proactive actions to address the CUOs' lack of awareness, knowledge and understanding regarding the risks can play a key role here. The BSI white paper places considerably more emphasis on the CSPs' responsibility to ensure security. Note that the BSI's recommendations are primarily intended to

Table 6.2 Key driving forces and actions influencing the EU cloud policy

Key players	Motivations and driving forces	Examples of actions
Vendors and industry groups	• Bring changes in cloud related policies and regulations in order to promote regional competitiveness, flexibility, growth and innovations.	• The ETNO, which represents 41 large telecom operators in 34 - European countries, lobbied for an international online privacy standard and simplification of rules governing data transfers. It argued that these measures would enable European companies to compete on the same level as those in the U.S. (Ingthorsson 2011). • The chief technology officer of the Paris-based company Capgemini expressed concern that most of the major CSPs in Europe are U.S.-based and argued that revision of EU data laws would help EU-based companies to sell cloud services to European users.
Activists, interest groups and user representatives	• Ensure reliability and availability of IT services and high level of data protection from various threats.	• In December 2014, 13 - non-governmental organizations, including the Romanian Association for Technology and Internet (ApTI), sent letters to Romania's president, the Romanian Parliament, the Romanian High Court of Cassation and Justice and the People's Advocate, which urged them to ask the country's Constitutional Court to review a cybersecurity legislation passed by the Parliament. The legislation would force businesses to provide national intelligence agencies with access to personal data without a court warrant (Constantin 2014). • A former Microsoft privacy chief warned that new EU data protection law proposals have no provisions for addressing such concerns.
EU national governments	• Prevent a situation in which CS-related policies are almost entirely influenced by the EU. • Respond to demands to harmonize and align legal systems and enforcement mechanisms with those of other EU countries.	• Romania's Committee for Information Technologies and Communications: proposed obligations need to be analyzed further to look for the possibility of reducing additional burdens.

(continued)

Table 6.2 (continued)

Key players	Motivations and driving forces	Examples of actions
International organizations (e.g., the EU)	• Respond to pressures from vendors, industry groups, consumers, activists, etc. • Provide an environment that promote the use of cloud computing • Harmonize and align legal systems and enforcement mechanisms.	• The EC Cloud strategy's focus areas: European Cloud Partnership (ECP), Cloud Computing Standards and Certification and Model Contract Terms for Cloud Computing. • The European Parliament emphasized the importance of opening EU-U.S. negotiations.

guide the actions of CSPs, which arguably have the means as well as the obligation to ensure adequate security on the cloud.

One observation is that in the cloud environment, the power is balanced in favor of the CSPs, since they are the ones who often stipulate the terms of the contract. It is thus a CUO's responsibility to make sure that the contract is formulated in accordance with the local personal data protection Act. For instance, the Swedish Personal Data Act makes it clear that a data processor (CSP) may process personal data only according to the instructions given by the Data Controller (CUO). Nonetheless, legal experts have indicated that in situations like this, the CUO needs to make sure that the terms are consistent with the requirements of the Act and explicitly stated in the contract (Runsten 2011).

6.3   Effects on the Private Sector and Consumers: A Comparison with the U.S.

Since the EU and the U.S. may serve as role-models for the formulation of national CS framework and strategy for other economies, in Table 6.4, we compare the effects of these two economies' CS regulation on the private sector and consumers. A really big difference between the EU and the U.S. concerns the reporting requirement in case of cyber-attacks against businesses. U.S. federal laws require that the victims of PII (e.g., credit card, SSN) be notified about breaches (blogs.wsj. com 2014). In the EU, any company offering services online will have to report cyber-attacks on their networks. For instance, it would require more than 42,000 firms in banking, transport, energy and healthcare sectors and Internet and public administrations to inform their respective national network and information security (NIS) authorities if their networks attacked (rt.com 2013). This means that whereas companies such as Apple, Google, Amazon, Sony, Microsoft, Facebook, Twitter, LinkedIn, DropBox, Flicker, Picasa and Wordpress are not required to report most security breach in the U.S., these companies' EU operations are required to report cyber-attacks. The EU Directive is thus likely to have more wide-ranging impact affecting all types of businesses.

Table 6.3 Guidelines and recommendations for strengthening cloud security in the EU's five biggest economies

Country (DPA)	Responsibilities of CUOs	Responsibilities of CSPs
France [Commission nationale de *l'informatique et des libertés* (CNIL)]	• Identifying the security measures and legal requirements based on the data and processing characteristics, assessing the risks involved, knowing the type of cloud services needed and selecting CSPs that gives sufficient guarantees (cloudsecurityalliance.org 2012).	• A CSP is generally considered as the data processor, but becomes a joint controller with the CUO if the latter lacks autonomy in the negotiation of the contract and in defining the manner data are processed (Maxwell 2012).
Germany [Bundesamt für Sicherheit in der Informationstechnik (*BSI*)]	• Assessing the risks associated with storing data and running applications in the cloud and identifying basic security issues and protection requirements. • Categorizing data, applications, systems and cloud services based on protection requirements. • Analyzing operational and legal framework for tackling cloud security issues.	• Addressing security issues with the CUO at an early stage, ensuring that the CUO understands the protection requirements and demonstrating security credentials transparently (bsi.bund.de 2011).
Italy (Garante per la protezione dei dati personali)	• Negotiating appropriate terms and conditions with CSPs in order to ensure adequate technical and organizational measures to avoid possible loss or unauthorized disclosure considering the fact that CSPs are just appointed as a data processor (Sforza 2012).	• CSPs take only the role of processor and are only part of the processing carried out by CUOs (Mantelero 2012).
Spain [Agencia Española de Protección de Datos (AEPD)]	• Being aware of the possibility and implications of a CSP providing services from locations that lack adequate data protection standards. • Having specifications in the contract for the CSP to subcontract services. • Being aware of issues of accountability and data portability (Fernandez-Samaniego 2013).	• Most CSPs will be considered as data processors. • It emphasizes that CSPs should review their contracts and make regular adaptation to comply. It reminds that CSPs may be liable for non-compliance (O'Donoghue and Kimoto 2013).

(continued)

Table 6.3 (continued)

Country (DPA)	Responsibilities of CUOs	Responsibilities of CSPs
The U.K. [Information Commissioner's Office (ICO)]	• Seeking assurances and guarantees that CSPs will keep the data safe. • Assessing the security of the cloud network and systems and the physical security of the CSP. • Having a written contract with the CSP that it cannot change the terms of the service without the CUO's agreement. • Having a written policy regarding the expectations from the CSP. • Obtaining customers' permission if the services are funded through ads targeted at the customers using their personal data. • Being aware about obligations associated with transferring data in foreign countries (ico.org.uk 2012).	• CSPs roles are not always clear and would need to be reviewed on a case-by-case basis. It also emphasizes the importance of determining whether a CSP is a data controller in its own right or is merely acting as a 'data processor' on behalf of the controller.

An important feature of the Data Protection Directive is that it restricts the transfer of EU citizens' personal data to jurisdictions that lack adequate protection. This has been a key source of the ongoing EU-U.S. conflict on the issues of CS. European politicians have criticized U.S. companies such as Facebook and Google for handing out European citizens' data to U.S. law enforcement agencies. In June 2014, the German government cancelled a contract with the U.S. telecoms firm Verizon Communications replaced it with Deutsche Telekom AG due to concern that Verizon was legally obligated to provide data to the U.S. government (reuters.com 2014a). According to Germany's new regulations, vendors bidding for public telecommunication and IT contracts cannot give data to foreign governments (Fouquet and Mawad 2014).

The EU's new privacy measures are likely may put foreign firms in general at a disadvantage and may challenge the U.S. firms' competitiveness. Under the new EU laws companies such as Facebook, Yahoo, and Google may face huge fines if they do not get approval from European officials before handing the data of European residents to U.S. agencies (Clayton 2014). U.S. firms are already feeling the negative consequences of EU's new regulations. Google reportedly notified The New York Times in September 2014 that in order to comply with the EU's "right to be forgotten, it removed links to five articles from its search results on the EU versions (Cohen and Scott 2014).

Since the EU economies' data privacy laws are among the strictest in the world, these economies' regulatory and enforcement attitude towards foreign CSPs deserve mention. European economies have exhibited some degree of

Table 6.4 Effects of CS strategies on the private sector and consumers

	EU CS strategy	US CS EO
Effects on expected roles and responsibilities of the private sector	• Further development of the European Public-Private Partnership for resilience (EP3R) for cooperation and information sharing with public authorities. • Investment on CS and development of best practices through Trust in Digital Life (TDL) and other initiatives. • Recommends businesses to adopt more robust, embedded and user-friendly security features in products and services. Cloud providers are expected to reduce reliance on foreign technology suppliers. • Member countries are required to enact laws that compel firms in industries such as transport, telecoms, finance energy, health and online infrastructure to disclose details of cyber-attacks to the national Computer Emergency Response Team (CERT).	• Defense and intelligence agencies would share classified cyber-threats data with companies. • Companies will receive incentives to follow security standards. • Companies are not required to publically disclose breaches unless PII is involved.
Effects on privacy and security interests of consumers	• Many privacy advocates consider the EU approach defensible and preferable in terms of promoting privacy and security interests of consumers.	• According to the White House senior administration officials the shared information would be limited to cyber-threats (e.g., malicious codes) and would not contain the contents of private emails. • The flow of data is one-way: Private-sector firms are not required to release information about their clients. • The EO would better protect privacy than the CISPA

heterogeneity in their orientation towards foreign CSPs. In June 2013, Sweden's DPA, Datainspektionen asked Stockholm's Salem Municipality to stop using Google Apps, email and calendar services. Datainspektionen argued that the data processor, Google, writes the contract and sets the ground rules for handling personal information, and, has too much room to use the data for purposes other than what is specified by the municipality (Tung 2013). Datainspektionen was concerned that the agreement gave Google too much power to process personal data for its own potential benefit. On the other hand, Norway, which is subject to the EU single market laws in all relevant areas except for those dealing with agriculture and fisheries, due to its membership in the European Economic Area (EEA) (http://

eeas.europa.eu/norway/index_en.htm) exhibited a more positive enforcement attitude towards foreign CSPs. In 2012, the Norwegian DPA, Datatilsynet approved local municipalities' use of Google Apps and Microsoft's Office365 except for handling personal information such as those related to taxation, public school, and healthcare (Tung 2012). One requirement was that the data were to be processed only in the EEA or the U.S. under the Safe Harbor principles.

Of special interest and significance is the revelation of the U.S. NSA PRISM internet surveillance program, which has motivated some of the recent concerns about foreign clouds' security. Following the revelation, Europe's top political elites including EC vice president Kroes (Finnegan 2013) and Germany's Interior Minister Hans-Peter Friedrich (Samson 2013) have indicated the possibility of a further deterioration of trust in U.S.-based CSPs. In July 2013, Germany's federal and state DPAs announced that they would strictly enforce privacy violations involving data transfers to countries outside the EU. The revelations regarding the accessibility of data stored by the U.S.-based CSPs such as Google and Microsoft to the NSA led them to call for the German government to suspend the participation in the U.S.-EU Safe Harbor Program (bna.com 2013). The German data protection commissioners also asked Chancellor Angela Merkel to pressure the EU to suspend the Program (Schuppert 2013). Note that the Safe Harbor Program provides streamlined process for U.S. companies to comply with the EU directive. It is sufficient to self-certify to the Department of Commerce that they would abide by EU data protection principles. Since there is no way to prove to the German DPAs regarding the sufficiency of privacy protection to make the data unreachable to foreign intelligence services such as the NSA, foreign CSPs are reported to be in a difficult position. In October 2013, in the negotiation of EU data protection regulation, Germany and France reportedly called for a new provision which specifically requires companies to inform the individuals if the NSA requires or asked to disclose their personal information (Taylor 2013).

The above said, the recent sentiment against foreign CSPs needs to be viewed more of an upward drift rather than a surge. The EC has made it clear that it is against closing the EU market to CSPs that are based and store data abroad and labelled the efforts to develop national or regional-only cloud framework are misguided and harmful (out-law.com 2013).

6.4   PPP and the Private Sector's Roles

The private sector is also gearing up to respond to the increased cyber-threats. In October 2014, the British Bankers' Association was reported to be working with BAE Systems Applied Intelligence to launch a Financial Crime Alerts Service. It is expected to cover the activities of cybercriminals and terrorists.

National and supranational bodies and states are teaming up with the private sector in CS initiatives and institutional arrangements have been established on this front. In September 2014, Europol's European Cybercrime Centre (EC3) and the

European Banking Federation (EBF), which is a federation of 32 national banking lobby groups with about 4500 banks as members, announced a memorandum of understanding to intensify CS cooperation. The cooperation is expected to allow them to exchange CS-related know-how, and strategic statistics and information (reuters.com 2014b).

In order to help organizations protect against cyber-attacks, in June 2014, the U. K.'s Department for Business, Innovation & Skills and Cabinet Office published a Cyber Essentials scheme (CES) (gov.uk 2014). The CES has been backed by the Federation of Small Businesses, the Confederation of British Industry (CBI) and a number of insurance organizations. The CES provides the details regarding the necessary technical controls, the independent assurance process and different levels of assessment required to achieve Cyber Essentials badges and guidance for CS professionals to carry out the assessments. In September 2014, the U.K. government announced that suppliers bidding for government contracts that handle sensitive and personal information are required to be CES certified from October 1, 2014 (Degun 2014).

Table 6.3 presented guidelines and recommendations for strengthening cloud security in the five biggest EU economies. In some cases, these guidelines were prepared by involving a number of stakeholders including the private sector. For instance, France's CNIL and Germany's BSI published their recommendations based on consultation with the industry and other key players (cloudsecurityalliance. org 2012).

6.5 Discussion and Concluding Remarks

In response to growing interests and demands of, and the interactions among the various players in the CS scene in Europe, new EU policy initiatives are likely to emerge that may address some of the major weaknesses of the EU approach to safeguarding data privacy. The new measures may also help EU economies take better advantage of modern ICTs such as BD and the cloud, which are considered a key to their progress and competitiveness.

Just like the U.S., the EU economies face a severe lack of CS professionals and their CS strategies have no special provisions for dealing with this shortage. For instance, according to the U.K.'s National Audit Office, which has responsibility to make sure the nation spends money wisely, it would take 20 years to bridge the country's CS skills gap (The Economist 2013).

Organizations handling personal data of customers and employees are likely to encounter complex issues concerning loss, unauthorized disclosure, and possible alteration of such data. The DPAs in EU economies have published guidelines and recommendations regarding the roles and responsibilities CUOs and CSPs. It seems clear that under the current EU regulations, a CSP acts as a data processor and a CUO is a data controller in the cloud environment. It is important to recognize that the primary responsibility to prevent the loss, unauthorized disclosure, and alteration of personal data resides with the organization handling the date rather than the CSP. Organizations processing personal data thus cannot delegate the burden, responsibility, and risk to a CSP. Given this, a CUO should ask tough questions to the CSP such as certification from auditing and professional organizations, locations of the data centers, and background check of its employees. This is especially important in the EU in light of the harsh sanctions and penalties for data breaches.

While the 1995 Directive intended to ensure a uniform data protection standard across the Member States, the EU is still far from achieving this goal. While the general principles are the same for all EU economies, significant heterogeneity in implementing and interpreting privacy regulations has been observed, which is unlikely to disappear anytime soon. For instance, analysts say that the Model Contracts for the transfer of personal data to third countries, which are based on the power given to the Commission by the Council and the European Parliament to decide that certain standard contractual clauses provide adequate safeguards with respect to the protection of the privacy, might no longer be acceptable to German DPAs (bna.com 2013).

The proposed strategy, to some extent, is expected to address the market fragmentation issue inherent in multiple jurisdictions among EU countries and lead to further harmonization of CS-related laws and enforcement in the 28 Member States. This may lead to the growth of local cloud firms. A further mechanism contributing to the growth of local firms is the increased local demand of cloud-based services as the users' privacy, security and reliability concerns are addressed by the local cloud providers compliant with EU regulations.

The proposed regulations can have important negative as well as positive effects on foreign firms offering services in the EU. The new strategy is likely to stimulate the creation of local cloud firms, which may emerge as strong competitors to foreign firms due to better knowledge of local market needs and preferences. The proposed certification schemes may also benefit non-EU providers as certification of EU compliance could ameliorate some of the negative country-of origin bias that has been shown to exist against U.S.-based firms.

References

Ashford, W. (2012). *Proposed EC data protection rules help cloud adoption.* http://www.computerweekly.com/news/2240114617/Proposed-EC-data-protection-rules-help-cloud-adoption-says-Kroes

blogs.wsj.com. (2014). *One CIO's guide to how board members can improve Cybersecurity.* http://blogs.wsj.com/cio/2014/09/29/one-cios-guide-to-how-board-members-can-improve-cybersecurity/

bna.com. (2013). *In wake of PRISM, German DPAs threaten to halt data transfers to non-EU countries.* http://tinyurl.com/m2frwrb

Brown, M. (2014). *Europe's new data laws will affect MSPs*. http://mspmentor.net/infocenter-cloud-based-file-sharing/082514/europe-s-new-data-laws-will-affect-msps; http://www.zdnet.com/europes-new-data-laws-just-how-many-cloud-vendors-would-comply-7000032499/

bsi.bund.de. (2011). *Security recommendations for cloud computing providers*. http://tinyurl.com/pdns54a

Clayton, M. (2014). *Five overlooked costs of the NSA surveillance flap, Christian Science Monitor, January 12*. http://www.csmonitor.com/World/Security-Watch/2014/0112/Five-overlooked-costs-of-the-NSA-surveillance-flap

cloudsecurityalliance.org. (2012). *CNIL (French data protection authority) recommendations on the use of cloud computing services*. http://tinyurl.com/pzvczy3

Cohen, N., & Scott, M. (2014). *Times articles removed from Google results in Europe*. http://www.nytimes.com/2014/10/04/business/media/times-articles-removed-from-google-results-in-europe.html

computerweekly.com. (2014). *European firms far from ready for new data rules, study shows*. http://www.computerweekly.com/news/2240231892/European-firms-far-from-ready-for-new-data-protection-rules-study-shows

Constantin, L. (2014). *Romanian version of EU cybersecurity directive allows warrantless access to data*, December 24. http://www.cio.com/article/2863633/romanian-version-of-eu-cybersecurity-directive-allows-warrantless-access-to-data.html

Degun, G. (2014). *UK government demands suppliers meet cyber security standards*. http://www.supplymanagement.com/news/2014/uk-government-demands-suppliers-meet-cyber-security-standards

Dowling, D. C. (2009). *International data protection and privacy law*. http://tinyurl.com/bgh4fza

dw.de. (2014). *Cyber summit reveals concerns over internet security*. http://www.dw.de/cyber-summit-reveals-concerns-over-internet-security/a-18038605

ec.europa.eu. (2013). *Digital Agenda for Europe*. http://tinyurl.com/cchnqpz

euractiv.com. (2013). *Statement of Wim Nauwelaerts reported in "Storm cloud emerges from EU cybersecurity strategy"*. http://tinyurl.com/avuq2bp

euractiv.com. (2014). *Europe under massive virtual cyber attack*. http://www.euractiv.com/sections/infosociety/europe-under-massive-virtual-cyber-attack-309623

europa.eu. (2013a). *IBE Committee vote backs new EU data protection rules*. http://tinyurl.com/q4dcxe7

europa.eu. (2013b). *EU Cybersecurity plan to protect open internet and online freedom and opportunity*. http://tinyurl.com/bhwgyuw

European Commission. (2013a). *Cybersecurity strategy of the European Union*. http://tinyurl.com/a6uomtz

European Commission. (2013b). *LIBE Committee vote backs new EU data protection rules*. http://tinyurl.com/q4dcxe7

European Commission. (2013c). *The European Commission's cybersecurity strategy – "An Open, Safe and Secure Cyberspace"*. http://tinyurl.com/cdejw3a

European Commission. (2013d). *Proposal for a directive of the european parliament and of the council*. http://tinyurl.com/ctkcfhu

European Parliamentary Research Service. (2014). *Mapping the Cost of Non-Europe, 2014-19*, July 2014.

Fernandez-Samaniego, J. (2013). *Spanish data protection agency issues guides on cookies and cloud computing*. http://tinyurl.com/oec8b25

Finnegan, M. (2013). *Prism harming US cloud provider business, European Commission claims*. http://tinyurl.com/mk6rsef

Fouquet, H., & Mawad, M. (2014). *France demonstrates security savoir faire as it enforces new cyber-security law*. http://www.chicagotribune.com/sns-wp-blm-news-bc-france-cyber06-20141006-story.html#page=1

gov.uk. (2014). *Cyber essentials scheme: Overview*. https://www.gov.uk/government/publications/cyber-essentials-scheme-overview

ico.org.uk. (2012). *Cloud on the horizon for data-handling outsourcing.* http://tinyurl.com/panlo23

Ingthorsson, O. (2011). *Regulations a barrier to cloud growth in Europe.* http://www.datacenterknowledge.com/archives/2011/08/29/enhancing-cloud-development-in-europe/

Jervell, E. E., Gummer, C. (2014). *U.S. web firms' expansion leaves Germans conflicted.* http://online.wsj.com/articles/amazon-to-launch-web-hosting-in-germany-1414075728

Kroes, N. (2012). *Cloud computing: building a European cloud partnership.* http://blogs.ec.europa.eu/neelie-kroes/european-cloud-partnership

Mantelero, A. (2012). *Cloud computing, trans-border data flows and the European Directive 95/46/EC: applicable law and task distribution.* http://tinyurl.com/nk47hy4

Maxwell, W. (2012). *CNIL cloud guidelines address controller vs. processor issues.* http://tinyurl.com/9boyl6y

O'Donoghue, C., & Kimoto, T. (2013). *Spanish data protection watchdog publishes one new guidance on cookies and two on cloud computing.* http://tinyurl.com/phrs425

out-law.com. (2013). *European Commission opposes 'Fortress Europe' approach to cloud but wants region to lead on data security trust.* http://tinyurl.com/lcyhu8b

Parliament of Romania. (2012). *Chamber of Deputies, Committee for information technologies and communications, The reform of the EU Data Protection framework.* http://tinyurl.com/bf5u6bd

reuters.com. (2014a). *German government cancels Verizon contract in wake of U.S. spying row.* http://www.reuters.com/article/2014/06/26/us-germany-security-verizon-idUSKBN0F11WJ20140626

reuters.com. (2014b). *European banks team up with Europol in cybercrime fightback.* http://uk.reuters.com/article/2014/09/22/uk-banks-cybersecurity-europe-idUKKCN0HH1RJ20140922

Robinson, N. et al. (2009). *Review of the European Data Protection Directive.* http://tinyurl.com/by7swsw

rt.com. (2013). *Net cost: EU cybersecurity reform blighted by price tag concerns.* http://tinyurl.com/aommfc2

Runsten, J. (2011). *Cloud services and the Swedish Personal Data Act.* http://tinyurl.com/qydmu2e

Samson, T. (2013). *Germany joins in voicing distrust of U.S.-based cloud services.* http://tinyurl.com/pendvhl

Schuppert, S. (2013). *German data protection commissioners push government towards suspension of U.S. – EU safe harbor regime.* http://tinyurl.com/my3epc3

Sforza, M. (2012). *Italian data protection authority's guide on cloud computing.* http://tinyurl.com/npuxkdt

Taylor, P. (2013). *Surveillance: Cloud users spooked by Washington's snooping.* http://tinyurl.com/kqc49pc

The Economist. (2013). To the barricades: How America and Europe are trying to bolster their cyber-defences. http://tinyurl.com/cnflnbz

Thiel, S., & Valpuesta, R. (2011). *U.K. Trails U.S. in public cloud adoption, Salesforce CEO Says.* http://www.sfgate.com/cgi-bin/article.cgi?f=/g/a/2011/09/13/bloomberg1376-LRILRH0YHQ0X01-3L8HOVDU01DK87C6RGOVTSL63E.DTL

Tung, L. (2012). *No personal data on Google Apps, Norway tells its councils as it clears cloud use.* zdnet.com.

Tung, L. (2013). *Sweden tells council to stop using Google Apps.* zdnet.com

Vaas, L. (2013). *Infosec pros give verdict on EU's new cybersecurity strategy: "Nice try".* http://tinyurl.com/atooylq/

whitehouse.gov. (2013). *Improving the security of the nation's critical infrastructure.* http://tinyurl.com/d9upafl

Chapter 7
Cybersecurity in China

7.1 Introduction

CS is embraced as a key national priority demonstrated by the fact that the president Xi Jinping has headed the newly formed Central Internet Security and Informatization Leading Group. Premier Li Keqiang and the First Secretary of the Central Secretariat of the Communist Party of China, Liu Yunshan were named as the Group's deputy heads. In the Group's first meeting, Xi emphasized the importance of building China into a cyber power (Wan 2014). According to Xi, domestic development of technology, the availability of vital and sound infrastructure and information services, "prosperous cyber cultures", high quality CS talents and international cooperation constitute the key foundations of cyber power. He also announced that the government will support the establishment of companies working in CS and related areas (xinhuanet.com 2014).

China has also introduced some policy changes in order to foster a cloud-based economy. In 2011, the Chinese government announced an investment of US$154 million to develop a cloud center for high-tech and start-up firms in Chongqing. The cloud computing Special Administrative Region (SAR) will be free of the country's strict internet censorship filters (Russell 2011).

China is also engaged with many other countries in bilateral as well as multilateral CS cooperation. In a policy paper released in April 2014, China announced its intention to work more closely with the EU in CS. China is especially trying to use its growing influence in developing countries to reshape the rules and institutions of CS-related international system to better serve its interests. A *China Daily* article of July 2014 noted that "further cooperation in improving CS will be a major focus of all BRICS states, all of which are inclined to alleviate dependence on Western technologies". The author of the article expressed dissatisfaction with the international institutions arguing that they have not been able to address the issue of "the US' pervasive cybersurveillance" (Yao 2014).

© Springer International Publishing Switzerland 2016   123
N. Kshetri, *The Quest to Cyber Superiority*, DOI 10.1007/978-3-319-40554-4_7

Despite these attempts, China's progress on many key aspects of CS so far has been slow. An international comparison would be informative and might help clarify China's ambiguous CS regulations and weak enforcement. In the 2012 Data Centre Risk Index issued by International consultancies Cushman & Wakefield and HurleyPalmerFlatt, China ranked near the bottom of the list: 26th out of 30 nations. The lack of an effective regulatory framework to address data theft and cybercrimes as well as tight government control over data contributed to China's low rank.

7.2   Cyber-Threats Facing China

A 2012 China Daily piece titled "Personal Data Protection" provided a succinct and valuable update on China's data privacy breaches' increasing prevalence and consequences (China Daily 2012). According to the editorial, illegal firms in the country specialize in collecting and selling personal information, acquiring information from subsidiaries of major telecommunication firms, and sending text messages for profit. Some bank and telecommunications company employees have been arrested for selling personal information to such firms. A China Internet Network Information Center report indicated that, in the first half of 2011, 121 million Chinese had their online account information stolen (Zhang 2012).

The abuse of personal information is widespread. A sizable and rapidly growing black market of personal information has reportedly emerged. A malicious actor can sell a database containing a specific type of information, for instance, phone numbers, for more than US$1500 on the black market. The illegal companies, in turn, charge their clients between US$1500 and US$150,000 for services such as private investigation, illegal debt collection, asset investigation, and even kidnapping (Yan 2012). The China Daily editorial warned that "the booming trade in personal information and its illegal use will finally ruin online economic activities and disturb even the order of off-line business activities" (China Daily 2012).

Thanks to high economic growth rate and a good political order internal security is relatively stable in China. In order to re-legitimize its rule and prevent the country's destabilization, the CCP is focusing on economic growth and patriotism. External security threats are thus viewed as a more challenging concern than internal security threats.

China is concerned about cyber-threats from foreign entities, both state and non-state actors. China views the great amount of metadata produced by smartphones and other devices as a key national security issue. Chinese state media have frequently criticized Apple. They have accused the company that it provided user data to U.S. intelligence agencies and called for a "severe punishment" against the company. In a July 2014 broadcast, the state-owned CCTV aired an interview of a researcher, who argued that iPhone's "Frequent Locations" function tracks and reveals "extremely sensitive data". The researcher further noted that the data could reveal the entire country's economic situation and "even state secrets" (reuters.com 2014a).

7.3 Informal Institutions and Non-state Actors

From the standpoint of CS Informal institutions are an especially intriguing and unique feature of China. Especially those born before 1960s either had a first-hand experience of the Japanese occupation (1930s and 1940s), or heard tales of horrors committed on the Chinese by the Japanese from their elders and the media or read in the history books (apcss.org 2001).

Some argue that the CCP regime has historically employed nationalism to bolster its legitimacy and public support and divert attention from domestic problems (Kalathil 2002). The state arguably does so through invoking a deep sense of "Chineseness" among citizens (Ong 1997). B. Sautman observed: "Nowhere is this more pronounced than in China, where these disciplines (Archaeology and paleoanthropology) provide the conceptual warp and woof of China's 'racial' nationalism" (Sautman 2001).

In recent years, online games are also being employed to infuse nationalism and generate "national spirit" among the youth (newsgd.com 2005). In 2005, the Chinese online gaming firm, PowerNet Technology and the China Communist Youth League (CCYL) collaborated to develop the game Anti-Japan War Online, which was based on the Japanese invasion of China during 1937–1945. Gamers can play simulations of key battles. They can, however, play only as the Chinese side.

Analysts also argue that the fact that China's "post-Tiananmen generation" has experienced little or no hardship has made this generation indifferent to democracy (Hvistendahl 2009). Chinese society is conditionally tolerant of the domination of civil society by a strong state. Thanks to China's Internet-driven nationalism, however, opposition to the West has become one of the defining values of this generation. When Chinese hackers see that the honour of their motherland is compromised, they consider it important to take necessary actions to restore their motherland's honour, glory and integrity. Following the collision of a U.S. surveillance plane and a Chinese fighter in 2001, a Chinese hacking group publicly released its plans for a "Net War," which was planned to continue until the May 7 anniversary of the bombing by the U.S. in the Chinese embassy in Belgrade. In 1999, a cyberwar broke out between Chinese and Taiwanese hackers when the then Taiwanese President suggested that Taiwan's relationship with Beijing needs to be conducted on a "state-to-state" basis. Initially, Chinese hackers defaced several Taiwanese websites with pro-China messages and said that Taiwan was and would always be a part of China (Denning 2000). Chinese hackers have also fought cyberwars with hackers from Indonesia and Japan (de Kloet 2002).

Note that because of the government's various control measures, nongovernment entities, special interest groups, and the civil society are organized loosely. There is little room for these groups to influence national policymaking.

Some nascent special interest groups, such as environmental and animal rights organizations and sports clubs, have placed new demands on the state and created competition for resources, attention, status, and legitimacy. Although such groups provide tremendous societal benefits, their potential for mobilizing people on a regional or even national scale has increased the government's nervousness. Although China's industrial leaders and state science and technology officials have repeatedly appealed to the government to take measures to increase the participation of trade, industry, and professional associations, the regime has responded with resistance to accept an increased role in the independent civil society.

The situation contrasts with India's. Trade associations, such as the National Association of Software and Services Companies (NASSCOM), have strengthened India's data privacy and security standards. For example, the Data Security Council of India—a self-regulatory member organization set up by NASSCOM—imposes a fine of up to US$1 million for member companies that fail to secure data.

The Internet Society of China (ISC) can be considered an entity analogous to NASSCOM. However, it's been described as a quasi-governmental organization and hence mostly acts under the government's guidance (MacKinnon 2012a). Under China's current institutional structures, trade associations and special interest groups are less prevalent than in India or the West, and those that exist aren't in a position to function like they do in the West or in India.

Indeed, the best way for trade associations such as the ISC to promote their interests has been to contribute to the government's cyber-control goals. Unsurprisingly, the ISC has developed and implemented sophisticated cyber-control strategies rather than help protect Internet users' security and privacy. In 2001, the ISC asked Internet companies to sign a voluntary pledge that required them to not disseminate information that could threaten state security or social stability. In 2009, the ISC awarded China's largest search engine company, Baidu, and 19 other companies the China Internet Self-Discipline Award for fostering and supporting "harmonious and healthy Internet development" (McLaughlin 2005).

Due to a strong state and a weak civil society there is little pressure to improve security and performance and develop appropriate industry standards in major industries, such as BD, the cloud and healthcare. Western initiatives such as the AICPA's role in accelerating cloud adoption among its members (Chap. 5) and cloud vendors' pressures on policymakers for sensible regulations (e.g., Oracle, Cisco, SAP, Apple, Google, and Microsoft lobbied to streamline the EU's fragmented national data protection laws) illustrate this point. Because of China's unique institutional arrangements, such initiatives and pressures are conspicuously absent in the country.

7.4   China's CS Legislation and Strategy to Fight Cyber-Threats

One complaint about China's CS regulation is its piecemeal approach that does not adequately provide systematic and comprehensive personal data protection (Hunton and Williams LLP 2011). CS issues in China have been governed by many regulations, legislation, and guidelines as well as industry-specific regulations. Table 7.1 lists key legislations governing CS in China. At a press conference, the NPC Standing Committee's spokesperson stated that the State Council had previously issued nine regulations in this area. In addition, various ministries and departments have issued more than 10 administrative rules regulating the Internet. The critics also complained that the data privacy provisions are often ambiguous and vague, making interpretation and enforcement difficult. In this regard, an NPC Standing Committee's spokesperson stated that the regulations would be reviewed and amended in accordance with the 2012 Decision.

A key driver of CS regulations is the public's increased awareness of the right to privacy. The new regulations have thus emphasized the protection of personal data. The Employment Services and Management Regulations require employers to keep certain employee data confidential. Similarly, "Certain Regulations on Standardizing the Order of the Internet Information Service Market" (2012 Regulations) provided a legal definition of personal information (see Table 7.1) (Lockyer 2013). Likewise, the 2012 Online Data Protection Regulation bans the sale and distribution of personal information without the owner's consent (Bloomberg 2013). It also requires ISPs to ensure the security of personal data and prevent misuse as well as provides consumers the right to seek deletion of personal data posted without consent and to sue for violations.

7.4.1   Tackling External Threats

China has pursued an integrated political, military, and economic strategy to deal with external threats. It is believed to have an extensive network of hacking groups that consist of a mix of independent criminals, patriotic hackers who focus their attacks on political targets, the intelligence-oriented hackers inside the PLA as well as other groups that are believed to work with the government (Barboza and Markoff 2011). The PLA's doctrine of cyber-warfare is to "knock out the enemy's information infrastructure" and its doctrine of CS is to "go on the offensive to defend itself against attacks" (economist.com 2013). In 2011, the Defense Ministry confirmed the existence of semi-independent units known as blue units (cyberspace special forces) in all military regions. The blue units operate according to Mao Zedong's Guerrilla warfare doctrine. The doctrine involves avoiding direct confrontation with powerful enemies such as the U.S. Note that Mao mobilized large peasant militias to fight small but powerful enemies and won the civil war by

Table 7.1 Key legislation governing CS in China

Legislation	Explanation/Main provisions
Chinese Constitution (1982)	Article 40: organizations and individuals can't infringe on the right of citizens' privacy (Zhu 1997).
The Measures for Security Protection Administration of International Networking of Computer Information Networks (1997) (wipo.int 1997)	Article 4: International networking can't be used to endanger state security, divulge state secrets, infringe on national, social, and collective interests and the legitimate rights and interests of citizens and engage in criminal activities.
The Telecommunication Regulations (2000) (International Financial Law Review 2012)	This piece of legislation provides the legal basis for telecommunications-related data protection, which supports users' freedom to use telecommunications and the privacy of communications.
The Regulation on Internet Information Service, promulgated by the State Council on September 25, 2000 (The Library of Congress 2013)	Article 14: Requires ISPs to keep records of each user including time spent online, account, IP address or domain name, phone number, and so forth, for 60 days and provide that information to the government authorities when required.
Measures for the Administration of Internet Email Services (2006) (Lehman and Xu 2006)	Article 3: Guarantees citizens' privacy in using Internet and email services. However, public security and prosecutorial authorities can access private information for protecting state security or investigating crimes.
The Employment Services and Management Regulations, issued by the Labor and Social Security Ministry, now known as the Human Resources and Social Security Ministry, effective January 1, 2008 (Abate 2012)	An employer is required to keep certain data relating to employees confidential. The regulation also limits the usage of such data by the employer.
Criminal Law amended in 2009 (Zhu 1997) (www.whitecase.com)	Many amendments include definition of acts related to data collection and privacy that can be considered as criminal offenses.
Tort Liability Law, effective July 1, 2010 (Zhu 1997)	Establishes data protection violations as a tort claim that recognizes that a party whose right to privacy is infringed can claim for the losses, profits arising from the breach, and damages associated with emotional distress.
Certain Regulations on Standardizing the Order of the Internet Information Service Market, issued 15 March 2012 (Lockyer 2013)	The regulations contain the first legal definition of personal information.

(continued)

Table 7.1   (continued)

Legislation	Explanation/Main provisions
The Decision of the Standing Committee of the National People's Congress to Strengthen the Protection of Internet Data, December 28, 2012 (Kitaev 2013)	Article 7: Prohibits sending commercial advertisements to telephones and email accounts without user consent.
	Article 8: Citizens may request ISPs to delete information that leaks individual identity, invades personal privacy, or infringes on other rights and interests.
	Article 9: The victims of criminal acts related to personal data can file an accusation with government authorities or a lawsuit in a court.
	Article 10: Requires ISPs to cooperate with the government and provide technical support upon inquiry from the authorized government authorities.
Information Technology Security—Guideline for Personal Information Protection Within Information Systems for Public and Commercial Services, issued February 1, 2013 (Yan 2012)	It provides further details and establishes eight basic principles regarding the protection and handling of personal information.

establishing strongholds in rural areas. The guerrilla groups frequently attacked the enemy (Chen 2011).

As discussed in Chap. 4, foreign manufactured ICT products remain a key security concern for China. In a white paper examining the state of the mobile Internet in China published in the early 2013, the China Academy of Telecommunication Research (CATR) expressed a concern regarding China's "serious … dependence" on Google's Android operating system. The paper also noted the difficulty associated with developing a new operating system due to the dominance of Android and Apple's iOS and their well-developed ecosystem.

A researcher at International Data Corp noted that the technology gaps between Chinese and overseas vendors are large, especially in the high-end enterprise use market (China Daily 2014). In 2013, China imported US$232 billion of semiconductor products, which was higher than the amount spent on petroleum. Contributing to the heavy reliance on imports is an underdeveloped domestic chip and semiconductor industry.

China has started programs to increase the state's investment in the semiconductor industry. It is also taking measures to gain expertise from foreign chip companies (Mozur 2014a). Vice Premier Ma Kai heads a task force that has been charged with making the Chinese chip industry a global leader by 2030. The task force is reported to have US$170 billion in government support to spend by 2025 (mckinsey.com 2014). There are some encouraging and favorable indications of potential progress in the Chinese semiconductor industry. In October 2014, China's Dawning Information Industry (also known as Sugon) announced that it developed the country's first homegrown servers, which was built using 100 % domestically produced technologies. The local chip maker Loongson Technology developed processor for the server. Quoting a top computing researcher in the country, a report of Xinhua asserted that the new servers would strengthen CS of China's military, financial and energy sectors and make sure that they are no longer under foreign control. Dawning was founded using local government-supported research, which is known for developing some of China's fastest supercomputers (Kan 2014).

Some progress has also been made on military innovations. According to a 2012 report of China's defense ministry, the country's military-related patents increased annually by 35 % during the previous decade (Locker 2014). In October 2014, the *PLA Daily* noted: "We will strongly advance the domestic and independent building of programs, and strengthen the foundations of our information security" (reuters.com 2014b).

7.4.2 Defensive and Offensive Motives

Just like in the conventional security (Huth 1988), states can have both defensive and offensive motives in their approach to cyberspace engagements. Defensive motives may include a desire to deny a rival state the opportunity to increase its power, prevent the escalation of a possible conflict, increase stability, or maintain the state's influence at the international level (Betts 1999). Dai Qingli's response in a letter to the *Financial Times*, arguing that Chinese police helped 41 countries investigate cybercrimes between 2004 and 2010 is an example of defensive intent (Chap. 1).

Offensive motives are concerned with a desire to extend the state's political, ideological and economic interests (Zartman and Touval 1996). The Chinese have viewed the U.S. approach as "capitalistic hypocrisy" and have expressed unhappiness and dissatisfaction with what they consider as the system of rules that are designed by the U.S. as to what are "legal" and illegal spying activities (Sanger 2014). Likewise, quoting to Chinese Internet insiders, a *China Daily* article on June 5, 2013 noted: "China has been the target of serious cyber-attacks from the United States, but Beijing has never blamed Washington or the Pentagon because such accusations would be 'technically irresponsible'" (Li 2012). China's approach has shifted toward more offensive strategies following Snowden's revelation of the PRISM surveillance program.

The Chinese government's response to internal security threats can also be interpreted in terms of these motives and attitudes. China's approach to CS has defensive motives, such as influencing consumers to use the Internet in a way that minimizes the threat to the CCP. For instance, in 2002, Internet cafes were required to install software that prevented access to up to 500,000 banned sites with pornographic "subversive" contents (BBC News 2002). Another example is the Green Dam Youth Escort firewall software program was launched in 2008. The Chinese government had announced a plan to make it mandatory to have the Green

Dam installed on all new PCs in the country. The stated goal of the mandate was to protect children from violent and pornographic content.

Chinese regulators have also responded to internal threats with offensive motives such as means for retaliation. For instance, it has been reported that the Chinese government reportedly sends a virus to attack banned sites (Guillén and Suárez 2005). Other offensive motives include attempt to mandate compliance with the CCP's viewpoint. According to the Berkeley China Internet Project, the government hides websites containing words or phrases such as 'freedom', 'democracy', 'China-liberal', and 'falun' (Foushee 2006). Following Google's withdrawal from China in 2010, contents posted by Chinese bloggers and social network users who expressed sympathy for Google's situation were deleted and blocked (MacKinnon 2012b). Likewise, the Chinese government has been suspected to engage in man-in-the-middle attacks in order to spy on citizens who performed Google searches over encrypted connections. It was reported that Chinese authorities used a fake security certificate, which redirected the traffic to a server they controlled. The traffics were then decrypted and analyzed. In some cases, they were blocked (techdirt.com 2014).

7.4.3   Cyber-Control as a Key Element

J.S. Nye predicted that the diffusion of power in the Information Age is likely to be much more challenging for states than the rival states' rise (Nye 2011). This observation is especially pertinent to authoritarian regimes such as China. China's relatively stable internal security does not mean that there is no danger of internal security threats. Chinese policymakers have given a high priority to cyber-control measures—that is, administrative, legislative, and technical measures as well as procedures and resources to monitor, control, and regulate users' access to and activities in cyberspace. According to Reporters without Borders, "China was one of the first countries to realize it couldn't do without the Internet, and so it had to be brought under control" (McLaughlin 2005). As noted above, the body formed in February 2014 to coordinate CS is headed by President Xi Jinping. Analysts interpreted this as a signal of the importance he placed on cyber-control (Bradsher and Mozur 2014). It is also argued that North Korea is the only country that has stricter Internet censorship than China (Bandurski et al. 2014).

As the second column in Table 7.1 shows, the stringent ISP recordkeeping requirements and the requirement to provide technical support to government authorities and prosecutorial authorities' power to access private information under various regulations reflect a strong emphasis on cyber-control measures. The National People's Congress (NPC) succinctly stated the rationale of the 2012 "Decision of the Standing Committee of the National People's Congress to Strengthen the Protection of Internet Data" (2012 Decision): "to protect network information security, protect the lawful interests of citizens, legal persons and other organizations, [and] safeguard national security and social order" (Kitaev 2013).

From a cyber-control point of view, the last point—safeguarding national security and social order—needs elaboration. Various cyber-control measures' stated goals have been to control information that is harmful to state security or social stability. Regarding the various cyber-control measures, government-sponsored Xinhua News Agency noted that the 2012 Decision "will help, rather than harm, the country's netizens" (China.org.cn 2012).

7.4.4   Enforcement of CS Regulations

Hacking has been a criminal offence in China since 1997. China has also made enforcement of CS and data privacy laws a priority. Regarding the enforcement, an observation made by a scholar about two decades ago is still true: "the law [in - China] is marginalized and the legal system relegated to a lowly position in a spectrum of meditative mechanisms, while at the same time available for manipulation by powerful sectors within the state and the society at large" (Myers 1996).

One of the most striking features of China is that the government's tendency has been to enforce the laws promptly and strictly when the criminals target the state secrets or state assets. For instance, in the first publicized hacking trial in China in 1998, two hackers broke into the website of a state-owned bank and stole less than US$100,000. One of the perpetrators was executed (economist.com 2013).

Likewise, in 2010, in the first criminal sentence for illegal acquisition of personal information under the amended Criminal Law, a Zhuhai court gave the alleged criminals monetary fines and jail sentences. The case involved illegal acquisition and sale of information related to 14 high-ranking government officials' telephone calls, which was used in extortion schemes.

A distinguishing feature of China's CS regulations and enforcement mechanisms is the sophisticated programs and systems that closely monitor cyber-activities of activists whose viewpoints challenge the Chinese Communist Party or its mainstream policies. China reportedly has the world's largest cyber–police force, with tens of thousands of government agents monitoring and controlling cyberspace activities (Stevenson-Yang 2006). Some reportedly pretend to be dissidents and participate in chat rooms, speaking out against the government. Thus, many Internet users are afraid to engage in online conversations on sensitive topics such as democracy, Japan, and religion.

The selective enforcement of existing regulations and intensification of cyber-control measures have led to the arrest of several democracy organizers, human rights activists, members of the spiritual organization Falun Gong, scholars, and other dissidents for alleged involvement in cybercrimes. On the other hand, the Chinese government has devoted relatively few resources to enforce data privacy measures.

7.5 Effects on Foreign IT Services Providers

China's uncertain legal environment and vague regulations have presented a big dilemma for foreign IT service providers because compliance with the Chinese government's requirements might infuriate stakeholders in home countries. Yahoo and Google faced criticism in the U.S. for complying with Chinese regulations and government demands. As noted in Chap. 4, Yahoo and its Chinese subsidiary faced lawsuits in the U.S. for their actions in China. In August 2013, Yahoo closed its email service in China (Shu 2013).

The upshot is that many foreign IT service providers have chosen not to operate in China. Compounded by problems such as severe air pollution in China's cities, some businesses are also transferring employees to regional hubs that have more open and speedier Internet access. In November 2013, General Motors announced its plan to move its international headquarters from Shanghai to Singapore. Singapore's unrestricted internet access and less risk to IP were among the key motivators for the move (Harris 2013). This, along with China's strict filtering system, has resulted in low-quality or unavailability of services from China's global IT service providers.

A number of foreign CSPs have located their servers in neighboring economies, such as Singapore and Hong Kong, to serve mainland China. Google has avoided mainland China for datacenter location due to the country's strict filtering policies. In 2011, Google purchased land in Changhua County in Taiwan, the Kowloon region of Hong Kong, and the Jurong West section of Singapore to develop datacenters. Likewise, Digital Realty Trust, Equinix, and Yahoo have built major datacenters in Singapore and other Asian locations to serve consumers from China and other Asian economies.

In 2010, Google closed its Chinese servers. Google's chief legal officer, David Drummond noted: "we have evidence to suggest that a primary goal of the attackers was accessing the Gmail accounts of Chinese human-rights activists" (newyorker. com 2013). Following its withdrawal from China, Google's search site for China was hosted on servers in Hong Kong, and Chinese users were redirected to the Hong Kong site, google.com.hk. Note that as a Special Administrative Region of the People's Republic of China, Hong Kong has a high degree of autonomy, except in defense and foreign policy. In particular, Hong Kong's mini-constitution guarantees its own political system, a high degree of autonomy, and Western-style civil liberties such as freedom of speech until 2047. Although the Hong Kong government does not censor google.com.hk, the Chinese government filters search results for users accessing the site from mainland China. In the early 2014, Google started encrypting searches. It made difficult for the Chinese government to track users searching for the banned topics. The Chinese government responded by blocking all Google services in May 2014. Since then, Google products have been reported to be more and more inaccessible in China. It was reported that Google's services in and out of China experienced sudden drop in traffic in the last week of December 2014.

According to a 2013 study of the Internet traffic analyst, Hitwise Gmail's share in the Chinese e-mail market was less than 2 % (Ford 2014).

7.6   Effects on Chinese Internet Users and IT Services Providers

Putting foreign cloud providers' servers in neighboring countries—thus requiring foreign-originated traffic to pass through China's firewall—leads to long loading times for Chinese consumers. A study of content delivery network provider CDNetworks indicated that China's firewall leads to an increase in load time by 450 ms or more for an object hosted on a server outside China. For a typical website hosted in Asian cities such as Hong Kong, Singapore, or Tokyo, the firewall adds 10–15 s. The average time to load an object from a Hong Kong datacenter is 50 % longer than in China. Websites hosted in the U.S. take 20–40 s to load (Kim 2013). Thus, accessing services provided by foreign CSPs such as Google Docs and Dropbox, is difficult or impossible.

There is still a big gap between the performances of foreign and domestic IT companies. Chinese consumers are becoming increasingly dissatisfied with inferior domestic offerings such as the Chinese search engine Baidu (Cronan 2014). According to its spokesperson Baidu has focused on indexing Chinese language websites as most of its users are Chinese speakers. Thus it is not possible to conduct research using Baidu due primarily to its limitations for searches in English and other non-Chinese languages (Bradsher and Mozur 2014). Scholars expressed disappointment that they were deprived of the knowledge regarding the latest findings in areas such as climate change since they were unable to access services such as Google Scholar (Cronan 2014). Even more frustrating, if a CSP's contents are on a server that also hosts content objectionable to the Chinese government, they might be blocked (MacKinnon 2012a).

Cyber-control has been a challenging task to implement for the Chinese government. Consequently, many enforcement mechanisms related to censorship are delegated to trade associations such as the ISC or individual service providers. Chinese consumers and service providers have exhibited a tendency toward noncompliance with government regulations (Kshetri 2013). For example, a 2011 regulation required microbloggers to register using their real names. Sina, a Nasdaq-listed Chinese online media company warned that the requirement would negatively affect user activity and threaten its popular microblogging service, Sina Weibo. Even after the March 16, 2012 deadline, Sina Weibo continued let users who hadn't registered their real names use its services.

In November 2014, at a meeting organized by the Cyberspace Administration of China (CAC), 29 major Chinese websites including Tencent.com, Sohu.com, 163. com and Xinhua News Agency signed a letter of commitment to manage user-generated contents. This commitment was made in response to the government's call for a clean Internet and requires the websites to ensure that users use real identity to register and post. They are also required to ensure that users abide by the "seven bottom lines", namely, law and rules, socialist systems, national interests, citizen's legitimate rights, social public order, morality and authenticity of information. The websites are also required to make sure that users do not release 18 categories of information that violate "basic principles established by the Constitution" (e.g., information jeopardizing national security and leaking national secrets) (news.xinhuanet.com 2014).

7.7 Comparing China's and Other Major Economies' CS Approaches

Two major approaches have been used to characterize data privacy regulations: the EU model and the U.S. model. As noted in Chap. 6, the EU set a baseline common level of privacy to protect its citizens' rights, irrespective of data location. Likewise, as described in Chap. 5, the U.S., on the other hand, prefers to rely more on voluntary self-regulation in an attempt to encourage firms' marketing and innovation. However, it has sector-specific strict regulations for sensitive data.

Along with Singapore and Thailand, China has broadly followed the U.S. model, which lacks comprehensive, mandatory regulations (Berry and Reisman 2012). This approach differs from those in other Asian economies such as India, Japan, Malaysia, South Korea, and Taiwan, which have followed the EU directive model and adopted some forms of comprehensive data privacy laws that apply to all types of personal data.

Table 7.2 compares CS regulations in China, the EU, and the U.S. in terms of salient features, drivers, and effects on IT providers and users. China has stricter data privacy regulations for sensitive personal information compared to other economic sectors. In the banking sector, the People's Bank of China (PBOC) issued a "Notice to Urge Banking Financial Institutions to Protect Personal Financial Information" (Notice) in 2011, which became effective May 1, 2011. The Notice requires domestic as well as foreign banks and other financial institutions operating in the country to follow these rules when they collect, process and store personal financial information (PFI). Among other things, the Notice prohibits banks from storing, processing or analyzing any PFI collected in China outside the country. It also forbids providing PFI collected in China to an offshore entity (Cheah 2011). It was reported that the PBOC branch in Shanghai subsequently issued a clarification, according to which branches of foreign banks could send such data outside China with written consent from customers (Rose 2011). Likewise, In May 2014, the National Health and Family Planning Commission issued the Management Measures for Population Health Information. According to the new regulation, an entity "in charge of the collection, utilization, management, security and privacy protection of population health information" cannot "store population health information

Table 7.2 A comparison of China, EU and U.S. CS regulations

Dimension	China	The EU	The U.S.
Salient feature	Encourages purely economic use of ICTs and strict cyber-control measures.	Strict enforcement of privacy rights through legislation.	Preference to rely mostly on voluntary self-regulation but with sector-specific regulations for sensitive data.
Key driving factors	Aims to balance economic modernization and maintenance of unity and stability through political control	Primarily due to World War II–era fascists' and post-War communists' use of secret files as the basis for nefarious activities, Europeans are more fearful of the prospect of personal information abuse	Encourages marketing and innovations
Effects on IT providers	Policies lack the specificity required for accurate understanding and compliance. The 2012 Online Data Protection Regulation is broad and vague and favors guiding principles over law. Many provisions, such as department or agency to supervise and enforce, are unclear. No specific details are provided about the nature and amount of penalties (Bloomberg 2013). Lack of enforcement means that there's little legal recourse for data theft by employees or equipment loss during police inspections.	Requirement for compliance with strict regulations and the lack of economies of scale due to market fragmentation have imposed inefficiencies and acted as a barrier to incentive for the development and diffusion of cloud and other technologies. The EU Directive, which is stricter than US regulations, is likely to have more wide-ranging impact on all business types.	There is a fear among some foreign consumers and activists that U.S. CSPs are required to disclose data stored in clouds to the U.S. government without the data owner's consent or knowledge.
Effects on IT users	Unavailability of some services has been a concern. Some foreign firms have located their servers in neighboring countries, which has caused a severe negative impact on service quality.	Users enjoy a high level of privacy but due primarily to the lack of choice and quality of cloud services, consumers are slower to adopt the cloud.	There have been some concerns related to the government's monitoring and companies' misuse of citizens' information.

in overseas servers, [or] host or rent overseas servers". In addition, such an entity is required to "establish a tracing management system under which any user who creates, modifies and accesses population health information shall be subject to stringent real-name identity authentication and authorization control" (Ferris et al. 2014). Likewise, according the Criminal Law, it is a crime for employees of government institutions and organizations in financial, telecommunications, transportation, education, and medical sectors to unlawfully provide personal information to third parties (Zhu 1997).

Another important difference between China and the U.S. is that China lacks the self-regulatory component in data privacy laws, which can be considered as a result of its strong state and weak civil society. China's regulations on data transfer to foreign countries also differ from that of the U.S., which has no general prohibition against transferring data outside its borders. As noted earlier in Chap. 5, in the U.S. sensitive data, such as healthcare and financial information, is regulated, and companies dealing with such data are expected to protect personal information irrespective of location.

Some similarities can be found in Chinese and U.S. data privacy and security approaches, including sensitive national security–related information, despite significant differences in the two economies' approaches regarding this issue. As noted earlier, some European policymakers and privacy activists have drawn attention to the fact that the U.S. Patriot Act and the Foreign Intelligence Surveillance Amendment Act allow U.S. surveillance and spying agencies to access to EU citizens' data stored in U.S. companies' clouds (Rauf 2011). However, important differences need to be noted regarding the two countries' data privacy laws and regulations' clarity and enforcement. Whereas the U.S. approach is based on relatively stronger rule of law, China's CS regulations are characterized by vagueness and ambiguity.

In recent decades, China has emphasized economic growth and prosperity. Its goal in the cyberspace is to control without jeopardizing economic development. The government's cost/benefit calculus associated with cyber-control measures might change over time. If the perceived risks of state insecurity or social instability increase, the government might adopt stricter enforcement measures.

Among other key forces, the cloud is shaping China's CS policies and practices. China's experience indicates that cloud-related policies must have a meaningful purpose, and introducing regulations that cannot be enforced is counterproductive. However, as indicated by key foreign cloud players' withdrawal from the country and foreign cloud services' unavailability and poor performance, there is a difficult tradeoff in controlling the information in the cloud and encouraging economically productive use of the technology. At the same time, Western technology companies' government-centric activities in China have led to a consumer backlash and even legal sanctions in their home country. Thus, regulatory and policy issues on cyber-control that arise in the context of the cloud might have strong bearing on foreign technology firms' ability to operate in China. The security risks are especially high for multinational firms handling sensitive information.

Despite recent awareness and understanding of privacy among key actors in China, the level of data privacy awareness is much less developed, and sector-specific regulations and enforcement mechanisms are lacking. For instance, although regulatory and security concerns are major barriers for the healthcare industry's adoption of public clouds in the US and other countries, such barriers are of less concern in China.

7.8   Cyber Cold-War with the U.S.

Cyber cold war with the U.S. represents a key feature that distinguishes China's approach to CS from that of other developing countries. Cybercrime is arguably the fastest-growing problem faced by China–U.S. cooperation (Schafer 2006). Allegations and counterallegations have been widespread in the U.S.-China discourse on the governance of cyberspace and there has been too little cooperation and too much conflict in this area.

As an example, in September 2012, Huawei's corporate senior vice-president, and ZTE's senior vice-president for North America and Europe testified at the U.S. House committee about the allegation that the two companies operations had posed CS threats to the U.S. In an interview after the U.S. House committee hearing of September 2012, ZTE's senior vice-president for North America and Europe noted that "many Congress members still harbor a Cold War mentality and know little about China's development" (Tan and Chen 2012).

According to a previous U.S. counterintelligence chief, in the last decade, over 2000 companies, universities, and government agencies in the U.S. have experienced cyber-attacks originating from China (Riley 2012). China has responded to this accusation by blaming the U.S. for cyber-attacks facing it. A *China Daily* article on June 5, 2013 noted that "the cyber-attacks from the US [on China] have been as grave as the ones the US claims China has conducted" (Li 2012).

Edward Snowden's revelation of the U.S. PRISM surveillance program constituted an important turning point in the China-U.S. relations involving the cyberspace. Commenting on the U.S. intelligence agencies' alleged hacking of China's major mobile companies and universities, an editorial in China's state-run Xinhua News Agency noted: "These, along with previous allegations, are clearly troubling signs. They demonstrate that the United States, which has long been trying to play innocent as a victim of cyber-attacks, has turned out to be the biggest villain in our age" (Ming 2013).

Among the most recent, the U.S. government in May 2014 indicted five high-ranking members of the PLA for committing cybercrimes against U.S. companies. The Chinese government questioned evidence used in the indictment and in response, suspended its participation in a CS working group with the U.S. (Mozur 2014b). China blamed the U.S. for disrupted CS cooperation between the two countries.

In October 2014, a Chinese Foreign Ministry spokesperson expressed dissatisfaction regarding "the United States' unjustified fabrication of facts in an attempt to smear China's name" and demanded the U.S. to "cease this type of action" (Khan 2014). In the same month, China's state councilor overseeing foreign affairs, Yang Jiechi told the U.S. secretary of state, John Kerry that resuming CS cooperation between two countries would be difficult because of "mistaken US practices". He emphasized that the U.S. "should take positive action to create necessary conditions for bilateral cyber security dialogue and cooperation to resume" (theguardian.com).

China also announced that it will perform national security inspections for imported technology products. China's nationalist bloggers described the announced inspections as a "hard blow to anti-China forces" and suggested that U.S. companies such as Cisco, IBM and Microsoft would be negatively affected (Lam 2014). In July 2014, anti-monopoly investigators raided four Microsoft offices and allegedly copied large amounts of the company's data (Cronan 2014).

Analysts suggest that China's cyber-warfare capabilities need to be analyzed in light of its emergence as a regional power with robust anti-access/area denial (A2/AD) capabilities. Such capabilities can be used to destroy or disable enemy's military assets from afar by combining cyber weapons with ground attacks, anti-ship missiles, submarines and anti-satellite weapons (economist.com 2012)

7.9 Discussion and Concluding Remarks

CS is an important national priority in China. It has implemented major policy improvements in areas such as cyber-control, international economic relations, and data privacy to create a cloud-based economy. The trend of rapid cybercrime growth has also resulted in a significant increase in China's CS investments. The Chinese CS market is forecast to reach US$4.9 billion by 2015 (wantchinatimes.com 2014).

China's CS laws and regulations reflect the tension it faces between using modern ICTs to maintain unity and stability via cyber-control and using them to stimulate economic growth and productivity. Policies that lack specificity regarding the agencies enforcing the laws and penalties, the government's engagement in cyber-control, and the restriction of foreign firms' participation have hindered this sector's growth.

Although China has initiated new regulatory efforts to address emerging data privacy problems, a closer look reveals Chinese policymakers' preference for vagueness and ambiguity. Despite some enforcement activities, there is an enormous gap between laws on the books and the government's capability and willingness to enforce these laws. While some limited reforms have been made on the cyber-control front, significant barriers exist for individuals and businesses to enjoy the Internet's full potential.

China's CS regulations contrast sharply with major economies owing to internal and external pressures the Chinese government faces. Whereas the EU places high priority on protecting personal data and the U.S. emphasizes self-regulation by businesses, China's regulations focus on cyber-control measures. The Chinese government's measures to protect personal information abuse, on the other hand, too often remain pure lip service. This is due to the fact that defending against internal security threats has been a key issue for the CCP. Just like the Russian government, Chinese government thinks that foreign powers can be a source of internal security threats.

A lesson from experience in other areas, such as infringement of IPR, is that CS violations in China are likely to be more a problem of enforcement than the absence of laws. The ignorance of law enforcement officials is also likely to hamper the enforcement. The gap between the law on the books and the law in action will likely be substantial.

References

Abate, D. A. W. (2012). *Privacy issues under PRC employment law.* www.mayerbrown.com/publications/Privacy-Issues-under-PRC-Employment-Law-01-19-2012

apcss.org. (2001). *Report from the conference on: Domestic determinants of security: Security institutions and policy-making processes in the Asia-pacific region, january 10-11, 2001 Honolulu, Hawaii.* http://www.apcss.org/Publications/Report_DomesticDeterminantsOfSecurity.html

Bandurski, D., Goldkorn, J., Creemers, R., & Qiang, X. (2014). *Can China conquer the internet?: A ChinaFile conversation.* http://www.chinafile.com/conversation/can-china-conquer-internet

Barboza, D., & Markoff, J. (2011). *Power in numbers: China aims for high-tech primacy.* http://www.nytimes.com/2011/12/06/science/china-scrambles-for-high-tech-dominance.html?pagewanted=all&_r=0

BBC News. (2002). *Behind China's internet Red Firewall.* http://news.bbc.co.uk/2/hi/technology/2234154.stm

Berry, R., & Reisman, M. (2012). Policy challenges of cross-border cloud computing. *Journal of International Commerce and Economics, 4*(2), 1–38.

Betts, W. (1999). Third party mediation: An obstacle to peace in Nagorno Karabakh. *SAIS Review, 19*(2), 161–183.

Bloomberg. (2013). *China enacts online privacy framework to protect data, but not user anonymity.* www.bna.com/china-enacts-online-n17179871719

Bradsher, K., & Mozur, P. (2014). Web barriers imposed by China are hampering businesses. *International New York Times*, p. 14.

Cheah, G. G. (2011). *Protection of personal financial information in China.* http://www.nortonrosefulbright.com/knowledge/publications/56148/protection-of-personal-financial-information-in-china

Chen, S. (2011). *Code blue for China's red army.* www.scmp.com/article/975063/code-blue-chinas-red-army

China Daily. (2012). *Personal data protection.* http://www.chinadaily.com.cn/opinion/2012-04/06/content_14987674.htm

China Daily – US Edition. (2014). IT vendors in search of new business code, July 24.

China.org.cn. (2012). *Nothing to fear from new internet ID policy.* www.china.org.cn/china/2012-12/28/content_27542923.htm

Cronan, B. (2014). China tightens censorship on Google; *The Christian Science Monitor.*

de Kloet, J. (2002). Digitisation and its Asian discontents: The internet, politics and hacking in China and Indonesia. *First Monday, 7*(9). http://firstmonday.org/issues/issue7_9/kloet/index.html

Denning, D. E. (2000). *Acktivism: An emerging threat to diplomacy.* American Foreign Service Association. www.afsa.org/fsj/sept00/Denning.cfm

economist.com. (2012). *The dragon's new teeth.* http://www.economist.com/node/21552193

economist.com. (2013). *Masters of the cyber-universe.* http://www.economist.com/news/special-report/21574636-chinas-state-sponsored-hackers-are-ubiquitousand-totally-unabashed-masters

Ferris, R. J., Lacktman, N. M., & Tianran, T. R. (2014). *Realizing the potential of telemedicine in China, part 2: Data privacy and security Health Care Law Today Yan, Foley & Lardner LLP*. http://www.lexology.com/library/detail.aspx?g=c8c9aa69-4efd-4686-a524-f52b98d98fc8

Ford, P. (2014). *Are Google and Gmail really the enemy of China?, December 29*. http://www.csmonitor.com/World/Asia-Pacific/2014/1229/Are-Google-and-Gmail-really-the-enemy-of-China

Foushee, H. (2006). Gray area: The future of Chinese internet. *Harvard International Review, 8* (2), 28.

Guillén, M. F., & Suárez, S. L. (2005). Explaining the global digital divide: Economic, political and sociological drivers of cross-national internet use. *Social Forces, 84*(2), 681–708.

Harris, D. (2013). *GM is leaving Shanghai. Why did it go there in the first place?* http://www.chinalawblog.com/2013/11/gm-is-leaving-shanghai-why-did-it-go-there-in-the-first-place.html

Hunton & Williams LLP. (2011). *Update: Privacy and the protection of personal information in China*. www.huntonprivacyblog.com/2011/02/articles/update-privacy-and-the-protection-of-personal-information-in-china

Huth, P. K. (1988). Extended deterrence and the outbreak of war. *American Political Science Review, 82*(2), 423–443.

Hvistendahl, M. (2009). The China syndrome. *Popular Science, 274*(5), 60–65.

International Financial Law Review. (2012). *Data privacy in telecom area*. www.iflr.com/Article/3093906/Data-privacy-in-telecom-area.html

Kalathil, S. (2002). Community and communalism in the information age. *Brown Journal of World Affairs, 4*(1), 347–354.

Kan, M. (2014). *China develops its first homegrown server amid cybersecurity concerns*. http://www.pcworld.com/article/2838692/china-develops-its-first-homegrown-server-amid-cyberse curity-concerns.html

Khan, M. (2014). *China: US is fabricating cyber attack claims*. http://www.ibtimes.co.uk/china-us-fabricating-cyber-attack-claims-1469302

Kim, J. (2013). How to do online business with China. *TechWeek Europe*. www.techweekeurope.co.uk/comment/how-to-do-online-business-with-china-108291

Kitaev, E. G. (2013). *China adopts privacy legislation strengthening online personal data protection*. http://www.dataprivacymonitor.com/online-privacy/china-adopts-privacy-legisla tion-strengthening-online-personal-data-protection/

Kshetri, N. (2013). Cyber-victimization and cybersecurity in China. *Communications of the ACM, 56*(4), 35–37.

Lam, O. (2014). *China to perform security inspections for tech products*. http://advocacy.globalvoicesonline.org/2014/05/28/china-to-perform-security-inspections-for-tech-products/

Lehman, Lee, & Xu. (2006). *Measures for the administration of internet e-mail services 2006*. www.lehmanlaw.com/resource-centre/laws-and-regulations/information-technology/mea sures-for-the-administration-of-internet-e-mail-services-2006.html

Li, X. K. (2012). *China is victim of hacking attacks*. http://english.peopledaily.com.cn/90883/8271052.html

Locker, R. (2014). Pentagon on watch for disruptive technology worldwide, *USA TODAY*. http://www.usatoday.com/story/nation/2014/01/08/technology-watch-horizon-scanning-pentagon/4240487/

Lockyer, V. (2013). *New developments in data privacy in China*. www.orrick.com/Events-and-Publications/Pages/New-Developments-in-Data-Privacy-in-China.aspx

MacKinnon, R. (2012a). *Consent of the networked: The worldwide struggle for internet freedom*. New York: Basic Books, p. 35'

MacKinnon, R. (2012b). Inside China's censorship machine. *National Post*. http://fullcomment.nationalpost.com/2012/01/29/rebecca-mackinnon-inside-chinas-censorship-machine

mckinsey.com. (2014). *Semiconductors in China: Brave new world or same old story?* http://
   www.mckinsey.com/insights/high_tech_telecoms_internet/semiconductors_in_china_brave_
   new_world_or_same_old_story
McLaughlin, K. E. (2005). China's model for a censored internet. *Christian Science Monitor 97*
   (210), 1–10.
Ming, J. W. (2013). *Commentary: Washington owes world explanations over troubling spying
   accusations.* http://news.xinhuanet.com/english/indepth/2013-06/23/c_132478464.htm
Mozur, P. (2014a). *Using cash and pressure, China builds its chip industry.* http://www.nytimes.
   com/2014/10/27/technology/using-cash-and-pressure-china-builds-its-chip-industry.html
Mozur, P. (2014b). *China questions evidence used in U.S. cybercrimes indictment.* http://online.
   wsj.com/articles/chinas-defense-ministry-questions-evidence-used-by-u-s-to-indict-five-peoples-
   liberation-army-officers-for-cybercrimes-1401359575
Myers, W. H. (1996). The emerging threat of transnational organized crime from the east. *Crime,
   Law and Social Change, 24*(3), 181–222.
news.xinhuanet.com. (2014). *Chinese websites promise to tighten comments management.* http://
   news.xinhuanet.com/english/china/2014-11/06/c_127186596.htm
newsgd.com. (2005). Anti-Japan war online' game to hit the market. www.newsgd.com/Specials/
   60thanniversaryofwaragainstjapaneseaggression/anniversarynews/200509010026.htm
newyorker.com. (2013). *Network Insecurity.* http://www.newyorker.com/magazine/2013/05/20/
   network-insecurity
Nye, J. S., Jr. (2011). *The future of power.* New York: Public Affairs Press.
Ong, A. (1997). Chinese modernities: Narratives of nation and of capitalism. In D. Nonini &
   A. Ong (Eds.), *Underground empires: The cultural politics of modern Chinese transformation.*
   New York, NY: Routledge.
Rauf, D. S. (2011). *Patriot act clouds picture for tech.* http://tinyurl.com/dy4lhcc
reuters.com. (2014a). *Apple iPhone a danger to China national security: state media.* http://in.
   reuters.com/article/2014/07/11/us-apple-china-idINKBN0FG0S520140711
reuters.com. (2014b). *China military calls for stronger cybersecurity, domestic software: State
   media.*   http://www.reuters.com/article/2014/10/08/us-china-military-tech-
   idUSKCN0HX12F20141008
Riley, M. (2012). SEC push may yield new disclosures of company cyber attacks. *Bloomberg
   News.* www.businessweek.com/news/2012-01-10/sec-push-may-yieldnew-disclosures-of-com
   pany-cyberattacks.html
Rose, N. (2011). *Protection of personal financial information in China.* http://www.nortonrose.
   com/knowledge/publications/56148/protection-of-personal-financial-information-in-china
Russell, J. (2011). *China to develop $154m tech centre free of web restrictions.* http://
   asiancorrespondent.com/58249/china-to-develop-154m-tech-centre-free-of-web-restrictions/
Sanger, D. E. (2014). Fine line seen in U.S. spying on companies. *New York Times.* http://www.
   nytimes.com/2014/05/21/business/us-snooping-on-companies-cited-by-china.html?_r=0
Sautman, B. (2001). Peking man and the politics of paleoanthropological nationalism in China.
   The Journal of Asian Studies, 60(1), 95–124.
Schafer, S. (2006). *A Piracy culture. Beijing continues to defy US and European efforts to stop IP
   theft, Newsweek (International Edition).* http://www.msnbc.msn.com/id/10756810/site/
   newsweek/
Shu, C. (2013). *Yahoo shuts down its email service in China?* http://techcrunch.com/2013/08/18/
   yahoo-shuts-down-its-email-service-in-china/
Stevenson-Yang, A. (2006). China's online mobs: The new red guard? *Far Eastern Economic
   Review, 169*(8), 53–57.
Tan, Y. Z., & Chen, L. M. (2012). *Telecom giants hit back at allegations.* http://usa.chinadaily.
   com.cn/china/2012-10/09/content_15802157.htm
techdirt.com. (2014). *Are Apple, Google, Microsoft and Mozilla helping governments carry out
   man-in-the-middle attacks?* https://www.techdirt.com/articles/20141106/05305729062/are-

apple-google-microsoft-mozilla-helping-governments-carry-out-man-in-the-middle-attacks.
    shtml
The Library of Congress. (2013). *China: NPC decision on network information protection*. www.
    loc.gov/lawweb/servlet/lloc_news?disp3_l205403445_text
theguardian.com. UN. *China says US must change 'mistaken policies' before deal on cyber
    security*. http://www.theguardian.com/world/2014/oct/19/china-cyber-security-cooperation-
    problematic-mistaken-us-policies
Wan, W. (2014). *Chinese President Xi Jinping takes charge of new cyber effort*. http://www.
    washingtonpost.com/world/chinese-president-takes-charge-of-new-cyber-effort/2014/02/27/
    a4bffaac-9fc9-11e3-b8d8-94577ff66b28_story.html
wantchinatimes.com. (2014). *IT giants vie for China's information security market*. http://www.
    wantchinatimes.com/news-subclass-cnt.aspx?cid=1206&MainCatID=12&
    id=20140826000106
wipo.int. (1997). China: Measures for security protection administration of the international
    networking of computer information networks. www.wipo.int/wipolex/en/text.jsp?file_
    id=182465
xinhuanet.com. (2014). *Xi Jinping leads Internet security group*. http://news.xinhuanet.com/
    english/china/2014-02/27/c_133148273.htm
Yan, Z. (2012). *Personal data crimes set to be defined*. www.chinadaily.com.cn/china/2012-07/04/
    content_15546503.htm
Yao, Z. Z. (2014). *Role of emerging economies*. http://usa.chinadaily.com.cn/opinion/2014-07/14/
    content_17756717.htm
Zartman, I. W., & Touval, S. (1996). International mediation in the post-cold war era. In C. A.
    Chester, F. O. Hampson, & P. Aall (Eds.), *Managing global chaos: Sources of and responses to
    international conflict* (pp. 445–461). Washington, DC: United States Institute of Peace.
Zhang, X. X. (2012). *China to further safeguard cyber security*. http://english.peopledaily.com.cn/
    90882/7704949.html
Zhu, G. (1997). The right to privacy: An emerging right in Chinese law. *Statute Law Review, 18*
    (3), 208–214.

Chapter 8
Cybersecurity in India

8.1 Introduction

As a response to domestic and international pressures to build CS measures, in July 2013, the Government of India released the National Cyber Security Policy (NCSP). The NCSP outlines the basic policies and strategies "to build a secure and resilient cyberspace for citizens, businesses and government". It set forth 14 objectives that included enhancing the protection of critical infrastructure, and developing 500,000 skilled CS professionals in the next 5 years (timesofindia. indiatimes.com 2013). The development of public-private partnership (PPP) efforts towards enhancing the CS is a key component of the NCSP. Note that PPPs are especially well-suited and justified for areas that require diverse types of expertise and knowledge in order to address complex problems (Yu and Qu 2012). This condition fits squarely with CS.

From the standpoint of CS, two key features of the Indian economy should be noted. First, due to rapidly growing IT and business process management (IT&BPM) sector and various instances of data breaches in this sector, India is facing an unprecedented pressure to strengthen CS from foreign offshoring clients as well as Western governments (e.g., the U.S. and the U.K.). In 2011, the U.S. and India signed a Memorandum of Understanding (MoU) to promote CS-related cooperation and exchange information (Office of the Press Secretary 2011). In bilateral talks held between the two countries in April 2012, the U.S. emphasized on India's capacity building in CS and especially to detect and investigate cybercrimes. As India is a major offshoring destination for back offices as well as other high-value business functions, CS orientation of Indian businesses has been an issue of pressing concern to U.S. businesses.

Second, India's CS initiatives have been hampered by insufficient investment in CS and insufficient law enforcement capability. According to Gartner, Indian organizations spent US$882 million in 2013 in CS, which is expected to increase to US$953 million in 2014 and US$1.06 billion in 2015. Over half of the CS

© Springer International Publishing Switzerland 2016 145
N. Kshetri, *The Quest to Cyber Superiority*, DOI 10.1007/978-3-319-40554-4_8

spending goes to consulting, implementation, support and managed services (techtarget.in 2014). As a point of comparison, China's CS spending is much higher, which is estimated to amount US$4.9 billion by 2015 (Chap. 7). Citing a study by the Indian CERT, an *indiatimes.com* article reported that Indian organizations faced a shortage of about 400,000 trained CS professionals in 2013 (economictimes.indiatimes.com 2014).

8.2   External and Internal Cyber-Threats Facing India

8.2.1   External Threats

China and Pakistan are viewed as the biggest external cyber-threats confronting India. For instance, the targets of a sophisticated cyberespionage network tracked in 2010 by U.S.- and Canada-based researchers, which they referred as the Shadow network, included the Indian Ministry of Defense and the Office of the Dalai Lama (Information Warfare Monitor/Shadowserver Foundation 2010). The malware installed in the computers of the Dalai Lama's Office reportedly turned on the microphones and cameras, controlled keyboards, and downloaded emails (Simmons 2011). Wikileaks pointed to the Chinese government as the perpetrator behind the attacks (Kazan 2010). In the same vein, McAfee's investigation of targeted attacks involving remote access tools, which some analysts suspected as China-originated, had at least 72 victims including the Indian government (Economist 2011).

Chinese firms' activities in India are viewed with suspicion and there is a widespread fear that activities of some of them are against India's national security interest. It was reported that, Xiaomi Redmi Note, the cellphone model developed by the Chinese firm Xiaomi, secretly sent Indian users' data to a China-based server (gadgets.ndtv.com 2014). In October 2014, due to CS concerns, India warned the military not to use devices manufactured by Xiaomi. In response, Xiaomi announced plans to open a data canter in India (bbc.com 2014).

Likewise, tests conducted in 2013 by the Guardian Project, which is a group of software developers, indicated that WeChat data generated in India was sent to Shanghai (Sternstein 2014). In 2001, India's Research and Analysis Wing (RAW) suggested that Chinese engineers working for Huawei in Bangalore (India) were involved in the development of state-of-the-art telephone surveillance equipment for the former Taliban regime in Afghanistan (Iype and Prema 2002). RAW also suggested that telecommunications software developed at Huawei's Bangalore R&D center allegedly ended up in the hands of the Pakistan government through Huawei's Afghan operations (Liu 2006).

While India has regarded China as the main source of cyber-threat, cyber-attacks from other countries have also victimized India. Especially, India–Pakistan cyberwars have been going on for some time. A hacker who defaced the state

Criminal Investigation Department's (CID) website in 2011 was traced to Pakistan (indiatimes.com 2011). In 1998, Indian army's website on Kashmir was "hijacked" by supporters of Pakistan's claim to the disputed territory. In the same year, hackers from the U.S., the U.K., the Netherlands, and New Zealand attacked India's Bhabha Atomic Research Center's website (Denning 2000).

8.2.2   Internal Threats

Some of the most serious internal cyber-threats to the Indian economy relate to insider breaches in the IT&BPM sector. The British Tabloid, *Sun* reported that an Indian call center employee sold confidential information of 1000 bank accounts to the Tabloid's undercover reporter. In another case, call center workers at the outsourcing services provider, Mphasis, transferred more than US$350,000 from four Citibank customers' accounts to their personal accounts. In major Indian cities, there are reportedly "data brokers," who obtain data illegally from people working in offshoring companies. In a case reported in March 2012, two "consultants", who claimed to be employed in Indian offshoring firms, met undercover reporters of *The Sunday Times*. They reportedly came with a laptop full of data and bragged that they had 45 different sets of personal information on 500,000 U.K. consumers. The information included credit card holders' names, addresses, phone numbers, start and expiry dates and security verification codes. Data for sale also included information about mortgages, loans, insurance, phone contracts and television subscriptions.

8.3   The Constraints Facing India in Dealing with Cyber-Threats

Most developing country governments are characterized by weak public administration, inadequate technical competence and political leadership in the implementation of economic and social policies (Pughm 1999). More importantly, the way the government is positioned (its subject position) does not allow it to spend state resources to support a newly developing area at the cost of competing sectors. If policymakers allocate disproportionately more resources to develop modern sectors such as IT&BPM, they may face stiff opposition from the mass of population that depends on the traditional economy. For instance, in India's Andhra Pradesh state in the early 2000s, political opponents attacked the then Chief Minister Chandrababu Naidu's decision to raise rice and electricity prices by cutting subsidies as anti-people. They also labelled his promotion of IT&BPM sectors and foreign capital as elitist. Naidu was voted out of the office in the 2004 election. Thus, for the majority of the Indian population, CS is irrelevant.

India is finding it difficult to put CS regulations into practice due to technology and human resources constraints. For instance, in 2011, India's Central Bank, the Reserve Bank of India (RBI) introduced a set of recommendations, which include the formation of separate information security groups within banks and maintenance of adequate CS resources based on their size and scope of operation. In order to enforce the RBI guidelines, however, India requires a large number of CS auditors to evaluate the adequacy of controls in the management of project and business processes and validate banks' CS practices (Bradbury 2013). An estimate suggested that India had only 60 CS auditors in 2013 (Doval 2013).

Likewise, in July 2014, the IT minister informed the lower house, Lok Sabha that all central and state/Union Territory government agencies had been asked to conduct CS auditing of their IT infrastructures, websites and applications. State governments were asked to build adequate technical capacity including infrastructure, cyber police stations and trained manpower (Doval 2013). Most Indian government agencies' websites are hosted by the National Informatics Centre (NIC), which was established by the government to promote IT culture among government organizations. It is argued that NIC-hosted websites are vulnerable to cyber-attacks due to a shortage of manpower. NIC outsources security audit works due to the lack of manpower.

A low degree of trust in different levels of state power and government agencies has been a major barrier in addressing CS problems. A survey to measure IT executives' confidence on the ability of their respective countries' authorities to prevent and deter potential cyber-attacks "No confidence" votes were highest for India (together with Brazil and Mexico). Moreover the confidence on the government deteriorated compared to the 2009 level (McAfee 2011). There is also a dramatically low level of trust in law enforcement agencies. For instance, a survey conducted by a research firm indicated that while most BPO firms in Gurgaon, had been cybercrime victims, about 70 % did not report to the police. Most organizations expressed doubt about competence, professionalism and integrity of the police in handling cybercrime cases. According to an *indiatimes.com* article published on November 6, 2011, about 50 % of the respondents not reporting thought that the cases were not dealt with professionally and 30 % noted that they had "no faith" in Gurgaon police. Cybercrime victims have also complained that the police follow a long and inefficient process to build a case. As a result, there is low reporting rate of cybercrimes. According to a *Hindustan Times* article of October 22, 2006, about 10 % of cybercrimes are reported. Of those reported about 2 % are registered. The conviction rate is estimated at 2 %. One reason behind the low rate of registration of cybercrime cases concerns the barriers, hurdles and hassles that confront the victims. There are reports that the police do not support the victims who want to file a cybercrime case and show unwillingness to investigate such crimes (Narayan 2010).

The Indian government severely lacks technology and human resources to develop and enforce CS-related regulations, standards, and guidelines. For instance, in 2011, the police cybercrime cell of the capital city, Delhi had only two inspectors. In 2012, the Delhi High Court criticized the lack of functionality of the Delhi

Police website, which according to the court was "completely useless ... obsolete and does not serve any purpose". Likewise, according to a Hindustan Times article of October 22, 2006, in 2004, of the 4400 police officers in Mumbai city, only five worked in the cybercrime division. The conviction rate in cybercrime cases was estimated at 2 %. As of 2006, no one charged for data fraud was convicted. As of August 2009, only four people were convicted for cybercrimes and until 2010, there was no cybercrime-related conviction in Bangalore, the country's biggest offshoring hub. The total number of convicted cases by 2010 was estimated at less than 10^3. According to an indiatimes.com article of February 16, 2013, 1630 people were arrested for cybercrimes in 2011, of whom only seven were convicted. Quoting a law enforcement officer, a *rediff.com* article of December 11, 2012 attributed the low conviction rates to the lack of technical skills and knowledge of the police stations and the lack of training to collect evidence. For instance, it was reported that when a police officer was asked to seize a hacker's computer, he brought the monitor. In another case, the police seized the CD-ROM drive from a hacker's computer instead of the hard disk.

   The state's weak regulatory role has negatively impacted key ingredients of CS. For instance, one estimate suggested that about 20 % of resumes submitted for IT&BPM positions in India are fake. The maximum risk faced by an individual in faking a resume is termination from employment. Due to India's s highly inefficient legal system, fraudsters are rarely caught and punished. The rule of law is weakly developed and often ignored with impunity. Getting an outsourcing job on the basis of a fake resume in general represents a high reward, low-risk activity because such jobs are better-paid compared to those in other economic sectors (Rai 2012).

8.4   The Private Sector's Role and the Conditions for PPP: The Case of IT&BPM Sector

8.4.1   The Establishment of the NASSCOM and the Data Security Council of India (DSCI)

As a result of the weak rule of law, India's IT&BPM sector is managing the CS risks through industry self-regulation. A highly visible private sector actor is the NASSCOM, which was established in 1988 as a not-for-profit organization funded by the industry to contribute to the software industry's development.

   As of the mid-2014, NASSCOM had over 1500 members compared to 650 members of the DSCI. While any company operating in the IT&BPM sector in India may have some incentive to join NASSCOM, the DSCI membership is especially important for companies for which CS is a key priority. NASSCOM membership fee varies from about US$450 to US$100,000 depending on the size of a member organization. Many of the NASSCOM's members are also global firms from the U.S. Europe, Japan, China and other countries. The NASSCOM thus has a fairly strong level of expertise and financial resources in order to take various CS measures.

Due primarily to the increase in data incidents, data security and privacy issues are becoming increasingly important for the success and vitality of the Indian IT&BPM sector. Realizing the importance of an organization with an exclusive focus on data protection, the NASSCOM established the DSCI in 2008, which is a self-regulatory member organization. A primary component of the DSCI's mission is to create trustworthiness of Indian companies as global outsourcing service providers. Its focus on CS is explained in the vision statement: "Harness data protection as a lever for economic development of India through global integration of practices and standards conforming to various legal regimes". The DSCI took over most of the CS-related activities performed by the NASSCOM.

The DSCI monitors member companies to ensure they adhere to CS standards. For instance, the DSCI increases CS compliance of its members by monitoring their security practices and providing training and education. It requires member companies to self-police and provide additional layers of security. The maximum fine for companies that fail to secure data is up to US$1 million. Non-compliant companies may also lose memberships in NASSCOM and DSCI.

8.4.2 The Context for PPP in the IT&BPM Sector

It is important to understand the enabling and constraining conditions that influence the success of PPP projects. Among the most important is the conduciveness of institutional environment to PPP. A government that is friendly to the private sector and willing to involve players in this sector in key national economic policies and interested to see this sector flourish is likely to be supportive of PPP initiatives. Broadly speaking these conditions exist in the IT&BPM sector in India, which has facilitated CS-related PPP in the country.

Prior research suggests that differences in the natures of strengths, expertise, and experience of the public and private sectors may lead to complementary roles they can play in meeting the developmental and social needs (Linder 1999). A unique strength of the state is that it is the most important institutional actor due to its ability to impose harsh sanctions and penalties to the violators of laws and regulations. Trade associations such as NASSCOM, on the other hand, may have a higher level of technical expertise and resources and do not face some of the constraints that limit the state's ability to monitor and control cybercrime activities.

Private and public sectors engaged in PPPs often have different objectives, agendas and interests (Posner 2002). For example, one of the goals of the public sector is to employ private sector's capital and technology and share risks with the latter in order to provide the delivery of public services or goods. On the other hand, by winning the support of the public sector, the private sector can increase profitability.

The Indian government and the private sector actors have partly overlapping motivation and objectives in strengthening CS. Since the IT&BPM sector plays a strategic role in the national economy the government is interested in promoting the development of this sector.

The NASSCOM partnered with the Ministry of Information Technology to draft data protection and data privacy laws to respond to privacy concerns of offshore clients. The goal is to bring Indian data protection laws to the same level as European and U.S. standards. In 2011, the DSCI announced a plan to set up a cloud security advisory group that would develop a policy framework. The group would also advise the government on cloud security and privacy issues.

8.4.3   The State's Weak Regulatory and Enforcement Mechanisms

One way to analyze the importance of the private sector is to consider their roles in addressing the regulatory vacuum in new sector such as CS. Note that compared to established industrial sectors, in nascent and formative sectors such as IT&BPM, there is no developed network of regulatory agencies (Powell 1993). There are a number of barriers and challenges in India to perform the functions of the regulatory state. The states have faced budget problems and failed to comply with federal directives to hire judges and upgrade legal infrastructures and court facilities. Factors such as ineffective national legal systems, ambiguous laws-on-the-books, lack of resources or the state's unwillingness to allocate them often severely hinder the ability of the state in controlling criminal activities. These observations are especially relevant for new types of crimes such as cybercrimes. As noted earlier, the greatest barrier to CS in India centers on the unavailability and ineffectiveness of law enforcement resources due primarily to the lack of and unwillingness to invest in such resources.

A major factor behind the low conviction rate concerns the law enforcement community's technological illiteracy and low level of cybercrime awareness. In one way, there is the development of a vicious circle: law enforcement agencies lack the skills, orientation and capability to address cybercrime related offenses, there are low cybercrime reporting rates because of the victims' lack of confidence in law enforcement agencies, and cybercriminals become more resourceful and powerful because their offenses are not reported and law enforcement agencies lack motivation or justification to improve their skills.

Many of the NASSCOM's and the DSCI's responses are the results of a hollow state and the thin institutions that are highly ineffective in dealing with CS challenges facing India. For instance, India lacks standard identifiers like the U.S. SSN making it difficult to check potential employees' backgrounds. It was reported that it cost up to US$1000 per employee to check backgrounds thoroughly. In response to the lack of such databases, in 2005, the NASSCOM announced a plan to launch a pilot employee-screening program called "Fortress India", which would allow employers to screen out potential workers who have criminal records. Subsequently it was developed into the National Skill Registry (NSR), which allows employers to perform background checks on existing or prospective employees. It is a voluntary registry for call center employees. While the NSR is incomplete since it does not include the profiles of most potential job seekers, it is at least an effort in the right direction.

8.4.4   The Role of a Participatory State

The state's willingness to work with the private sector is critical for the success of PPP. This can be explained by introducing the concept of a participatory state, which captures the extent to which policies and institutions represent the wishes of the members of society. In such a state, in order to protect their independence and autonomy, businesses may participate in the national policy making and work closely with state agencies. India's PPP initiatives in the area of CS are largely a product of a participatory state. The economic liberalization undertaken since 1991 has been a major driving force behind the growth and increased importance of groups such as trade associations. There has been a shift from a state-dominated economic policy framework towards a decentralized one. Religious, social, economic and political associations have offered a viable set of examples encouraging the development of many new trade and professional associations. A strong mutual interdependence between the state and the private sector, particularly organized business groups, has developed quickly. The liberalization thus resulted in more room for associations to flourish and to have a strong voice and increased their participation in national policy development and planning processes (Frankel 2006).

The Indian government's relationship with the private sector has involved a high level of trust and partnership in CS-related matters. As early as in 2000, the NASSCOM established a CyberCop Committee to provide CS services to the government and the private sector. In 2006, the NASSCOM drafted plans for new legal measures to safeguard IP and prevent data theft.

The government has made efforts to create a favorable climate for a higher participatory involvement in CS. For instance, a Joint Working Group (JWG) on CS was established with representatives from government agencies and the private sector, which was mandated to come up with recommendations for consideration by the government on PPP in capacity building and policy making. The JWG released its report "Engagement with Private Sector on Cyber Security" in October 2012. The NASSCOM expressed satisfaction that many of the recommendations of the JWG report as well as that of a NASSCOM-DSCI report titled, "Securing Our Cyber Frontiers" released in April 2012, were incorporated in the NCSP. For instance, both the JWG report and the NASSCOM-DSCI report had placed high level of emphasis on the formulation of PPP to address CS issues, which is also a key element of the NCSP (Jain 2013).

As a further sign of an improving climate for participatory involvement of the private sector, in October 2012, India's National Security Advisor announced a plan to establish a permanent working group on CS with representatives from the government and the private sector. The working group would implement the country's cyber-defense framework. The NSA advisor noted that this would mark the first time that the Indian government allowed the participation of the private sector in national security matters.

8.5 Responses to External Threats

India has encountered and grappled with external cyber-threats. Since 2005, India started focusing attention on cyber-warfare due primarily to a growing concern over the cyber-threats from Pakistan and China (Pandit 2005).

Like many countries, India has imposed several protectionist measures in order to protect against foreign cyber-threats. As noted earlier, India is among the countries actively discussing data localization laws. The RBI guidelines prohibit storing customer data outside India, which limits cloud adoption by financial services company (Aggarwal 2014). In February 2012 India's Ministry of Communications and Information Technology released a notification, which outlined preferential market access policy for domestically manufactured electronic goods. CS is the main rationale for the Policy, which is applicable to procurement of telecommunications products by government ministries and departments (Das 2014).

Because of India's suspicion of Huawei's ties with China's intelligence apparatus and military and the fear that it conducted electronic eavesdropping operations for the Chinese Embassy in India, Indian Telecommunications Ministry blocked the company's application for a license to bid as an equipment supplier for Indian telecom projects run by state-owned service providers (Simons 2006).

Indian policymakers know full well that the country lacks indigenous technology and patents related to CS. CS systems of Indian government organizations including that of the Prime Minister's Office are believed to the weakest among the G20 nations and below global benchmarks. A major problem is the lack of a domestic company that can offer a CS system to prevent foreign espionage activities (Bhattacharjee 2014). Facing this reality, the Indian government announced the possibility of providing financial assistance to Indian firms for acquiring foreign firms with high-end CS technology. The Ministry of External Affairs would explore possible targets worldwide through Indian embassies and missions (Thomas 2012). The fact that Indian government agencies have been under cyber-attacks, suspected from foreign governments, has provided a major motivation for this move. The Indian company which owns the technology gained through the acquisitions is required to give the government agencies access to the IPR for their use.

8.6 Discussion and Concluding Remarks

Some have rightly labeled India's CS policy as "incomplete" and "all words and no action" (Desai 2013) due to a lack of national CS action plan document or any guidelines regarding how the policy will be implemented. For instance, there is no clear action plan as to how the various goals proposed by the NCSP are going to be achieved. Overall, the NCSP lacks details of tangible actions and specific guidance, direction and procedures in order to achieve the vision of a secure cyberspace. The director of Israel's Military and Strategic Affairs Program and director of the cyber-warfare program at the Tel Aviv University's Institute for National Security Studies (INSS) noted: "India has published its strategy.., but it is far away from what I call strategy ... It does not have the substance ... (and is) a very generic, high-level paper" (Alawadhi 2014).

India's CS measures largely reflect its response to perceived external CS threats (mainly from China and Pakistan) as well as external pressures from the clients of the IT&BPM sector to strengthen CS. Thanks to pressures from Western clients, unbelievable as it may sound, most Indian firms in the IT&BPM sector are reported to have the same CS levels as Western firms. Commenting on CS measures in the Indian IT&BPM sector, a report of the UK's Banking Code Standards Board (BCSB) noted: "Customer data is subject to the same level of security as in the UK. High risk and more complex processes are subject to higher levels of scrutiny than similar activities onshore" (Rao 2006). Citing the findings of the BCSB and Forrester Research, the NASSCOM's then president, Karnik, asserted that security standards in Indian call centers were among the world's best and there were more CS breaches in the U.K. and the U.S. in 2005 than in India (AFX News 2006). The NASSCOM initiated its crime fighting efforts in response to the jolts or trigger events in the Indian IT&BPM sector that acted as catalysts to strengthen CS measures.

India has benefitted greatly from the NASSCOM's and the DSCI's expertise in the interpretation, implementation and application of the CS principles, and their role as a repository of experience and source of best practices and cutting-edge knowledge. They have been exemplary self-regulatory bodies, which have played key roles in strengthening CS orientation of the IT&BPM sector and have been a driving force in affecting India's CS profile. In sum, while the government lacks resources, expertise and legitimacy to develop new template, monitor the behaviors of industries and enforce laws, trade associations' influences are likely to be more readily apparent. With well-focused priorities, trade associations are likely to be better, more effective and more efficient institutions. While sectoral business organizations such as trade associations are generally numerous and exist in almost every country their level of development and influence on national policy making and implementation vary greatly. The NASSCOM is probably among the most influential and effective trade associations, which has been successful in strategi-cally solving collective CS problems of organizations in the Indian IT&BPM sector. Inter-firm linkages such as trade associations in emerging economies can establish moral legitimacy of the industry in Western economies. For instance, developed world-based offshoring clients may rely on trade associations such as the NASSCOM than on the weak, ineffective state.

A PPP is the distinguishing mark of India's CS landscape, which is an appropriate institutional means to deal with underdeveloped regulative institutions. The NASSCOM and the DSCI have played an important role in the PPP initiatives. They have worked with the government and law enforcement agencies in the formulation and enforcement of CS-related legislation. While the government has expressed a high degree of willingness to involve in the PPP, the resource constraint constitutes a significant barrier to the effective enforcement of the legislation. India's experience thus shows that in a state characterized by weak regulatory and monitoring capability, trade associations may fill the vacuum. Nonetheless, there are many things critical in strengthening CS of the IT&BPM sector that are beyond the NASSCOM's control. India's experience provides novel and unique insights regarding the role of PPP in CS.

While the DSCI's measures in strengthening data protection in the IT&BPM sector have been largely successful and can serve as a model for other developing economies, the effect is not noticed outside this sector.

Whereas firms in the IT&BPM sector have tools and procedures in place to provide strong CS, the economy as a whole is characterized by an extremely weak CS level against cyber-attacks. For instance, India experienced a high Stuxnet infiltration rate but it exhibited comparatively low implementation of counter-Stuxnet measures (McAfee 2011). The country is thus characterized by a high degree of intersectoral heterogeneity in CS performance. That is, the IT&BPM sector has been an enclave economy separated from the rest of the economy.

While the DSCI's codes of behavior are irrelevant outside the IT&BPM sector, training and education to law enforcement personnel could be one of the key mechanisms to strengthen the national CS profile. One reason behind the extremely low cybercrime conviction rate could be that the training programs provided by the DSCI often are insufficient to develop law enforcement officers' measurable competence in cybercrime investigation. A majority of the initiatives are special lectures or 3–5 day programs. More comprehensive training programs will allow them to master cybercrime investigation techniques, and feel confident about their ability to deal with cybercrimes. While most of the current programs mainly focus on police officers, the DSCI and the government need to place more emphasis on educating prosecutors, judges and lawyers using practical and layman's language.

References

AFX News. (2006). India could process 30 pct of US bank transactions by 2010 – report, September 27. http://www.finanznachrichten.de/nachrichten-2006-09/7050839-india-could-process-30-pct-of-us-bank-transactions-by-2010-report-020.htm

Aggarwal, V. (2014). *Microsoft may become first MNC to set up cloud data centre in India.* http://articles.economictimes.indiatimes.com/2014-08-06/news/52514307_1_cloud-services-data-centre-cloud-adoption

Alawadhi, N. (2014). *Cyber security policy must be practical: Experts.* http://articles. economictimes.indiatimes.com/2014-10-22/news/55318902_1_cybersecurity-digital-india-national-cyber-security-policy

bbc.com. (2014). *Xiaomi to open India data centre to allay privacy fears.* http://www.bbc.com/news/technology-29786324

Bhattacharjee, S. (2014). *In the fight against black money, cyber security remains a weak link.* http://indianexpress.com/article/business/business-others/in-the-fight-against-black-money-cyber-security-remains-a-weak-link/#sthash.HimI9Nxs.dpuf

Bradbury, D. (2013). *India's cybersecurity challenge.* http://www.infosecurity-magazine.com/view/34549/indias-cybersecurity-challenge/

Das, D. (2014). *PMA policy and COAI recommendations.* http://cis-india.org/internet-governance/blog/pma-policy-and-coai-recommendations

Denning, D. E. (2000). *Hacktivism: An emerging threat to diplomacy.* American Foreign Service Association. www.afsa.org/fsj/sept00/Denning.cfm

Desai, V. V. (2013). *Is India's cyber policy all words and no action?* http://searchsecurity.techtarget.in/news/2240207148/Is-Indias-cyber-policy-all-words-and-no-action

Doval, P. (2013). *Govt orders security audit of IT infrastructure.* http://timesofindia.indiatimes.com/tech/tech-news/Govt-orders-security-audit-of-IT-infrastructure/articleshow/38398644.cms

economictimes.indiatimes.com. (2014). *Shortage of over a million cyber security experts globally.* http://articles.economictimes.indiatimes.com/2014-01-20/news/46374805_1_cyber-security-web-hosting-attack-surface

Economist. (2011). Black hats, grey hairs, 399(8745):49–50, 2.

Frankel. R. (2006). *Associations in China and India: An overview.* European Society of Association Executives, http://www.esae.org/articles/2006_07_004.pdf

gadgets.ndtv.com. (2014). *Xiaomi redmi 1s and redmi note to launch soon in India; prices revealed.* http://gadgets.ndtv.com/mobiles/news/xiaomi-launches-redmi-1s-and-redmi-note-in-india-1-558833

indiatimes.com. (2011). *Kolkata top cop's mail Id hacked.* Retrieved from http://timesofindia.indiatimes.com/city/kolkata/Kolkata-top-cops-mail-id-hacked/articleshow/10562881.cms

Information Warfare Monitor/Shadowserver Foundation. (2010). Shadows in the Cloud: Investigating Cyber Espionage 2.0, Joint Report: Information Warfare Monitor Shadowserver Foundation, JR03-2010, April 6. www.utoronto.ca/mcis/pdfshadows-in-the-cloud-web.pdf

Iype, G., & Prema, R. (2002). RAW wants 95 Chinese software engineers expelled, *India Abroad,* August 23, (47), A20.

Jain, R. (2013). *Welcoming the National Cyber Security Policy (NCSP).* http://blogs.nasscom.in/welcoming-the-national-cyber-security-policy-ncsp/

Kazan, C. (2010). *China hacked Google—and the Dalai Lama.* http://www.dailygalaxy.com/my_weblog/2010/11/china-hacked-googleand-the-dalai-lama.html

Linder, S. H. (1999). Coming to terms with the public–private partnership: A grammar of multiple meanings. *American Behavioral Scientist, 43*(1), 35–51.

Liu, M. (2006). High-tech hunger; The goal: Make China a technology powerhouse--critics say by any means necessary. Inside Beijing's '863 program, *Newsweek International Edition.*

McAfee. (2011). *In the dark: Crucial industries confront cyberattacks.*

Narayan, V. (2010). *Cyber criminals hit Esc key for 10 yrs.* http://timesofindia.indiatimes.com/city/mumbai/Cyber-criminals-hit-Esc-key-for-10-yrs/articleshow/6587847.cms

Office of the Press Secretary. (2011). *United States and India Sign Cybersecurity Agreement.* http://www.dhs.gov/news/2011/07/19/united-states-and-india-sign-cybersecurity-agreement

Pandit, R. (2005). Army gearing up for cyber warfare, *Times of India,* 7 July.

Posner, P. L. (2002). Accountability challenges of third-party government. In L. M. Salamon (Ed.), *The tools of government: A guide to the new governance* (pp. 523–551). New York: Oxford University Press.

Powell, W. W. (1993). *The social construction of an organizational field: The case of biotechnology*. Paper presented at the Warwick–Venice Workshop on perspectives on strategic change, University of Warwick.

Pughm, C. (1999). Getting good government: Capacity building in the public sectors of developing countries. *Urban Studies, 36*(2), 400–402.

Rai, S. (2012). *How bogus resumes raise questions about Indian outsourcing skills.* http://www.techrepublic.com/blog/cio-insights/how-bogus-resumes-raise-questions-about-indian-outsourcing-skills/

Rao, H. S. (2006). *Outsourcing thriving in Britain despite India bashing.* http://www.rediff.com/money/2006/oct/07bpo.htm

Simmons, B. A. (2011). International studies in the global information age. *International Studies Quarterly, 55*(3), 589–599.

Simons, C. (2006). The Huawei Way; The telecom giant is either a security menace or a real comer--or it could be a house of cards. Or all of the above, *Newsweek International Edition*.

Sternstein, A. (2014). *Should Feds be afraid of a popular Chinese chat app?* http://www.nextgov.com/cybersecurity/2014/10/should-feds-be-afraid-popular-chinese-chat-app/95696/?oref=ng-relatedstories

techtarget.in. (2014). *Indian businesses wake up to IT security risks.* http://searchsecurity.techtarget.in/news/2240225781/Indian-businesses-wake-up-to-IT-security-risks-consumers-still-in-the-dark

Thomas, T. K. (2012). *Govt will help fund buys of foreign firms with high-end cyber security tech.* http://www.thehindubusinessline.com/industry-and-economy/info-tech/article3273658.ece?homepage=true&ref=wl_home

timesofindia.indiatimes.com. (2013). *Government releases National Cyber Security Policy 2013.* http://timesofindia.indiatimes.com/tech/it-services/Government-releases-National-Cyber-Security-Policy-2013/articleshow/20874965.cms

Yu, J. X., & Qu, Z. Y. (2012). PPPs: Inter-actor relationships two cases of home-based care services in China. *Public Administration Quarterly., 36*(2), 238–264.

Chapter 9
Cybersecurity in Japan

9.1 Introduction

As late as 2012, Japan had not officially acknowledged cyber-attacks as a security threat (Yatsu 2012). Part of Japan's CS laggardness can be attributed to the fact that the country's political and military elites, until not long ago, failed to recognize the seriousness and significance of this issue. A British official involved in CS went as far as saying that Japan has "zero capability" in CS and the country severely lacked a "situational awareness" (Villar 2013).

CS issue has become a far more prominent part of the national discourse and dialogue in the past few years. Due primarily to high profile cyber-attacks facing the country as well as internal and external pressures, Japan has revised CS strategies and new CS practices are being implemented. Japan's policy-makers have also realized that the country's CS regulations have acted as a barrier to utilize modern technologies such as BD and the cloud effectively and are taking measures to revise them.

An even more striking and important point is that, Japan is planning to push through measures as drastic as constitutional reform. There has been a discussion about changing the country's war-renouncing Article 9 of the constitution in order to develop effective defense capabilities to protect the cyberspace as well as land, sea, air and space. For instance, in his 2014 New Year's message to the nation, the Prime Minister Shinzo Abe said that the country's post-World War II constitution, which limits the use of military force to situations involving self-defense, could be amended by 2020. Cyber-threats facing the nations have provided one of the rationales behind the motivation for the proposed amendment.

The rapidly growing cyber-threat has also spurred some high-profile initiatives in the private sector aimed at improving the country's CS profile. According to a November 2014 online article of the *Nihon Keizai Shimbun*, NEC has announced plans to expand its CS services for the industry and government. The company is expected to increase CS professionals to 1200 by March 2018. It also wants to

© Springer International Publishing Switzerland 2016

N. Kshetri, *The Quest to Cyber Superiority*, DOI 10.1007/978-3-319-40554-4_9

increase the domestic sales of its CS services by 2.5-folds to ¥35 billion by 2016 (nikkei.com 2014a).

Japan is also engaged in international cooperation in the development of cyber-defense capabilities. For instance, Japan and the U.S. have planned to launch joint military drills against cyber-attacks. Japan is also planning to send its officers to the U.S. for CS-related trainings. Likewise, in December 2013, Japan and the ASEAN agreed to jointly develop mechanisms in order to fight cyber-attacks (Mie 2014).

As to the external security, the view that the cyberspace has emerged as a new venue for warfare has been echoed by Japan. For instance, a Japanese military panel's ruling in 2012 defined cyberspace as "a 'territory' where various activities such as information gathering, attack, and defence occur, on the same way as land, sea, air and space". *The Defense Posture Review Interim Report* published by the MoD in July 2013 identified CS as one of Japan's defense priorities.

From the CS standpoint, a key political development arguably was the 2012 victory of the Liberal Democratic Party (LDP). A striking development is the Japanese government's attempt to change its interpretation of the war-renouncing Article 9 of the constitution to lift self-imposed ban on exercising the right of collective self-defense. The exercise of "collective self-defense" would include sanctioning counterattacks by Japanese forces against attackers of allied forces. Note that Japan's current constitution prohibits such measures. In October 2013, Japan and the U.S. agreed to revise defense cooperation guidelines by the end of 2014. Cyber-threat, along with China's growing military capability and North Korea's nuclear and missile development was identified as a trigger that prompted its intention to revise the guidelines. The LDP government thinks that the proposed change would strengthen the SDF's powers and enhance the security of the cyber-space and the physical space.

9.2 Cyber-Threats Facing Japan

Japan has witnessed a rapid escalation of cyber-attacks in recent years. It was reported that the government networks faced 3000 cyber-attacks every day in 2012, which is more than double the 2011 level (japandailypress.com 2013). The 2011 high profile cyber-attacks on defense contractors including Mitsubishi Heavy Industries, which were believed to be the first of their kind, were an eye-opening event. According to Mitsubishi, the perpetrators gained access to 83 computers and servers at 11 locations, which included Tokyo headquarters, many factories, and a R&D center (Tabuchi 2011). The attacked involved over 50 types of viruses and malware products. Other defense contractors such as IHI and Kawasaki Heavy Industries also reported cyber-attacks. Around the same time, cyber-attackers stole user ID and passwords of the Lower House Diet members and their secretaries, which gave the perpetrators access to e-mails and documents possessed by the Diet's 480 lawmakers and other personnel for at least a month (ajw.asahi.com 2011a).

Studies of the National Police Agency (NPA) and other authorities have indicated that 97 % of cyber-attacks targeted at Japanese institutions in 2013 originated from foreign countries (Kyodo News International 2014). According to Trend Micro's Q2 2014 Security Roundup: Turning the Tables on Cyber-attacks, Japan was the country most susceptible to the theft of banking information (Braue 2014). Of equal concern are foreign organized cybercrime groups. According to the NPA, 90 % of bank accounts in Japan that received fraudulently transferred money online were opened under Chinese names. The Agency suspected that Chinese-organized crime groups were behind these frauds.

As noted in Chap. 3, internal security is viewed as an issue of less concern for Japan. Nonetheless, in recent years, domestic organized crime groups are becoming increasingly active in the cyberspace. The organized-crime groups, Yakuza, which has 84,000 members, for instance, reportedly hired Russian hackers to attack law-enforcement agencies' databases (economist.com 1999). Due to the global financial crisis as well as enhanced law enforcement efforts, the Yakuza's revenues from traditional activities such as gambling, prostitution and loan-sharking have severely declined, which has forced them to switch to cybercrime, deposit fraud, money laundering and other white collar crimes (Demetriou 2009).

9.3 Challenges and Barriers Facing Japan in Strengthening CS

The above threats can be partly attributed to organizations' weak defenses against cyber-threats. Japan's performance is poor in key indicators related to CS such as R&D spending and technology manpower in this area.

According to the NISC, only half of Japanese companies had a CS policy and less than a quarter had a business continuity plan in case of a cyber-attack (Humber and Reidy 2014a). MM Research Institute's 2014 survey of information security investments conducted among 300 Japanese and 300 U.S. companies found that Japanese companies' average investment was ¥2.4 billion in FY 2014, which was 30 % lower than those of U.S. companies and about the same amount as U.S. companies investments 2 years ago (scan.netsecurity.ne.jp 2014). Likewise, according to a PwC Global Information Security Survey 2015 released in November 2014, in the average Japanese companies annually invested ¥210 million on CS compared to the global average of ¥420 million. The survey also found that only 41 % Japanese companies had board members who emphasized on the importance of CS compared to 64 % worldwide (PwC 2014). Likewise, according to the NISC, 60 % of the working engineers lacked enough skills to counter a new virus (Aoki 2014). It was reported that when a Japanese computers parts maker was informed that its computers were virus infected, the maker's CS chief did not have knowledge to respond (Ishima et al. 2014).

Japan cut R&D spending on CS by nearly 50 % during 2006–2010 whereas many countries increased such spending (ajw.asahi.com 2011b). A growing number of observers have linked some industrialized countries' weak cyber-defense mechanisms to their outdated bureaucratic structure. In Japan's case, the Finance Ministry was reluctant to allocate funds for the MoD's cyber-defense capabilities for several years (Kallender-Umezu 2013). The MoD's FY 2014 budget for cyber-related activities was ¥20.5 billion (US$200.5 million) (Ministry of Defense 2013). As a point of comparison, the Japanese government's CS spending is significantly lower than South Korea's (Chap. 1).

We noted earlier that most Western economies are facing a shortage of skilled CS professionals. The same is true of Japan. Japan's cyber-defense ability is likely to be hampered by highly insufficient and unqualified human resources at various levels. A Tokyo-based IT security firm's chief technical officer noted: "There's no one at the Defense Ministry who understands cyberspace" (Villar 2013). According to the Information-technology Promotion Agency, Japan faces a shortage of at least 80,000 technical experts and among the country's 265,000 experts, 160,000 need further education and training (Miller 2013).

It was reported that the MoD was having difficulty in finding qualified personnel for its 100 member planned CDU (wn.com 2012). A Japanese intelligence specialist pointed out that the CDU's staff are likely to be recruited internally, who are likely to be insufficiently trained, and may lack sufficient specialized skills and a "strong cyber warrior mentality" (Kallender-Umezu 2013). He also maintained that the CDU needs at least 2000–3000 dedicated cyber warriors, and some of them need to be "white hat" hackers recruited from the private sector.

The DoF's original plan was to recruit 100 people, who would be responsible for collecting information about malware and viruses and identifying ways to respond to cyber-threats. The CDU launched in March 2014 had 90 SDF personnel.

9.4   Jolts and Shocks Encountered by Japan

Until not long ago, Japanese politicians did not consider CS as an issue of national importance. Of the eleven political parties, only three had statements about CS issues in their manifestoes for the Upper House election in 2010 (Yatsu 2012). However, recent political and regulatory developments have introduced a complexity of new forces which are transforming the Japanese CS landscape.

As noted earlier in Chap. 2, initiating events or triggers also known as disruptive events, shocks, jolts, or discontinuities often lead to institutional changes. Especially the 2011 high-profile cyber-attacks Mitsubishi and other defense contractors were major jolts and shocks that woke the country up to a new level of CS awareness. The attacks also led to external pressures on Japan to enhance CS. For instance, following the attacks, the U.S. showed serious concern about the country's cyber-defense capabilities. The pressures from the U.S. are obvious since Japanese companies build U.S.-designed missiles, warships and military aircrafts. For instance, Mitsubishi works closely with Boeing and has built the U.S.-designed F-15 fighter jet and missile systems including Patriot batteries under license (Kallender-Umezu 2013).

The 2020 Olympics constitutes another major force that is likely to transform Japan's CS landscape. The Japanese government is determined to close the CS gaps (Aoki 2014). In order to enhance its ability to fight cybercrime to prepare for the 2020 Tokyo Olympics, in October 2014, Japan announced plans to launch bilateral talks by March 2015 with France, Australia, Israel and Estonia (Kyodo News International 2014).

9.5 Political and Regulatory Developments

Table 9.1 presents key events and milestones in Japan's CS initiatives. Attempts have been made to develop an extensive network of CS-related rules, regulatory bodies and enforcement agencies. In 2005, Japan set up the National Information Security Center (NISC) within the Cabinet Secretariat. Its goal was to monitor, analyze and counter internal and external cyber-attacks facing the Japanese ministries. The center has been working with organizations such as the NPA and the MoD.

The NISC, however, lacked a legal foundation to perform in the way it was envisioned (Mie 2014). Regulatory measures have been taken to address the shortcomings. In the proposed law, which passed the lower house and was awaiting a vote in the upper house, the NISC would be the cabinet's primary CS coordinator. Companies are required to report all incidents to the NISC (Humber and Reidy 2014b). According to a September 2014 article published by Nihon Keizai Shimbun, the National Information Security Center (NISC) would start hiring white hat hackers from April 2015 in order to strengthen cyber defense. They will be hired as short-term contractors (nikkei.com 2014c). A tentative outline of the basic CS bill seeks to enhance cooperation among the country's 13 critical infrastructure operators in key industries such as finance, electricity, petroleum and transportation (Mie 2014).

In July 2014, the Japanese government announced a plan to create a new CS policy headquarters by 2015. The new body will be headed by the chief Cabinet secretary, which will be equivalent to Vice Minister (reuters.com 2014) and will report directly to the cabinet. It will work closely with the National Security Council, devise a unified CS strategy for the government and implement measures across ministries. The ruling coalition also announced a plan to submit a bill before the Diet session, which would make it mandatory for all government ministries and agencies to report cyber-attacks to the new headquarters (Mie 2014). The new CS strategy aims to reduce the shortage of CS professionals to half by 2020 (Aoki 2014).

Three major categories of responses and actors in the government sector deserve mention in Japan's efforts to fight against cyber-threats and enhance economic

Table 9.1 Key events and milestones in Japan's CS initiatives

Time	Event	Explanation
2005	The NISC was established under the Cabinet Secretariat	A concern was that the NISC lacked a legal foundation to perform its envisioned
2005	The Personal Information Protection Law was enacted	It requires companies that handle personal data on 5,000 or more individuals to designate a CPO.
2011	Mitsubishi Heavy Industries and the Diet experienced cyber-attacks	Other defense contractors such as IHI and Kawasaki Heavy Industries also reported cyber-attacks.
2012	A Japanese military panel's ruling redefined cyberspace.	Cyberspace is defined as "a 'territory' where various activities such as information gathering, attack, and defence occur, on the same way as land, sea, air and space".
June 2013	The NISC released its CS strategy.	It described the roles of key actors such as the government, providers of critical infrastructure providers, businesses, individuals, and technology providers.[a]
July 2013	The Defense Posture Review Interim Report published by the MoD.	It identified CS as a priority.
January 2014	In 2014 New Year's message to the nation, Prime Minister Abe said that the country's post-World War II constitution could be amended by 2020.	Cyber-threats facing the nations have provided one of the rationales behind the motivation for the proposed amendment.
March 2014	The CDU was launched.	It started with 90 SDF personnel.
November 2014	The government decided that Japan's Information Security Policy Council will become the Cyber Security Strategy headquarters in January 2015.[b]	It will be headed by the chief Cabinet secretary, which will be equivalent to Vice Minister[c] and will report to the cabinet.

[a]Ng (2013)
[b]nikkei.com (2014b)
[c]reuters.com (2014)

competitiveness: a) cybercrimes which fall under the purview of the national police; b) industrial policies, such as the standardization and codes and other protection measures, which are mainly handled by the Ministry of Economy, Trade and Industry (METI) and the Ministry of Internal Affairs and Communications (MIAC); and c) national security in which the MoD is the key players (The National Institute for Defense Studies 2012). In addition an emerging network of academic institutions and the private sector interested in CS has begun to develop.

9.5.1 Anti-cybercrime Initiatives

In 2004, the NPA installed the Cybercrime Division as well as the High-Tech Crime Technology Division in each Prefectural Info-Communications Department. In March 2013, the NPA announced the launch of nationwide police task force consisting of 140 staff. In addition, the Police have played a key role in public education about CS.

9.5.2 Industrial Policies and Other Protection Measures

The METI established the Personal Data Working Group under the IT Integration Forum in November 2012. In its report released in May 2013, the working group recommended to utilize intermediary organizations that provide consumers with information regarding businesses' credibility and help businesses to handle personal information in an appropriate manner. The working group also pointed out a deficiency of the current framework which requires consumers to disclose personal information required by the businesses according to the latter's terms in order to use the services. The working group recommended a framework which involves businesses providing different levels of services based on the type of information consumers want to disclose. That is, consumers are given the choice to select the "disclosable information". Likewise, starting November 2012, the MIAC held the Research Society for Use and Circulation of Personal Data. The Research Society released its official report in June 2013, which favored transparency, user participation, and proper means of data collection and management of user information, among other things (International Policy Division 2013).

9.5.3 National Security

The government has realized that ensuring the stability of the cyberspace is critical for the JSDF to achieve its missions. In April 2013, the MoD announced that it would set up a new CDU by March 2014 with a budget of US$142 million (Kallender-Umezu 2013). In March 2014, the SDF activated the CDU (saiba boeitai), whose task is to monitor and respond to attacks on the MoD's networks. Some of the key goals that the SDF is expected to achieve through the CDU include protecting its own information systems and contributing to the government's response to cyber-threats facing the country by advancing relevant knowledge and skills.

9.6 The Japanese Culture from the CS Perspective

Japan is a high-trust culture, where people and businesses generally place trust in the government, the police and the legal system. This has also been the case in CS. A November 2010 survey conducted in 14 countries to measure IT executives' confidence on the ability of their respective countries' authorities to prevent and deter potential cyber-attacks revealed that Japan had the highest confidence from the executives. Due primarily to the increased focus on regulation and audits, 83 % expressed confidence in the authorities in 2010 compared to 56 % in 2009 (McAfee 2011). To take an example, Japan was among the countries, which implemented highest levels of counter-Stuxnet security measures despite a relatively low rate of Stuxnet infiltration in the country (McAfee 2011). CS legislation is less likely to face impediment and opposition from privacy groups, business community and opposition parties.

A final point that should be stressed is the prevalence of lifetime employment and low worker mobility in high technology industries. Ryusuke Masuoka, a Senior Fellow at the Tokyo-based Center for International Public Policy Studies (CIPPS) noted that CS specialists in Japan have an extremely low tendency to move across the private sector, public sector, and the academia. This is unlike in the U.S. where experience in public service would help government workers to move to lucrative private sector jobs. He further noted that unlike the FBI and other U.S. government agencies, the Japanese government agencies are not likely to hire hackers (Rigoli 2013).

9.7 Similarities and Differences with Major World Economies

Some major similarities and differences between Japan's CS landscape and those of the EU and the U.S. are summarized in Table 9.2. Japan has followed some elements of the EU directive mode. For instance, just like the EU, it has established a detailed regulatory framework and requires its ministries to implement it in all types of personal data. Another similarity with the EU is that due to concerns about privacy and data protection, most Japanese companies' use of BD and cloud computing has been limited (O'Donoghue and Kimoto 2013). In connection with this point, some of the recent initiatives (e.g., recommendations of the METI's Personal Data Working Group and the MIAC's Research Society for Use and Circulation of Personal Data) would help enhance the national economic competitiveness by encouraging Japanese firms to benefit from these technological advances.

There are also a number of key differences between the CS approaches of Japan and the EU. While it is necessary to obtain the individual's ("data subject") consent in the collection, processing and transfer of personal data in the EU (contrary to law

Table 9.2 Japan's CS landscape: Key similarities and differences with the EU and the U.S.

	The EU	The U.S.
Similarities	•No sector specific regulations • Due to concerns about privacy and data protection, most Japanese companies' use of BD and cloud computing has been limited compared with the U.S.[a]	• To some extent relies on private sector self-regulation • Facing major cyber-attacks originated from foreign countries
Differences	• Collection, processing and transfer of personal data do not require the individual's consent. • Businesses have no general obligation to delete personal data after the use. • Unlike in the EU, a company offering services online is not required to report cyber-attacks on its networks.	• Does not have a privacy commission or an agency equivalent to the FTC. • CS specialists have an extremely low tendency to move across the private sector, public sector, and the academia.

[a]O'Donoghue and Kimoto (2013)

in the U.S.) (Hultsch 2011), the Personal Data Protection Law in Japan requires enterprises only to state the purpose of use. That is, consent of the data subject is not necessary in Japan. Likewise, businesses in Japan have no general obligation to delete personal data after the use. Finally, unlike in the EU, a company offering services online is not required to report cyber-attacks on its networks.

At the same time, just like the U.S., Japan relies, to some extent, on private sector self-regulation. The Personal Information Protection Law enacted in 2005 has stated a set of obligations for companies handling personal data, which includes the requirement to designate a corporate privacy officer (CPO) and other staff in companies that handle personal data on 5000 or more individuals. A manager who fails to comply with the regulation faces fines of up to ¥300,000 or jail sentences of up to 6 months.

A further similarity with the U.S. is that Japan's major CS-related responses are attributable to high-profile cyber-attacks facing the country. In connection with the point, there is a common thread that binds Japan and the U.S. together: national elites and policy makers in both countries believe that organizations in both countries have been victimized by China-originated cyber-attacks. A *Financial Times* commentator in 2010 had suggested that cyber-threats might serve as a common ground, which would lead policy-makers in Japan and the U.S. to realize the importance of an increased military security alliance (Alkire 2010).

The 2011 cyber-attacks on the Mitsubishi Heavy Industries and the Diet reportedly originated from China (Yee 2012). The historical and political animosities between China and Japan are linked to major cyber-attacks faced by the country. A *Telegraph* article noted that the cyber-attacks on the Diet coincided with the 80th anniversary of the so-called Manchurian Incident of September 18, 1931 (Ryall 2011). On that day, a small amount of dynamite damaged a portion of the railroad operated by Japan's South Manchuria Railway in today's Chinese city of Shenyang in Manchuria in the Liaoning Province. Note that this incident was used by the Japanese Army as a pretext to launch a full invasion of Manchuria.

Triangulation of information from a number of U.S.-based computer security firms and other sources gives more validity to the notion that sophisticated cyber-espionage activities allegedly originated from China have targeted organizations in Japan and the U.S. Based on the experiences and findings gathered from research Taiwanese CS specialists offered their viewpoint that Chinese hackers planning highly-targeted cyber-attacks aimed at stealing sensitive data from organizations in big countries such as Japan and the U.S. first rehearse the attack scenario to Taiwanese organizations. The founder of a Taiwanese internet security company was quoted as saying: "We'll see a specific attack signature here, and then six months later see the same signature in an attack on the States" (Gold 2013).

Finally there are major differences between Japan and the U.S. A really big difference, as noted earlier, is that Japan does not have a privacy commission or an agency equivalent to the FTC. As of April 2008, there were 37 guidelines established in 24 fields under various ministries according to the Article 8 of the Personal Data Protection Law. The entities involved are supervised by the relevant ministries. While the guidelines are not binding, most businesses abide by the guidelines. As noted earlier, another key difference is that CS specialists in Japan have lower job mobility.

9.8 Discussion and Concluding Remarks

Japan failed to act early on the CS front. The lack of awareness and low perception of cyber-attack risks among Japan's political and military elites can be attributed to the country's poor CS policies and performance. The low level of preparedness of Japan is particularly striking given its technological prowess and the seriousness of this issue. Nonetheless, Japan has intensified regulatory and policy measures on the CS front recent years and is planning to push through measures as drastic as constitutional reform. The interplay of external and internal factors such as high-profile cyber-attacks on the country's large defense contractors and legislative bodies, pressures from foreign governments and threats posed by organized crime groups has shaped the company's CS responses.

Networks of interaction between universities and the private sector are also being established in order to promote discussions, and work collectively to strengthen human and technological capabilities in CS, which are also sought after and encouraged by the government. A report on long-term CS strategy released in the mid-2013 by a government panel of experts emphasized on upgrading specialized CS education at universities and other institutions (Mainichi Japan 2013). Boeing and other companies have also announced plans to provide CS training to support Japan's need for more experts as well as CS-related solutions (Hoover 2012).

While significant CS measures have been initiated and implemented in recent years Japan's performance has been poor compared to key benchmarks and those of major world economies such as the U.S., China, Russia, Israel and South Korea. Compared to South Korea's, Japan's CS plan is less ambitious. In March 2014, Ichita Yamamoto, the country's cabinet minister in charge of IT policy noted that despite the recent CS efforts, Japan lags behind the U.S. on the CS front (Kelly and Kubo 2014). Moreover, Japan's CS initiatives are mainly oriented toward external threats. In general, Japan requires greater investment and attention in facilitating the awareness, skill, and capabilities for CS, especially among the law enforcement, and defense officials.

References

ajw.asahi.com. (2011a). *Cyber-attack from server in China targets Lower House.* http://tinyurl.com/lr8rg6r

ajw.asahi.com. (2011b). *Editorial: Japan should play active role against cyber attacks.* http://tinyurl.com/n8fh7eg

Alkire, J. (2010). *Cyber threats can unite Japan and America.* http://tinyurl.com/kxzk73w.

Aoki, M. (2014). New SDF unit shores up thinly protected cyberborders. *The Japan Times.*

Braue, D. (2014). *Japan's banking malware surge pushes Australia out of top 10.* http://www.cso.com.au/article/552261/japan_banking_malware_surge_pushes_australia_top_10/

Demetriou, D. (2009). *Japanese yakuza gangsters hit by recession.* http://tinyurl.com/bwgw2ke

economist.com. (1999). *Crime without punishment.* http://www.economist.com/node/234642

Gold, M. (2013). Taiwan a 'testing ground' for Chinese cyber army. *Reuters.* http://tinyurl.com/m5axceh

Hoover, M. (2012). *Boeing inks partnership for Japanese cyber initiative.* http://tinyurl.com/17hflf4

Hultsch, C. (2011). *Basic principles of European Union consent and data protection.* http://tinyurl.com/la8nonn

Humber, Y., & Reidy, G. (2014a). *Yahoo hacks highlight cyber flaws Japan rushing to thwart.* http://www.bloomberg.com/news/2014-07-08/yahoo-hacks-highlight-cyber-flaws-japan-rushing-to-thwart.html

Humber, Y., & Reidy, G. (2014b). *Japan takes its first step to fight hackers.* http://www.businessweek.com/articles/2014-07-24/proposed-law-would-fix-japans-lax-cybersecurity

International Policy Division. (2013). *Official announcement of report from Research Society for Use and Circulation of Personal Data.* http://tinyurl.com/k3dyhex.

Ishima, T., Kamizono, M., & Shimbun, Y. (2014). Cybersecurity 'experts' lacking in numbers, skill. *The Japan News, 22935*, 2.

japandailypress.com. (2013). *Japan's cyber-defense problems to be highlight of security talks.* http://tinyurl.com/lbmtb33

Kallender-Umezu, P. (2013). *Experts: Japan's new cyber unit understaffed, lacks skills.* http://tinyurl.com/l5b5wbf

Kelly, T., & Kubo, N. (2014). *Japan holds first broad cybersecurity drill, frets over Olympics risks.* http://www.reuters.com/article/2014/03/18/us-japan-cybercrime-idUSBREA2G1O920140318

Kyodo News International. (2014). *Japan to launch cybersecurity talks with 4 nations by March.* http://www.globalpost.com/dispatch/news/kyodo-news-international/141005/japan-launch-cybersecurity-talks-4-nations-march

Mainichi Japan. (2013). *Japan promoting programs to produce more hackers for cybersecurity.* http://tinyurl.com/pcm2cye.

McAfee. (2011). *In the dark: Crucial industries confront cyberattacks.*

Mie, A. (2014). Ruling bloc readies bill to bolster cybersecurity amid growing attacks. *The Japan Times.*

Miller, J. (2013). *Japan's new cybersecurity strategy: Implications for the Alliance. Forbes.* http://www.thecre.com/fnews/?p=6668

Ministry of Defense. (2013). *Defense programs and budget of Japan, overview of FY2014 budget.* Tokyo: Defense Planning and Programming Division, Bureau of Defense Policy Finance Division, Bureau of Finance and Equipment.

Ng, K. (2013). *Japan releases national cyber security strategy.* http://www.futuregov.asia/articles/japan-releases-national-cyber-security-strategy

nikkei.com. (2014a). *NEC、*セキュリティー人材倍増　18年3月期本画http://www.nikkei.com/article/DGXLASDZ19HJR_Z11C14A1TJ2000/

nikkei.com. (2014b). サイバー攻撃対策で戦略本部　政府、15年1月にも設置. http://www.nikkei.com/article/DGXLASFS25H3G_V21C14A1PP8000/

nikkei.com. (2014c). 政府、ホワイトハッカー採用へ　サイバー攻撃対応で　15年度めど. http://www.nikkei.com/article/DGXLASDE06H07_W4A900C1PE8000/

O'Donoghue, C., & Kimoto, T. (2013). *Japan promotes the use of big data.* http://tinyurl.com/kevjxa6

PwC. (2014). *PwC's Global Information Security Survey 2015 - Japanese companies are behind the global standard.* http://www.pwc.com/jp/ja/advisory/press-room/news-release/2014/information-security-survey141105.jhtm

reuters.com. (2014). *Japan cyber attacks on government sites surge, government mulling steps to respond.* http://www.reuters.com/article/2014/07/10/us-japan-cybersecurity-idUSKBN0FF1OR20140710

Rigoli, E. (2013). *Insights into Japan's cybersecurity and other global views.* http://tinyurl.com/lnyy4tl

Ryall, J. (2011). *Cyber attacks coincide with 80th anniversary of Manchurian incident.* http://tinyurl.com/438fogl

scan.netsecurity.ne.jp. (2014).日本企業の情報セキュリティ投資額は米国の2年前の水準に相当 (MMRI). http://scan.netsecurity.ne.jp/article/2014/09/29/34898.html

Tabuchi, H. (2011). *U.S. expresses concern about new cyberattacks in Japan.* www.nytimes.com

The National Institute for Defense Studies. (2012). *East Asian strategic review 2012: Chapter 7: Japan: Toward the establishment of a dynamic defense force.* Tokyo: The National Institute for Defense Studies.

Villar, R. (2013). *Japan-U.S. security talks likely to highlight Tokyo's cyber-defence woes.* http://tinyurl.com/kmhghy7

wn.com. (2012). *SDF seeks white-hat hackers/Cyberdefense skills hard to cultivate, especially at SDF wages.* http://tinyurl.com/kzfqzs7

Yatsu, M. (2012). *Will Japan's legal framework be a red light stopping the cyber defense?* http://tinyurl.com/k4rgawn

Yee, A. (2012). *International cyber war: Limits and possibilities.* http://www.eastasiaforum.org/2012/03/14/international-cyber-war-limits-and-possibilities/

Chapter 10
Cybersecurity in South Korea

10.1 Introduction

As is the case of other industrialized countries, South Korea's highly digitized economy makes it an attractive target for financially motivated hackers. A unique aspect of South Korea is its hostile and tense relationship with North Korea, which has special implications for the CS. The two countries are still technically at war. Defense specialists have argued that by combining cyber-warfare with other asymmetric assets such as hovercraft, chemical, biological, and radiological weapons, North Korea is likely to drastically strengthen its warfare capabilities (Kim 2012). In 1999 then leader Kim Jong Il reportedly said: "The basic key to victory in modern warfare is to do well in electronic warfare" (Bermudez Jr 2005). Consistent with this observation, South Korea's military, government agencies, businesses, nonprofit organizations and consumers have faced a number of high-profile cyber-attacks. While there are technical challenges in attribution of cyber-attacks and thus it is impossible to prove with certainty, based on indirect and circumstantial evidence, South Korea has accused North Korea for most of the major cyber-attacks facing the country.

In October 2013, quoting the South Korean Defense Ministry (SKDM), Rep. Chung Hee-soo of the ruling Saenuri Party, noted that North Korea launched over 6000 cyber-attacks against the South since 2010 (Hern 2013). According to the South Korean government, North Korea's cyber-attacks cost the country over US $805 million between 2009 and 2013 (globalpost.com 2013).

© Springer International Publishing Switzerland 2016   171
N. Kshetri, *The Quest to Cyber Superiority*, DOI 10.1007/978-3-319-40554-4_10

Table 10.1 Major cyber-attacks experienced by South Korea in recent years

Time	Explanation
July 2009	Starting July 4, South Korean and U.S. government and financial websites were disrupted by distributed denial of service (DDoS) attacks for many days with millions of requests per second, which was the first major attacks facing the country.[a] The websites of the presidential office, the SKDM and the National Assembly were among the key targets.
March 4, 2011	A second major cyber-attack launched malware, which erased computer hard drives of one of the largest banks and left 30 million customers without ATM services for many days.[a] Cyber-attacks that were believed to be originated from North Korea jammed South Korean GPS signals during joint U.S.-South Korean military drills in March 2011, which lasted for 10 days.[b]
April 2011	Nonghyup Agricultural Bank experienced service outages for 3 weeks due to cyberattacks. 273 of its 587 servers were down.[c]
April-May 2012	North Korea allegedly launched jamming attacks, which affected GPS navigation of 337 commercial flights, 122 ships, and a number of vehicle owners.[d]
June 2012	Databases containing articles and photos and editing production system of two conservative South Korean newspapers were destroyed by hackers. It took place 1 week after the KPA had criticized them for negative coverage.[c]
March-April, 2013	Three broadcasters KBS, MBC, YTN, three banks Shinhan, Nonghyup and Jeju, and two insurance firms reported cyber-attacks to their networks to the National Police Agency. The attacks disabled anti-virus software. ATMs across the country stopped functioning and online banking systems froze for many days. Authorities found the use of *hard-drive wiper malware* in the attacks called DarkSeoul. Hard drives of about 30,000 computers were wiped out.[e]
June 25-July 1, 2013	A series of cyber-attacks paralyzed the country's 69 government offices, major banks such as NongHyup and Shinhan, major telecommunications companies, news outlets, broadcasters, and other institutions. In addition, the attacks also victimized the presidential office website, which stored massive personal data 2.5 million members of the ruling Saenuri Party, 300,000 military personnel and 200,000 registered users.[f] The cyber-attacks coincided with the 63rd anniversary of the Korean War, which started on June 25, 1950.
December 2014	South Korea's nuclear power plant operator, Korea Hydro and Nuclear Power Co Ltd (KHNP), which runs the country's 23 nuclear power reactors, faced cyberattacks. The KHNP noted that only non-critical data was stolen.[g] The hackers had used 300 different types of malware. They released power plant blueprints, testing data and payroll information.

[a]Clayton (2013)
[b]chosun.com (2011)
[c]Beach-Westmoreland (2014)
[d]Kovacs (2012)
[e]Cain (2014)
[f]beSUCCESS (2013)
[g]Cho (2014)

10.2 Cyber-Threats Facing South Korea

Table 10.1 presents major cyber-attacks experienced by South Korea in recent years. A survey of government institutions, banks, businesses, and schools indicated that **in 2003**, 26,000 hacking incidents were reported to the **South**'s Ministry of Information and Communication which was 178 times the level in 1996 (Ho 2004). The president of the Korea Internet and Security Agency (KISA) described the recent cyber-attacks as APTs, in which the perpetrators carefully studied the targets for a long period to develop their tactics (koreaittimes.com 2013). The NIS has also accused the North of manipulating the South's online opinion by engaging in activities such as posting blogs and e-mailing journalists (chosun.com 2013).

North Korea is reported to have the cyber-warfare capabilities required to jam GPS and to inject false GPS coordinates (HP 2014). South Korea's unique geographic position bordering North Korea makes it especially vulnerable to some types of cyber-attacks. For instance, regarding numerous GPS attacks against the South allegedly carried out by the North, geography has an important role to play. In the 2012 GPS attacks, the jamming signals were identified as coming from Kaesong in North Korea about 10 km from the South Korean border and 50 km from the Incheon International Airport (Kovacs 2012).

Quoting an NIS official briefing her, a lawmaker, who served the country's intelligence committee, noted that most of the websites facing cyber-attacks belonged to conservative South Korean organizations that support a hard-line approach to North Korea (Table 10.1). However, a number of other big companies have faced cyber-attacks. For instance, a major target in the June–July 2013 cyber-attacks was South Korea's Hyundai Merchant Marine (HMM). This has been puzzling mystery for some analysts due to the lack of explanation of obvious benefit to North Korea from cyberespionage against HMM. An analyst concluded that a more probable explanation of the cyber-attacks against HMM would be that North Korea might have been hired by China to do so. Other possible explanations could be that North Korea launched the attack with a different motivation: to sell the information to China. Still another explanation offered was that China may have launched the attack but did in such a way that it looked like one that was perpetrated by North Korea (Ulsch 2013).

While the North has a drastically lower level of economic development, the asymmetric nature of cyber-attacks means that actors with limited financial and technical resources possess capability to compromise high-value targets. North Korea has reportedly developed advanced cyber-warfare capabilities and its substantial workforce is allegedly involved in the Internet's dark side activities with the explicit support of the state. In its annual report on the state of North Korea's military released in March 2014, the U.S. DoD observed that North Korea shifted its focus towards offensive cyber operations (OCO) and other asymmetric tactics (Panda 2014). South Korea views the North's cyber-warfare capabilities as a "terroristic threat" (HP 2014).

In 2004, North Korea allegedly gained access to 33 of 80 South Korean military wireless communication networks (HP 2014). In March 2014, the SKDM reported that it detected a hacking attempt allegedly from North Korea to steal military data, which used a journalist's computer. According to the Ministry, the journalist covered defense issues, whose computer was connected to the SKDM network (Agence France-Presse 2014).

Cyber-attacks on South Korea that are believed to be associated with the North are also motivated by material and monetary gains. According to a South Korean security official, North Korea's hacking organizations and a network of spies operate from China, Japan and other countries. The South Korean police also estimated that each North Korean hacker operating from China sends about US $500 per month to the "Office 39" or "Bureau 39", which is a secretive branch of the North Korean regime that provides financial support to the country's leadership in part through alleged engagement in illicit activities (economist.com 2011).

10.3   South Korea's Asymmetric Strengths and Weaknesses

From South Korea's perspective North Korea is seen as the principal source of cyber-threat and danger. It is thus relevant to compare the two Koreas' asymmetric strengths and weaknesses.

10.3.1   Positive Asymmetries

South Korea undoubtedly demonstrates a higher level of resourcefulness in developing greater levels of cyber-offense and defensive capabilities. For instance, according to the UN, in 2012, South Korea's per capita Gross National Income (GNI) was US$23,180 compared to North Korea's US$583 (United Nations 2014). This huge difference thus has the consequence that North Korea would face difficulty in matching the South in resource-intensive strategies and tactics.

South Korea's major local antivirus firms such as HAURI and AhnLab have capabilities to detect and stop cyber-attacks. In October 2013, AhnLab detected DDoS attacks on local companies which infected over 10,000 computers.

Finally South Korean can effectively leverage its collaboration with global cyber-powers into a cyberspace advantage. For instance, the SKDM announced that it would work with the U.S. in the development of cyber-offense capabilities (Tae-gyu 2013). Note that the U.S. has teamed up with South Korea and other allies such as Japan in addressing the threats associated with North Korea and China (Ong 2008). In recent years, the cooperation has been extended to the cyber domain. South Korea and the U.S. have started holding joint cyber-defense exercises regularly and are training professionals to protect from the cyber-threats. In the annual war exercise of August 2012, military forces of the two countries conducted first basic cyber-warfare operations, which were viewed as a step to enhance cyber-defenses (koreatimes.co.kr 2012).

10.3.2 Negative Asymmetries

A big concern is a general lack of CS orientation among individuals, businesses and government agencies. As discussed in Chap. 1, the country's businesses and government agencies have failed to invest in CS systems adequately and they have a poor CS orientation. This is a serious concern, given the widespread use of ICTs in the South. One estimate suggested that daily online banking transactions in South Korea amounted US$29.3 billion in 2013 (beSUCCESS 2013). Likewise, car navigation, air traffic control as well as U.S. and South Korean military systems heavily rely on the GPS navigation system (Waterman 2012). South Korea's information superiority makes its networks extremely lucrative targets and highly vulnerable to cyber-threats.

There are other constraints and challenges. For instance, the nationalist left and other North sympathizers may oppose attacks against the North (Firn 2013). According to an opinion poll reported in the *Munhwa Ilbo* newspaper in May 2005, 48 % of South Koreans said that they would back the North if the U.S. bombed it (Miller 2006). Especially young people, who did not experience the Korean War, are found to be more sympathetic to North Koreans (Kwony 2013). Another poll conducted among 15–25 year olds in South Korea, which was published by the *Chosun Ilbo* newspaper in August 2005, reported that about two-third of the respondents said they would support the North in a war with the U.S. (Miller 2006). These factors are seen as significant constraints and difficulties in dealing with cyber-threats associated with the North.

Politically motivated cyber-attacks on South Korea are not just external since it also has internal political dissidents (Koo 2013). For instance, some of the malware used in the attacks against the South Korean targets was traced to a computer in Seoul. Some of the codes also came from the U.S. and three European countries (Lee 2012). North Korea may thus launch cyber-attacks and avoid sanctions and retaliatory attacks. In this way, North Korea can use its cyber-warfare capability to harm enemies without potential negative consequences (McGee 2011).

North Korea's United Front Department is allegedly engaged in cyber psychological warfare. There are reportedly about 200 agents whose job is to post online comments to weaken the morale of South Koreans. They allegedly do so through about 140 websites that have servers in 19 countries. In 2011, these agents were reported to post about 27,000 propaganda items against South Korea. The number of such items was estimated to exceed 41,000 in 2012 (Kwony 2013). In this way, some view that the North practicing aggressive pressure and intimidation tactics via cyber-attacks on the South Korea at a low cost, without the deployment of troops and tanks, which has direct impact on the public (Clayton 2013).

A final consideration is the reputation damage that the South Korean cyber-warfare command suffered from the alleged engagement in psychological warfare capabilities on its own population, which may also lead to a reduced public support for the organization. Critics have noted that a major weakness of South Korea is its politicized military (Drennan 2003). It was accused that the South Korean military tried to influence voters during the 2012 presidential elections (bbc.com 2014). According to the SKDM, at least 11 officials at its cyber-warfare command spread online political messages, which praised President Park Geun-hye and her party or attacked the opponents before the 2012 election (Sang-Hun 2013).

10.4   Policy Framework and Strategic Plan for Preparedness and Response to Cyber-Threats

South Korea has been among economies to initiate early regulatory actions on some CS areas. For instance, following foreign hackers' alleged cyber-attacks in 2004, **South Korea** made it mandatory for Internet-related firms to report hacking incidents (Ho 2004). The country became one of the first in the world to introduce such regulations.

In recent years, South Korea has introduced a number of legal, regulatory and organizational structures to deal with cyber-threats. In 2010 South Korea developed and implemented a cyber-strategy. The first part of the plan, which was up and running as of the early 2014, focused on protecting networks (Keck 2014). It established a cyber-command in January 2010 and a cyber-protection policy team at the SKDM in March 2011 (Sang-ho 2012). The SKDM also established a Cyber Policy Department in 2013. The NIS announced that its Third Department[1] would give greater attention to "monitoring of cyberspace and telecommunications" (Tae-gyu 2013). The South Korean government also announced a plan to appoint a secretary of CS.

The cyber command has focused its efforts on psychological warfare activities against the North's propaganda and other cyberspace tactics that it considers as offensive. Its online propaganda strategy involves posting to North Korean social networking and social media websites. The SKDM plans to further build its psychological warfare capability (Eun-jung 2014). South Korea also blocks access to North Korean websites and broadcasts (Boynton 2011).

The second phase of the plan involves developing cyber-weapons that can be deployed to physically damage North Korean nuclear plants and missile facilities. In February 2014, the SKDM outlined its aim to develop weapons to attack the North's nuclear facilities, which will be similar to the Stuxnet worm (bbc.com 2014). It also announced a plan to create a new Cyber-Defense Command to carry

---

[1]The first department focuses on gathering foreign intelligence and anti-communist, anti-terror and anti-espionage efforts remain within the second department's purview.

out these missions. In addition, the South Korean military has announced plans to set up the Cyber Tactics Department under the Joint Chiefs of Staff (JCS) by January 2015. The new Department will control and command military operations in the cyberspace. It is considered as a part of efforts to change cyberspace operations from defensive to proactive and preventive (shanghaidaily.com 2014).

According to a *Dong-A Ilbo* article, between 2010 and July 2014, the South Korean military and law enforcement agencies blocked access to 125 websites and 1622 pro-North Korea social networking service (SNS) accounts, which praised the Kim Jong-un regime and defamed the South Korean government. More than 90 % of the websites and SNS servers were believed to be located in China and some in Japan, the U.S., and Europe. The South Korean intelligence community believed that these websites and services were run by the North Korean regime (japanese.donga.com 2014).

The South Korean government has also engaged in public-private collaboration in CS. In 2012, its army teamed up with Korea University to open a cyber-defense school, which enrolls 30 students per year. Courses included in the 4-year program include breaking malicious codes, psychological preparation for cyber-warfare and other techniques to protect against cyber-attacks (Agence France-Presse 2011).

Military theorists and analysts have argued that the category of asymmetric strategic means should be such that the adversary cannot effectively counter (Metz and Johnson 2001). This is especially important for asymmetries that are deliberately created than those that arise by default (Kshetri 2010). South Korean policy makers believe that cyber-threat is a serious problem facing the country and worthy of serious efforts and strategies to combat it. If there is one thing that North Korea is unable to effectively replicate, it is South Korea's resourcefulness and technological might. As noted in Chap. 1, in July 2013, South Korea announced that it would double its CS budget and spend $8.76 billion by 2017. It also plans to train 5000 CS experts by that time.

South Korea is taking a number of measures to strengthen its offensive and defensive capabilities. The military has established a special alert level system called Information operations condition (INFOCON), which measures CS threat levels. As noted in Chap. 3, South Korea is making efforts to enhance its GPS system capability.

South Korea is intensifying international collaboration and cooperation in CS areas. In March 2013, the SKDM announced that it would increase cyber-warfare forces and team up with the U.S. to develop deterrence scenarios (Eun-jung 2013). In October 2013, South Korean Minister of National Defense and U.S. Secretary of Defense announced that the two countries would strengthen CS cooperation. They also signed an agreement to establish a working-level council for CS policy (businesskorea.co.kr 2013).

The South Korean government has introduced legal and regulatory measures and economic incentives for strengthening organizations' CS measures. The KISA, which is a governmental agency established to promote the Internet, Security and International Cooperation, has made it mandatory for public agencies to implement the government-backed Information Security Management System. In August

2014, South Korea's Ministry of Science, ICT, and Future Planning announced the creation of an index for private companies to evaluate the information security level. Companies will be graded between B to AAA. A KISA spokesperson announced that the government was considering tax cuts and other benefits for companies with high scores (zdnet.com 2014). A probe of the Ministry of Security and Public Administration conducted of state-run agencies and civilian firms in the first half of 2014 indicated that the organizations were engaged in excessive collection of personal information and insufficient data management. The ministry announced its plan to revise the related laws to increase punitive damages for companies that fail to protect data, which will be up to three times the damage caused by data breaches (Min-sik 2014).

South Korea has also enacted data localization laws that require storage and analysis of sensitive data within the country. For instance, unless given written consent to do otherwise by their clients, South Korea requires banks and financial institutions to process data within South Korea. Its trade agreements with the EU and the U.S., however, provide exceptions to this rule.[2]

The regulatory developments that have occurred in South Korea in response to the North-originated cyber-attacks have far reaching implications. For instance, while Google Maps can provide directions for public transport in South Korea, they cannot do so for driving. In order to block from falling into North Korean hands, South Korean security restrictions put in place after the Korean War prohibit the export of map data. Thus Google and other foreign companies are not allowed to provide driving maps for South Korea (Pfanner 2013). In 2013, the government relaxed some of the restrictions. The new regulation allows foreign companies to provide English-language maps but they cannot be made available in high resolutions. Moreover, the map data is required to be processed in servers inside the country's borders (Newton 2013). In this way, South Korea's CS policies are driven by the need to address real and perceived geopolitical threats.

10.5   Discussion and Concluding Remarks

South Korea faces unique CS challenges and threats. North Korea is the most pronounced source of cyber-threats facing the country. CS also has a prominent link with geopolitical threats in South Korea. The two countries are asymmetrically motivated to respond to adversaries in the cyberspace. Each country is also attempting to destroy the honor of the other through cyber-attacks and cyber-warfare strategies and tactics.

---

[2]European Union Chamber of Commerce in Korea (EUCCK), Trade Issues and Recommendations 2011, Free Trade Agreement Between the United States of America and the Republic of Korea, Annex 13–B, Section B and Article 7.43. Each agreement allows a phase-in period of two years for the commitment.

The Mongolian warrior and conqueror, Genghis Khan famously said that one of the main goals of the war was "to rob them [the enemies] of their wealth, [and] to see their near and dear bathed in tears", which provided him "the greatest pleasure" (Royle 1990). To put things in context, the North Korea rulers may derive pleasure from the cyber-attacks-led sufferings of businesses, consumers and government agencies in South Korea. Regarding the targets, cyber-attacks on the banks can be viewed as an effective way to inflict damage and destruction of the South Korean economy. Likewise, South Korean media companies may be viewed as mouthpiece of anti-North Korean sentiments and thus are selected as targets of North Korea-originated hackings (Cain 2014).

It is fair to say that the two Koreas' intentions and actions on the cyber front point toward the possibility that these countries have engaged in cyber-warfare against each other. Each country has been attempting to fight the dominance of the other in the cyberspace. Each is also bolstering its ability to defend the cyberspace against the threats posed by the other.

Moreover, gains from cyber-attacks on South Korea targets may also strengthen North Korean rulers' economic position. An analysis of the North Korean regimes' use of cyber-attacks as a means of raising money for the ruling elites provides ample evidence to confirm the views of the skeptics, from economics and political science fields, who have questioned the effectiveness of international economic sanctions in producing desired economic and political consequences in the target country (Kaempfer and Lowenberg 1988).

The North's cyber-warfare capabilities may be more sophisticated and complex than many analysts give the country credit for. While it severely lacks the capability to match the South in terms of technological resources, it may have surpassed the South in terms of some aspects of cyber-warfare capability. For one thing, North Korea's alleged engagement in the Internet's dark side activities is likely to produce high externalities and spillover effects for cyber-attacks. The North has also displayed strong will and confidence in cyber-attacks.

South Korea's CS regulations and the development of cyber-offense and cyber-defense capabilities are principally a response to vulnerabilities associated with the North. It is taking measures to develop symmetric advantage by matching its adversary (North Korea) in terms of strategic resources and is attempting to make adequate institutional, financial, and policy preparations for strengthening CS.

South Korea's case demonstrates that adoption of an appropriate combination of institutional, financial and policies are needed to deal with cyber-threats. Some of the recent initiatives and actions taken by South Korea would help the country maximize positive asymmetries and minimize vulnerabilities of negative asymmetries. Nonetheless, some key challenges and critical issues still need to be addressed. For instance, South Korea's planned Stuxnet-like worm is likely to produce a number of negative spill-over effects (Chap. 1). Given these limitations of such a worm, some analysts have suggested that a more effective approach for the South would be to intensify its "information operations" so that North Koreans have access to outside news and information, which can change their perception of the country's socio-political and economic development status (Raska 2014).

South Korea also needs to make further efforts to improve CS orientation of businesses, consumers and government agencies. Some laws that cannot keep pace with technological development are of concern. For instance, a South Korean law requires anyone using online banking to use a "digital certificate" issued by a bank. This process requires an ActiveX plug-in, which is an outdated technology associated with Microsoft Internet Explorer. This is ignored by web developers in other countries and is incompatible with other internet browsers. According to StatCounter, in 2014, 76 % of South Koreans used the Internet explorer instead of other more reliable browsers. Note that in April 2014, the U.S. government suggested to avoid using explorer after a program flaw was discovered (Mundy 2014). A final challenge for the country's military is the cyber-warfare command's engagement to influence voters during the 2012 presidential elections, which is especially puzzling and intriguing. In this case, the importance of internal political agenda seems to have superseded the need to combat external threats.

References

Agence France-Presse. (2011). *South Korea to open cyber warfare school*. http://gadgets.ndtv.com/others/news/south-korea-to-open-cyber-warfare-school-225865

Agence France-Presse. (2014). *S. Korea detects suspected N. Korea hacking attempt*. http://www.globalpost.com/dispatch/news/afp/140327/s-korea-detects-suspected-n-korea-hacking-attempt

bbc.com. (2014). *South Korea to develop Stuxnet-like cyberweapons*. http://www.bbc.com/news/technology-26287527

Beach-Westmoreland, N. (2014). *If North Korea did hack Sony, it's a whole new kind of cyberterrorism*. December 23, http://www.wired.com/2014/12/why-america-must-answer-north-korea/

Bermudez, J. S., Jr. (2005). SIGINT, EW, and EIW in the Korean people's army: An overview of development and organization. In A. Y. Mansourov (Ed.), *Bytes and bullets in Korea*. http://www.apcss.org/Publications/Edited%20Volumes/BytesAndBullets/CH13.pdf

beSUCCESS. (2013). *South Korea cyber security concerns go far beyond financial industry*. http://e27.co/south-korea-cyber-security-concerns-go-far-beyond-financial-industry/

Boynton, R. S. (2011). *North Korea's digital underground*. http://www.theatlantic.com/magazine/archive/2011/04/north-koreas-digital-underground/308414/

businesskorea.co.kr. (2013). *Strengthened cyber security: Korea and US lay institutional foundation for cooperation in cyber security*. http://www.businesskorea.co.kr/article/1601/strengthened-cyber-security-korea-and-us-lay-institutional-foundation-cooperation-cyber

Cain, G. (2014). *North Korea: How the least-wired country became a hacking superpower*. http://www.sbsun.com/general-news/20141208/north-korea-how-the-least-wired-country-became-a-hacking-superpower

Cho, M. (2014). *South Korea official says cannot rule out North's hand in hack of nuclear operator*. December 23, 2014, http://www.reuters.com/article/2014/12/23/us-southkorea-cybersecurity-usa-idUSKBN0K100D20141223

chosun.com. (2011). *Seoul's makeshift answer to N. Korean jamming attacks*. http://english.chosun.com/site/data/html_dir/2011/09/23/2011092300630.html

chosun.com. (2013). *KSTN. Korea boosting cyber warfare capabilities*. http://english.chosun.com/site/data/html_dir/2013/11/05/2013110501790.html

Clayton, M. (2013). *In cyberarms race, North Korea emerging as a power, not a pushover.* http://www.csmonitor.com/World/Security-Watch/2013/1019/In-cyberarms-race-North-Korea-emerging-as-a-power-not-a-pushover/%28page%29/4

Drennan, W. M. (2003). North Korea's non-military threats. *East Asia: An International Quarterly, 20*(2), 48–59.

economist.com. (2011). *North Korean computer hackers: Black hats for hire.* http://www.economist.com/blogs/banyan/2011/08/north-korean-computer-hackers

Eun-jung, K. (2013). *S. Korean military to prepare with U.S. for cyber warfare scenarios.* http://english.yonhapnews.co.kr/national/2013/04/01/20/0301000000AEN20130401004000315F.HTM

Eun-jung, K. (2014). *S. Korea pushes to develop offensive cyberwarfare tools.* February 19, http://english.yonhapnews.co.kr/national/2014/02/19/3/0301000000AEN20140219003100315F.html

Firn, M. (2013). *North Korea builds online troll army of 3,000.* http://www.telegraph.co.uk/news/worldnews/asia/northkorea/10239283/North-Korea-builds-online-troll-army-of-3000.html

globalpost.com. (2013). *Damage from N.K. cyber attacks estimated at 860 bln won: lawmaker.* http://www.globalpost.com/dispatch/news/yonhap-news-agency/131015/damage-nk-cyber-attacks-estimated-at-860-bln-won-lawmaker

Hern, A. (2013). *North Korean 'cyberwarfare' said to have cost South Korea £500m.* http://www.theguardian.com/world/2013/oct/16/north-korean-cyber-warfare-south-korea

Ho, S. (2004). Haven for hackers. *Foreign Policy, November/December,* 145.

HP. (2014). *Companion Report: HP Security Briefing Episode 16: Profiling an enigma: The mystery of North Korea's cyber threat landscape.*

japanese.donga.com. (2014). 海外にサーバー、1784の「親北サイバー基地」摘発. http://japanese.donga.com/srv/service.php3?biid = 2014091109418

Kaempfer, W. H., & Lowenberg, A. D. (1988). The theory of international economic sanctions: A public choice approach. *American Economic Review, 78*(4), 786–793.

Keck, Z. (2014). *S. Korea seeks cyber weapons to target North Korea's nukes.* http://thediplomat.com/2014/02/s-korea-seeks-cyber-weapons-to-target-north-koreas-nukes/

Kim, D. (2012). The Republic of Korea's counter-asymmetric strategy. *Naval War College Review, 65*(1), 55–74.

Koo, S. (2013). *Cyber security in South Korea: The threat within.* http://thediplomat.com/2013/08/cyber-security-in-south-korea-the-threat-within/

koreaittimes.com. (2013). *Responses to cyber threats and future tasks – IPAK seminar,* July 11. http://www.koreaittimes.com/story/30252/responses-cyber-threats-and-future-tasks-%E2%80%93-ipak-seminar

koreatimes.co.kr. (2012). *Korea, US mull regular cyber warfare drills.* http://www.koreatimes.co.kr/www/news/nation/2013/07/205_119780.html

Kovacs, E. (2012). *Navigation affected after North Korea launched GPS jamming attack.* http://news.softpedia.com/news/Navigation-Affected-After-North-Korea-Launches-GPS-Jamming-Attack-268714.shtml

Kshetri, N. (2010). *The global cyber-crime industry: Economic, institutional and strategic perspectives.* Heidelberg: Springer.

Kwony. (2013). *North Korea's vast cyber warfare army.* http://cybersecurity.mit.edu/2013/09/north-koreas-vast-cyber-warfare-army/

Lee, D. (2012). *North Korea: On the net in world's most secretive nation.* http://www.bbc.co.uk/news/technology-20445632

McGee, J. (2011). *The difficulties of assessing North Korea's cyber strategy.* https://csis.org/blog/difficulties-assessing-north-koreas-cyber-strategy.

Metz, S., & Johnson, D. V. II. (2001). *Asymmetry and U.S. military strategy: Definition, background, and strategic concepts.* Carlisle Barracks, PA.: US Army War College, Strategic Studies Institute, January.

Miller, O. (2006). *North Korea's hidden history.* http://www.isj.org.uk/?id=166

Min-sik, Y. (2014). *Korea to punish lax personal data protection.* The Korea Herald.

Mundy, S. (2014). *South Korea suffers poor cyber security controls.* http://www.ft.com/intl/cms/s/0/7ae2b288-e29a-11e3-a829-00144feabdc0.html#axzz3JAV1TRou

Newton, C. (2013). *Why Google can't give you driving directions in South Korea.* http://www.theverge.com/tech/2013/10/13/4835026/why-google-cant-give-you-driving-directions-in-south-korea

Ong, R. (2008). South Korea and China's security objectives in East Asia. *Asia-Pacific Review, 15* (2), 102–119.

Panda, A. (2014). *Pentagon North Korea report for 2013: Unimpressive hardware, focus on cyber attacks.* http://thediplomat.com/2014/03/pentagon-north-korea-report-for-2013-unimpressive- · hardware-focus-on-cyber-attacks/

Pfanner, E. (2013). *Google jousts with wired South Korea over quirky Internet rules.* http://www.nytimes.com/2013/10/14/business/international/google-jousts-with-south-koreas-piecemeal-internet-rules.html?_r=1&amp

Raska, M. (2014). *Cyberwars on the Korean Peninsula.* http://www.aljazeera.com/indepth/opinion/2014/04/cyberwars-korean-peninsula-2014422531782925.html

Royle, T. (1990). *A dictionary of military quotations.* New York: Simon & Schuster.

Sang-ho, S. (2012). *S. Korea strives to bolster cyber combat capabilities.* http://www.koreaherald.com/common_prog/newsprint.php?ud=20120610000219&dt=2

Sang-Hun, C. (2013). *South Korean officials accused of political meddling.* http://www.nytimes.com/2013/12/20/world/asia/south-korean-cyberwarfare-unit-accused-of-political-meddling.html

shanghaidaily.com. (2014). *S.Korean military to set up cyber operation team next year*, December 23. http://www.shanghaidaily.com/article/article_xinhua.aspx?id=260343

Tae-gyu, K. (2013). Spy agency ups capabilities against cyber attacks. *Korea Times.* www.koreatimes.co.kr/www/news/nation/2013/04/116_133851.html

Ulsch, M. (2013). *The axis of cyber evil: A North Korean case of cyber espionage.* http://www.hstoday.us/blogs/critical-issues-in-national-cybersecurity/blog/the-axis-of-cyber-evil-a-north-korean-case-of-cyber-espionage/3072be3aacf419cc494e3910a62107b2.html

United Nations. (2014). *National accounts main aggregate database.* http://unstats.un.org/unsd/snaama/resCountry.asp

Waterman, S. (2012). North Korean jamming of GPS shows system's weakness. *Washington Times.* www.washingtontimes.com/news/2012/aug/23/north-korean-jamming-gps-shows-systems-weakness

zdnet.com. (2014). *ZDNet Staff Korea introduces security readiness guideline for private sector.* http://www.zdnet.com/korea-introduces-security-readiness-guideline-for-private-sector-7000032626/

Chapter 11
Cybersecurity in Gulf Cooperation Council Economies

11.1 Introduction

The six oil rich Gulf Cooperation Council (GCC) economies—Bahrain, Kuwait, Oman, Qatar, Saudi Arabia, and the United Arab Emirates (UAE)—are intensifying CS efforts. For instance, Saudi Arabia's CS spending during 2007–2018 is estimated to exceed US$33 billion (Karasik 2013). In February 2014, the UAE announced a plan to double security spending in the next 10 years, majority of which is expected to be on CS (Mustafa 2014). Similarly, Bahrain worked with the U.S. DoD in developing civilian and military CS capabilities, including manpower development (Ratnam 2014). Likewise, Oman was reported to attract foreign investors in developing CS capabilities in an attempt to establish itself as a regional CS hub (Mustafa 2014).

First, the region's oil-fueled prosperity and availability of liquid money make them attractive targets for financially motivated cyber-attacks. Low level of user awareness, the lack of technical and legislative capabilities and a lack of experience in CS lead to further vulnerability of these economies (El-Guindy 2013; Fielding-Smith 2013). Experts have pointed out that cyber-threats facing the energy sector of these economies and lack of sufficient awareness of such threats among key actors in the region are problems of special concern (Burgers et al. 2014).

GCC governments have adopted a number of measures in response to high profile attacks facing these economies. CS regulations in these economies are shaped by a variety of factors, such as Shari'ah principles, drive to modernize the economy and increasing international orientation.

GCC economies which had a combined GDP of US$1.6 trillion in 2013 are *attractive markets for ICT products*. Especially consumers and organizations in these economies are rapidly adopting cloud computing. According to the research firm, Gartner, public cloud services in the Middle East and North Africa (MENA) increased by 24.5 % to reach US$462.3 million in 2013. ICT infrastructure market was estimated to reach US$3.9 billion in 2013. Gartner noted that the data center

© Springer International Publishing Switzerland 2016   183
N. Kshetri, *The Quest to Cyber Superiority*, DOI 10.1007/978-3-319-40554-4_11

market in the Middle East is mainly driven by increased construction of data centers in GCC economies such as Saudi Arabia and the UAE, primarily driven by multinational corporations (gartner.com 2013). For instance, the UAE's cloud market is expected to experience a compound annual growth rate of 43.7 % until 2016 (gitex.com 2013).

The rapidly growing CS market in the region has also created opportunities for global ICT firms. For instance, in 2013, the U.S. International Trade Administration sent a delegation of 13 companies focusing on CS and critical infrastructure protection to Saudi Arabia and Kuwait to market their products, technologies and services to government agencies and private businesses (Eduard 2014).

Due to the strategic attractiveness of the GCC economies, cyber-threats facing them as well as their responses, resources, capabilities and limitations have significant global implications and thus deserve close observation and evaluations. For instance, the 2012 cyber-attacks on Saudi Arabian state oil company are major factor that reportedly influenced the U.S. Pentagon's plan to expand the CS force in the DoD's Cyber Command from about 900 personnel to 4900 over the next several years (Nakashima 2013). To take another compelling example, when the Saudi national oil company Aramco experienced cyber-attacks in 2012, oil traders from all over the world reported that they needed to communicate with Aramco by telex and fax (Burgers et al. 2014).

11.2   Threats, Vulnerabilities, Risks and Challenges Facing GCC Economies

GCC economies are currently facing a number of challenges and uncertainties in strengthening CS capabilities. A look at the ICT strategies of organizations indicates a lack of CS orientation, which has hindered their CS posture. These issues are of special concern for banks and financial institutions, which are found to have lax policies and procedures regarding electronic transactions. Problems such as the lack of protection of ATMs, implementation of mobile payments without giving sufficient security consideration to payment cards are more pervasive in the region compared to other economies (El-Guindy 2013). Likewise, the region's firms are engaged in outsourcing of sensitive and critical data to offshore vendors without paying much attention to the security policies and reputation of the vendor.

These economies' CS measures are also hindered by the lack of resources, experiences and training for participants in the criminal justice and law enforcement system, such as judges, police officers and prosecutors. In a cybercrime seminar organized by Oman's state-run Informational Technology Authority (ITA), the participants recommended that judges should be trained in cybercrime cases and the Royal Oman Police (ROP) should be trained in the prevention, detection and investigation of cybercrimes (gulfnews.com 2012). A lack of coordination among government ministries and a lack of leadership to coordinate a national CS strategy make the task equally challenging and difficult (scidev.net 2013).

The lack of skilled human resources is another barrier that GCC economies have experienced in their CS initiatives. For instance, based on the U.S. experience and the size and structure of the Saudi economy, Naef Bin Al-Saud (2012) argued that the country needs to train up to 3000 Saudi CS experts with the highest levels of skills and experience as well as "tens of thousands" of people with basic skills. As another example, Qatar had secured the commitment of a U.S.-based consulting company to develop a cyber-operations center. However, it was found later that the intent was to run the center with U.S. personnel (Schwentker 2013). The efforts stopped pretty much right there.

Financially motivated cybercriminals see GCC economies as *attractive crime targets*. In May 2013, US$45 million was stolen from banks in the UAE and Oman in a debit card cyber-attack scheme (Smythe 2013). There are reports that some Eastern Europe- and China-based cybercrime organizations focus exclusively on targets in GCC economies. Especially the UAE's Dubai has become an attractive target for these hackers due to its advanced financial center and most developed connectivity (financierworldwide.com 2013).

In addition to economic attractiveness, geopolitical positions of these economies are also linked to cyber-threats. These economies have also exposed to damage from politically motivated cyber-attacks. For instance, Saudi Arabia's enmity with Iran, Israel, Syria and Yemen contributed significantly to the cyber-threats facing the country (scidev.net 2013). The Syrian Electronic Army, which is a hacking group loyal to the Syrian President Bashar Al Assad, was believed to attack several Qatari websites in 2013 (The peninsulaqatar 2014).

The GCC economies as well as other countries in the Middle East are modernizing the natural gas and petrochemical industry, which involves heavy investment in computing platforms (Nusca 2014). CS remains a key security concern for this industry. According to Symantec, the global energy industry ranks among the top five for targeted cyber-attacks (businessweekme.com 2014). In August 2012, the Saudi national oil company Aramco, which is the world's largest oil and gas company supplying a tenth of the world's oil, experienced cyber-attacks, which were arguably the most severe cyber-attack on the country. The attacks, which were attributed to a virus called Shamoon, wiped out the hard drives of 30,000 computers or 85 % of the oil giant's devices and shut the company's business down for 2 weeks (Knickmeyer 2013). The costs associated with replacement and incident response were estimated to exceed US$15 million (Carr 2012). Several months *following* the first attacks, the Shamoon malware reportedly tried to attack the *oil and gas flow networks* in an attempt to disrupt international supplies (Cornwell 2014).

Shamoon is arguably the most significant cyber-attack against the oil and gas industry (Bronk 2014). Some argued that since Aramco is a state-owned company, a cyber-attack against it can be considered as equivalent to an attack against Saudi Arabia (Carr 2012). In the same month, Qatar's liquid natural gas company RasGas also experienced cyber-attacks, which was caused by the same virus. It led to the shutdown of the website and computer servers of RasGa (Schwentker 2013).

U.S. officials and the Middle East-based private sources attributed the cyber-attacks on Aramco, Qatar's Ras Gas to the Iranian government (Brenner 2013). One view was that Iran saw Saudi Arabia and Qatar as U.S. proxies. The attacks took place not long after Saudi Arabia expressed its intention to increase oil production to counter any supply problems caused by sanctions on Iran. Some analysts cite this incident to illustrate the convergence of the political and economic perspectives (Binham 2013).

Businesses and government agencies in the region too often fail to realistically assess the cyber-threats facing them and adequacy of their security measures. For instance, according to Microsoft, the location with the largest malware infect rate, as measured by Computers Cleaned per Mille (CCM) in the first quarter of 2011 was Qatar, which had a CCM of 61.5 (Rains 2011). This means that for every 1000 systems that the Microsoft Malicious Software Removal Tool (MSRT) executed in Qatar, 61.5 systems were found to be infected with malware. Policymakers in Qatar, however, are in denial regarding the seriousness of cybercrimes. For instance, the chairman of Economic Crimes Department at Qatar's Ministry of Interior noted that cybercrimes in the country are "manageable" and "effective measures" have been taken to protect the country's computers (menafn.com 2011). According to a 2014 survey of SafeNet, 66 % of decision makers in the Middle East believed their CS measures were sufficient, while 48 % of them had faced hacking attempts (Saudi Gazette 2014).

11.3 CS Regulations and Strategies

Despite the existence of cybercrime and CS laws and constitutional rights to privacy, a major shortcoming of most GCC economies concerns the lack of specific national laws to govern data protection and privacy (financierworldwide.com 2013). CS is of special concern outside the free trade zones. In recent years, a number of factors have acted as drivers and facilitators in strengthening GCC economies' CS initiatives. Especially numerous high-profile attacks against targets in the region have triggered CS measures. The president of Qatar Foundation Research and Development cited the August 2012 attacks on Saudi Aramco and Qatari Natural Gas Company have served as a jolt that has triggered increased efforts to strengthen CS in the region (scidev.net 2013).

CS regulations in GCC economies are rapidly evolving. There are sector specific laws in banking, healthcare, telecommunications and other industries. CS issues have been identified among the highest priorities in some GCC economies. According to the chairperson of Qatar Foundation, which has its mission to support the country's efforts to transform into a knowledge economy, CS has been identified as among the three priority challenges (together with energy security and water security) to be confronted (thepeninsulaqatar.com 2013).

In general, constitutions in these economies recognize an individual's right to privacy. For instance, Saudi Arabian Constitution clearly recognizes *individual dignity*. It guarantees the privacy of telephone, telegraphic, postal and other forms of communications and prohibits surveillance or eavesdropping of such communications (Elliott 2012). The 2007 Anti-Cyber Crime Law provides *civil and criminal sanctions* for violations o of personal data privacy including the interception of data transmitted through information networks and the unauthorized access of financial data in digital form.

GCC economies have realized a need to integrate with the outside world, which has helped strengthen CS initiatives. The region has a number of free zones with more developed regulations and guidelines in general as well as regulations to protect personal data. For instance, the Dubai International Financial Center (DIFC) has its own legal system and courts with jurisdiction over corporate, commercial, civil, employment, trusts and securities law matters, which are different from those of the UAE in general. Another free zone is Dubai Healthcare City (DHC), which serves as a free zone for medical services. Likewise, the Qatar Financial Centre (QFC), which was established by the Qatari government to attract international financial services, follows legal structure based on English common law. These free zones have enacted data protection laws to regulate the processing, storage and transfer of personal data by organizations that operate within these jurisdictions (Cornish 2013). These laws are modelled after the EU data protection directive.

The U.S.-Bahrain Free Trade Agreement (USBFTA), which was signed in 2004, has "Data Protection" provisions, which are especially relevant in the drug development and approval process. A drug is required to be approved by a regulatory agency (e.g., the FDA in the U.S.) before it can be sold. The FDA requires extensive testing before approval. The Data Protection" provisions require the developer to ensure the protection of data related to clinical trials and other tests (ustr.gov 2004).

As noted earlier, data protection laws in the QFC and other free zones are modelled on the EU data protection directive. Likewise, the U.S.-Bahrain Free Trade Agreement (USBFTA) has influenced Bahrain's data protection laws (ustr. gov 2004). CS-related regulations in these economies also draw from other sources. For instance, Oman's Electronic Transactions Law (Royal Decree 69/2008) and Qatar's Electronic Commerce and Transactions Law (Law No. 16 of 2010) draw on the UN Model Law on Electronic Commerce and the Model Law on Electronic Signatures (O'Connell 2012).

Some GCC economies are building CS capabilities with direct help from foreign countries. The U.S. is reportedly helping GCC countries, especially those that are involved in intelligence gathering about Iranian arms and providing the U.S. with such intelligence, to defend against cyber-attacks. Saudi Arabia, the UAE and Bahrain are believed to receive such assistance (jpost.com 2013).

Political, legal and law enforcement structures have been key ingredients in the set of policies that have brought to tackle internal CS threats. For instance, Reporters Without Borders has named some of the GCC states as "The Enemies of the Internet". The countries included in the 2012 list were Bahrain and Saudi Arabia. These countries "combine often drastic content filtering with access restrictions, tracking of cyber-dissidents and online propaganda". Some observers have noted that Saudi authorities' *vigilance* toward and crackdown against online activists has reached "extremely worrying levels" (globalvoicesonline.org 2014). Human rights defenders in the country face threats, harassment, arbitrary detention, imprisonment and torture. The *fabrication of judicial proceedings* against them has been a concern. In July 2014, the Saudi human rights activist Waleed Abulkhair was sentenced to 15 years, fined a large sum of money and banned from leaving the country for another 15 years. He faced these harsh punishments for his comments on social media and remarks to the news media regarding the country's miserable human rights record (washingtonpost.com 2014). In June 2013, Saudi Arabia also banned Viber, which allows users to call for free, send messages and share photos. In 2006, Google Translate and Wikipedia were blocked, which translated blocked sites and were used to bypass the filters (dnaindia.com 2013).

Cultural security has also been an instrument of national strategic priorities on the cyber front. A 2002 study conducted by Harvard Law School found that proxy servers in Saudi Arabia filtered and blocked "sexually explicit" contents (Hermida 2002). In 2013, the Communications and Information Technology Commission (CITC) reportedly blocked about 400,000 pornographic sites (arabnews.com 2014). In August 2014, the Commission for the Promotion of Virtue and Prevention of Vice asked the Ministry of Interior to arrest cyber-offenders who insult Allah. The commission reported that in 2013/14, it received complaints on 9341 pornographic websites, 2743 websites that contained faith violations and 132 cases of electronic blackmail (saudigazette.com.sa 2014).

11.4   Organizational Initiatives

Government agencies and the private sector have also taken organizational *and technological measures to* enhance CS and data protection. Saudi government bodies such as the Capital Markets Authority, Riyadh city government launched in-house, or contracted, efforts to protect their data (Knickmeyer 2013). Among other policy, institutional and technical capacity-building measures, CERTs have been established in Oman, Saudi Arabia, Qatar and the UAE in order to safeguard information and communications systems and assist organizations in response to CS breaches. On a regional level, the GCC-CERT initiative was launched in 2008 to provide a framework for regional cooperation. Likewise, Qatar has established a Cybercrime Investigation Centre and an Information Security Centre.

Researchers in Qatar are also investigating the types of attacks, technologies employed and their origination that could be used to attack the oil and gas industry (scidev.net 2013). They are also upgrading their capabilities, through collaboration with multinationals. In July 2013, IBM and Saudi Arabia's Mobily collaborated on a secure online operations center, which is IBM's first, top-security global operations center in the Middle East (Knickmeyer 2013).

Growing cyber-threats have contributed to a steep increase in CS investments. In the UAE, sensitive sectors such as the public sector, oil and gas, banking, finance and insurance are driving demand for CS products, especially cloud security solutions. According to Frost and Sullivan, revenue from cloud security services in the UAE is was US$8.7 million in 2012, which will increase to US$72.3 million by 2019 (Khaleej Times (United Arab Emirates) 2014). Following the attacks on Saudi Aramco and Qatar's RasGas operations, big firms in the regions are taking drastic security measures. For instance, the Saudi Electricity Company increased its CS investment by about 20 % following the attacks (Allison 2013). The company is placing special emphasis on IT security of its operational part—the electricity generation and transmission systems. Until not long ago, the Saudi Electricity Company viewed the production side as a separate, closed system and did not consider as outward facing. After realizing that the production side is also exposed to cyber-threats, the company revised the traditional view. The company hired the consulting company Devoteam to provide a comprehensive assessment and recommendations of its network security, which included all areas of operations (arabianindustry.com 2013).

CS is being considered as a critical organizational function. Some are building their own CS teams instead of outsourcing to a third party. Following the 2012 attacks, Aramco moved the outsourced IT services to in-house.

Some organization in the GCC economies have also implemented CS measures because of competitive and customer imperatives rather than regulatory compliance issues. For instance, as early as in 2007, most private sector companies offering online products and services in Kuwait had privacy policies and consumer rights on their websites. These measures were also directed towards raising their clients' awareness. Especially companies in the telecommunications and financial sectors take strict measures such as deployment of the latest security products to ensure that electronic transactions meet international standards (United Nations 2007).

11.5 Similarities and Differences with Major World Economies

Some major similarities and differences between GCC economies' CS landscape and those of the EU and the U.S. are summarized in Table 11.1.

11.5.1 A Comparison with the EU

As a point of similarity between the GCC economies and the EU, as noted earlier, comprehensive data protection laws exist in the free zones of DIFC, QFC and DHC. These laws are modelled on the EU Data Protection Directive.

Just like the EU, some GCC economies mandate companies to obtain users' consent to collection, processing, and transfer of personal data. According to Oman's Electronic Transactions Law, issued by the Decree 69/2008, a government

Table 11.1 GCC economies' CS landscape: key similarities and differences with the EU and the U.S.

	The EU	The U.S.
Similarities	• Comprehensive data protection regimes in the free zones. • Restrictions on transferring personal data originated from DIFC to most jurisdictions. • Requirement of users' consent in some economies (e.g., Oman's Electronic Transactions Law)	• Sector specific laws deal with data privacy in certain circumstances: Qatar (Labor Law, Banking Law, E-Commerce and Transactions Law, Telecommunications Law). • Transfer of personal data originated outside the free zones (Saudi Arabia: No specific laws apply to the transfer of personal data outside the country).
Differences	• Outside the free zones, no specific national laws to govern data protection and privacy. • Lack of intra-GCC consistency in data protection laws: no pan-GCC/pan-Arabic laws.	• Vagueness and uncertainty regarding the exact nature of measures to be taken by a company to prevent data disclosure. • No privacy commission or an agency equivalent to the *FTC*.

agency or a service provider may collect personal data only with explicit approval of the concerned person. Moreover, it is not permitted to process or use such data for any purpose other than that for which it was collected (ITA 2011).

A final similarity is that, just like the EU, there are restrictions on transferring personal data originated in the free zones to most jurisdictions. For instance, personal data that originates within the DIFC may only be transferred to jurisdictions outside the DIFC that are considered to have an "adequate level of protection."

As a first difference with the EU, GCC economies have no specific national laws governing data protection and privacy, and there are no unified set of laws (financierworldwide.com 2013). Yet another difference is that while there is some heterogeneity in implementation and interpretation the Data Protection Directive in EU member countries (Kshetri and Murugesan 2013), the differences are more prevalent in the GCC region. There has been a lack of pan-GCC or pan-Arabic laws governing data protection and privacy in the region (Cornish 2013). GCC economies also differ widely at the current state of such regulations and the rate at which they are developing. For instance, as of 2008, Bahrain, Kuwait, Oman and Saudi Arabia had no data protection and privacy rules, whereas Qatar and the UAE had articles and specific rules on these issues (Qatar's Telecom Law 2006-Decree 34 and the UAE's Data protection Law 2007) (Idlebi 2008).

11.5.2   A Comparison with the U.S.

As a first point of similarity between the GCC economies and the U.S., sector-specific regulations play an important role in shaping CS policy initiatives. For

Table 11.2 Sector-specific data protection regulations in selected GCC economies

Economy	Sector-specific data protection regulations
Kuwait	The Central Bank of Kuwait Law provides higher level of protection for data related to banks and their customers (KPMG 2012).
Bahrain	While there are no specific regulations and guidelines for data protection, regulations mandate strengthening data protection measures in financial institutions.
Qatar	It has a number of sector-specific laws. They include Labor Law (requirement to keep record for employers), Banking Law (requirement for QCB-regulated financial institutions to protect their clients' information), E-Commerce and Transactions Law (control on e-commerce service providers' collection, use, retention and disclosure of customer information) and Telecommunications Law (requirement for telecommunication service providers to protect customer information and also controls regarding the collection, use, retention and disclosure of such information) (Cornish 2013).

instance, as discussed in Chap. 5, visions and priorities of the U.S. EO on CS include combating cyber-attacks and cyber-espionage on government agencies and critical sectors such as banking, power and transportation industries and U.S. companies. Commercial IT products and consumer IT services are excluded from critical infrastructures and thus are less likely to be affected (Kshetri and Murugesan 2013). Just like the U.S., sectoral differences can be observed in these economies' CS regulations (Table 11.2).

Another similarity between GCC and the U.S. concerns the transfer of personal data, especially those originated outside the free zones. In Saudi Arabia, for instance, there are no specific laws that apply to the transfer of personal data outside the country.

A difference is that CS-related laws and regulations in the region are more vague and uncertain than in the U.S. For instance, while the UAE Penal Code, Labor Law, and industry-specific legislation make disclosure of data a criminal offence in many cases, the exact nature of measures to be taken by a company or employer is to prevent such disclosure is not specified. A further difference is that GCC economies do not have a privacy commission or an agency equivalent to the U.S. *FTC*.

11.6 Discussion and Concluding Remarks

This chapter described a number of developmental and structural aspects of the GCC economies' CS landscape. A high proportion of the cyber-attacks targeting the region are politically motivated. Some argue that hackers targeted Saudi Aramco due to Saudi Arabia's close connection and interdependence with the U.S.

An important, unique, and distinctive attribute of GCC CS landscape is the prevalence of religious and cultural dimension in the region's CS strategy. Measures are also aimed at strengthening political security by increasing political authority, and governing capacity. Despite the lack of comprehensive and specific national laws or regulators governing data protection and privacy, these issues are regulated through constitutions, statutes, and other legal codes. While data protection laws and regulations in these economies are still relatively new and developing, they are increasingly reflecting the growing global recognition of the importance of such protection. The lack of pan-GCC or pan-Arabic laws governing data protection and privacy means that managers struggle with a number of compliance challenges.

CS is usually an afterthought and a low priority. The evidence from the surveys cited above (e.g., MSRT 2014 and SafeNet) suggests GCC businesses and government agencies have a tendency to underestimate the vulnerability to cyber-attacks of their firms and they are unable to assess a realistic situation regarding the CS. The increasing cyber-threats facing the region provide compelling reasons to rethink the current policy of spending disproportionately less on CS compared to that in telecommunication networks. Capacity-building efforts, including CS skill development and enhancing educational awareness at various levels, need to be designed with the aim of enhancing cyber-offense and cyber-defense capabilities.

For the U.S. and other Western countries, the strategic significance of GCC economies' CS initiatives is growing due to the fact that these economies are involved in intelligence gathering and sharing about key issues such as Iranian arms, and their rapidly growing CS market due primarily to some of the high profile cyber-attacks faced by some of the GCC economies has created opportunities for Western technology firms specializing in CS.

National data protection and CS laws exhibit a lower *degree of specificity and comprehensiveness* in GCC economies. In the absence of comprehensive laws covering an issue, the court's judgment may be influenced by Shari'ah. Given the clear and important role of Shari'ah law, it will be of considerable interest to understand some of the key features of this law. An important point to mention here is that it is against Shari'ah principles to invade an individual's privacy and disclose secrets without his/her permission, especially if it is not in the public interest to do so (financierworldwide.com 2013). The punishment for data breach related crimes are likely to be unpredictable and unclear as they fall under the judge's discretion.

References

Allison, A. (2013). The hidden value of IT departments. *MEED: Middle East Economic Digest, 57* (18), 41.

Al-Saud, N. B. A. (2012). Cybersecurity strategies. *JFQ: Joint Force Quarterly, 64*, 75–81 (1st Quarter).

arabianindustry.com. (2013, August 1). *Saudi Electricity Company's IT transformation.* http://arabianindustry.com/utilities/features/2013/aug/1/saudi-electricity-companys-it-transformation-4391218/#.VA8IPVcaTIY

arabnews.com. (2014). *400,000 porn sites blocked by CITC.* http://www.arabnews.com/news/598441

Binham, C. (2013). *The hacker hunters.* http://www.ft.com/intl/cms/s/2/bccc8f3c-523c-11e3-8c42-00144feabdc0.html#axzz37vVS6Nvw

Brenner, J. F. (2013). Eyes wide shut: The growing threat of cyber attacks on industrial control systems. *Bulletin of the Atomic Scientists, 69*(5), 15–20.

Bronk, C. (2014). *Hacks on gas: Energy, cybersecurity, and U.S. defense.* The James A. Baker Iii Institute For Public Policy, Rice University.

Burgers, R., Baars, H., Adriaensen, M., & Raja, A. (2014). Middle East needs cyber security from within utilities face energy threat. DNV KEMA Energy & Sustainability.

businessweekme.com. (2014). *Fallout from the Saudi Aramco breach continues.* http://businessweekme.com/Bloomberg/newsmid/190/newsid/35

Carr, J. (2012). *Why wasn't Saudi Aramco's oil production targeted?* http://jeffreycarr.blogspot.de/2012/09/why-wasnt-saudi-aramcos-oil-production.html

Cornish, J. (2013). *Data protection and privacy laws in the Middle East.* Latham & Watkins LL. http://www.jdsupra.com/legalnews/data-protection-and-privacy-laws-in-the-24928/

Cornwell, A. (2014). *Cyber attacks an increasing threat for Mideast oil and gas.* http://gulfnews.com/business/oil-gas/cyber-attacks-an-increasing-threat-for-mideast-oil-and-gas-1.1399982

dnaindia.com. (2013). *Saudi Arabia to ban WhatsApp soon.* http://www.dnaindia.com/scitech/report-saudi-arabia-to-ban-whatsapp-soon-1850251

Eduard, K. (2014). *Website of Kuwait's Ministry of Interior Hacked and Defaced.* http://news.softpedia.com/news/Website-of-Kuwait-s-Ministry-of-Interior-Hacked-and-Defaced-435068.shtml

El-Guindy, M. N. (2013). *Middle East Cyber Security Threat Report 2014.* http://netsafe.me/category/cybercrime/

Elliott, S. (2012). *Privacy and data interception in Saudi Arabia.* http://www.privacydatasecurityblog.com/2012/06/08/privacy-and-data-interception-in-saudi-arabia/

Fielding-Smith, A. (2013). *Middle East cyber crimes force concerted response from banks.* http://www.ft.com/intl/cms/s/0/28010fda-25f1-11e3-8ef6-00144feab7de.html#axzz2osZmvj8v

financierworldwide.com. (2013). *Talking point: Cyber security and data protection in the Middle East.* http://www.financierworldwide.com/article.php?id=11296&page=2

gartner.com. (2013). *Gartner says The Middle East and Africa IT infrastructure spending to reach US$ 4 billion.* http://www.gartner.com/newsroom/id/2347215

gitex.com. (2013). *MENA outpacing most of world in cloud computing growth.* http://www.gitex.com/Content/MENA-outpacing-most-of-world-in-cloud-computing-growth

globalvoicesonline.org. (2014). *7 Cases that prove online activism is under siege in Saudi Arabia.* http://advocacy.globalvoicesonline.org/2014/07/15/7-cases-that-prove-online-activism-is-under-siege-in-saudi-arabia/

gulfnews.com. (2012). *Oman forum calls for tough laws against cybercrime.* http://gulfnews.com/news/gulf/oman/oman-forum-calls-for-tough-laws-against-cybercrime-1.1035332

Hermida, A. (2002). *Saudis block 2,000 websites.* http://news.bbc.co.uk/2/hi/technology/2153312.stm

Idlebi, N. (2008, February). *Cyber legislation in the ESCWA region security issues.* UN-Economic and Social Commission for Western Asia, Data Protection and Privacy (DP&P)

ITA. (2011). *Electronic transactions law.* Information Technology Authority (ITA). http://www.ita.gov.om/ITAPortal/MediaCenter/Document_detail.aspx?NID=56

jpost.com. (2013, June 9). *US aids Gulf allies to counter Iran cyber-attacks.* http://www.jpost.com/Iranian-Threat/News/US-aids-allies-defend-against-Iran-cyber-attacks-315903

Karasik, T. (2013). *Saudi Arabia's defense posture is robust.* http://english.alarabiya.net/en/views/news/middle-east/2013/09/23/Saudi-Arabia-s-defense-posture-is-robust.html

Khaleej Times (United Arab Emirates). (2014, August). *GCC cloud market to post seven-fold growth by 2020.* http://www.khaleejtimes.com/article/20140821/ARTICLE/308219895/1037

Knickmeyer, E. (2013). *After cyberattacks, Saudi steps up online security.* http://blogs.wsj.com/middleeast/2013/08/26/after-cyberattacks-saudi-steps-up-online-security/

KPMG. (2012). *International executive services: Thinking beyond borders Kuwait*. KPMG International.

Kshetri, N., & Murugesan, S. (2013). EU and US cybersecurity strategies: Impacts on businesses and consumers. *IEEE Computer, 46*(10), 84–88.

menafn.com. (2011). *Rate of cyber crimes in Qatar negligible: Official, MENAFN, The Peninsula*. http://www.menafn.com/menafn/qn_news_story_s.aspx?storyid=1093423127

Mustafa, A. (2014). *UAE to double security budget, focus on cyber*. http://mobile.defensenews.com/article/302240015

Nakashima, E. (2013). *Pentagon to boost cybersecurity force*. http://www.washingtonpost.com/world/national-security/pentagon-to-boost-cybersecurity-force/2013/01/19/d87d9dc2-5fec-11e2-b05a-605528f6b712_story.html?hpid=z4

Nusca, A. (2014). *It's time for corporate boards to tackle cybersecurity. Here's why*. Fortune.com. 1-1.

O'Connell, N. (2012). *Data protection and privacy issues in the Middle East*. http://www.legal500.com/c/united-arab-emirates/developments/17454

Rains, T. (2011). *The curious case of Qatar*. http://blogs.technet.com/b/security/archive/2011/11/22/the-curious-case-of-qatar.aspx

Ratnam, G. (2014). *Pentagon aiding allies on cybersecurity in Gulf to Asia*. http://www.bloomberg.com/news/2014-03-31/pentagon-aiding-allies-on-cybersecurity-in-gulf-to-asia.html

Saudi Gazette. (2014). *38 percent Saudi companies unsure about cyber security*. https://en-maktoob.news.yahoo.com/38-percent-saudi-companies-unsure-cyber-security-084219081.html

saudigazette.com.sa. (2014). *Haia asks ministry to arrest blasphemers*. http://www.saudigazette.com.sa/index.cfm?method=home.regcon&contentid=20140819215183

Schwentker, R. B. (2013). Cyber warfare – The new reality. *Infrastructure, 52*(3), 1–5 (cover story).

scidev.net. (2013). *Gulf countries 'need early-warning on cyber attacks'*. http://www.scidev.net/global/technology/news/gulf-countries-need-early-warning-on-cyber-attacks.html

Smythe, C. (2013). *Eight charged with debit card cyber-crime targeting banks*. http://www.bloomberg.com/news/2013-05-09/eight-charged-with-debit-card-cyber-crime-targeting-banks.html

The peninsulaqatar. (2014). *Cyber attacks: Qatar third most targeted*. http://thepeninsulaqatar.com/news/qatar/303181/cyber-attacks-qatar-third-most-targeted

thepeninsulaqatar.com. (2013). *Energy, water and cyber security top goals*. http://thepeninsulaqatar.com/news/qatar/262025/energy-water-and-cyber-security-top-goals

United Nations. (2007, August). *National profile of the information society in Kuwait*. Economic and Social Commission for Western Asia (Escwa), United Nations.

ustr.gov. (2004). *U.S.-Bahrain FTA: Fact sheet on access to medicines*. http://www.ustr.gov/about-us/press-office/fact-sheets/archives/2004/september/us-bahrain-fta-fact-sheet-access-medicines

washingtonpost.com. (2014). *Saudi Arabia continues its outrageous repression of human rights activists*. http://www.washingtonpost.com/opinions/saudi-arabia-continues-its-outrageous-repression-of-human-rights-activists/2014/08/26/dc6404fa-2258-11e4-958c-268a320a60ce_story.html

Chapter 12
Cybersecurity in Brazil

12.1 Introduction

Brazil's social, economic, political, and cultural characteristics provide unique and fascinating insights into the key drivers of cybercrimes and the nature of CS measures. The country is both a major source and a target of cyber-attacks. Some of the world's well-known cybercriminal gangs operate from the country. For instance, in 2004, two-thirds of the world's paedophile pages were reportedly hosted in Brazil (Leyden 2004a). Economic losses related to cybercrime were estimated at US$8 billion in 2012 (Symantec 2012). The country also faces politically motivated internal cyber-threats. For instance, Brazilian government agencies' websites have been attacked frequently by the Anonymous and other hacking groups (Southern Pulse 2011). Likewise, although Brazilian officials have denied, CS experts outside the country have suggested that the 2009 blackouts which affected over 60 million people, and similar blackouts in Espirito Santo State in 2007 and Rio de Janeiro in 2005 may have been caused by cyber-attacks (Libicki 2013).

CS is becoming a high profile policy and political issue in Brazil. In November 2012, Brazil approved cybercrime legislation and made other policy improvements. Development of CS policies is one of the six key areas of in the priorities for 2014 set by the Ministry of Science, Technology and Innovation (MCTI) for the development of the country's basic technology policies (Mari 2014a).

12.2 Cyber-Threats Facing Brazil

Table 12.1 presents some examples of real and perceived cyber-threats facing Brazil. Brazil has earned its reputation as the "king of the banking Trojan" (Theriault 2011). Whereas cybercriminals mostly rely on a small number of

Table 12.1 Real and perceived cyber-threats facing Brazil: some examples

	Internal	External
Political	• 2013: Anonymous Brazil defaced the website of the Brazilian Air Force (Kovacs 2013). • 2014: Anonymous Brazil's attack on Brazilian government websites to protest against 2014 FIFA world cup.	• The NSA's alleged interception of President Rousseff's private communications. • 2013: Indian hackers defaced Brazilian websites.
Economic	• 2014: Cyber-attack on Boleto Bancário system. • February 2012: A coordinated attack which coincided with quarterly earnings reports victimized most major Brazilian banks (Lincoln 2013).	• The NSA's alleged industrial espionage on the oil giant Petrobras. • According to the Brazilian television OGlobo, Canadian spy agencies tracked the Brazil's Mines and Energy Ministry e-mails and phone calls as well as communications to other countries, including the Ecuador-based Latin American Energy Organization (OLADE) (Caldwell 2013). • 2012: A cyber espionage campaign targeted high-profile oil companies including those of Brazil according to Dell SecureWork CTU.

malware products in most other parts of the world (e.g., Zeus or Citadel in Europe), the Brazilian malware landscape is more diverse. Bancos, the well-known password stealing Trojan, which is designed to steal banking information mainly from Latin American consumers, is believed to be originated in Brazil and originally targeted Brazilians. Other well-known banking Trojans such as ZeuS, SpyEye and CARBERP are also reported to be increasingly common in Brazil (Robertson 2013).

As early as 2004, losses from online financial fraud in Brazil were estimated to exceed losses through bank robberies (Leyden 2004b). A PwC study revealed that hackers stole US$1 billion from Brazilian companies in 2011 (Geromel 2012). According to the Brazilian Federation of Banks or Federação Brasileira de Bancos (Febraban), cybercrime accounts for 95 % of losses incurred by Brazilian banks. The Febraban estimated that US$1.4 billion was lost to electronic fraud in 2012 (Perlroth 2014). In a high profile cyber-attack reported in the mid-2014, Brazil's popular payment method, Boleto Bancário was a target. Note that Boleto can be issued online and paid through a number of channels such as banks and supermarkets. The criminals attempted to steal US$3.75 billion although it is not clear what proportion of that was actually stolen. Researchers from the Internet security company, RSA traced the bolware to a criminal gang in Brazil (Perlroth 2014).

Brazil is also exposed to politically-motivated internal cyber-threats. In 2008, hackers attacked a government website, which affected over 3000 employees for more than 24 hours, and compromised valuable documents. The hacker demanded US$350 million in ransom money. The ransom was not paid but it took more than a week to regain control of the website (Mylrea 2009). In the first 10 months of 2011, government websites were attacked more than 1250 times in Brazil (Wyss 2011). In June 2011, significant cyber-attacks affected websites of Brazilian government agencies (Southern Pulse 2011).

One reason is that many Brazilians are concerned about the disproportionate political power held by the government. Brazil is also reported to be among the top countries in terms of the government's actions to control and monitor citizens' activities online. For instance, Google has reported that Brazil is among the countries making highest numbers of requests to obtain user information or to block search results through legal actions. According to Brazil's speech laws, public officials have the power and authority to decide what is considered as libel, slander or defamation of character (Southern Pulse 2011). In 2012, the director of Google Brazil was arrested for failing to remove two videos that criticized Alcides Bernal, who was a candidate for mayor of Campo Grande. In March 2014, Bernal was removed from office for alleged public corruption (latimesblogs.latimes.com 2012).

Regarding the data localization initiatives, due to this reputation of the Brazilian government, experts debate over whether keeping the data within the Brazilian jurisdiction would make individuals' data more secure. Some argue that increased localization would make it easier for the Brazilian government to track and censor its citizens (King 2014). Ronaldo Lemos, director of the private Institute for Technology and Society and a professor at the Rio de Janeiro State University, who conceived of the Marco Civil in 2007 noted: "Until we have better laws in terms of data protection and other civil rights protections, it actually harms these rights to have them located in Brazil" (King 2014).

Since the 1990s, in an effort to bridge the digital divide, the Brazilian government took a number of measures to introduce ICTs in the poorer areas. Due primarily to these efforts, Brazil is reported to have the world's second-highest Twitter usage behind the U.S. Due to its anonymity, and the ability to reach a wide audience, Twitter has been one of the most popular tools for recruiting volunteers for hacktivist organizations such as Anonymous. Some of the well-known Twitter accounts for publicizing Anonymous-related news are reported to have tens of thousands of followers (Olson 2012).

The Brazilian government fined Google for failing to reveal information about an Internet user. The public's confrontation with expanding state power and the authority and a general cultural indifference towards hacking and cyber-attacks also deserve mention. A report of the IT security company, Imperva noted that "strong government or corporate resentment in a population is a key factor" behind the escalation of cyber-attacks in Brazil (p. 5). In their early years of existence, Brazilian hacktivists attracted the attention of many Brazilians. Brazilians perceived that many of their targets deserved attack. Imperva notes: "In the minds of many Brazilians, the cyber mayhem was no crime" (Imperva 2012). In this way, the relative lack of external and internal stigma associated with hacking, which is related to culture and ethical attitudes, has been a crucial factor in driving hacking and cyber-attacks in Brazil.

In June 2014, as a protest against the 2014 FIFA World Cup, the hacker group Anonymous Brazil defaced a number of Brazilian government websites. The Foreign Ministry's server was attacked which compromised emails and attachments. It also attacked top FIFA partner sites, such as the Korean car manufacturers Hyundai. A hacker, who claimed to be a member of the Anonymous emailed Reuters: "Companies and institutions that work with a government that denies the basic rights of its people in order to promote a private, exclusive and corrupt sports event will be targeted" (Gaskell 2014). The website of Mato Grosso state government was also attacked.

Regarding the NSA's alleged industrial espionage on the oil giant Petrobras, while the U.S. has denied spying for commercial advantage, many Brazilians do not seem to be convinced. President Dilma Rousseff argued that if the allegation of the NSA's breaking into Petrobras computers is true, then gathering economic information would be the motive (McDonald 2014). The networks of Ministry of Mines and Energy were also hacked, which, together with Petrobras, was involved in the auction of oil fields (Purkayastha and Bailey 2014). Specifically, Brazilians think that the company's data on Brazil's offshore oil reserves and plans for allocating licenses for exploration to foreign companies were the intended targets (Sanger and Perlroth 2014). In September 2013, Brazil's Congress opened an investigation and questioned oil industry regulator Magda Chambriard on whether the alleged spying by the NSA could have given U.S. companies the edge in bidding for offshore production rights to be auctioned in October 2013. In 2012, the Dell SecureWorks Counter Threat Unit (CTU) research team tracked a cyber-espionage campaign that targeted a high-profile oil companies in a number of countries including those in Brazil (Cutler 2012). In 2013, a group of Indian hackers defaced 37 Brazilian websites. The attacks were claimed to be in retaliation to cyber-attacks on Indian government's websites by Brazil-based hackers (timesofindia.indiatimes.com 2013).

12.3   The Brazilian Approach to CS

A major drawback of the Brazilian CS landscape is the ineffective legislative systems. According to Brazil's legislation enacted in 1988, a hacker cannot be charged for breaking into a site, or distributing a virus, unless it is proven that the action resulted in a crime (Smith 2003). A cybercrime bill introduced in the Brazilian congress in 2005 had been pending for over 6 years (Theriault 2011). The bill became unpopular with lawmakers due to a concern that it may facilitate the government's spying on citizens (opennet.net 2008).

Recent CS developments have given rise to significant regulatory activities in the CS arena. The Internet Bill of Rights known as "Marco Civil da Internet", which was proposed in the Brazilian Congress in 2011, received new significance following the NSA spying. It was passed by the Brazilian Senate in April 2014 and signed by the president in the same month (Stankey 2014). It intends to provide privacy protections for Internet users, and limit the amount of metadata that can be gathered on Brazilians. Disclosure of personal data to third parties requires the user's informed consent. Companies collecting personal data from residents of Brazil are subject to Brazil's laws and courts in cases involving information on Brazilians irrespective of the location of data storage (Stankey 2014). In order to get opposition support, the government agreed to withdraw a provision in the proposed Internet law, which would have required foreign Internet companies to host data of Brazilians in the country (Ribeiro 2014).

Brazil is also taking actions to ensure the enforcement of Internet users' privacy rights. In July 2014, Brazil's consumer protection regulator fined the telecom company Oi SA US$1.6 million for allegedly failing to notify Internet users that it would track their browsing activities and provide to the data advertisers. According to the Justice Ministry, Oi failed to fully disclose how its partnership with the British online advertising company Phorm would affect consumers. The partnership involved creating a tool that allowed Oi to track consumer data traffic and compile profiles, which could be sold to third parties (Grande 2014).

In September 2013, Brazilian communications minister Paulo Bernardo noted that Brazil could require telecommunications companies to use equipment in their networks that is designed and produced in Brazil (Leahy 2013). Bill Woodcock, executive director of Packet Clearing House, described this as the most controversial element of the Brazilian plan. This requirement is expected to address the fear that equipment manufactured in foreign countries may come with back doors installed (Woodcock 2013). Rousseff had also asked the Congress to introduce regulations to require foreign companies to store data generated by Brazilians on local servers (Brooks and Bajak 2013).

The proposed regulation faced strong resistance and criticism from foreign companies. In October 2013, 47 organizations representing diverse industries worldwide *sent* a letter *to selected* Brazilian Congress members, which pointed out several unintended consequences of the proposed data center localization plan. Their criticism focused on four main points: decreased security (data security depends on how data is protected and a focus on physical location may distract from the reality), higher costs (not being able to enjoy economies of scale, which would increase costs for end users), decreased competitiveness (isolation from the world's innovative and efficient cloud services and strong computing power around the world) and harm to consumers (denial of cloud services available around the world).

Foreign technology companies warned the Brazilian government that the requirement of local data centers may lead to closure and divestment of their facilities and operations. Google criticized and opposed the legislation on the grounds that data is more secure if it is stored in multiple locations. The company also argued that storing data in one location slows the services and increases customer inconvenience. Google's director of law enforcement and information security, Richard Salgado noted that Brazil's proposed law to require all data of Brazilian citizens and companies to be stored in the country would be difficult to comply and argued that Google "could be barred from doing business" in Brazil

(Miller 2014a). Testifying before the Senate Judiciary Subcommittee on Privacy, Technology and the Law Hearing, Salgado noted: "If data localization and other efforts are successful, then what we will face is the effective Balkanization of the Internet and the creation of a 'splinternet' broken up into smaller national and regional pieces, with barriers around each of the splintered Internets to replace the global Internet we know today" (Miller 2014a). Among U.S. companies, while Microsoft announced in December 2013 that it would allow Brazilian cloud customers to store locally, Facebook and Google have viewed the proposals with concern and disapproval (Mari 2013a).

In October 2013, Rousseff requested all federal government bodies to deploy a secure electronic communications system in order to strengthen privacy and security. Brazil's IT policy secretary discussed the possibility that the Brazilian government may store sensitive data locally rather than in the cloud (bbc.co.uk 2013). Brazil is replacing the Microsoft Outlook by a custom-made system, Expresso V3. Expresso V3 was developed by the Federal Service of Data Processing or Serviço Federal de Processamento de Dados (SERPRO), which is an organization that offers Information Technology and Communication Services to the public sector. Expresso V3 runs on the cloud platform maintained by the SERPRO and aims to protect official emails from all types of surveillance. In April 2014, the Ministry of Defense started the installation of a secure digital communication network for federal government offices. The system included instant messaging, web conferencing and other functions, which is expected to be fully installed throughout federal government offices by the end of 2014 (arabtoday.net 2014). As of September 2013, SERPRO had spent US$3.9 million to purchase network equipment, new servers, security systems and a data link of 10 Gbps to connect its three datacenters (Mari 2014a).

The revelation of the NSA spying is likely to result in a significant diversion of trade flows away from the U.S. Brazil has been among the most vocal critics of the NSA surveillance programs. Rousseff postponed her planned state visit to the U.S. because of anger at the revelations that the NSA had intercepted her private communications. In a speech to the UN General Assembly in September 2013, she condemned the NSA's spying as a breach of international law (Constantin 2014). Rousseff also called for a global multilateral Internet governance meeting. It led to the NETmundial event held in April 2014 in Sao Paulo, Brazil, which was attended by 1000 on-site and 500 remote participants (Purkayastha and Bailey 2014).

U.S. firms in defense, telecom, energy and aviation are affected by Brazil's proposed measures. During Rousseff's October 2013 planned visit in the U.S., the two countries were expected to negotiate and sign trade and investment deals in areas such as oil exploration, biofuels technology, and fighter jets. Boeing was expected to sell 36 Super Hornet jet fighters fighter worth more than US$4 billion to the Brazilian Air Force (Paulo 2013). Brazilian officials were reported as saying that Brazil could not buy from an untrustworthy country (Boadle 2013). In January 2014, defensenews.com reported Brazil's decision to purchase the Swedish Gripen plane instead of the McDonnell Douglas (now Boeing) F/A-18. According to

Brazilian officials, the NSA scandal played a key role in this decision (Brattberg 2014).

Brazilian policy makers view that a major factor that enabled the NSA to record conversations of Rousseff and other leaders in Latin America concerned the region's dependence on the U.S. for communication routes and infrastructure (Woodcock 2013). Brazil is taking measures to avoid U.S.-based data centers, and routers. For instance, as of 2013, about 90 % (18–19 Gbps) of data originating from and destined to Latin America and the Caribbean (LAC) were routed through Miami's Network Access Point (NAP), which connects the LAC economies with more than 148 countries. In an attempt to keep sensitive data beyond the reach of the U.S., Brazil has backed a plan to create the Brics Cable, a 34,000 km fiber-optic link connecting Brazil's Fortaleza with Vladivostok in Russia. It will pass through Africa and Asia and connect with cables running to mainland Europe and the Middle East. The Brics Cable's organizers are expecting the link to be ready by 2015 (bbc.co.uk 2013). While there will be a link between Fortaleza and Miami, data will not need to go through NAP. The Brazilian president's office also noted that "negotiations are underway in South America for the deployment of land connections between all nations".

The NSA scandal also highlighted the need for closer cooperation between the EU and Brazil, which agreed to lay a direct undersea communications cable between Europe and Brazil (Emmott 2014). In February 2014, Brazil and the EU decided to build cables between Brazil and Portugal. It is not surprising and is consistent with Brazil's measures to avoid U.S.-based data centers and routers. Prior to that, they had used U.S. undersea cables for intercontinental communication. They gave the contract to Brazilian and Spanish companies (Miller 2014b).

12.4 Similarities and Differences with Major World Economies

Some major similarities and differences between Brazil's CS landscape and those of the EU and the U.S. are summarized in Table 12.2. It is clear that Brazil has many points of similarity, as well as critical points of deep and significant differences with the EU. Just like the EU, Brazil lacks sector specific regulations. To some extent, CS strategies of Brazil as well as the EU economies are driven by the concern that the NSA's PRISM program is a key threat. Finally, Brazil's "Internet Bill of Rights" can be viewed as similar to the EU Data Protection Directive.

As a key difference with the EU, as of the early 2014, Brazil lacked legislation which made it mandatory to report cybercrimes. That is, if a customer's financial information is stolen by cybercriminals in a corporate data breach incident, the company is not required to inform the victim, the public, or the government about the incident. Argentina, Colombia and a number of other countries in Latin America, on the other hand, have enacted regulations which make it mandatory to report

Table 12.2 Brazil's CS landscape: key similarities and differences with the EU and the U.S.

	The EU	The U.S.
Similarities	• No sector specific regulations. • CS strategies driven by the concern of the NSA's PRISM program. • In some way, the "Internet Bill of Rights" is similar to the 1995 EU Data Protection Directive.	• The DPDC is an agency equivalent to the U.S. FTC.
Differences	• Not mandatory for organizations to report most cybercrimes. • Domestically originated attacks, both financially and politically motivated, are of concern.	• A higher proportion of domestically originated cyber-attacks in Brazil. • No reliance on private sector self-regulation for CS.

a cyber-attack. Another difference concerns a much higher proportion of domestically originated cybercrimes in Brazil compared to both the EU and the U.S.

A key similarity between Brazil and the U.S. is that they both have a federal data protection agency. Brazil's Department of Consumer Protection and Defense (DPDC) is an agency equivalent to the U.S. FTC. A main difference with the U.S. is that Brazil does not rely on private sector self-regulation measures for CS.

12.5 Local Capacity Building

Brazil has also realized that much of the success on the CS front will depend on local capacity building and making a major push on this front. Its postal service announced plans to create an encrypted email service by 2014, as an alternative to Gmail and Yahoo. In October 2013, the secretary of IT policy at the MCTI announced the creation of funding pools for new ventures in the CS sector. According to the secretary, the MCTI would nurture 10–15 CS companies, which can get up to R$200,000 (about US$92,000) in funding as well as mentoring. A key motivating factor for the creation of such companies was to use their expertise in CS threats facing Brazil such as the NSA spying. The government is especially interested in companies focusing in encryption technology (Mari 2014a).

Brazil's CS strategy is also linked to economic security. The development of a domestic ICT sector has been a key priority. It has taken a number of initiatives such as high import tariffs and tax breaks to protect homegrown industries. While these policies have led to a dramatic increase in the prices of electronics such as smartphones, they have played a key role in creating thousands of startups and major manufacturing plants. Moreover, friendly tax policies have attracted global companies such as Microsoft and Lenovo (Toor 2013). A recently launched program Startup Brasil aims to attract foreign entrepreneurs with visas and seed money and offers as much as US$78 million in investment for domestic and foreign high-tech companies (Ungerleider 2013). The switch from the Microsoft email system to

Serpro's new technology is also viewed as a safeguard of national economic security. The Minister for Communication, Paulo Bernardo Silva viewed the switch as an economic option for Brazil (argentinaindependent.com 2013).

12.6 Key Constraints Facing Brazil

In some sense, the country's CS initiatives are characterized by a lack of vision and a cohesive strategy and a common set of priorities. While different government departments have developed initiatives and projects, their activities lack coordination (Mari 2014b). Some government agencies have showed a low degree of internalization of CS measures. For instance, in the first half of 2013, only about R$8 million (US$3.7 million) out of the R$90 million (US$41.4 million) CS budget for 2013 was spent by the military. Moreover, about half of the money that was spent went to physical assets such as vehicles, buildings, and physical security items like locks, metal detectors and signs for locations dedicated to CS (bloggingsbyboz.com 2013).

Brazil's cybercrime setting presents security professional with a significantly more challenging landscape. Most of the malware products are developed locally and then modified and tweaked (Lincoln 2013). Unlike their Eastern European counterparts, Brazilian cybercrime groups have not realized the need to internationalize their operations due to Brazil's well-developed financial sector. A study suggested that many banking Trojans are interested in targeting only Brazilian IP addresses (Theriault 2011). Brazilian cybercriminals implement a vast range of Trojans with a very low degree of detectability. They employ techniques to maintain stealthiness. They use "bulletproof" hosting and techniques that identify the IP addresses of potential victims. Knowing the IP address of a user that visits the infected web page would enable them to perform targeted attacks and hide malware from antivirus companies (Bestuzhev 2012). If someone from a computer outside of Brazil visits an infected webpage, the malware would not infect it. The user may see a 404 "page not found" error or a website with pictures of Brazilian girls in bikinis (Theriault 2011). In this way, CS specialists outside Brazil are less likely to have access to malicious codes used in Brazil. This makes it harder to detect the malware products and protect from them.

A low degree of public trust in the government is likely to hinder CS measures and efforts. As noted in Chap. 8, Brazil ranked among the countries at the bottom in terms of IT executives' confidence on the ability of their respective countries' authorities to prevent and deter potential cyber-attacks. Moreover the confidence on the government deteriorated compared to the 2009 levels (McAfee 2011).

In 2011, Brazil ranked seventh among the world's most violent nations (huffingtonpost.com 2013). Only 5–8 % of crimes are solved in Brazil compared with 80 % in France (huffingtonpost.com 2013). This remarkable situation is a direct consequence of the scarcity of law enforcement resources. A prevailing culture of violence in cities such as São Paulo, Rio de Janeiro and Brasília have taken most of the available resources, and left little law enforcement resources to enforce cybercrimes.

In the 2013 BSA Global Cloud Computing Scorecard, Brazil ranked 22nd of the 24 economies considered in the study (BSA 2013). The scorecard considered Data Privacy, Security, Cybercrime, IPR, Support for Industry-Led Standards, & International Harmonization of Rules Promoting Free Trade and ICT Readiness, Broadband Deployment. Likewise, a 2012 report by the law firm Cushman and Wakefield and hurleypalmerflatt noted that high energy prices and shortage of skilled manpower increase risks to build datacenters in Brazil (Mari 2014a). Brazil has not signed the WIPO Copyright Treaty, which means the lack of strong regulations to protect new technologies.

12.7 Organizations' CS Orientation

On the plus side, Brazilian firms are characterized by a high degree of security awareness and orientation. For instance, According to a BT-sponsored survey released in February 2014, which was conducted by Vanson Bourne among medium-to-large organizations in seven economies (the U.K., France, Germany, the U.S., Brazil, Hong Kong and Singapore), Brazil topped the list in terms of the attitudes of IT decision makers to CS. It was followed by the U.S. (Donnelly 2014).

Petrobras is among organizations with strongest CS measures. Before proceeding further, it is important to stress that thanks to intensive research and investment of billions of dollars, Petrobras has been a global leader in deepwater drilling and oilfield development technologies. The company's key strength is especially in exploiting pre-salt reservoirs. In addition, Petrobras is leading development of many major projects, which are expected to contribute to a new production of about 2 million barrels/day of to the global market over the next decade. Following the revelation by Edward Snowden that the company had been targeted by the NSA, the Brazilian oil giant Petrobras announced that it would heavily invest in CS. In 2013, the company planned to spend US$1.8 billion in CS. Among the company's more than 86,000 employees (http://www.petrobras.com.br/en/about-us/profile/), 3000 worked in CS in 2013 (Leahy 2013). The IT software solutions general manager of Petrobras, Marcel José Kaskus noted that the company made some uses of private clouds but not public clouds. He expressed his concerns related to security of clouds. Petrobras also prefers to deploy proprietary systems and Brazilian-developed software (Ozores 2013). It further announced another US $9.5 billion CS investment by 2017 (Kovacs 2014). The company's sensitive data is stored in a highly secure processing center, access to which is controlled with biometrics such as thumb readers, weight monitoring, and video surveillance. It was also reported to be studying and piloting holography, and 3D motion capture (Ozores 2013). Scientists and others with access to data are prohibited from transferring critical data such as seismic studies of the company's oil reserves through the Internet (Leahy 2013). Moreover, a large number of potentially malicious emails are blocked. For instance, of the 195 million emails sent to the company's systems during August 9–September 9, 2013, only 16.5 million reached their destination (Kovacs 2014).

The above said, a substantial difference between large and small firms can be observed in terms of CS orientation. An estimate suggested that in 2006, about three million Brazilian SMEs or more than half of such enterprises in the country, lacked anti-virus software in their PCs (Business Wire 2006). Moreover, a large proportion of Brazilian computer users do not take remedial actions such as patching the systems. For instance, it is reported that many Brazilian computers are still infected by the Conficker worm, which spread worldwide in 2009. A difficulty is also a widespread use of unlicensed versions of Windows, which don't have access to security updates (Robertson 2013). For instance, while Microsoft issued a patch to fix the vulnerability exploited by earlier versions of Conficker, the worm remains active in infected machines with unlicensed Windows. In 2010, Brazil was among the top two sources of Conficker attack traffic (Lemon 2010).

12.8   Discussion and Concluding Remarks

Unlike in the U.S., IP theft and industrial espionage are not currently a major concern in Brazil. The country is, however, exposed to significant cyber-threats thanks to the country's financially and politically motivated cybercriminal gangs. Brazil has not been able to devote a significant amount of resources to implementation and enforcement issues. Equally problematic has been the lack of spending on core CS assets. The military and other government agencies may need to divert from generally ineffective spending on physical assets to core CS assets.

Criminal groups targeting Brazil are focusing on cyber-attacks that can be quickly monetized. One of the most intriguing characteristics of Brazilian cybercrime landscape is that most cyber-attacks are domestically originated, which would make threat detection a difficult exercise. For instance, since Boletos are not used outside Brazil, it might have made security companies less vigilant about the threat. Likewise, the perception among many Brazilians that government agencies exercise undue power over the citizens and businesses *has led* many hackers to target government agencies' websites.

While organizations such as Petrobras have exemplar security system and policies in place, a large proportion of Brazilian SMEs lack latest anti-virus software and other CS measures. In connection with this point, efforts should also be directed toward upgrading the unsecure old technology and deploying CS tools among SMEs. In Brazil, the large movement toward increasing CS has been mostly a response to the revelation of the NSA spying activities. Yet Brazil may encounter difficulty in following through on those intentions. Some argue that, in light of its high inflation and economic difficulties, a trade war with the U.S. might further worsen the current economic situation (rmprofessional.com 2013). This is because the two countries are important trading and investment partners of each other. The

WWW creator Tim Berners-Lee referred the requirements for local data storage as an "emotional reaction" to the NSA spying and noted that it will have no practical impact in reducing cyber-espionage risks (Mari 2013b).

The NSA scandal marked an important turning point in Brazil's CS policy and strategy. President Rousseff has been one of the most vocal critics of the PRISM program. In order to avoid possible security risks and compromises, Brazil is trying to keep itself away from U.S.-based data centers, equipment and technologies. Experts have, however, noted the CS-related measures announced following revelation of the NSA monitoring scandal are emotional, rather than rational responses and will do little to strengthen CS and lead to economic harms.

Since formal and informal institutions have been both linked to cybercrime and CS in Brazil, it is important to examine the differences in the rates at which these two components of institutions are likely to change. Douglas North noted that "although formal rules may change overnight as the result of political and judicial decisions, informal constraints embodied in customs, traditions, and codes of conduct are much more impervious to deliberate policies" (North 1990). To put things in context, changing the culture that is indifferent towards hacking and cyber-attacks and development of trust in government and public institutions are likely to be more challenging and more painful than enacting CS-related laws and regulations.

References

arabtoday.net. (2014). *Brazil installs spy-proof email network*. http://www.arabtoday.net/~arabtode/internet/brazil-installs-spy-proof-email-network.html

argentinaindependent.com. (2013). *Brazil: Government to implement new 'spy proof' email system*. http://www.argentinaindependent.com/tag/expresso-v3/

bbc.co.uk. (2013, September 20). *Brazil data plan aims to keep US spies at bay*. http://www.bbc.co.uk/news/technology-24145662

Bestuzhev, D. (2012). *Brazil: A country rich in banking Trojans*. http://www.securelist.com/en/analysis/204792084/Brazil_a_country_rich_in_banking_Trojans?print_mode=1

bloggingsbyboz.com. (2013). *Brazil's cybersecurity budget is a mess*. http://www.bloggingsbyboz.com/2013/07/brazils-cybersecurity-budget-is-mess.html

Boadle, A. (2013, August 22). *Brazil's Rousseff calls off state visit to U.S. over spying*. http://www.reuters.com/article/2013/09/17/us-usa-security-snowden-brazil-idUSBRE98G0VW20130917

Brattberg, E. (2014, August 22). *Commentary: NSA scandal hurts US exports: Underscored by Brazilian fighter bid loss*. http://www.defensenews.com/article/20140107/DEFREG02/301070018/Commentary-NSA-Scandal-Hurts-US-Exports?odyssey=navlhead

Brooks, B., & Bajak, F. (2013). *Brazil looks to break from US-centric*. http://www.sfgate.com/news/world/article/Brazil-looks-to-break-from-US-centric-Internet-4819946.php

BSA. (2013). *2013 BSA Global cloud computing scorecard a clear path to progress*. http://cloudscorecard.bsa.org/2013/index.html

Business Wire. (2006). SMBs in Brazil to spend $260USM on IT security in 2007; Up to 72 % of Brazil-based SMBs cited enhanced data security and privacy as key factors influencing IT purchases. AMI Partners Study Finds.

Caldwell, J. (2013, August 22). *Canada spies on Brazil's mines and energy ministry*. http://ithinkmining.com/2013/10/08/canada-spies-on-brazils-mines-and-energy-ministry/

Constantin, L. (2014). *Brazil to fortify government email system following NSA snooping revelations.* http://www.computerworld.com.au/article/529008/brazil_fortify_government_email_system_following_nsa_snooping_revelations/

Cutler, S. (2012). *The Mirage campaign.* http://www.secureworks.com/cyber-threat-intelligence/threats/the-mirage-campaign/

Donnelly, C. (2014). *UK lagging behind US & Brazil in cyber security.* http://www.itpro.co.uk/security/21588/uk-lagging-behind-us-brazil-in-cyber-security

Emmott, R. (2014, August 22). *Brazil, Europe plan undersea cable to skirt U.S. spying.* http://www.reuters.com/article/2014/02/24/us-eu-brazil-idUSBREA1N0PL20140224

Gaskell, H. (2014, August 22). *Hackers bring down World Cup websites.* http://www.itp.net/mobile/598576-hackers-bring-down-world-cup-websites

Geromel, R. (2012). *Hackers stole $1 billion in Brazil, The worst prepared nation to adopt cloud technology.* http://www.forbes.com/sites/ricardogeromel/2012/03/02/hackers-stole-1billion-in-brazil-the-worst-prepared-nation-to-adopt-cloud-technology/

Grande, A. (2014). *Brazilian telecom giant fined $1.6M for online tracking.* http://www.law360.com/articles/560776/brazilian-telecom-giant-fined-1-6m-for-online-tracking

huffingtonpost.com. (2013). *Brazil, 7th most violent country in the world, had 1.1 million murders between 1980 and 2011.* http://www.huffingtonpost.com/2013/07/19/brazil-most-violent-country-murders_n_3618704.html

Imperva. (2012). *Imperva's hacker intelligence summary report: The anatomy of an anonymous attack.* Redwood Shores, CA: Imperva.

King, G. (2014, August 25). *The Marco Civil da Internet.* http://www.cpj.org/reports/2014/05/halftime-for-brazilian-press-censorship-violence-marco-civil-da-internet.php

Kovacs, E. (2013). *Brazilian Air Force website hacked and defaced by anonymous.* http://tinyurl.com/o8kuan5

Kovacs, E. (2014, August 25). *Brazil's Petrobras to invest billions in Cybersecurity in light of NSA spying allegations.* http://news.softpedia.com/news/Brazil-s-Petrobras-to-Invest-Billions-in-Cybersecurity-in-Light-of-NSA-Spying-Allegations-384874.shtml

latimesblogs.latimes.com. (2012, August 25). *Google executive detained in Brazil for YouTube videos.* http://latimesblogs.latimes.com/world_now/2012/09/brazil-google-youtube-videos-executive-arrested.html

Leahy, J. (2013, August 22). *Brazil's Petrobras to invest heavily in data security.* http://www.ft.com/intl/cms/s/0/f3195d0a-2081-11e3-9a9a-00144feab7de.html#axzz3AlFqmIaB

Lemon, S. (2010). *Conficker worm still spreading, Akamai says.* http://www.infoworld.com/d/security-central/conficker-worm-still-spreading-akamai-says-077

Leyden, J. (2004a, August 25). *Brazil "Tops Cybercrime League": Cybergeddon or cyberFUD?* http://www.theregister.co.uk/2004/09/15/brazil_cybercrime_shocker/

Leyden, J. (2004b). *US credit card firm fights DDoS attack.* http://www.theregister.co.uk/2004/09/23/authorize_ddos_attack

Libicki, M. C. (2013). *Don't buy the Cyberhype: How to prevent Cyberwars from becoming real ones.* http://www.foreignaffairs.com/articles/139819/martin-c-libicki/dont-buy-the-cyberhype

Lincoln, C. (2013). *What security managers can learn from Brazil: Frontline in the global cyber wars.* http://www.infosectoday.com/Articles/Brazil.htm

Mari, A. (2013a). *Google and Facebook express concern over data protection laws in Brazil.* http://www.zdnet.com/google-and-facebook-express-concern-over-data-protection-laws-in-brazil-7000019508/

Mari, A. (2013b). *Web creator criticizes Brazil's local storage plans.* http://www.zdnet.com/web-creator-criticizes-brazils-local-storage-plans-7000024041/

Mari, A. (2014a). *Brazilian government outlines technology priorities for 2014.* http://www.zdnet.com/brazilian-government-outlines-technology-priorities-for-2014-7000025306/

Mari, A. (2014b, August 25). *Brazil struggles to create cybersecurity policies.* http://www.zdnet.com/brazil-struggles-to-create-cybersecurity-policies-7000026701/

McAfee. (2011, April 19). *In the dark: Crucial industries confront cyberattacks.* https://blogs. mcafee.com/business/in-the-dark-crucial-industries-confront-cyberattacks/

McDonald, J. (2014). *China suspends cooperation in joint task force over Cyberspying charges.* http://www.huffingtonpost.com/2014/05/20/china-suspends-cooperation-us-_n_5356447.html

Miller, C. C. (2014a). *Google pushes back against data localization.* http://bits.blogs.nytimes. com/2014/01/24/google-pushes-back-against-data-localization/?_php=true&_type=blogs&_php=true&_type=blogs&_r=1

Miller, C. C. (2014b). *Revelations of N.S.A. spying cost U.S. Tech companies.* http://www.nytimes. com/2014/03/22/business/fallout-from-snowden-hurting-bottom-line-of-tech-companies.html?_r=0

Mylrea, M. (2009). *Brazil's next battlefield: Cyberspace.* http://www.foreignpolicyjournal.com/ 2009/11/15/brazils-next-battlefield-cyberspace/

North, D. C. (1990). *Institutions, institutional change and economic performance.* Cambridge, MA: Cambridge University Press.

Olson, P. (2012, August 22). *How Twitter helped Brazil become a hotbed for hacktivists.* http:// www.forbes.com/sites/parmyolson/2012/02/27/how-twitter-helped-brazil-become-a-hotbed-for-hacktivists/

opennet.net. (2008). *Censura Não!: Brazilian bloggers protest new cybercrime bill.* https:// opennet.net/blog/2008/07/censura-n%C3%A3o-brazilian-bloggers-protest-new-cybercrime-bill

Ozores, P. (2013). *Petrobras on cloud: "We are conservative".* http://www.bnamericas.com/ news/technology/petrobras-on-cloud-we-are-conservative

Paulo, S. (2013, August 25). *More in sorrow than anger.* http://www.economist.com/blogs/ americasview/2013/09/brazil-and-united-states

Perlroth, N. (2014). *Cybercrime scheme uncovered in Brazil.* http://www.nytimes.com/2014/07/ 03/technology/cybercrime-scheme-aims-at-payments-in-brazil.html?_r=0

Purkayastha, P., & Bailey, R. (2014). U.S. control of the internet. *Monthly Review: An Independent Socialist Magazine, 66*(3), 103–127.

Ribeiro, J. (2014). *Brazil to drop requirement that Internet firms store data locally.* http://www. networkworld.com/article/2175352/data-center/brazil-to-drop-requirement-that-internet-firms-store-data-locally.html

rmprofessional.com. (2013). *Cyber security boost for Petrobras amid spy claims.* http://www. rmprofessional.com/content/news/cyber-security-boost-petrobras-amid-spy-claims

Robertson, J. (2013). *Why are hackers flooding into Brazil?* http://www.bloomberg.com/news/ 2013-09-13/why-are-hackers-flooding-into-brazil-.html

Sanger, D. E., & Perlroth, N. (2014). *New Russian boldness revives a cold war tradition: Testing the other side.* http://www.nytimes.com/2014/10/31/world/europe/new-russian-boldness-revives-a-cold-war-tradition-testing-the-other-side-.html?_r=0

Smith, T. (2003). *Technology; Brazil becomes a cybercrime lab.* http://query.nytimes.com/gst/fullpage. html?res=9F02E3DA1131F934A15753C1A9659C8B63&sec=&spon=&pagewanted=2

Southern Pulse. (2011, August 25). *Spy vs. spy: Cybercrime, surveillance on rise in Latin America.* http://insightcrime.org/insight-latest-news/item/1478-spy-vs-spy-cyber-crime-surveillance-on-rise-in-latin-america

Stankey, R. (2014). *Brazil enacts "Internet Bill of Rights," including net neutrality and privacy protections.* http://www.jdsupra.com/legalnews/brazil-enacts-internet-bill-of-rights-36906/

Symantec. (2012, September 5). *Norton Cybercrime Report.*

Theriault, C. (2011). *Brazil's Cybercrime evolution – It doesn't look pretty.* http://nakedsecurity. sophos.com/2011/10/05/brazils-cybercrime-evolution-it-doesnt-look-pretty/

timesofindia.indiatimes.com. (2013, August 22). *Indian hackers retaliate, attack Brazilian websites.* http://timesofindia.indiatimes.com/tech/tech-news/Indian-hackers-retaliate-attack-Brazilian-websites/articleshow/19593356.cms

Toor, A. (2013, September 25). *Cutting the cord: Brazil's bold plan to combat the NSA.* http:// www.theverge.com/2013/9/25/4769534/brazil-to-build-internet-cable-to-avoid-us-nsa-spying

Ungerleider, N. (2013). *Brazil offering foreign startups visas, funding.* http://www.fastcompany.
com/3008348/fast-feed/brazil-offering-foreign-startups-visas-funding

Woodcock, B. (2013). *On internet, Brazil is beating US at its own game.* http://america.aljazeera.
com/articles/2013/9/20/brazil-internet-dilmarousseffnsa.html

Wyss, J. (2011, August 25). *Political hackers are one of Latin America's newest headaches.* http://
www.miamiherald.com/2011/10/31/2481360_p2/political-hackers-are-one-of-latin.html

Chapter 13
Cybersecurity in Russia

13.1 Introduction

Russia is viewed as one of the top three global cyber powers along with the U.S. and China (Shafa 2014). It was reported that in 2013, President Vladimir Putin asked the Russian Security Council to strengthen CS (Itar-Tass 2013). If we believe what many Western CS experts have to tell us, Russia has seen its cyber power as an opportunity to combine with its conventional power to engage in military actions and operations. One example of Russia's alleged exploitation of cyber power is the 2008 Russia-Georgia war, in which Russia combined its cyber power with traditional military operations (Bonner 2014).

The Russian government's view and perception of the CS problem is different from most Western nations. As is the case of China, internal threats have been recognized as a potential source of instability and regime change in Russia. Russia, like China, views information security as much broader than CS issue. According to Russia's Information Security Doctrine, adopted in 2000, information security is defined as "the state of protection of its national interests in the information sphere defined by the totality of balanced interests of the individual, society, and the state" (Thomas 2001). A real purpose behind it is arguably to increase the state's capacity and legitimacy for cyber-control and censorship. Nonetheless, Russia does not want to be perceived internationally as a as a politically repressive country (Boiten 2014). A Russian presidential aide noted that the Russian government did not consider "China's experience on tough regulation of virtual space as an example" (itar-tass.com 2013). Compared to China's so-called "great firewall" designed to deal with the internal threats, which restricts access to information for the Chinese population, Russia has employed more subtle and indirect means.

According to Timothy L. Thomas, a *former U.S. Army lieutenant colonel* and an expert on Russian and Chinese cyber-warfare strategies, Russia's military doctrine has been to break "information operations" (IO) issues associated with external threats into two components: "information-technical" and "information-

© Springer International Publishing Switzerland 2016
N. Kshetri, *The Quest to Cyber Superiority*, DOI 10.1007/978-3-319-40554-4_13

psychological" (Thomas 2001). The information-technical component has the same meaning and interpretation as the U.S. conception of cyberwar. The information-psychological component has a broader meaning, which encompasses the potential usefulness of the Internet in affecting beliefs and attitudes of the adversary, including military, political leaders and the civilian population (Ford 2010). According to Russia's Information Security Doctrine, key elements of information security threats includes the security of the state, society and the individual. Thus contents, information and technologies that threaten citizens' cultural, spiritual, and psychological values or to critical technologies and resources are considered information security threats (Thomas 2001).

Russian political elites have also seen the cyber power as an opportunity to engage in war with neighboring states and use as a weapon against political opponents. Some analysts believe that anyone opposing the government or supporting the opposition may faces cyber-attacks. There was also an accusation that the country's cybercriminals have been co-opted by the intelligence agencies. The intelligence agencies allegedly use criminals' expertise or their networks of virus-infected computers for political purposes (Kramer 2010). Russian websites of organizations with anti-government positions have been victims of DDoS attacks. A 2002 cyber-attack on Kavkaz.org, the website of Chechen separatist fighters, was among the first indications of such approach, in which students of the Tomsk city were reportedly involved. The local department of the Federal Security Service was apparently aware of the perpetrators, which issued a press release describing the attack as an "expression of their position as citizens, one worthy of respect". Since then the so called "hacker patriots" have allegedly launched DDoS attacks against independent media sources in Russia as well as at government agencies in Estonia, Georgia, and Lithuania (Soldatov 2011). Cyber-attacks against Georgia in 2008 and on Estonia in 2007 were widely believed to be carried out by hackers with connection to the Russian government. Regarding the 2008 cyber-attacks on Georgia, the Georgian Ministry of Foreign Affairs noted: "A cyber warfare campaign by Russia is seriously disrupting many Georgian websites, including that of the Ministry of Foreign Affairs".

13.2   Cyber-Threats Facing Russia

13.2.1   External Threats

Among the Russian political elites there has been heightened concern and focus on external threats facing the country. At a 2012 U.N. convention to fight cybercrime and terrorism, Russia said that 120 countries were planning cyberwar capabilities and developing cyber-attack strategies (reuters.com 2012). A Russian presidential aide noted that Russia "must not allow the Russian segment of the Internet to be switched off from outside. Now such a threat is real enough" (itar-tass.com 2013).

Russia's deputy Prime Minister Dmitry Rogozin *was reported to mention* Pentagon computer games, which showed that strikes by some 3000–4000 precision-guided munitions used against Russia could destroy up to 80–90 % of the country's nuclear potential (Maksimov and Kuksin 2013). The concerns were further highlighted when it was revealed that among the alleged targets of the NSA spying were the Russian natural gas company Gazprom and Russian airline Aeroflot (Bershidsky 2014).

Putin warned that "certain countries", which dominate the cyberspace, were trying to use their "soft power" to achieve "economic, military and political goals" (phys.org 2014).

As is the case of China, external threats are considered as more acute for Russia due primarily to problems related to territorial conflicts (Boiten 2014). For instance, the cyber-attacks between Ukraine and Russia escalated following the overthrow of the Yanukovych government in Ukraine and the subsequent annexation of Crimea to Russia. State forces, criminal groups, independent patriotic hackers and activists were believed to participate in the cyber-warfare. The cyber-attacks attempted to destroy computer systems, steal intelligence, spread online propaganda and cause other damages (Farmer 2014).

13.2.2 Internal Threats

As noted in Chap. 1, hacktivism has become a major headache for the Russian government. In March 2014, websites of the Kremlin, the central bank and the Foreign Ministry experienced cyber-attacks. A group, which called itself Anonymous Russia, was believed to be behind the attack. The same group claimed that it attacked the website in May 2012 to protest against Putin's return as the president for a third term. Social networks were also widely used by protesters for this purpose (bbc.com 2014). The websites of a number of Russian media outlets, which supported Putin, also experienced similar attacks (Heritage and Tsvetkova 2014). The attacks left the Russian *government red-faced and were described as* "a minor triumph" for the attackers. The hactivist group, Anonymous Caucasus took responsibility for the cyber-attacks on the websites of Channel One and the news outlet *LifeNews*. It accused the latter as the *"lapdogs of the FSB [Russian security service]"* (RT 2014a). Russia-24 TV channel also faced similar attacks.

13.3 Russia's CS Strategies and Regulatory Frameworks

13.3.1 Dealing with the External Threats

Russia has stepped up plans to *build a significant cyber army*. In the early 2013, the Russian Defense Minister, Sergei Shoigu reportedly gave the General Staff several months to complete proposals for creating an army "cyber command" (Lvov 2013). In November 2014, Russia was reported to establish a cyber-warfare division in order to carry out offensive and defensive operations with an initial investment of US$500 million. The division was reported to be recruiting cyber-forces with foreign, especially English, language skills. Among the main tasks of the division are to monitor and process of information coming from foreign sources, and fight against cyber-threats and attacks (Gerden 2014). Sergei Shoigu, Russia's Minister of Defense noted: "We are starting a "major search" for programmers and IT experts. This need is dictated by the volume of IT and security technologies that are intended to be integrated in the national army over the next 5 years. We need a new generation of young people who will develop the science of warfare" (Gerden 2014).

CS concerns are also reflected in the bias of Russia's rules and regulations against foreign technology providers, especially those from the U.S. A Russian lawmaker said that he would force Google to register a subsidiary in Russia and comply with Russian laws due to its alleged cooperation with foreign governments (RT 2014b). The Russian Ministry of Communications and Mass Media asked Apple to reveal its source codes to Russian experts. As noted earlier, Microsoft revealed its source codes to Russian authorities in 2003. In March 2014, Russia prohibited its Cabinet members to use iPads. Instead, Samsung tablets were promoted arguing that they perform better in protecting confidential information (themoscowtimes.com 2014). Citing Izvestia, a Russian publication, a *Newsweek* article reported in December 2014 that the Russian military had banned its personnel from using iPhones (Mosendz 2014a). According to a report published in November 2014, starting 2015, a new Russian law would prohibit retailers from selling devices such as iPhone and iPad that use Apple's iCloud. The rationale behind the ban was that the iCloud data is not stored locally (Rathinavel 2014).

As noted earlier, Russia is concerned about possible cyber-attacks on critical systems such as *nuclear and missile*-related technologies. In October 2014, the spokesperson of the Strategic Missile Forces announced the creation of Sopka (*System of Detection and Prevention of Computer Attacks*) teams in order to detect and prevent cyber-attacks (en.ria.ru/military_news 2014). In the same month, the Defense Ministry also announced the creation of a new unit of anti-hackers to protect the IT systems of all Russian nuclear weapons stockpiles. The Russian Strategic Missile Forces (SMF), which oversees the country's nuclear weapons, is *adopting new digital technologies in weapon, troop control and other areas. It is increasing the use of electronic document management* (rt.com/news 2014).

A bias against foreign technology products is also nurtured and sustained by the actions and discourses of political elites. For some political elites, the foreign dominance of the cyberspace domain has clearly become an issue of cultural security. State Duma Deputy Sergei Zheleznyak described the situation as an "information war that was unleashed against our country and our values" (Eremenko 2014). Likewise, the head of Russia's Chechen Republic, Ramzan Kadyrov, urged Russians to abandon iPhone due to its link to U.S. culture. The use of U.S. ICT products is also framed as a threat to the country's military security. For instance, Kadyrov reportedly argued in his message on Instagram that Russian citizens were spending "tens of millions" of dollars to buy iPhones, "thus financing the U.S. military industrial complex" (Mosendz 2014b).

13.3.2 Handling the Internal Threats

As noted in Chap. 1, CS strategy is affected by national political system and context. In general, authoritarian states lack incentives to strengthen non-governmental actors, which are seen as a force to undermine regime stability (Ebert and Maurer 2013). This feature has special relevance for the cyberspace. An additional feature of the post-Soviet Russia that is important from a practical point of view is that it is characterized by weak state and strong state officials (Thompson 2002).

Russian government officials view cyber-control as an essential dimension in confronting the internal threats facing the regime. They know full well that the Internet has the *capability to change a regime* as has happened in Tunisia, Ukraine, Georgia, Kyrgyzstan and other countries (Deibert and Rohozinski 2010). In some ways, Russia has learned from the lessons of authoritarian regimes such as those of Kazakhstan and Belarus, which have compelled websites to register with authorities. If the websites do not comply, their licenses may be revoked. Website owners who do not want to go through the hassle of registering with authorities face legal sanctions if the website is viewed as carrying illegal contents. If foreign content providers such as BBC and CNN have local audience, they are also required to register. A dilemma for foreign content providers is that their contents can be filtered for "noncompliance" if they do not register. On the other hand, if they register, the contents on their websites are subject to local laws. In some cases, contents on foreign websites may be deemed *unacceptable, slanderous*, derogatory, insulating or immoral according to the local laws (Deibert and Rohozinski 2010). Such contents can be blocked. In December 2014, the Russian communications regulator, Roskomnadzor announced that Facebook had agreed to block a Facebook page promoting a Russian opposition rally (Khrennikov and Meyer 2014). A Roskomnadzor spokesman further noted that the regulator had been seeking to prevent access to other Facebook pages calling for mass protests and posts on other social networks such as VKontakte and Twitter.

In 2014, the Russian Parliament's both houses approved the data localization legislation, which requires data operators to store personal data of Russian citizens on servers inside the Russian territory. The legislation was signed by the President on July 9, 2014. Data operators, which collect personal data of Russian citizens, will be required to use servers based in Russia to store personal data by September 2016. Companies that do not comply with this regulation will be blocked from the Internet (Gulyaeva and Sedykh 2014).

Observers noted that the data localization legislation was enacted when Russian intelligence agencies were pressuring foreign Internet companies to provide data on Ukrainians who supported the overthrow of the president, Viktor Yanukovych, who was backed by Russia (Hill 2014). President Putin also reportedly remarked that the Snowden disclosures had showed that the Internet was a "CIA project" (MacAskill 2014).

According to a researcher at IDC, in order to comply with the legislation, Western companies such as Facebook and Twitter are required to rent up to 1500 additional servers and spend as much as US$45 million a year (Khrennikov 2014). The new legislation is likely to benefit local data-center providers such as OAO Rostelecom and OAO MegaFon (MFON). In this way, the new regulatory framework, to some extent, is likely to address the economic security concern associated with the cyber-threats.

Under the Russian online content law, which became effective on August 1, 2014, all "organizers of dissemination of information over the Internet" are required to register with Roskomnadzor and store information about the users and electronic messages for 6 months. The information needs to be provided at the request of government investigators and law-enforcement authorities (Gulyaeva and Sedykh 2014). Roskomnadzor asked Facebook, Google's Gmail and Twitter to register as "organizers of information dissemination" (Khrennikov 2014).

Analysts argue that authoritarian governments (e.g., Russia, China, and Iran) tend to pursue broad data localization rules, which apply to all citizen data. Such data localization laws are viewed as an effective means for information control in order to monitor their citizens' activities (Hill 2014). Commenting on data localization laws, a lawmaker for the pro-Putin United Russia party said: "The Internet is widely used to influence people and stage street revolutions. Therefore, we are urging companies working in Russia to transfer their servers into the national jurisdiction" (Khrennikov 2014).

In most Western countries, *blacklisted websites sites are often those* that contain child pornography or distribute copyrighted materials. Russia has shown a significant deviation in its approach to blacklist and ban websites. The banned sites in Russia include a number of independent news sites such as the online newspaper *Grani*, Garry Kasparov's opposition information site *kasparov.ru*, Alexei Navalny's *livejournal* and the web pages of the radio station Ekho Moskvy (Galperin and O'Brien 2014). The Prosecutor General's Office said that the Russian-language pages of the social networking website *VKontakte* advocated terrorism by providing an open access to the materials, which called for extremist and terrorist activity (en.itar-tass.com 2014a). In 2014, its founder fled the country under pressure from the law enforcement agencies (phys.org 2014). The new anti-extremism legislation became effective on February 1, 2014. In less than 3 months following the legislation's introduction, Russian prosecutors blocked access to about 100 websites. Some of the blocked sites included those that called for protests over the crisis in Ukraine (Nechepurenko 2014). Moreover, a government agency can block websites blacklisted for extremism without a court order (phys.org 2014).

The government has emphasized the importance of strengthening its regulatory control over the Internet and mass media. The state goal of this approach has been to protect the majority of the population from harmful information (Nechepurenko 2014). For instance, Russian regulations also prohibit "gay propaganda" on the Internet and other media (Eremenko 2014). The government has *argued that* the compulsory identity verification for social networks *would defend citizens against* identity thieves (en.itar-tass.com 2014b).

While the Russian government has demonstrated a certain level of sophistication in cyber-control measures to deal with political threats, the country's cybercrime fighting measures is less impressive. A piecemeal and fragmented approach to law enforcement is reflected in CS. The Interior Ministry's Directorate K is the lead agency to deal with CS. The lack of cooperation and turf wars between the Directorate K and local agencies are clearly visible (Warren 2011).

13.4 International Engagements

Russia has rejected the CoECoC arguing that it violates the country's constitution by permitting foreign law enforcement agencies to conduct Internet searches inside its borders. Since 1998, Russia has put forward resolutions for consideration by the UN calling for prohibition of "information aggression", which is interpreted to mean ideological attempts and the use of ideas to undermine the stability of the regime (Deibert and Crete-Nishihata 2012). In 1998, Russia introduced a draft resolution to the UN Security Council, entitled "Developments in the field of information and telecommunications in the context of security". In September 2011, Russia, and other SCO members (Tajikistan and Uzbekistan) also submitted a draft International Code of Conduct for Information Security to the 66th UN General Assembly Meeting. The code called on nation states to "cooperate in . . . curbing dissemination of information which incites terrorism, secessionism, extremism or undermines other countries' political, economic and social stability, as well as their spiritual and cultural environment". This was interpreted by some analysts as an attempt to counterbalance the U.S. dominance on the cyberspace (Spade 2011). In 2011, then Prime Minister Vladimir Putin also stated that Russia's goal was to establish international control over the Internet using the ITU's "monitoring and supervisory capabilities" (Government of the Russian Federation 2011).

The environments of tension, distrust, and conflict, which characterized the U. S.-Soviet cold war relationship, have been the typical features of the U.S.-Russia relationship on CS (Kshetri 2013). In March 2012, following a meeting of the SCO Regional Antiterrorism Structure (RATS), Russia's first deputy director of the Federal Security Service, Gen. Sergei Smirnov told reporters that Western intelligence agencies have used cyber-attacks to damage Russia and other SCO members. He also noted that the RATS was taking measures to counter cyber-attacks (Gertz 2012).

In addition to the SCO, Russia is also engaged in international cooperation with other emerging economies *through the BRICS initiatives*. All the BRICS countries have been concerned about the U.S. cyberspace dominance and are seeking to change the status quo by engaging in and fostering new international alliances and making efforts to reformulate norms and standards (Noss 2005).

While Russia has shown a tendency to avoid U.S.-based companies due to CS concerns, it has signed important bilateral cooperation with China. Russia's relationship with China in the fields of ICT and communications is characterized by increasing collaboration and engagement. In May 2014, Russia's state telecom company and the Chinese company Huawei signed a US$60 million deal. Under the deal, Huawei would build an underwater communication line in Russia's Far East. In August 2014, Russia and China reached in an agreement to increase exports of Russian software to China and imports into Russia of servers made by Chinese companies. The servers made by China's Inspur Group will be used by the Russian government in systems used to produce passports and manage elections (huffingtonpost.com 2014).

The Russian newspaper *Kommersant* had reported that, during Vladimir Putin's state visit to China in November 2014, the two countries were expected to sign the *"two-sided agreement on cooperation in the field of information security"*. According to the draft treaty, two countries oppose the use of ICTs to interfere in the internal affairs of independent states and to weaken national sovereignty and political, economic and social stability and public order (rt.com 2014). It was subsequently reported that the two countries were working to make the agreement "more extensive and practical" and are expected to sign it in the first half of 2015 (defenseworld.net 2014).

13.5 Discussion and Concluding Remarks

It is clear that Russia's viewpoint and approach regarding CS and the governance of the cyberspace are different from those of the Western economies. Likewise, despite a wide variety of measures used by the Russian government to control citizens' cyberspace activities, it is noteworthy that the governments of Russia and China differ significantly in the way in which they have used cyber-control measures to grapple with internal political threats. For instance, Russia's internet control measures are much less sophisticated compared to China's great firewall.

Regarding the BRICS initiatives, it is important to note that while all BRICS economies share common concerns and experiences regarding the international governance of the cyberspace, they have different emphasis and priority. In order to compare similarities as well as deviations between the two authoritarian states (China and Russia) and the three democratic states (India, Brazil, South Africa), it is important to look at the approach adopted by the IBSA Dialogue Forum. Note that the IBSA Dialogue Forum is an international group for promoting international cooperation among India, Brazil, South Africa, which describe themselves as "vibrant democracies". All of them are concerned about the dominance of the West in the global ICT industry. For instance, in the Brasilia Declaration of IBSA in 2003, the three countries "agreed to intensify their cooperation in information and communication technology, including in international efforts and initiatives towards narrowing the digital divide" (IBSA 2003). China's and Russia's emphasis on information security is an important dimension on which these two economies deviate significantly from Brazil, India, and South Africa (Noss 2005). Observers have noted that important differences between IBSA and BRICS meetings. For instance, issues related to human rights and civil society are not discussed when the BRICS economies meet (Stuenkel 2012).

Finally, it is worth noting that while all BRICS economies prefer the ITU over the ICANN, they have diverse motivations. A lawyer for Center for Technology and Democracy was quoted as saying that while authoritarian regimes such as China and Russia are interested in controlling the Internet, other more democratic nations such as Brazil, India and South Africa have felt that they lack voice in the ICANN-governed Internet (Sullivan 2012).

References

bbc.com. (2014). *Russian MPs back law on internet data storage*. http://www.bbc.com/news/world-europe-28173513

Bershidsky, L. (2014). *Why U.S. should bring Snowden home*. http://www.bloombergview.com/articles/2014-05-30/why-u-s-should-bring-snowden-home

Boiten, E. (2014). *Nations want to be the ruler of the internet—at least within their own borders*. http://phys.org/news/2014-11-nations-ruler-internet-borders.html

Bonner, E. L., III. (2014). *Cyber power in 21st-century joint warfare*. http://ndupress.ndu.edu/Media/News/NewsArticleView/tabid/7849/Article/9094/jfq-74-cyber-power-in-21st-century-joint-warfare.aspx

defenseworld.net. (2014). *Russia, China to sign cyber security pact in 2015*. http://www.defenseworld.net/news/11492/Russia__China_To_Sign_Cyber_Security_Pact_In_2015#.VIYy0WdINmc

Deibert, R. J., & Crete-Nishihata, M. (2012). Global governance and the spread of cyberspace controls. *Global Governance, 18*(3), 346.

Deibert, R., & Rohozinski, R. (2010). Control and subversion in Russian cyberspace. In J. Palfrey, R. Rohozinski, & J. Zittrain (Eds.), *Access controlled: The shaping of power, rights, and rule in cyberspace*. Cambridge: MIT Press.

Ebert, H., & Maurer, T. (2013). Contested cyberspace and rising powers. *Third World Quarterly, 34*(6), 1054–1074. doi:10.1080/01436597.2013.802502.

en.itar-tass.com. (2014a). *Russian prosecutors urge limiting access to VKontakte over inciting extremism*. http://en.itar-tass.com/russia/756707

en.itar-tass.com. (2014b). *Publishing private information of Russian social network users without consent to become illegal.* http://en.itar-tass.com/russia/699283

en.ria.ru/military_news. (2014). *Russian strategic missile forces create Cybersecurity units: Defense Ministry.* http://en.ria.ru/military_news/20141016/194157367/Russian-Strategic-Mis sile-Forces-Create-Cybersecurity-Units.html

Eremenko, A. (2014). *Russia to make internet providers censor content*—Report. http://www. themoscowtimes.com/news/article/russia-to-make-internet-providers-censor-content-report/ 512475.html

Farmer, B. (2014).*Ukraine cyber war escalates alongside violence.* http://www.telegraph.co.uk/ news/worldnews/europe/ukraine/10860920/Ukraine-cyber-war-escalates-alongside-violence. html

Ford, C. A. (2010). The trouble with cyber arms control. *New Atlantis: A Journal of Technology, 29,* 52–67.

Galperin, E., & O'Brien, D. (2014). *Russia blocks access to major independent news sites.* https:// www.eff.org/deeplinks/2014/03/russia-blocks-access-major-independent-news-sites

Gerden, E. (2014). *$500 million for new Russian cyber army.* http://www.scmagazineuk.com/500- million-for-new-russian-cyber-army/article/381720/

Gertz, B. (2012). *Russian intelligence director accused west of cyber attacks as NATO conducts cyber attack exercise.* http://www.infowars.com/russian-intelligence-director-accused-west- of-cyber-attacks-as-nato-conducts-cyber-attack-exercise/

Government of the Russian Federation. 2011. *Prime Minister Vladimir Putin meets with Secretary General of the ITU Hamadoun Toure.* https://itunews.itu.int/En/1444-Prime-Minister-Vladi mir-Putin-reaffirms-the-Russian-Federations-support-for-ITU.note.aspx

Gulyaeva, N., & Sedykh, M. (2014). *Russia enacts data localization requirement; new rules restricting online content come into effect.* http://www.hldataprotection.com/2014/07/arti cles/international-eu-privacy/russia-enacts-new-online-data-laws/

Heritage, T., & Tsvetkova, M. (2014). *Kremlin website hit by 'powerful' cyber attack.* http://www. reuters.com/article/2014/03/14/us-russia-kremlin-cybercrime-idUSBREA2D16T20140314

Hill, J. F. (2014). *Lawfare research paper series 2(31) the growth of data localization post-snowden: Analysis and recommendations for U.S. policymakers and industry leaders.*

huffingtonpost.com. (2014). *Why Russia and China see eye-to-eye on cybersecurity.* http:// www.huffingtonpost.com/worldcrunch/why-russia-and-china-see-_b_6071528.html?utm_hp_ ref=world

IBSA. (2003). *Brasilia declaration.* http://www.ibsa-trilateral.org/index.php?option=com_con tent&task=view&id=48&ltemid=27. Accessed 2 Dec 2012.

Itar-Tass. (2013). *Putin calls to strengthen protection against cyber attacks.* Johnson's Russia List 122.

itar-tass.com. (2013). *Russia praises China's initiative to host first global Internet conference.* http://en.itar-tass.com/world/760667

Khrennikov, I. (2014). *Google to visa face Russia rules, boon to local data centers.* http://www. bloomberg.com/news/2014-09-25/google-to-visa-face-russia-data-rules-in-boon-to-local-oper ators.html

Khrennikov, I., & Meyer, H. (2014). *Facebook page for Russia rally blocked as putin cracks down,* December 23. http://www.bloomberg.com/news/2014-12-23/facebook-page-for-russia-rally- blocked-as-putin-tightens-control.html

Kramer, A. E. (2010). *E-mail spam falls after Russian crackdown,* October 26. http://www. nytimes.com/2010/10/27/business/27spam.html

Kshetri, N. (2013). Cybercrimes in the Former Soviet Union and Central and Eastern Europe: Current status and key drivers. *Crime Law and Social Change, 60*(1), 39–65.

Lvov, A. (2013). *Russian army developing cyberattack defenses.* http://rbth.co.uk/politics/2013/ 02/27/russian_army_developing_cyberattack_defenses_23313.html

MacAskill, E. (2014). Putin calls internet a 'CIA project' renewing fears of web breakup. *The Guardian.* http://www.theguardian.com/world/2014/apr/24/vladimir-putin-web-breakup-inter net-cia

Maksimov, I. & Kuksin, S. (2013). Russia will not be a bystander in the arms race. *Rossiyskaya Gazeta*. Johnson's Russia List 122.

Mosendz, P. (2014a). *In Russia, the iPhone is coming under fire*. http://www.newsweek.com/russia-iphone-coming-under-fire-289671

Mosendz, P. (2014b). *Chechnya leader denounces iPhones*. http://www.newsweek.com/chechnya-leader-denounces-iphones-288196

Nechepurenko, I. (2014). *Russian internet 'one step away' from Chinese firewall*. http://www.themoscowtimes.com/news/article/russian-internet-one-step-away-from-chinese-firewall/499121.html

Noss, E. (2005). A battle for the soul of the internet. *CNET News*. http://news.cnet.com/A%20battle%20for%20the%20soul%20of%20the%20Internet/2010-1071_3-5737647.html

phys.org. (2014). *Russia to develop cyberspace 'security' without 'total control*. http://phys.org/news/2014-10-russia-cyberspace-total.html#nRlv

Rathinavel, P. (2014). *Apple iPhones and iPads will be banned in Russia from new year's day 2015*—Report. http://au.ibtimes.com/articles/571776/20141105/apple.htm#.VFoHq1dINmc

reuters.com. (2012). *Russia says many states arming for cyber warfare*. http://www.reuters.com/article/2012/04/25/germany-cyber-idUSL6E8FP40M20120425

RT. (2014a). *Hackers down Russian presidential site in 'powerful cyber-attack'*. http://rt.com/news/kremlin-site-attack-hackers-790/

RT. (2014b). *MP urges 'nationalization' of Google over security fears*. http://rt.com/politics/186364-russian-google-nationalization-fyodorov/

rt.com. (2014). *Russia, China prepare to sign unique cybersecurity treaty—Report*. http://rt.com/politics/197812-russia-china-network-security/

rt.com/news. (2014). *Cyber security units to protect Russia's nuclear weapons stockpiles*. http://rt.com/news/196720-russia-missile-forces-cybersecurity/

Shafa, E. K. (2014). *Iran's emergence as a cyber power*. http://www.strategicstudiesinstitute.army.mil/index.cfm/articles/Irans-emergence-as-a-cyber-power/2014/08/20

Soldatov, A. (2011, December 9). *Vladimir Putin's cyber warriors*. http://www.foreignaffairs.com/articles/136727/andrei-soldatov/vladimir-putins-cyber-warriors

Spade, J. M. (2011). *China's cyber power and America's national security*. Philadelphia, PA: US Army War College.

Stuenkel, O. (2012). Keep BRICS and IBSA separate. *The Diplomat*. http://thediplomat.com/the-editor/2012/08/13/keep-the-brics-and-ibsa-seperate/. Accessed 27 Feb 2013.

Sullivan, B. (2012). *Is Flame virus fallout a Chinese, Russian plot to control the Internet?* http://redtape.nbcnews.com/_news/2012/06/12/12172042-is-flame-virus-fallout-a-chinese-russian-plot-to-control-the-internet?lite

themoscowtimes.com. (2014). *Russia suggests apple reveal its source codes*. http://www.themoscowtimes.com/news/article/russia-suggests-apple-reveal-its-source-codes/504269.html

Thomas, T. L. (2001). *Information security thinking: A comparison of U.S., Russian, and Chinese concepts*. Fort Leavenworth, KS: Foreign Military Studies Office. http://fmso.leavenworth.army.mil/documents/infosecu.htm

Thompson, W. (2002). Putin's challenge: The politics of structural reform in Russia. *Europe-Asia Studies, 54*(6), 933–957.

Warren, P. (2011). *Russia proposes new plan to defeat online hackers*, December 22. http://1070www.telegraph.co.uk/sponsored/russianow/technology/8972805/Russia-plan-defeat-online-hackers.html

Chapter 14
Lessons Learned, Implications and the Way Forward

14.1 What Do We Know About Global CS?

A heightened concern and awareness of CS issues have led to a number of regulatory responses and driven the development and implementation of national CS strategies. In addition to governments and regulators, CS issues are also receiving greater attention from other stakeholders. For instance, there have been industry-wide private sector initiatives on the cyber front.

It is important to recognize the presence of highly complex forces at play in the global CS landscape. From the material ends perspective, J. Hirshleifer (1998) expressed a sense of optimism that nations' chance of engaging in war has diminished due to the rising costs of and low potential benefits from a war compared to those that can be realized form peaceful trade and commerce. However, compared to potentially high costs associated with a physical war, in terms of human lives and suffering and longer term development, some regimes may view cyber-attacks as a considerably cheaper and more attractive option. This issue is especially critical since some nations have viewed cyber-threats pose the same level of threats as posed by terrorism and others are contemplating measures as serious as a nuclear attack *as a deterrent* to adversaries' possible cyber-attacks and any challenge to their interests in the cyberspace. *What is making the current cyber-conflict a potentially dangerous* game is that in many cases, CS-related concerns are based more on perception and fear rather than on reality, scientific evidence and fact.

Prior researchers have noted that drastic changes in the environment such as those associated with the current cyber-conflicts may create confusion and uncertainty and produce an environment that lacks norms, templates, and models about appropriate strategies, structures, and legitimacy. A significant change also creates ambiguity in cause effect relationships, making learning difficult and inhibiting the ability to undertake a rational search for solutions (Newman 2000). Moreover, it is difficult to learn from experience during a period of significant institutional change, because past experience is not an appropriate guide for future actions (Weick 1979).

© Springer International Publishing Switzerland 2016
N. Kshetri, *The Quest to Cyber Superiority*, DOI 10.1007/978-3-319-40554-4_14

These conditions fit squarely in the context of cyber-conflicts, which are a recent phenomenon. Under such conditions, "superstitious learning" may occur (Levitt and March 1988), and nations may engage in strategically confused behavior. A country's *operations in the cyber* domain may also be complicated by the lack of an accurate assessment regarding the possible response of the rival.

The consequences of the Stuxnet worm deployment is probably the most appropriate way to illustrate the above concepts. The worm attacked Siemens control systems used in a number of facilities such as electrical generation plants, factories and water treatment works (bbc.com 2014). While its unambiguous target was the Iranian nuclear program, it also disrupted the operations of industrial control computers in plants in China, India and Indonesia (Fildes 2010). In 2012, it was discovered that Stuxnet had infiltrated systems of the U.S. oil producer Chevron (businessweekme.com 2014).

Especially authoritarian regimes are facing unique threats in BD and the cloud and are responding in a hostile or defensive fashion to the challenges presented by their opponents' increasing utilization of these technologies. Some defenders of freedom and democracy have chosen the Internet as a means of challenging and reacting against tyrannical regimes. The experiences of China and Russia indicate that cyberspace can be difficult but is not impossible to control. *Even in a democratic nation such as South Korea, rulers' temptation* to use the cyber power to gain political advantage seems to persist. Overall, a proper balance between security and freedom has been a key issue on the cyber-front (Ebert and Maurer 2013).

Countries and organizations differ in terms of the degree of long-term orientedness and resources committed to fight cyber-attacks. The low level of CS preparedness among firms in industrialized economies such as the EU and the U.S. is particularly striking. CS-related measures are hindered by serious *resource constraints (e.g., India) and ineffective* use of existing resources (*e.g.*, Brazil). The most important barrier to utilize the Internet's potential in China has centered on the government's strict cyber-control measures. Possible negative impacts of CS frameworks on economic growth and productivity have been observed. While nations are interested in ensuring CS without compromising economic growth and national competitiveness, the experiences of some economies such as Japan and the EU indicate that they face a tricky trade-off between economically productive uses of emerging technologies (*e.g.*, cloud computing, social networking, mobile applications and data analytics) and an enhanced CS profile.

From cyber-offenders' standpoint, nations and organizations have differing levels of appeal and various characteristics that make them attractive targets. As South Korea's case suggests, background conditions such as geopolitical location may be linked to the likelihood that a nation faces some forms of cyber-attacks (*e.g.*, GPS jamming). Target attractiveness is also related to economic systems of organizations' country of origin (*such as capitalism*). Some categories of cyber-threats are strongly linked to cultural norms and values. For instance, cultural indifference to hacking is believed to be especially pronounced among Brazilians, which has been a key driver of internally originated cyber-attacks in the country. As discussed in Chap. 12, cyber-attacks against government agencies are culturally more justifiable in Brazil than in most industrialized countries. The difference can be also partly attributed to a lower degree of trust in the government in Brazil. The Brazilian case thus underscores the importance of *strengthening citizens' trust in government* in order to strengthen national CS profile.

Due to CS-related concerns, many industrialized as well as developing countries have initiated and adopted a number of protectionist measures, especially in the ICT sector. A related point is that businesses are becoming what a former Israeli intelligence officer described as "unwilling pawns" in cyber-warfare (Regalado 2014). For instance, China's Huawei became the world's largest seller of telecom equipment in 2013. Its U.S. market share has been low due primarily to the U.S. government concern that its products act as a Trojan horse for China's intelligence services. Now U.S. firms are facing similar situation. Chinese businesses and customers are avoiding their products for similar reasons. The *blurred boundary between the responsibilities* of the private sector and the nation state has also contributed *significantly to the current confusion* about appropriate CS measures. To take an example, as yet, there are no established norms, and rules regarding the measures and counter-measures to be taken by a commercial bank and the state when the offender targeting a financial institution is a state actor.

Finally, the lack of sufficient number of CS specialists is among the most glaring shortcoming facing most economies. Experts say that many CS specialists with practical computer expertise are often self-taught rather than being trained by the universities (Risen 2014). Some have emphasized for the professionalization of CS. A report of the Pell Center for International Relations and Public Policy called for the creation of an association to set professional standards and influence CS-related education and training (Spidalieri and Kern 2014).

14.2 Action Agenda for Cyberspace Participants

The battle against cybercrimes, cyber-attacks and cyber-warfare must be waged on many fronts. Various cyberspace participants have distinct roles to play to make the *cyberspace safe and* secure.

14.2.1 Implications for National Governments

In light of the apparent disconnection between research and national CS policies (Choucri and Goldsmith 2012), the frameworks developed in this book can provide a prescription for policy-making. In order to fight cybercrimes associated with some economies, a higher level of priority needs to be given to dealing with the fundamental sources of the problem. Some such sources have been identified in earlier chapters. In some cases, these sources are largely economic such as the lack of employment opportunities for ICT professionals. In other cases, the real source concerns some economies' lack of sufficient integration and willingness to cooperate with the West. They have not been able to participate in the global discourse on CS. It would be in the interest of the West to provide support, encouragement and incentives to emerging economies for meaningful participation in the formulation of formal international frameworks on CS as well as other broader international agreements.

Growing cyber-attacks have indicated the need for urgent CS-related regulatory measures. The experiences of major economies indicate that the establishment of *sound CS-related regulatory framework,* by its very nature, involves working with the private sector (*e.g.*, India), national governments (*e.g.*, the EU) as well as other political parties (*e.g.*, the U.S.) to establish policies and procedures beyond vested national or *political party* interests. At the same time ambiguous and complex regulations have been a problem in many cases. A reason why many businesses do not comply with compliance standards is that such standards are often lengthy, confusing and contain a lot of technical jargon *that* no one without a technical knowledge can understand (Fields 2014). Thus important CS laws and regulations need to be formulated in simple, easily readable and unambiguous language and formats.

Since geographic dispersion of data is an important factor associated with cost and performance in technologies such as the cloud, an issue that deserves mention relates to regulatory arbitrage. That is, IT vendors can take advantage of loopholes in regulatory systems of certain jurisdictions to reduce risks. At least for the short run, countries are likely to update their laws individually rather than acting in a multilateral fashion. Jurisdictional arbitrage is often higher for new technologies such as BD and the cloud compared to other industries in general. Critics are concerned that CSPs may store sensitive information in jurisdictions that have weak laws related to privacy, protection and availability of data (Edwards 2009). Given the significance of these new technologies to economic competitiveness and national security, policy makers need to look at developments in formal institutions in other countries and take proactive measures to enact and enforce relevant laws.

It is clear that shortage of CS professionals is a critical weakness that has severely limited most nations' efforts to strengthen CS. Corporate support and training programs and national programs aimed at the creation of awareness and knowledge about CS and change in people's attitude and behavior related to CS are equally important. Some experts think that it is important to start CS education in primary schools (dw.de 2014).

Finally, some forward-looking governments are devoting increasing attention to developing a good CS ecosystem by encouraging domestic and foreign investments in this sector with policy interventions such as subsidies, low corporate taxes, and other incentives. As discussed in Chap. 1, a prominent example is Israel. A strong relationship between military intelligence and the private industry has been a key force in the country's prominence in the world CS market. The Israeli army's military intelligence and technological units such as Unit 8200 provide much of the training and experience needed for the country's success on the CS front (Moskowitz 2014). In 2014, Israel accounted for 7 % of the global CS market and

13 % of new R&D in the sector. These numbers were three times more than the 2010 levels. There has been about a fourfold increase in CS-related VC investment in the country during 2010–2014 (Cohen 2014). This is despite export restrictions in the global CS market. IBM, Cisco, and GE made large acquisitions and investments in Israeli CS companies in 2013 (Hiner). Israel's strong entrepreneurial spirit and top technical universities have been key ingredients of the country's global leadership in CS. The government has provided favorable tax incentives and subsidies, which have amounted as much as 40 % of some companies' staff salaries (Barnes 2014).

A similar example is Singapore. The Singaporean government noted that, in 2015 Boeing will launch the first Cyber Analytics Centre outside the U.S. in Singapore (Nirmala 2014). Companies such as Boeing are attracted to Singapore due to its cutting-edge IT infrastructure, availability of IT experts and government incentives (Arnold 2010).

14.2.2   Implications for Board of Directors and Top Management Teams

Cyber-threats facing an organization are changing in a way that has made CS an increasingly critical function. CS has become an issue that affects every aspect of a business. Organizations are expected to establish effective data privacy and consumer information security systems and practices. Nonetheless, in most countries, no specific CS laws provide the clarity and definitive guidance on identifying the steps and procedures needed to establish such systems and practices.

In order to understand the *criticalness and* significance of CS consider the impact of the 2013 cyber-attacks on Target. As of July 2014, Target's expenses related to the data breach in the 2013 holiday season reached US$146 million. Over 100 lawsuits relating to the breach had been filed against the company. The company blamed the attack for the company's sales decline in the fourth quarter of 2013 (Stanford 2014). In May 2014, proxy advisory firm Institutional Shareholder Services (ISS) suggested that seven of ten directors at Target be removed from office because they did not take sufficient actions to prevent a massive data breach of December 2013 (Harrison 2014). In December 2014, a judge in the U.S. state of Minnesota rejected Target's motion to dismiss the lawsuit brought against the company by several banks. The judge argued that the retailer's actions were negligent since it failed to give careful attention to warnings from a security alerting system and disabled some security features (Vijayan 2014).

The contours of global cyber-attacks are not well known. *Hackers are using new aggressive* and *sophisticated social engineering* tactics to defeat organizations' defense mechanisms. Corporations are also facing regulatory pressures to change their business models so as to minimize real and perceived vulnerabilities of negative asymmetry. Consequently businesses are revamping their organizational

structures and CS specialists have started holding key positions in the organizational hierarchy. For instance, in September 2014, General Motors announced that
it hired first product CS chief. The company's response was in light of the
technological complexity in the automobiles industry (Bennett 2014). JPMorgan's
CS spending is expected to be about US$250 million in 2014 with 1000 dedicated
workers. The company's plan is to double CS spending over the next 4–5 years
(Glazer 2014). Likewise, Citigroup's annual CS budget in recent years is estimated
to be over US$300 million (Huang et al. 2015).

While the above are good signs, more remains to be done. Many organizations'
CS strategies reflect the misguided belief that strong CS measures are needed only
for businesses that exhibit a high degree of digitization. For instance, it was
reported that when Home Depot's CS team asked for new software and training
in order to strengthen CS measures, the top management's response was: "We sell
hammers" (Creswell and Perlroth 2014). No business sector or industry is immune
from cyber-threats. *CS is thus* as much important for the *sellers of hammers and
axes* as it is for *banks and financial institutions.*

In order to effectively carry out their duties and responsibilities, CEOs, directors,
and other employees need to design an appropriate CS strategy and tactics. Some
regulatory requirements are also driving such needs. For instance, a SEC Commissioner called for corporate boards to oversee CS risks, which is now a critical
component of risk management. The case of Target indicates that CEOs and board
members can be blamed and held responsible if a company facing cyber-attacks
lacks an effective strategy. CEOs and boards need to become more involved in CS
instead of delegating the responsibility *to other* managers or other *organizations.
They* must have an *in-depth understanding of the issue. It may be helpful to ask the
CIO and* IT managers *explain the company's CS measures in clear and simple*
terms. It is also necessary to document the extent, degree and types of possible
cyber-threats faced by organizations.

Since there is no such thing as foolproof CS and providing 100 % security is not
realistic and feasible, what is important is having all possible safeguards in place
and following appropriate processes to strengthen CS rather than the outcome or
end product. It is important to document and justify CS measures and steps taken to
choose the measures. A high priority must be given to protect the most valuable
assets. Most critical, probably is to have a well-developed plan for post-breach
resilience in order to quickly return to normal business operations (Barrett 2014).
For instance, regarding the data breach at Sony Picture, in addition to weak cyber-
defense mechanisms, many employees blamed the company for its lack of cyber-
disaster recovery provision. Current and former employees complained that they
did not get information about registering for free credit monitoring and identifying
protection measures offered by the studio (Fritz 2014).

Most often firms need to exceed the regulatory requirements or *the auditing*
standards *that are* generally accepted. For instance, the process by which banks
audit their IT system is an area that needs improvement. Often it is not possible for
auditors to cover an entire banking application in a single audit. They thus rely on
random sampling to assess a bank's CS profile. A problem is that auditors do not

vary their sampling techniques to ensure a wider CS test. For this reason, it is important for banks to exceed rather than just to be in compliance with an IT audit (Gabberty 2014).

A lesson from the CS readiness test of the big investment-management firm reported in Chap. 1 and similar experience is that growing cyber-threats make it important to revisit key organizational objectives such as providing better services, enhancing customer satisfaction and retention, increasing employee satisfaction, motivation, operational efficiency, productivity and reducing turnover. Rapid growth in cybercrime also requires serious rethinking about the way employees are viewed, valued, and rewarded. For instance, some analysts suggest that a simpler way to prevent insider cyber-attacks would be to pay more in order to prevent an employee from becoming disgruntled (Schrager 2014).

There are also positive motivations for strengthening CS measures. The director for CS on the White House National Security Council predicted that by 2020, CS insurance will be standard for businesses just like property or liability insurance (Sternstein 2014). Strong CS capabilities are likely to lead to lower cyber-insurance premiums. For instance, insurance underwriters may ask whether a retailer complies with the payment card industry data security standard (developed by PCI Security Standards Council) (businessinsurance.com 2014).

Two types of capabilities—functional and cultural (Hall 1993)—need to be developed in the CS context. Functional capability entails an organization's ability to *perform* specific things effectively. In the CS context, this type of capability results from the CS-related knowledge, skill and experience of employees, as well as those in the value chain (*e.g.*, suppliers, vendors, distributors, stockbrokers, lawyers, and advertising agents). For instance, from the CS standpoint, CSPs are key members of value chain. A company can be held liable in case of a breach of customer data stored with a CSP. Cultural capability related to the organization's employees CS-related habits, attitudes, beliefs, values and behaviors. It is important to instill a general CS culture in the organization. CS practitioners have emphasized the importance of building a "human firewall", which entails clearly defined CS responsibilities for every employee through awareness and training (forbes.com 2014). In many cases, the first victim is often an administrative assistant or an accountant, who may require special training (symantec.com 2014). Overall, when the organization's culture leads to a high CS standard, it contributes to a competitive advantage.

14.2.2.1 Need for Clear Organizational Rules and Safeguards

Organizational rather than technology issues are becoming increasingly important in successfully protecting and defending digital assets. According to the FBI, insider cyber-attacks from current and former employees are among the biggest threats organizations face, which has risen in recent years. Such attacks have led to "several significant FBI investigations". Some current and former employees are found to use their access privilege to destroy and steal data, obtain confidential information about customer and engage in frauds using customer accounts (Strohm 2014).

Employees that have no bad intention or no malicious thinking also pose significant risks (Yadron 2014). Some serious CS breaches can be attributed to employees' failure to follow organizational CS rules and policies. For instance, employees may use external thumb drives in their work computers without thinking whether they are violating organizational policy. Likewise, employees may leave their computers without logging out, when they take a short break. Organizations are required to monitor the adherence to security measures more closely (Gabberty 2014). They may have to use self-regulatory strategies instead of waiting for data protection laws.

14.2.2.2 CS of the Value Delivery Networks

It is also important to evaluate the activities of the members of the value delivery networks such as distribution channels and supply chain partners from the standpoint of CS. It is important to make sure that supply chain partners have at least the same CS standard that companies set for themselves with compliance mandated in contracts (Progressive Media 2014). A survey conducted among British companies found that 23 % of retailers and consumer companies attributed CS incidents to current service providers and contractors and 45 % attributed to former partners (Medland 2014). The case of Sony discussed in Chap. 2 makes it clear that if a company uses public clouds, it may be important to make sure that cyber-insurance will also cover when a cybercriminal uses the CSP's service to attack the company's system. This issue is even more important in developing economies that lack well-developed regulative institutions. For instance, for U.S. companies doing business in China, it may be even more important to carefully evaluate their Chinese partners' systems for handling customer data to avoid the privacy and data protection risks and compliance with existing privacy laws.

14.2.2.3 Understanding the Unique Risks and Threats and Assessing Objective Vulnerabilities

Making sound investment decisions about CS has been a major challenge facing organizations. A global survey of PwC indicated that only 38 % of the organizations had a methodology to prioritize CS investments based on risk and impact to business strategy. Overall there is a *lack of proactivity in the management* of CS issues and most companies follow a reactive strategy. Verizon's 2012 survey indicated that 69 % of breaches were discovered by third parties (Verizon 2013). Even among major government organizations and big companies, cyber-defense has not been a proactive drive to enhance CS. For instance, the U.S. government was reportedly alerted by a "friendly ally" regarding the cyber-attacks on the White House computer systems that was reported in October 2014 (Sanger and Perlroth

2014). Likewise, JPMorgan increased cyber-defenses after an attack in August 2014 (Son 2014). While complete *prediction and prevention may not* be achievable, organizations can benefit from some degree of proactivity.

There are a number of ways to describe the observed inter-firm and inter-industry heterogeneity in the nature and extent of cyber-attacks faced and the CS performance. Industries and organizations differ widely in terms of the threats and vulnerabilities faced and the degree of risk tolerances. Brian Finch argues that there is no "cyber-alchemy formula" to accurately determine the cyber tools and CS spending needed to dramatically increase CS. He makes the case for a process-based model. The formula in such a model is to use a risk-based strategy, where risk equals "threat plus vulnerability plus consequences" (Finch 2014). A *threat* is a danger related to cyber-attack that has the potential to cause harms to an organization. *Vulnerability refers to the d*egree to which an organization is susceptible to harm from cyber-attacks. A number of factors such as a firm's *jurisdiction, physical* location, nature of business, and symbolic significance are related to the degree of vulnerability.

In making strategic CS decisions, knowing the nature of threats is critical. For most firms it may make no sense to take preventive security measures against some categories of cyber-threats such as those coming from nation-states or groups that have access to tools with the same level of sophistication as used by countries. For instance, according to the FBI, almost *no security measure would* have stopped the type of cyberattacks that was launched against the Sony Pictures in November 2014 (Gibbs 2014). The cyber-threats associated with amateur criminal gangs, who use readily available well-known tools, or insiders attracted in selling corporate IPR on the other hand, can be minimized.

An understanding of the of the likely adversary's motivations, tools, tactics and practices can help design measures to boost cyber-defense and resilience. Cyber-attacks are driven *by what psychologists refer as intrinsic motivations such* as revenge as well as extrinsic/economic *motivations such as extortion.* Extrinsically motivated hackers are likely to attack networks of companies with higher digitization of values (higher potential financial incentives). For instance, online casinos, banks, and e-commerce hubs are a sweet spot for cyber-extortionists. Intrinsically motivated hackers' attacks, on the other hand, are often directed towards organizations with symbolic significance and criticalness. For instance, quoting an NIS official briefing her, a lawmaker, who served South Korean's intelligence committee, noted that most websites targeted by the attacks originated from the North belonged to conservative South Korean organizations that support a hard-line approach to North Korea (Olsen 2009). While many companies have become "unwilling pawns" in cyber-warfare, the case of hacks on Sony Picture indicates that companies can also become the *direct and main target of a cyber-warfare.*

Hackers backed or employed by the state are more interested in intelligence with strategic value. Hackers contracted by governments or companies for IP theft are behind information such as oil-drilling maps, software source codes, military technology or next generation fighter jets (Summers 2014). Cyber-attacks on critical infrastructure are likely to be motivated by politics whereas the aims on attacks in the finance and retail to steal something of value (Vinton 2014). In addition to nationalism and religion, hackers' interests are also framed by fight against global capitalism (de Kloet 2002). Such hackers are likely to attack networks of big multinationals.

Cyber-attacks are likely to follow any key economic or political events affecting the global economy. Organizations need to consider their subject positions in relation to such events. For instance, in a cyberwar, firms that are viewed as an economic symbol of a country's modernization and development are likely to be targeted by an enemy nation. Some hackers' interests are also framed by fight against global capitalism (de Kloet 2002), who are likely to attack networks of big multinationals.

It is important to note that vulnerability has two dimensions: objective and subjective (Busetta and Milito 2009). The objective vulnerability is related to political, social, economic, and demographic characteristics of an entity that determine the vulnerability to cyber-attacks. The subjective vulnerability refers to an entity's self-perception related to the risk of becoming a cyber-attack victim. It is important to increase the overall accuracy of the assessment of objective vulnerability. A vulnerability analysis entails the systematic examination of factors such as security mechanism of third party vendors, as well as software and hardware used in the company. For instance, a third-party service provider's weak cyber-defense mechanism is likely to expose a company's PII.

Organizations that deploy technologies and systems used by other more attractive cyber-attack targets also expose themselves to higher degree of vulnerability. To take an example, most of the computing platforms used in natural gas and petrochemical industry in Arab countries run on common operating systems that businesses and consumers widely use in other parts of the world. This means that any computing *problem faced by the Arab* gas and petrochemical industry *is likely to spillover* to the whole world (Fortune.com 2014). This is just one of many observations which reflect the existence of possible spillover effects of cyber-attacks across jurisdictional boundaries.

Finally consequences of possible cyber-attacks need to be evaluated in terms of factors such as reputational damage, financial loss, and possible physical harm. It is thus important for firms with higher probabilities of potential negative consequences to take measures such as information sharing internally and externally to gain intelligence on fast-evolving cyber threats, development of threat-specific policies and enhanced training and workforce messaging to boost CS awareness in order to minimize the impacts.

14.2.2.4   Managing Demands from Multiple Constituencies

In some cases CS-related pressures from various constituencies are complementary and compatible. In other contexts, demands of these constituencies are conflicting and CS-related concerns create uncertainty and ambiguity for organizations. While there are clearer regulatory requirements in some countries, others lack regulatory guidance, due primarily to the newness of this phenomenon. Organizations thus often face pressures for non-isomorphic responses that "involve departure from established structures, practices, and utterances of other actors in the environment" (George et al. 2006). In such situations, the appropriate level of isomorphism/non-isomorphism with respect to a given constituency is a function of resources associated with and importance of maintaining control over the constituency. An understanding of the natures of concerns of various constituencies and cost-benefit analysis associated with complying with their demands and requirements would help take appropriate actions.

The relative powers of different organizational and institutional interests would determine the nature of the response. For instance, Internet companies' responses to the government's pressure to create a controlled cyber environment in China have varied widely. Among foreign technology companies, Yahoo followed a strategy of compliance with local institutional requirements. Yahoo's then CEO, Jerry Yang said that he had to make a decision to help Chinese authorities arrest a journalist in order to do business in China (McLaughlin 2005). It can, however, be argued that unlike many Chinese technology companies, which may have unconsciously adhered to local rules, the strategy of compliance of foreign technology companies such as Yahoo is consciously and strategically chosen to comply with institutional pressure in anticipation of self-serving benefits or access to resources. In the early, 2000s, other foreign companies such as Google and AltaVista responded differently. These companies' response to institutional pressure related to the Chinese cyber-control can be described as avoidance, which is an "attempt to preclude the necessity of conformity" or escape, which entails exiting "the domain within which pressure is exerted" (Oliver 1991). Moreover, some organizations have changed their strategies to deal with government pressures. Among foreign affiliates, Yahoo followed the strategy of 'acquiescence' from the beginning, obeying rules and norms, and cooperating with the government. Some portals and search engines such as Google and Altavista, on the other hand, defied or actively resisted the institutional processes and were blocked in the country in 2002 (Singer and Friedman 2014). Put differently, they exited the Chinese cyber-control field in 2002. Subsequently, however, Chinese authorities won agreements from Google for filtering and screening out sensitive words. For instance, when Google operated in China, it shut down when a user looked for banned words (McLaughlin 2005). Google thus re-entered the Chinese cyber-control field. China's unfavorable environment, however, again led to Google's withdrawal from the country in 2010.

14.2.2.5 Operating in Foreign Countries

Accurately or not, increasingly policy makers in many states argue for the need for keeping sensitive data within their jurisdiction in order to strengthen CS. CSPs are thus likely to face more and more pressures and demands to open local data centers to store their citizens' information. Likewise, since regulative institutions related to liability and other issues are not well developed, CSPs may feel pressures to obtain endorsements from professional societies. As discussed in Chap. 2, AICPA's endorsements have driven the diffusion of cloud applications among some CPA firms.

By understanding the concerns raised by the governments and other actors, firms can make their strategy more specific to the factors that have led to the barriers. An understanding of context and mechanisms related to newly emerging CS-related barriers to trade and investment would help companies avoid wasting resources and time on ineffective actions. Concerns related to specific products can be relatively easy to deal with. For instance, in 2003, Microsoft signed an agreement to share Windows source code with the Chinese Government (SinoCast 2003). Microsoft also opened Windows XP, Windows 2000 and other systems programs to government technical security experts of Russia, and the U.K. (Menn 2003).

CS concerns associated with broader issues such as suspicion regarding a company or its operation are difficult to overcome. For instance, for companies suspected to be engaged in cyber-espionage, giving a simple reassurance may not be enough. Huawei and ZTE have engaged in public relations efforts but have not been able to assuage the concerns of U.S. policy makers. For instance, in September 2012, Huawei issued a report on CS which pledged that it would not involve *in any type of spying* acts (washingtonpost.com 2012). Huawei also engaged in various lobbying activities in the U.S. and also appointed a former U.S. State Department officer as its vice president for external affairs. This has, however, produced little or no change in the U.S. government's response.

CS-related barriers are often established on the basis of perception rather than reality. Attention thus needs to focus on the factors that lead to the perception. For instance, in some cases, measures are needed to reduce the perceived closeness with the government in the home country. Cautions should also be practiced in doing businesses with some foreign governments in high technology related products and services. In other cases, a firm's development of capabilities to address CS-related barriers to trade and investment in a foreign country may act as a source of competitive advantage. For instance, U.S. businesses are forced to implement new data privacy practices due to the EU restrictions. In the long run, U.S. businesses would be in an advantageous position as compared with firms without such practices from other countries. The real or perceived engagement in cyber-espionage by firms from an economy may act as a source of the negative country of origin for other technology firms from the economy. Economies with such effects are likely face higher barriers as governments across the world become more CS oriented.

14.2.3 Implications for Consumers

The newness and uniqueness of new technologies such as BD and the cloud often mean that clients would not know what to ask for in investment decisions. Most users are functioning on the assumption that vendors possess a reasonable capability and are willing to protect privacy and security of their data (Wittow and Buller 2010). However, against the backdrop of the institutional and technological contexts, this assumption may not always be realistic. Users may need to ask tough questions to vendors regarding certification *from auditing* and professional organizations, *data center locations, and background checks of employees.*

A one-size-fits-all approach may not work for all user organizations' decisions to adopt the cloud, BD and other technologies. For instance, organizations may have to make decisions concerning combinations of public and private clouds. A public cloud is effective for an organization handling high-transaction/low-security or low data value (*e.g.*, sales force automation). Private cloud models, on the other hand, may be appropriate for enterprises and applications that face significant risk from information exposure such as financial institutions and health care provider or federal agency. For instance, for medical-practice companies dealing with sensitive patient data, which are required to comply with the HIPAA rules, private clouds may be appropriate.

Other issues of particular relevance and concern are government overreach and the potential of BD and the cloud to be the *ultimate spying machine.* There are stories of espionage activities' successful transition to cyber-espionage2.0 and national and international security issues. A *Google report* released in April 2010 is especially timely and enlightening. The company described how government authorities around the world request the company for private information and to censor its applications.

There have been concerns about possible overreach by law enforcement agencies. In the U.S., for instance, thanks to the 2001 Patriot Act, the federal government can ask **service** providers for details of a user's activities without telling the user. The FBI's audits indicated the possibility of overreach by the agency in accessing Internet users' information (Zittrain 2009). For some analysts, the biggest concern has been the government's increased ability to access business and consumer data, and a lack of constitutional protections against these actions (Talbot 2010). Especially, BD and the cloud are likely to provide authoritarian regimes a fertile ground for cyber-control and spying activities.

14.3 Directions for Future Research

This section proposes a number of future research needs and directions. First, many smaller and poorer economies currently lack CS-related regulatory frameworks and strategies. This book's focus is on major world economies. An intriguing avenue for future research is thus to examine the likely sources of influences when countries with different political, cultural and historical contexts formulate their CS frameworks and strategies.

As noted above, companies' responses to CS-related barriers in foreign countries differ widely. As discussed above, U.S. companies' response to the Chinese government's pressure to create a controlled cyber-environment varied widely such as compliance, avoidance, escape and defiance. In this regard, future research might examine differences in organizations' responses to CS-related trade and investment barriers and changes in such responses over time. The roles of factors such as the nature of the top management team and businesses and history of the company in their responses to the government's CS-related pressures might be worthwhile target of study.

One issue that was raised in this book but not fully developed was the actions of various interest groups and other actors that lead to CS-related barriers to trade and investment. In this regard, another area of future research concerns the processes and mechanisms associated with actions of these actors that lead to regulations and policy developments surrounding CS-related barriers to trade and investment in the home and the host countries. For instance, Chinese hackers' alleged attacks on the networks of the U.S. DoD, which used 3Com intrusion-detection products was a concern raised by a U.S. lawmaker in his argument to oppose Huawei's deal to buy 3Com (Gross 2008).

The role of PPP in strengthening countries' CS profiles also has not been dealt in detail. This book documented numerous examples of PPPs in CS in a number of countries such as India, Israel, and South Korea. In future research scholars need to consider the possible motivations and contexts in which PPPs are taking place in CS-related areas.

While many governments have regulations and legislation to restrict data flows outside their countries, they are likely to be driven by different factors. For instance, authoritarian and democratic regimes may differ widely in their motivations associated with data localization. In this regard, another intriguing avenue for future research is to examine governments' diverse motivations and interests associated with data localization laws in countries with diverse institutional and legal settings.

Finally this book focused mainly on CS framework and strategy from a nation's perspective. In recent years, corporate CS strategy is becoming rather important due to the rapid escalation of high profile cyber-attacks targeting organizations. The consequences involving data breach at Target indicate that CEOs and board of directors can be held responsible if an organization lacks an effective CS strategy. Despite the importance of understanding the elements of an effective corporate CS strategy, in little research have scholars examined this issue. In future research scholars need to consider CS strategy using a company as the unit of analysis and examine the key characteristics and elements of CS strategy that can give the company potential competitive advantage.

14.4   Final Thought and Conclusion

A number of forces have evolved in recent years, which have dramatically altered the global CS landscape. CS strategy is increasingly becoming a central aspect of the national security systems of most major economies. Nonetheless most developing and least developed economies lack clearly formulated and detailed national

CS strategies. In this regard, the economies analyzed in this book may serve as role-models for the formulation of national CS framework and strategy.

As examples presented in this book suggest, the perpetrators may find it more attractive to focus their efforts on countries that have more lax regulations, weaker enforcement and Internet users with a lack of proper cyber-defense mechanisms. A critical and urgent step for nations is to strengthen CS by enacting new rules and regulations, enhancing enforcement measures and practices, promoting public education and awareness initiative related to CS and participating in international collaborations and cooperation. These factors are likely to alter the cost-benefit analysis of cybercriminals and other perpetrators targeting the country.

A critical practical challenge that organizations face in the digital economy concerns the ability to function effectively by protecting their digital assets from cyber-threats and balancing conflicting CS-related goals of consumers, interest groups, the government and other actors. Keeping networks secure has been extremely tough, and *even businesses with the strongest* defense mechanisms such as JPMorgan Chase have been victimized. It is not possible to avoid cyber-attacks facing an organization completely but they can be reduced and adverse effects can be minimized by taking proactive actions based on an accurate assessment of objective vulnerability facing the organization. The increasing cyber-threats facing organizations also provide the most convincing evidence regarding the need to revisit and update key organizational objectives.

References

Arnold, W. (2010). *Regulations and security concerns hinder Asia's move to cloud computing.* http://www.nytimes.com/2010/10/11/technology/11cloudasia.html

Barnes, J. (2014). *Israel utilises its cyber security expertise.* http://www.ft.com/intl/cms/s/0/8b6e572c-97e7-11e3-8dc3-00144feab7de.html#axzz3EnpyGV6S

Barrett, P. M. (2014). *The Cybersecurity myths that small companies still believe.* http://www.businessweek.com/articles/2014-11-24/the-cyber-security-myths-that-small-companies-still-believe

bbc.com. (2014). South Korea to develop Stuxnet-like cyberweapons. http://www.bbc.com/news/technology-26287527

Bennett, J. (2014). *GM hires Cybersecurity chief to help in vehicle development.* http://online.wsj.com/articles/gm-hires-cybersecurity-chief-to-help-in-vehicle-development-1411499354

Busetta, A., & Milito, A. M. (2009). Socio-demographic vulnerability: The condition of Italian young people. *Social Indicators Research, 97*(3), 375–396.

businessinsurance.com. (2014). *Target data breach prompts insurers to scale back cyber coverage for retailers.* http://www.businessinsurance.com/article/20140330/NEWS07/303309967/target-data-breach-prompts-insurers-to-scale-back-cyber-coverage-for

businessweekme.com. (2014). *Fallout from the Saudi Aramco breach continues.* http://businessweekme.com/Bloomberg/newsmid/190/newsid/35

Choucri, N., & Goldsmith, D. (2012). Lost in cyberspace: Harnessing the Internet, international relations, and global security. *Bulletin of the Atomic Scientists, 68*(2), 70–77.

Cohen, T. (2014). *Israel turns defense capabilities into cyber security tech gold.* http://www.haaretz.com/news/diplomacy-defense/1.617461

Creswell, J., & Perlroth, N. (2014). *Ex-employee say Home Depot left data vulnerable*. http://www.nytimes.com/2014/09/20/business/ex-employees-say-home-depot-left-data-vulnerable.html

de Kloet, J. (2002). Digitisation and its Asian discontents: The internet, politics and hacking in China and Indonesia. *First Monday, 7*(9). http://firstmonday.org/issues/issue7_9/kloet/ index.html

dw.de. (2014). *Cyber security should start in primary school*. http://www.dw.de/cyber-security-needs-to-start-in-primary-school/a-18032036

Ebert, H., & Maurer, T. (2013). Contested cyberspace and rising powers. *Third World Quarterly, 34*(6), 1054–1074.

Edwards, J. (2009). Cutting through the fog of cloud security. *Computerworld, 43*(8), 26–29.

Fields, J. (2014). *Cyber security: 5 steps to defend your business*. http://www.tennessean.com/story/money/2014/09/18/cyber-security-steps-defend-business/15853617/

Fildes, J. (2010). *Stuxnet worm "targeted high-value Iranian assets"*. http://www.bbc.co.uk/news/technology-11388018

Finch, B. (2014, December 11). *Why Cybersecurity must be defined by process, not tech*. http://blogs.wsj.com/cio/2014/12/11/why-cybersecurity-must-be-defined-by-process-not-tech/

forbes.com. (2014). *5 Ways to reinforce your company's cybersecurity program today*. http://www.forbes.com/sites/symantec/2014/11/03/5-ways-to-reinforce-your-companys-cybersecurity-program-today/

Fortune.com. (2014). *It's time for corporate boards to tackle cybersecurity. Here's why*. Nusca, Andrew, 1–1.

Fritz, B. (2014). *Victims of Sony breach left fuming*. http://www.wsj.com/articles/victims-of-sony-breach-left-fuming-1418082738

Gabberty, J. (2014). *How banks can step up to bat on cybersecurity*. http://www.americanbanker.com/bankthink/how-banks-can-step-up-to-bat-on-cybersecurity-1070900-1.html

George, E., Chattopadhyay, P., Sitkin, S. B., & Barden, J. (2006). Cognitive underpinnings of institutional persistence and change: A framing perspective. *Academy of Management Review, 31*(2), 347–385.

Gibbs, S. (2014, December 12). *FBI: 90% of US companies could be hacked just like Sony*. http://www.businessinsider.com/fbi-90-of-cyber-security-systems-out-there-would-not-have-been-able-to-block-the-sony-hackers-2014-12

Glazer, E. (2014). *J.P. Morgan CEO: Cybersecurity spending to double*. http://online.wsj.com/articles/j-p-morgans-dimon-to-speak-at-financial-conference-1412944976

Gross, G. (2008). Bain/Huawei's bid to buy 3Com is scuttled by security issues. *Network World, 25*(8), 30.

Hall, R. (1993). A framework linking intangible resources and capabilities to sustainable competitive advantage. *Strategic Management Journal, 14*, 607–618.

Harrison, E. E. (2014). Boards need to oversee cybersecurity risk says SEC official. *Inside Counsel* (formerly *Corporate Legal Times*).

Hiner, J. *How Israel is rewriting the future of cybersecurity and creating the next Silicon Valley*. http://www.techrepublic.com/article/how-israel-is-rewriting-the-future-of-cybersecurity-and-creating-the-next-silicon-valley/

Hirshleifer, J. (1998). The bioeconomic causes of war. *Managerial and Decision Economics, 19* (7/8), 457–466.

Huang, D., Glazer, E., & Yadron, D. (2015). *Financial firms bolster cybersecurity budgets*. http://online.wsj.com/articles/financial-firms-bolster-cybersecurity-budgets-1416182536

Levitt, B., & March, J. G. (1988). Organizational learning. *Annual Review of Sociology, 14*, 319–340.

McLaughlin, K. E. (2005). China's model for a censored internet. *Christian Science Monitor, 97* (210), 1–10.

Medland, D. (2014). *Cyber security and the danger of ostriches in the boardroom.* http://www. forbes.com/sites/dinamedland/2014/10/02/cyber-security-and-the-danger-of-ostriches-in-the-boardroom/

Menn, J. (2003). Microsoft opens windows to China. *Los Angeles Times.* https://www.latimes. com/technology/la-fi-micro1mar01,0,1547577.story?coll=la-headlines-technology

Moskowitz, J. (2014). *Cybersecurity unit drives Israeli Internet economy.* http://www.csmonitor. com/World/Passcode/2014/1205/Cybersecurity-unit-drives-Israeli-Internet-economy

Newman, K. L. (2000). Organizational transformation during institutional upheaval. *The Academy of Management Review, 25*(3), 602–619.

Nirmala, M. (2014, September 26). *S'pore to beef up cyber security ecosystem; Move part of coordinated plan to thwart cyber crooks.* http://digital.asiaone.com/digital/news/spore-beef-cyber-security-ecosystem

Oliver, C. (1991). Strategic responses to institutional processes. *Academy of Management Review, 16,* 145–179.

Olsen, K. (2009). *Cyber attackers used IP addresses in 5 nations: South Korea.* http://www. huffingtonpost.com/2009/07/10/cyber-attackers-used-ip-a_n_229376.html

Progressive Media. (2014, May 29). *Company News, US organisations not battle ready in war against cybercrime.* http://www.cbronline.com/news/cybersecurity/data/us-organisations-not-battle-ready-in-war-against-cybercrime-4280918

Regalado, A. (2014, May/June). *Spying is bad for business.* Technology Review, 1099274X, 117.

Risen, T. (2014). *FCC adds cybersecurity to its oversight.* http://www.usnews.com/news/articles/ 2014/10/24/fcc-adds-cybersecurity-to-its-oversight

Sanger, D. E., & Perlroth, N. (2014). *New Russian boldness revives a cold war tradition: Testing the other side.* http://www.nytimes.com/2014/10/31/world/europe/new-russian-boldness-revives-a-cold-war-tradition-testing-the-other-side-.html?_r=0

Schrager, A. (2014). *Underpaid employees are a Cybersecurity risk.* http://www.businessweek. com/articles/2014-10-06/underpaid-employees-are-a-cybersecurity-risk

Singer, P. W., & Friedman, A. (2014). *Cybersecurity and cyberwar: What everyone needs to know.* New York: Oxford University Press.

SinoCast China Business Daily News. (2003, March 13). Scott McNealy to come to China.

Son, H. (2014). *JPMorgan boosts customer data protections after attack.* http://www. businessweek.com/news/2014-08-28/jpmorgan-boosts-defenses-against-hackers-after-attack

Spidalieri, F., & Kern, S. (2014). *Professionalizing cybersecurity: A path to universal standards and status.* New Port: Pell Center for International Relations and Public Policy, Rhode Island.

Stanford, D. D. (2014). *Kmart says card data stolen in latest retail cyber hack.* http://www. bloomberg.com/news/2014-10-10/sears-s-kmart-says-hackers-stole-payment-card-data-in-attack.html

Sternstein, A. (2014). *WH Official: Cyber coverage will be a basic insurance policy by 2020.* http://www.nextgov.com/cybersecurity/2014/09/wh-official-cyber-coverage-will-be-basic-insurance-policy-2020/93503/

Strohm, C. (2014). *Unhappy workers hacking employers on the rise, FBI says.* http://www. bloomberg.com/news/2014-09-23/unhappy-workers-hacking-employers-on-the-rise-fbi-says. html

Summers, D. J. (2014). *Fighting in the cyber trenches.* http://fortune.com/2014/10/13/cold-war-on-business-cyber-warfare/

symantec.com. (2014). *Francophoned—a sophisticated social engineering attack.* http://www. symantec.com/connect/blogs/francophoned-sophisticated-social-engineering-attack

Talbot, D. (2010). Security in the ether. *Technology Review, 113*(1), 36–42.

Verizon. (2013). *Data breach investigations report. Study conducted by the Verizon RISK team.* www.verizonenterprise.com/DBIR/2013/

Vijayan, J. (2014). *Target ruling raises stakes for cybersecurity vigilance.* http://www.csmonitor. com/World/Passcode/2014/1209/Target-ruling-raises-stakes-for-cybersecurity-vigilance

Vinton, K. (2014). *Hacking gets physical: Utilities at risk for Cyber attacks*. http://www.forbes. com/sites/katevinton/2014/07/10/hacking-gets-physical-utilities-at-risk-for-cyber-attacks/

washingtonpost.com. (2012). *Chinese telecoms gear maker Huawei calls for cybersecurity cooperation, promises no spying*. http://www.washingtonpost.com/business/technology/chinese-telecoms-gear-maker-huawei-calls-for-cybersecurity-cooperation-promises-no-spying/2012/09/05/5e32fc20-f718-11e1-a93b-7185e3f88849_story.html

Weick, K. E. (1979). *The social psychology of organizing* (2nd ed.). Reading, MA: Addison-Wesley.

Wittow, M. H., & Buller, D. J. (2010). Cloud computing: Emerging legal issues for access to data, anywhere, anytime. *Journal of Internet Law, 14*(1), 1–10.

Yadron, D. (2014). *Miscommunication as a Cybersecurity threat*. http://online.wsj.com/articles/miscommunication-as-a-cybersecurity-threat-1413751067

Zittrain, J. (2009). Lost in the cloud. *The New York Times*, p. A19.

Printed in the United States
By Bookmasters